The Illusion

Also by Jürgen Thorwald

The Century of the Detective

Science and Secrets of Early Medicine

The Century of the Surgeon

The Triumph of Surgery

Crime and Science

The Patients

Jürgen Thorwald
SOVIET SOLDIERS

TRANSLATED FROM THE GERMAN

A HELEN AND KURT WOLFF BOOK

The Illusion

IN HITLER'S ARMIES

BY RICHARD AND CLARA WINSTON

HARCOURT BRACE JOVANOVICH | NEW YORK AND LONDON

Printed in the United States of America

The quotations from *Against Stalin and Hitler 1941–1945*
by Wilfried Strik-Strikfeldt, copyright © 1970 by
David Footman, are reprinted by permission of
the publishers, The John Day Company and Macmillan Publishers Ltd., London.

Library of Congress Cataloging in Publication Data

Thorwald, Jürgen.
    The illusion: Soviet soldiers in Hitler's armies.

    "A Helen and Kurt Wolff book."
    Bibliography: p.
    Includes index.
    1. World War, 1939–1945—Russia.   2. World War,
1939–1945—Germany.   3. Russkaia osvoboditel'naia
armiia.   4. Vlasov, Andreĭ Andreevich, 1900–1946.
I. Title.   10-13-76
D764.T455613   940.53'47   75–14033
ISBN 0-15-144085-9

First edition
B C D E

Contents

068693

And so we National Socialists consciously draw a line beneath the foreign policy tendency of our pre-War period. We take up where we broke off six hundred years ago. We stop the endless German movement to the south and west, and turn our gaze toward the land in the east. At long last we break off the colonial and commercial policy of the pre-War period and shift to the soil policy of the future.

If we speak of soil in Europe today, we can primarily have in mind only Russia and her vassal border states. . . . The giant empire in the east is ripe for collapse. And the end of Jewish rule in Russia will be the end of Russia as a state.

Hitler, *Mein Kampf*
Volume II, Chapter XIV
Translated by Ralph Manheim
(Houghton Mifflin Sentry Edition, pp. 654f.)

Fundamentally, what matters is to cut up the huge cake into convenient slices so that we can first control it, second administer it, and third exploit it. . . .

The formation of a military power west of the Urals must never be permitted again, even if we have to wage war on that account for a hundred years. All successors of the Führer will have to realize that the security of the Reich depends on there being no foreign military force west of the Urals. . . . No one in those parts may ever again be permitted to bear arms except the Germans. . . . Otherwise they will inevitably turn against us some day. Only the Germans may bear arms, not the Slavs . . . not the Cossacks, not the Ukrainians. . . .

Martin Bormann's record of a conference held in the Führer's headquarters on July 16, 1941 (Present: Hitler, Göring, Rosenberg, Bormann, Keitel, Lammers)

Preface

This book began on an autumn evening of the year 1950, in Munich, where I was living at that time. My telephone rang, and an unfamiliar voice spoke to me in fluent German with a noticeable American accent. The caller explained that he had read my book published the previous year, *Es begann an der Weichsel** and had been particularly struck by a sentence in it about General Reinhard Gehlen. Then he said: 'I suppose you don't know the general, do you?"

I said I did not and asked who he was. "That doesn't matter at the moment," he replied. "But it would surely be interesting for you to meet the general."

Up to that time, I had attributed little importance to the name Gehlen. The few lines about him in *Flight in the Winter* (*Es begann an der Weichsel*) were based on information from General Heinz Guderian, who had been chief of staff of the German army in the winter of 1944–1945, when the German eastern front collapsed and the Soviet armies on the Vistula and the Oder launched their great advance into eastern and central Germany. Since my book had dealt with that advance, and the flight of the East German population with all those geographical, human, demographic, and power-political consequences that go on into the present, I had called on Guderian in his modest postwar refuge in Dietramszell Monastery in Bavaria. In the course of our talk, he mentioned the name of Gehlen as the chief of the Foreign Armies East (Fremde Heere Ost) department in the German General Staff. During the Second World War, this department was responsible for probing the

* Published in English as *Flight in the Winter* (London and New York, 1951.)

enemy's strength and intentions. Guderian had stressed Gehlen's great abilities as a director of intelligence. In particular, he had spoken of the accuracy with which Gehlen had predicted the last major Soviet offensive of January 16, 1945, which had sealed the fate of East Germany and had, in fact, determined the present state of Eastern Europe.

I asked the stranger whether Gehlen wanted to offer any amendments to what had been said about him in my book. He replied: "No, but the general has a proposal to make to you." He then asked whether I had a car, asked the model and what the license plate number was, and finally suggested that I park, on a particular evening, under a street light on Harthauser Strasse in Harlaching, a suburb of Munich.

I still had not the faintest notion of what had become of Gehlen after the German collapse. I did not know he had been convinced that the Soviet-American wartime alliance was bound to fall apart and had coolheadedly made approaches to the American Secret Service. In fact, he had continued the work that his Foreign Armies East department had been doing all along, except that now the camouflaged "Gehlen Organization" operated on the basis of a special agreement with the American Secret Service.

Knowing nothing of all this and beset by doubts, I drove out to Harlaching with some trepidation and waited uneasily on the deserted, dimly illuminated street. At last, a big black Opel drove up behind me, a man I had never seen before got out, came to the window, and asked me to take the seat beside the driver of the Opel. He would follow along with my car, he said. The shadowy figure in the driver's seat introduced himself as General Gehlen.

We drove to Nymphenburg in a rather heavy mist, parked on Montenstrasse, and walked a short distance to a large private house of a somewhat older vintage than the other houses in the vicinity. A man in civilian dress, who had the air of an orderly, opened the door. Inside, in the "drawing room," three men were waiting. Henry Pleasants, a CIA liaison officer attached to the Gehlen Organization, was the man who had telephoned me. The second man was Gehlen's deputy, von Mellenthin, formerly a general in the artillery. The third was Heinz Danko Herre who had been a colonel in the Foreign Armies East department and who was now one of Gehlen's closest associates in his secret organization.

Gehlen was cool, restrained, and laconic. Mellenthin, on the contrary, was so excessively sociable that I could tangibly feel the incompatibility of their two characters. Herre, extremely thin and highly intelligent, seemed burning with fierce ambition and painfully checked impetuosity.

Pleasants used the camouflage of music critic to conceal his secret assignment; what is more, he actually was a dedicated musician.

After a prolonged conversation, the background of the mysterious meeting became apparent to me. At the beginning of 1942, they reminded me, in spite of the vast territory the German armies had taken in their initial drive, every clearheaded person had recognized that there was no longer any hope of a German military victory over the Soviet Union. At that time Gehlen and Herre had been members of a group of German General Staff officers who undertook to prevent an otherwise certain defeat by launching a political and military experiment.

They had, however, underestimated Hitler's determination to annihilate the Soviet Union. For Hitler, Russia was not only the supposed center of "Jewish world bolshevism" (a favorite concept of his), but also the sphere he was going to transform into a Germanic empire. He meant to reduce the population to the status of a colonial people, and just at the time the colonial empires of the British and French were beginning to slip from their grasp, Germany would win a great colonial realm which would serve it for "living space." The war in the West seemed to have come to a halt at the English Channel, and that standstill had intensified Hitler's resolve. For a vast empire in the East would make Germany economically and militarily invincible, and thus force the Anglo-Saxons to bow to the facts and conclude peace.

For anyone with eyes in his head, the plans of these General Staff officers seemed utterly obvious. Stalin's rule had degenerated in the thirties into a cruel depotism. It had aroused widespread repressed hostility in the masses of the Soviet population, and among intellectuals and military men as well. As soon as opportunity offered, that antagonism to the regime was sure to break out into the open. And it was already doing so. The German successes in 1941 had to be attributed to a considerable extent to the Russian people's reluctance to fight for that regime. Historical studies made since that time have shattered the legend of the superiority of the German armored units. In reality, these units were dispatched with barely 3100 tanks, of which 1700 were already either outmoded or light models, or were seized from the Czechs. With this meager force, they were supposed to conquer a gigantic country that already had 20,000 tanks at its disposal, including 100 T-34's which were superior to the best German tanks.

The reception many German formations encountered was also highly significant, for they were hailed by the populace, and not only in the rural districts and in the traditionally separatist regions—the Ukraine, the

Caucasus, and the regions of White Russia—and in the Baltic countries that had been annexed to the Soviet Union only in 1939 and 1940. With no knowledge of German intentions at the highest level, in fact with very little knowledge of the Germans at all (except for the tales of fathers and grandfathers about the efficiency of these Westerners), millions upon millions of people accepted the German propaganda promising the Soviet population liberation from Stalinism. To be sure, many of those who spread the propaganda believed it themselves, and a good many intellectuals in the Soviet Union failed to anticipate the price that would be paid for this liberation: subjection to a foreign despot named Hitler. To many intellectuals the idea of a new Russia, socialist still, but more humane, had great appeal. A vast human potential was prepared to work for this end and, with German support, to fight for it as well.

Up to the spring of 1942, the German troops in the East, except for the top staff officers, knew nothing about Hitler's neocolonialist plans. But on their own initiative, because of the manpower shortage and the scarcity of reserves, they had "absorbed" into the German forces some 700,000 former Red Army soldiers, including an estimated six thousand officers and former commissars. This had happened without much thought being expended on the political aspects of such recruiting.

These Red·Army soldiers served in German uniform, some of them in auxiliary units known as "Hiwis" (pronounced "hee-vees"), an abbreviation of the German word for "auxiliary volunteers" (*Hilfsfreiwillige*). As much as a quarter—and more—of many German divisions were made up of former Red Army men. The High Command of the German Armed Forces (OKW) knew nothing about these unauthorized enlistees. Only a small part of them consisted of opportunists bent on escaping the murderous conditions in the German prisoner-of-war camps. The camps had become veritable graveyards, partly deliberately—the guards having been steeped in the Nazi doctrine of the inferiority of all Slavs—partly because of sheer overcrowding. And it was in the camps that the Russian prisoners first began to realize in what contempt they were held by the supposed German "liberators."

In the initial period, the majority of the defectors to the Germans were not separatists. Those did not appear until after the German conquest of the Caucasus in 1942. Rather, the Russians were manifesting their willingness to fight against Stalinism—not against their native land and not against socialism. Amazingly enough, they were still of this mind even after the first German defeat at the gates of Moscow.

In the light of all this, Gehlen and the officers who shared his views had tried to persuade the German top leadership of the necessity, given the military situation, of abandoning the by now patent colonialist aims and equipping a Russian liberation army to fight its own battle. Some notable Soviet figure would have to be found who, in return for assurances of future freedom of action and German abandonment of territorial claims, would lead this army and later become head of an anti-Stalinist government. The ultimate goal, which at present was still rather vague, was a "new" non-Stalinist Russia friendly to and allied with Germany, at least on the economic plane. This approach would make it possible to call a halt to the hostilities on many fronts and allow Germany to emerge from the war at least intact, though not victorious in the sense of Hitler's grandiose Pan-Germanic empire. The group around Gehlen entertained all sorts of notions, from fighting on in the West and in the Mediterranean region to making peace offers that would preserve the territorial integrity of Germany as of 1939. There were also as yet unexpressed ideas about returning to the status of 1938.

Those efforts, and the mark they made on events during the years between 1942 and 1945, were still largely unknown as late as 1950. Ultimately, more than a million Red Army men served on the German side. Pleasants and other CIA agents had been informed of this only after the creation of the Gehlen Organization. At this time they also heard something more about General Vlasov, a man of barely forty in 1942, bearer of the Order of the Red Flag and successful army commander in the 1941 Battle of Moscow. On Stalin's personal order, he had been appointed acting commander in chief of the Soviet northwest front, and in the spring of 1942 had become commander in chief of the Leningrad forces. There he was captured by the Germans. Embittered and disillusioned by his experiences under Stalin, he had been ready to assume the role of leader of the "liberation government" and the "liberation army." For two years some officers in the German army tried in vain to persuade Hitler to change the policy toward the East. In 1944, they at last managed to organize by stealth a tiny portion of the Russian soldiers in German uniform into a farcical formation known as the Vlasov Army. On November 14, 1944, Vlasov—urged on by Himmler, who was frightened by the prospect of imminent defeat—issued a manifesto proclaiming the dawn of a new Social Democratic Russia. The manifesto filled in some of the blanks in the vague outline of what was to be done with Russia and for Russia. Only a few units of the prospective army under Vlasov were actually raised, and these soldiers, like the majority of the former Red Army men and Soviet civilians who had served the Germans, attempted, when Germany collapsed, to make their way to the British and American forces.

These Russians had earlier been deceived by German officers, who were themselves laboring under an illusion. Their own hopes now deceived them again when they turned to the Western powers as authentic fighters in the vanguard of freedom. The Russians reasoned that the Anglo-American alliance with Stalin could not possibly survive the end of the war, and that by joining the Allied side they could continue to pursue their own anti-Stalinist aims. A great many of them, it is true, were already so thoroughly disillusioned and fatalistic that all they wished for was shelter and work in any non-Soviet part of the world. They fully realized that to Stalin and a victorious Soviet Union they would necessarily seem traitors and would be condemned to death or to penal camps if they attempted to return home.

There was no comfort to be had, however, from the Western powers. Misconceptions about Stalin's character and intentions, and the assumption that Stalin's aid would be needed to defeat Japan, led Roosevelt and Churchill at Yalta to agree that all Soviet citizens captured by British or American forces, people who had "collaborated with the enemy," would be turned over to the Soviet Union. And so it was.

Now, in 1950, in the era of the Cold War, American military and intelligence authorities, some of whom had participated in the surrender of those hapless Soviet citizens, became interested for the first time in this already forgotten episode in the recent war. They were suddenly intrigued by this scheme which Hitler had flubbed (although, of course, he could never have backed it), since they might some day want to try a similar approach: that of threatening the now powerful and imperialistic Soviet political system from within, by enlisting the aid of the Russian population. They suddenly realized that the story of Red Army men in German uniform might contain valuable lessons should the Cold War ever develop into a hot one.

By 1950, Pleasants and a group of Gehlen's associates had decided that it was important to record the story of German mistakes and crimes in the Soviet Union, and the story of the Russian volunteers, while there were still living witnesses. Their idea was that such a history might serve as a "textbook" in case of a military confrontation between East and West. Pleasants had read *Flight in the Winter,* which was based largely on interviews with surviving witnesses, a procedure relatively new in those days. He thought that I would be the "right fellow" to write the variegated, many-faceted history of this particular chapter of German Eastern policy.

These gentlemen proposed to turn over to me the available material on the Russian volunteer movement and on German policy in the occupied eastern territories. They would also undertake to assemble all the surviving witnesses who could be reached, and bring them to a place yet to be determined. There I would be able to interview these witnesses in depth and to obtain stenographic records of their accounts, to be used as sources for the projected history.

Late that night we parted in superficial agreement; but at bottom there was certainly a misunderstanding. For what I had in mind was hardly a political textbook or manual. What tempted me was the opportunity they put in my way to uncover hitherto unknown historical events which preceded in time the tempestuous happenings recorded in *Flight in the Winter*. That background alone could explain much that had happened since: the ruthlessness of the Soviet counteroffensive in the German eastern provinces, from East Prussia to Silesia; the expulsion or flight of the German inhabitants of those provinces; the annexations; and the splitting of the remaining territory of Germany into two parts.

Herre was appointed the liaison man; he promised to keep in touch with me. I never saw Gehlen himself again. A few weeks after the meeting, Herre informed me that we were all set. At the turn of the year I moved into the lonely, snow-covered and almost snowed-in country house of Herre's aged parents, situated in the hills above the village of Krün, near Mittenwald, and enjoyed their hospitality for some time. Two secretaries took turns recording the interviews, and at regular intervals a gray Opel limousine brought witnesses of that chapter of history to the quiet house and took them away again after I had learned what I could from them.

It was a remarkably smooth operation that brought people from all over Germany. Many of them came under bond of secrecy because they were living in what was then the Soviet zone of occupation, or because they were Russians who had contrived not to be turned over to the Soviet authorities and had since gone underground.

On several occasions, I myself set out in the gray Opel, with a chauffeur and one of the secretaries, to call on witnesses who for reasons of health, occupation, idiosyncrasy, or status (in some cases obviously because of tensions or rivalries with Gehlen), could not or would not come to Krün. In one case, I saw old General Köstring in Unterwössen who, until 1941, had been German military attaché in Moscow and later, as "General of the Volunteers," had become more or less by accident the caretaker for the million or so ex-Soviet soldiers in the German forces. Another time, I went to see the highly interesting and controversial Wilfried Strik-Strikfeldt, a Baltic German who acted as liaison officer among Gehlen, the German Army General Staff, and Vlasov. And finally I interviewed a close associate of Vlasov who referred to Vlasov as "my starets"—"my saint."

Before the first quarter of 1951 was over, thousands upon thousands of pages of "interrogations" had been taken down by the stenographers. I had studied voluminous documents and diaries, taken many notes, and was fairly well acquainted with the whole field. Since I did not wish to write a dry and heavy treatise, but a work of historical reportage as faithful as I could make it in setting, atmosphere, characterization, and dialogue, and as far as possible reproducing the thinking of the actors, my interviews were far more thorough than those I had used for *Flight in the Winter*. In the cases of a wide variety of individuals all the way up to Rosenberg, Himmler, and Hitler, I had explored the circumstances and obtained the texts of important discussions and negotiations, so that I could vouch for what had been said by these people, in many instances even to the exact wording. Some conversations had taken place in privacy, with no one present but the principals, and these people were no longer alive. But usually at least one of the participants would have informed his friends or associates about the course of the conversation. This kind of research explains the form of this book, which may at times sound like fiction but in fact represents a special method of historical writing.

The voluminous first version of the book was written in a single year—Herre kept hurrying me, as though he felt history could still make up for what he regarded as the "wasted opportunity." Our book, he thought, could serve as a sort of "manual" on how to deal with the Russians. This first version showed some of the effects of such haste, and a severe illness also gave the work a peculiar cast.

As the book grew, it became steadily more apparent that it was going to prove a great disappointment to the men who had initiated the project. When the first version was published in 1952, in a tiny edition under the title of *Wen sie verderben wollen* . . . (*Whom the Gods Wish to Destroy* . . .), it was a far cry indeed from a "textbook." Rather, it was a survey of Hitler's intemperate "neocolonialist" Eastern policy, which stood revealed as having been as foolish as it was inhumane: a blind failure to appreciate the real forces operating in the area. Presently this policy had forced Stalin to undertake a desperate mobilization of the country's total resources, which he had never intended; so that far from annihilating the Soviet Union and colonizing its vast domains, Hitler had helped bring forth the Soviet empire of today, with all the consequences for Germany, Europe, and the world.

My book tried to recount the tragedy of the Russians, Ukrainians, Cossacks, and other Soviet nationals who either lost their lives as volunteers or later paid heavily in Soviet camps for their trust in Germany or in individual Germans. Back then, I could not yet take the full measure of the effects of the Yalta Conference; but I could pass judgment on the political naïveté of the Anglo-Americans in acceding to Stalin's demands on this particular point.

Finally, my book was a history of those Germans who belatedly tried to move away from the policy of conquest toward a policy of cooperation. In telling their story I had to raise the question, though gingerly, of their having seduced Soviet citizens into playing a fatal game between Hitler and Stalin, although some of these Germans should have seen, given their military or political positions, that there was no real chance of changing Hitler's political ideas.

Since the book criticized the German side and, toward the end, the Anglo-American side as well, it forfeited a large part of its effectiveness. No participating generation reads charges against itself—not in Germany, not in England, and not in America. Back then, America was still far away from the bitter disillusionments, the shocks, and the scathing self-examinations of the present. In the end, the only value of my work seemed to be that it had amassed some historical documentation which otherwise would have passed into oblivion.

Two decades have gone by since then. But although my attention turned to altogether different subjects, I still retained my interest in the episode involving those million or so former Red Army soldiers who fought for the German (and yet not on the German) side. I seemed to have the topic to myself, however. The Gehlen circle was no longer pursuing this particular line. After years of collaboration with American intelligence, Gehlen had switched to the service of Germany again and had founded the Federal Republic's intelligence service. But my brief connection with him stood me in good stead when, in 1955, a weekly newspaper asked me for a story on the mysterious espionage chief. I deemed it advisable to contact the Gehlen Organization and inquire how it felt about publicity, whether it would care to release some reliable data

I could use for my article. Apparently, they were not averse to this and gave me the information I was seeking. But I gathered that they no longer saw any relevance in the story of the Russian defectors. By now, they were convinced that there was no way for the "West" to infringe upon the existing reality of the Soviet empire, let alone—as they once had dreamed—"rolling back" the sphere of Soviet influence. Thus there was no longer any point in analyzing that ill-fated experiment of the war years, which seemed already very far away.

When I again had an occasion to talk with Herre, more than a decade later, I found him a general and in charge of the intelligence section at the German embassy in Washington. He was on the point of retiring and returning to his familiar country house where I had been put up, long ago, when I was collecting my material. Herre was not the man to deceive himself about the extent of genuine progress toward peace. Nor did he, like many Germans, regard the years of the Cold War as a block to world peace or to the longed-for reunion of Germany. On the contrary, he saw those years as a historical phase that had at least preserved the status quo between East and West and had decisively checked the expansionistic policy that, to his mind, the Soviet leadership had never really abandoned. He also continued to think that the governmental system of the Soviet Union, in spite of its impressive consolidation since the war, still did not rest upon the firmly rooted affection of the masses of its peoples, still less of those in the satellites.

Despite the lapse in time, Herre's recollection of events between 1942 and 1945 still filled him with bitterness. He could not forget his farewells with Soviet citizens who, in 1945, had nothing to look forward to but extradition. For he knew that he himself was partly responsible for their fate. He considered it the irony of history that countries like South Africa and Australia were going to great lengths, as he put it at the time of our conversation, to lure white immigrants as workers when they could have taken in ample numbers of stateless Russians in 1945.

By this time, the book that had once been entitled *"Whom the Gods Wish to Destroy . . ."* had long since undergone a good many transformations, either because I learned certain things that prompted changes and improvements, or because I had been able to check statements more carefully against other evidence or variant accounts. Frequently I undertook radical cutting and tightening of the manuscript, although I did not want to alter its fundamental style or tenor. In the course of time, a new title suggested itself: *The Illusion.* For the entire episode seemed to be characterized by this element. Certainly illusion marked the conduct of the Germans, who were attempting a maneuver over the heads of their superiors, and should have known this was a game they could not win. The word also applied to the Soviet citizens who dreamed of liberating their native land and "humanizing the Soviet system." The title also was a reference to Hitler's monstrous fantasy of conquest and colonization in the Soviet Union. Finally, it was a commentary on those people in England and America who, for a wide variety of reasons, had regarded the alliance with Stalin as something more than an act of political and military necessity and who dreamed of an idealized friendship with the Soviet Union which would become the basis for a new order in a peaceful world. They had been sadly deluded.

It is an old truism that peoples and individuals need time and distance to come to an unemotional and unbiased evaluation of certain historical events. That principle was proved anew in 1970 in regard to the Soviet "volunteer movement." In that year, a book was published entitled *Against Stalin and Hitler,* subtitled *Memoir of the Russian Liberation Movement 1941–1945,* by Wilfried Strik-Strikfeldt. As presumably the first German publication on the subject, it was published in translation in London and New York. In the British Commonwealth and America, it evoked a certain intellectual interest, although also a good measure of sharp criticism, if not incredulity. In the fifties, some books written in English and touching on the subject had appeared; but in the psychological atmosphere of that period, considerable numbers of Soviet citizens could have defected to the Germans. If so, they must have been nasty traitors, like Quisling, Mussert, or Dagrelle. That was how the question looked to most people, for Hitlerism was held in total abhorrence and little was understood of the subtle distinctions within the Nazi system.

Besides, people would ask, would it have made sense for Soviet citizens opposing Stalinism to turn instead to a country with a dictatorship of its own? One might have replied that, in the given situation, there was no other country they could have turned to. But that answer would have been scornfully dismissed. Back then, it was not yet known that Hitler's totalitarianism, unlike the tightly closed system of Stalin, had all sorts of shadowy nooks and crannies among its competing power groupings and its disparate ideologies where, within narrow limits, there were possibilities of speaking and even acting somewhat freely. To persons who have grown up under totalitarian systems, things of this sort have a significance that at the time could not be comprehended in liberal countries. To this day, democracies dealing with dictatorships have not entirely appreciated these complexities.

Socialist and Marxist writers, though themselves outspoken opponents of the Stalinist deviation, were apt to condemn anyone who made any compromise with fascism for whatever reasons. In the Soviet Union itself, the matter of the mass defections necessarily remained a taboo subject. Those who returned from Germany vanished, if they even survived, into penal and labor camps. If Vlasov was mentioned at all, as he was by Ilya Ehrenburg, for example, he was branded a criminally ambitious traitor who, out of thirst for power, had sold out to the Hitlerian fascists. An otherwise excellent and, for Germans, highly instructive book, Alexander Werth's *Russia at War 1941–1945,* devoted only a few lines in its eleven hundred pages to the startling fact that a million soldiers changed sides. Werth held to the simple thesis that the Russians had let themselves be impressed into the German army because they feared the misery and death that awaited them in German prison camps.

The attention, hostile though it was, that Wilfried Strik-Strikfeld's *Against Stalin and Hitler* received indicated the onset of a new phase in the historiography of the period 1941–1945. Another book, *Wlassow— Verräter oder Patriot* ("Vlasov—Traitor or Patriot?") contributed to the revaluation. Its author, Sven Steenberg, was like Strik-Strikfeldt of Baltic German descent; his book constituted the first biography of Vlasov. Although he based his work on the documents accumulated between 1950 and 1952 for my own *"Whom the Gods Wish to Destroy . . . ,"* he had gone to such pains to discover a host of new details that his book must be regarded as a basic text on the Russian renegades. But both books focused upon Vlasov and his army. Unquestionably, that was an important part of the story of Russian citizens and soldiers living, acting, hoping, and suffering against the barbarous and, to them, inconceivable background of German policy in the East. But it was by no means the only aspect. *The Illusion* is an attempt to widen the picture, to let other voices be heard besides those of Vlasov's forces, and to explore the inhuman (and, in hindsight, incomprehensible) reaction of Hitler and the men around him, a reaction that ultimately destroyed them.

The Illusion

The Thinkers and the Fighters

I.t was the morning of April 20, 1942, and the guests had already lined up to congratulate the Führer on his fifty-second birthday. Hitler shook the hands extended to him. He murmured a few inconsequential words to each of the congratulants, interrupting his monotonous, rather absent-minded mumbling only when Reichsleiter Alfred Rosenberg stepped forward. At this time, Rosenberg held the posts of chief of the Office for Total Intellectual and Ideological Supervision of the National Socialist German Workers Party (NSDAP) and editor in chief of the party's newspaper, *Völkischer Beobachter*.

According to reports of a number of surviving witnesses, Hitler said "Rosenberg, stay on a bit afterwards."

It was a long time since Rosenberg had been singled out for favor. After years of mounting disappointment and helpless vexation, he had taken to complaining that Hitler merely looked "askew" when he was in the room. He would also put it in telephone parlance: "Hitler no longer hears my ring."

Rosenberg stepped aside to make room for Gauleiter Sauckel. With a look of worry on his pulpy face, Rosenberg went over to one of the windows. There he looked for something to lean on. The tubercular degeneration of his bones, which often made him limp, troubled him particularly in the spring. The others in the "court," who were taking their turns in the line of birthday well-wishers, glanced sidelong at Rosenberg. They had not failed to notice that Hitler had singled him out for a remark.

They had long ceased to regard Rosenberg as a rival for posts of any real importance. In their eyes—and they knew that their opinion was shared by Hitler—Rosenberg was an unworldly dogmatist who was still entirely engrossed in his Nordic and "Eastern" theories. To all these men, whose overriding concern was the struggle for power, he seemed a crackpot who had "not yet outgrown political puberty."

These men in Hitler's entourage had heard Hitler making fun of the whole idea of a Nordic race. "What good is a mane of blond hair to me if it's a horse's mane?" Often they had heard him comment "pigheaded ass" when he came across some of those ideological arguments in Rosenberg's books that ran counter to his tactical aims in power politics. They had seen how Rosenberg on such occasions took refuge in insulted silence. They, too, had noted how Hitler looked "askew" in Rosenberg's presence. Hitler's policy seemed to be to keep Rosenberg isolated but protected in his curious offices on Margaretenstrasse, as if Rosenberg were a kind of national monument. There the ideologue could write, publish, and distribute pamphlets, and believe in the overwhelming success of his *Myth of the Twentieth Century,* concerning which Hitler had said often enough: "I can't read that bosh."

Rosenberg had to wait another twenty minutes. He watched the antics of his enemies, people such as Foreign Minister Ribbentrop who more than once had tried to "close down for good Rosenberg's half-assed Foreign Office." Or Goebbels, who had called Rosenberg a "cultural Congo nigger." Nevertheless, Goebbels had stolen Rosenberg's arguments about the oneness of Judaism and bolshevism and the mission of the Nordic, Germanic race to serve as the bulwark of the civilized world against the bolshevistic Slavic imperialism of the East.

At last, they all left the room except for Göring and Reich Minister Lammers. Hitler invited Rosenberg to be seated.*

"Rosenberg," he said, "I'm well aware that in February 1938 you were deeply disappointed when I didn't promote you from chief of the party Foreign Policy Office to government foreign minister. I hope that in the interval you've realized my decision was right. In these turbulent times I need the sort of foreign minister who knows how to use his fists and elbows."

Hitler watched closely to see the effect of his words.

"I know, Rosenberg," he went on, "that the tough way we have to

* The conversation that followed was reconstructed from diary entries of Rosenberg's intimates and from statements made by members of Göring's and Lammers' staff.

4

conduct our foreign policy never suited you. But there is a reward for the trial of patience I've put you through. I now have a task for you that is going to give you pleasure. You are the man who first directed my attention to the possibilities for Germany in the East. You're our party specialist on Russia. Now I'm going to tell you something that up to this moment has been known to very few people inside and outside the party. We are soon going to put an end to the bolshevist menace. We shall sweep aside Stalin and bolshevism with the victorious might of our Wehrmacht and make what arrangements in the East *we* desire."

Rosenberg, who knew nothing of the impending campaign against the Soviet Union, showed signs of shock.

"I intend," Hitler said, "to appoint you Reich Minister for the eastern territories our army will soon occupy. And you will be independent; with two exceptions, no other cabinet minister and no other party bureau will be allowed to interfere with your work.

"The first exception concerns Göring as commissioner for the Four-Year Plan. Once the Soviet Union has collapsed under the smashing blows of our army—and that will be a matter of a few months—the vast economic energies of the East will be at our disposal. We will then be in a position to force England to make peace and to set up a German empire with inexhaustible resources whose power can no longer be shaken. With the occupation of the eastern territories, Göring will have a great deal more to handle."

Hitler began speaking faster, as was usual with him when he embarked on one of his monologues.

"All the raw materials of the East will have to be mobilized and transported to Germany. As chief of the Four-Year Plan, Göring must be able to issue directives and orders on his own. The East must be for Germany what the British Commonwealth is for England. The other exception involves Himmler. I would not want to charge you, Rosenberg, with the task of eliminating bolshevistic subhumanity. This sort of operation calls for Himmler's ruthless hand. Himmler, too, must therefore be given a special position in accordance with the tremendous tasks awaiting him in the East. But I shall insist he cooperate with you on a basis of mutual confidence."

Hitler was now finished with what he had to say; with a look he encouraged Rosenberg to reply.

"I thank you, my Führer," Rosenberg said in a low voice. As so often when he was agitated, his German had a distinctly Baltic accent. "Thank you for this sign of your trust in me."

5

Hitler stood up. "That will be all for today. I shall expect you to submit precise plans to me."

After Rosenberg had shuffled out of the room, Göring tapped his forehead. "This is the happiest day in his life," he said sardonically. "This appointment is your decision, my Führer. But I must repeat what I told you earlier: Rosenberg is utterly incompetent in organizational matters. . . . He won't be able to scurry up a single cow from the East, and like all these bookworms he'll be scared to death when his own theories will be applied to the Russians."

"I can't keep him a wallflower forever," Hitler replied. "Let him be. In the East he can do less harm than in his office here. At last he will have something to keep him busy and we won't have to have his sourpuss face around. We will be deciding what happens in practice, nobody else."

Swooped suddenly from the lowly state of ideological mentor to the dignity of a cabinet minister, Rosenberg descended the steps of the Chancellery in a state of exultation that abruptly gave way to acute anxiety. It was years afterward, when everything was over and all was lost, that he confessed to an intimate this fit of sheer funk. He admitted that at the moment something within him had warned him against letting himself be thrust into the harshness of wartime reality, against entering a battlefield where defeats awaited him.

For decades he had sat in his study developing theories on how to overcome bolshevism and divide up the vast area of the Soviet Union. Now he suddenly shied away from the process of translating those theories into realities. He stepped into his car and drove to Number 17 Margaretenstrasse, the solid, old-fashioned building that housed his offices, along with the neighboring building. In the vestibule Ukrainian, White Russian, and Caucasian exiles would be waiting to discuss dreams of their future "liberated homelands"—to talk either with Rosenberg himself or with Schickedanz, the stooped, bespectacled staff chief (a party rank). An old friend of Rosenberg's from the Baltic, he was a victim of stomach trouble and a shrewish wife. He seldom came up with any constructive ideas; sterile intellectual negation was his forte. Or else the visitors would talk with Georg Leibbrandt, an antibolshevist writer from the Ukraine who was the "specialist for Russian questions." He had no gift for practical or organizational work, but was a tough, obstinate man and wielded an adroit pen.

Rosenberg entered his office, patted the head of his Alsatian, who as usual welcomed him effusively, and slumped into his desk chair. As he later told the friend in whom he confided, at that moment, which after years of vain hopes and humiliations seemed to be the peak of his career, a host of images out of his past life seemed to come creeping from the corners of the room.

Early on he had developed the view that bolshevism was one facet of the Jewish world conspiracy against Western civilization, a cunning Jewish exploitation of the latent Russian and Slavic urge for imperialistic expansion.

Then Munich—years of intimate association with Hitler who looked up to him as the specialist on bolshevism and the East. It was he who had supplied Hitler with what seemed a simple solution to all German economic problems. There in the East was ample living space for Germans, and seizing it would simultaneously be a service to the Western world.

Acting as stand-in for Hitler while the Nazi party chieftain was imprisoned in Landsberg, Rosenberg had for the first time encountered mutterings in the party about his organizational ineptitude. But what did the opinions of such ruffians matter to him? Thronging around Hitler for their own selfish ends, all they wanted was to edge him out of power, shunt him off on a sidetrack as the "philosopher of the Movement."

For Rosenberg was filled with the proud confidence that he had given birth to the ideas they were feeding on—in his books *The Myth of the Twentieth Century* and *Paths for German Foreign Policy,* in which he had formulated the antibolshevist mission in the East. It would require fraternal racial collaboration among all the Germanic peoples, the English, the Dutch, the Flemings, the Swiss, Norwegians, Swedes, and Danes, joined together in a great league to save Western civilization. What was needed was peace in the West while the Germanic nations battled in the East against the "forces of decline."

In recognition of his leading role, Hitler had appointed him chief of the Foreign Policy Office of the party. Thus in 1933, when the Nazis took over the government, Rosenberg expected to be made foreign minister. But those "blockheads" around Hitler—as he bitterly put it—were incapable of really understanding his doctrines; they would sell their souls for power and were ripe for any kind of compromise. For a time he had clung to the hope that Hitler himself would summon him as soon as the first real Nazi foreign minister replaced the old nationalist conservative, Baron von Neurath.

At this time he moved his headquarters to the buildings on Margaretenstrasse and gathered around him assistants who seemed to share his views and goals, so that he would be prepared when his hour came. However, his attempt to visit "Germanic England" and personally pave the way for the union of the Germanic countries had failed. No Englishman of any consequence had been willing to receive him. But that had only confirmed his idea that malicious enemies in Hitler's entourage had been intriguing against him. Given his admiration for the British and his faith in his doctrines, he could conceive of no other explanation.

On February 4, 1938, Ribbentrop had been appointed the first Nazi foreign minister. Rosenberg wrote to Hitler: "I feel publicly compromised and dishonored. . . . Forgive my mentioning this, but what is involved is the prestige and honor of a man who has served you for eighteen years. . . ." But Hitler did not even bother to reply. And Rosenberg began to hate the men who had stolen his intellectual property and treated him as a laughing-stock, above all Ribbentrop and Goebbels.

Rosenberg had withdrawn into his own world. In 1939 he hailed the break-up of Czechoslovakia and the war against Poland, seeing this as a road to the destruction of the Soviet Union. But instead of crushing bolshevism, Hitler and Ribbentrop had divided Poland with the Soviet Union and concluded a pact of friendship with Stalin and an economic alliance. The Hitler-Stalin pact was like a blow in the face to all Rosenberg stood for. The war with France and England, especially with England, had struck him a further blow. He was sure this war would never have come about if Hitler had appointed him foreign minister from the start. He would have been able, he believed, to convince England and France as well that there was only one great peril to their existence, bolshevism, the Soviet Union's bolshevist imperialism combined with traditional Russian imperialism. He would have persuaded them that in spite of the wounds of Versailles there need not be any further problems between them and Germany, no colonial demands, no naval rivalry, no call for the return of Alsace-Lorraine; and that Germany had only one aim—to defeat the Soviet Union and impose a new order on the territory in the East.

Ever since 1939 Rosenberg had withdrawn into a sterile, isolated world in which he went on forging plans for which there was no context. This had gone on for one and a half years, until the sudden change of this April day.

The Führer had not forgotten him! The Führer had summoned him.

. . .

Surrounded by some collaborators, Hitler stood silently at the table on which Rosenberg had spread out maps illustrating his plans for the partition of the East. It was the afternoon of May 9, 1941. Under his maps lay others of the Balkans, where the German campaign against Yugoslavia and Greece was proceeding. There was also a map of Crete, for the parachute-troop assault on that island was being prepared.

"My Führer," Rosenberg started out,* "may I present you with the results of the preliminary studies of my temporary bureau for the administrative division of the occupied eastern territories." He said "occupied eastern territories" as though the impending operation were already completed. "I would like to review once more the conception that my associates and I have developed in years of work in order that the West in the future may be freed not only from the bolshevist menace but from any and all threats issuing from the East. Were we now to annihilate bolshevism alone but permit the Russian empire to continue, we might soon be facing another peril, namely that a White tsar might rise up again out of those intelligent strata of the Russian population which have an admixture of Germanic blood. Such a tsar would spawn a new Russian, though not bolshevist, imperialism and in thirty or forty years require fresh sacrifices of Teutonic lives. The only way to avert this danger is for us to splinter the vast Russian area. We must shear away those large border nations that have been violently subdued by both bolshevist and tsarist Moscow; the Ukrainian, the White Russian, and the Caucasian. We must either colonize these regions with Germanic peoples or set them up as independent entities under Germanic influence. In this way a bulwark against the Russians will arise. For the Russians must be diverted from Europe and turned toward Siberia. The plans I wish to present to you now, my Führer, are based upon this conception.

"The occupied eastern territories will be partitioned into five large governments. The northernmost of these will be given the name 'Ostland' and will embrace the former Baltic countries of Estonia, Latvia, and Lithuania which were occupied by the Bolsheviks in 1940. It will also include White Ruthenia. Latvia and Estonia, however, will be considerably enlarged toward the east, so that Estonia extends to the gates of Leningrad. White Ruthenia will also be enlarged so that it includes the

* This account is based on notes and statements of one of Rosenberg's assistants.

ancient historic city of Smolensk. As you can see on the map, my Führer, the old German trading port of Novgorod also belongs to Ostland; we shall rename it Naugard.

"The Ostland government with its Latvians and Estonians will contain about six million Germanically tinged inhabitants. In addition, there are German colonies in Lithuania and Germanic offshoots in White Ruthenia, all of whom together will provide a good nucleus for Germanization of Ostland. If, my Führer, you agree that the entire Ostland region shall be made an area for future German settlement, we shall have to work toward this goal from the very first. Latvians, Estonians, and Lithuanians must not be encouraged to think that they will regain the independence they had until 1940. We must take care that a large part of the intelligentsia, especially among the Latvians, are deported eastward into the remnant of Russian territory, which I will discuss presently. And then measures must be taken to encourage Germanic immigration. I could conceive, for example, that Norway would send Germanic immigrants into Ostland. The settlement of Danes, Dutch, and Flemings might also be considered, and after the victory over England, of Englishmen as well. In this way, after one or two generations, the Ostland could be regarded as Germanized territory. In some manner I shall have to leave to you, my Führer, we will directly unite Ostland with the German Reich."

As Rosenberg droned on, Hitler became visibly restless. Not that the content of Rosenberg's plan disturbed him, as it disposed of the destinies of nations and individuals with the total insensitivity of the theoretician; but he found Rosenberg's manner hard to take.

Rosenberg's hand now traced the southern portion of the map. "My Führer, let me now turn to the second government, the Ukraine. Its western boundary corresponds to that of the present Soviet Ukraine. Thus it also embraces Galicia, which one and a half years ago"—there was a faintly reproachful note in this allusion to the Hitler-Stalin pact—"after the partition of Poland, was assigned, with its oil wells, to the Soviet Union and became a part of the Ukraine. Galicia is highly important for the Ukraine, not only because of the oil but above all because of Ukrainian nationalism. Most of the advocates of Ukrainian independence who are still alive today live in Galicia. It is also the home of the OUN, the Ukrainians' militant revolutionary organization under Melnik and, recently, Bandera. For our purposes this group is too nationalistic and we therefore cannot use it. But the potential for moderate forces may also be found in Galicia. If, therefore, we wish to set up a Ukraine closely allied to Germany but relatively independent as a mighty bulwark against future Russian cravings for power, we must include Galicia in the Ukraine."

Rosenberg seemed impervious to the signs of Hitler's impatience.

"I have also expanded Ukrainian territory far to the east," he continued. "I propose to include the Crimea, which now belongs to Russia, in the Ukraine, although the population is heavily Russian and, in the south, Tatar. In this area a resettlement of the population eastward must take place. . . . Naturally the Ukraine must also include the German Volga Republic. There are already three hundred thousand Germans living in the Ukraine; in this way we would add to them the approximately four hundred thousand Volga Germans. Together with deserving German soldiers, who could be given land in the region, these would constitute the abutments for a strong Germanic bridge into the Ukraine. Unfortunately, we lack the manpower to think of Germanizing the Ukraine itself. For the present, the liberated Ukraine would have to assume the form of a German protectorate and then slowly evolve, under a pro-German leadership, into a self-governing state, perhaps into a kind of dominion. Russian pressure from the east would naturally force the Ukraine to enter into a lasting alliance with Germany. I have added such a wide band of Russian territory to the Ukraine precisely in order to provoke such pressure. The dispute over this band will keep the hostility alive forever, thus making the Ukraine a bulwark and a supplier of raw materials and food to us for all time."

So lost had Rosenberg become in his exposition that Hitler's first objection made him start in surprise and alarm.

"Does that mean," Hitler asked, "that you intend to stimulate Ukrainian nationalism? We should all be cured of engaging in such experiments. Think of what happened when we tried to establish a Ukrainian state at the end of the First World War. The Ukraine interests me solely as a reservoir that we need as other colonial nations need their colonies. Nationalistic ambitions there would only be a nuisance. Keep clear of that."

Rosenberg, flustered, tried to resume the thread of his discourse. "My Führer," he protested, "according to all the programs I have been working out with your approval during the past twenty years, the aim of this campaign in the East is to smash once and for all this Russian colossus, which is as dangerous to us in the bolshevist as in the tsarist form. Therefore we must fragment it by exploiting the irredentist tendencies of non-Russian regions which were annexed by force to the tsarist empire. Naturally all these regions will be dependent on Germany. But we will be restricting the Russians to their own territory and thrusting their center of gravity far back to the east, as far as the Urals. In this way the Russian peril will be once and for all . . ."

With controlled but unmistakable annoyance Hitler interrupted Rosenberg: "Never mind the dogmas," he grumbled. "In a few months we will have our victory in the East and ethnic boundaries will be totally unimportant. We shall extend our own power beyond Moscow. At the moment I cannot predict where the eastern frontier of the German or Germanic or European empire will lie. Perhaps the Japanese will lay claim to Siberia. Of course, I would not be delighted if the Japanese were to claim all of Siberia as far as the Urals, but we must show consideration for our ally in the Far East."

Hitler dropped the red pencil he had been holding, turned his back on Rosenberg, and stalked over to the window. "All right, set up your Ukraine government then," he said. "I've already told you that in that part of the world you can do as you please. But no stirring up of Ukrainian nationalism.

"Incidentally, I don't like the name 'government,' " Hitler continued. "That's a term that goes back to tsarist Russia. I would favor Reichskommissariat."

"My Führer!" Rosenberg said in a tone of offended helplessness. "The term 'kommissariat' will remind everyone of the bolshevist tyranny. Russia swarms with commissars who represent the Soviet state and who are feared by the populace."

"All the better," Hitler snapped. "They must fear us if our rule is to be solidly established. In that regard I have given radical orders to the army and to Himmler's SS squads. All commissars and Asiatic criminal types are to be shot by these Einsatzkommandos. Jews are to be collected and locked up in ghettos. Naturally, the army will try to slide out of these assignments. Our soldiers are always too soft. But a comprehensive program of education and propaganda will change all that and teach them to employ the necessary firmness in their encounters with bolshevist Jewish subhumans. Very well then, let us agree on Reichskommissars and Reichskommissariats."

Rosenberg hesitated, but only for a moment; then he was carried away by Hitler's stronger will and unbounded hubris. He resumed his lecture. "Adjacent to the Ukraine, and to the southeast, lies the Caucasus government—I beg your pardon, my Führer, I meant to say the Caucasus Reichskommissariat—so that the Russian heartland will be completely cut off from the Black Sea. The Caucasian peoples, who were not conquered by Moscow until the nineteenth century, not only reject bolshevism but also have a long tradition of hatred for the Russians. They will hail a political bond with Germany, since the backing of the powerful Greater German Reich will mean that they no longer need fear reprisals from the Russians."

"Very good," Hitler said, visibly forcing himself to be patient. "Do what you like with these savages. What interests me is the oil. Baku oil will be German property the way Persian oil belongs to the English, and it will remain German property."

Rosenberg forged on: "Then there would remain the Russian Reichskommissariat and possibly one for Turkistan," he said. "The eastern frontier of Reichskommissariat Russia, with Moscow as the center, is a matter I have left open for the present, since I do not know how far our army will advance. In order to be prepared, however, I have sketched an administrative division as far as the Urals. Russia also conquered most of the Turkistan areas only in the nineteenth century. These must, therefore, be separated from the body of Russia. The remaining Russia must be systematically weakened during the occupation. Since we will have possession of all the areas with food surpluses, a famine will arise automatically. Carrying out such a program will call for firmness and character on our side. The Russians will necessarily look eastward for help, will cease to regard Europe as the goal of their dynamic ambitions, and will direct their remaining vital energies toward Siberia."

"Rosenberg," Hitler interrupted in a mixture of sternness and condescension, "I am gratified to hear you talk of firmness, but I do not propose to get stuck in Russia. I have ordered the army to advance as far as the Astrakhan-Archangelsk line. Once we have occupied this line, bolshevism is done for, and what is left of Russia will no longer play any part in world politics. The Russians can tend to their own affairs in turning to the East. We don't have to send administrators into no-man's-land for that purpose. I am much more interested in the Reichskommissars who will be carrying out our policy on the spot. They must be carefully selected."

"As Reichskommissar for the Ostland, I should like to suggest Party Comrade Lohse," Rosenberg said. "In his capacity as gauleiter of Schleswig-Holstein he has dealt with questions of the North European Germanic stock. He would be excellent for the task of carrying out the Germanization of the Ostland."

"Lohse!" Hitler clasped his hands behind his back. "I don't give a damn whether or not Lohse knows anything about the Germanic stock. But he is supposed to be a hard-driving man. That's the important thing. I would have no objection to him."

"For the Ukraine," Rosenberg continued, "I've thought that Gauleiter Meyer of Münster would be the man. Dr. Meyer is an Old Fighter and has a balanced temperament. I think I would get on well with him, although so far he has not had any contact with Eastern problems."

"Out of the question," Hitler snapped. "Meyer in the Ukraine? The fellow should have been an office manager. In the Ukraine we're going to need a personality with iron fists who'll know how to extract the wealth of the country. Haven't you anybody but these third-raters?"

"Well, I was also thinking I might fit Meyer into my ministry as assistant secretary. . . ."

"That's all right with me. But for the Ukraine . . . ?"

"I was also thinking of Gauleiter Sauckel."

"Sauckel would certainly be stronger. But there must be still more energetic people. What have you been doing all this time you've been working on the problem? I'll settle it with Göring. Whom do you have for the Caucasus?"

"My staff chief, Schickedanz. It's true that he doesn't know Russia, but from working in my bureau he's acquired a great deal of information."

"I don't know him at all. Is he familiar with economics and oil?"

"He has had a great deal of political training and is accustomed to working with me. . . ." Rosenberg trailed off; his voice plainly betrayed how offended he was.

"If he has no background in economics I can't use him there. So I'll have to talk with Göring about the Caucasus also. Incidentally, I want you to find a place for Party Comrade Kube somewhere in the East. I've forgiven him his extravagances as gauleiter of Brandenburg."

As Rosenberg related immediately after the interview, he realized fully that in recommending these "hard-driving" men, Hitler was forcing him to collaborate with his enemies.

"Personally, I don't particularly like Kube," he protested. "But if you wish it . . ."

"Indeed, I wish it," Hitler said. "For the rest, I'll instruct the Army High Command to check with you about the demarcations of the military and civil administrations. The occupied eastern territories will remain under military administration for two hundred kilometers behind the battlefront; in that zone, too, Göring and the Reich Minister of Food will have the same special rights they'll enjoy in your zone. The country behind the two-hundred-kilometer area will be turned over to you piece by piece. So you still have time. I'll let you know what I decide about the Reichskommissariats. I guess that is all."

Dr. Otto Bräutigam, the German consul general for Soviet Transcaucasia, whose offices were located in Tiflis, had just completed his annual cure in Karlsbad—he suffered from a gastric disorder—when he received a telephone call from Number 14 Margaretenstrasse in Berlin. The caller was Rosenberg's Russian specialist, Leibbrandt, who urgently asked Bräutigam to call on him before returning to Tiflis.

Bräutigam knew Leibbrandt from the years when he had served as German consul in Kharkov. At that time Leibbrandt had undertaken a study tour among the German population of the Ukraine. Since Bräutigam in any case had to report to the Foreign Office, he agreed, and two days later was in Berlin.

Bräutigam was immediately struck by a change in Leibbrandt. He had an air of nervous bustle. As soon as the two men were alone, Leibbrandt announced to Bräutigam that the decisive battle with bolshevism was impending.

If this were so, it naturally reduced Bräutigam's further work in Tiflis to a shadow play. But even before Bräutigam had fully digested Leibbrandt's statement, he was informed that the German armed forces were completing their deployment in the East and that Hitler was counting on defeating the Soviet Union within three to four months at the latest. Of course, there were some skeptics, Leibbrandt said; they were to be found among the diplomats in Moscow and also among the high-ranking generals. They had been persuaded, however, that Stalin and the Soviet Union must not be allowed the time to prepare a surprise attack on Germany while she was still involved in the war with England. The 1939 pact with the Soviet Union had only been a ceasefire that the Russians would break as soon as Stalin felt strong enough. Now the German Wehrmacht was still in a position to achieve military destruction of the Soviet Union and eliminate the bolshevist menace once and for all. The Führer had assigned Alfred Rosenberg the task of reconstruction of the conquered eastern areas and had therefore created the Ministry for the Occupied Eastern Territories.

"Of course, we are having a hard time finding the needed top personnel," Leibbrandt said, fixing Bräutigam with a questioning look through his thick glasses. "I was thinking of you. Aside from you, I know of no one so well acquainted with the East; I'd like to have you as my deputy and head of the Department for General Policy. You've often told me that you think the majority of the Ukrainians want separation from Russia and an independent Ukrainian state. Creation of just such a Ukraine will be one of the main pillars of our policy. I have already recruited the head of our Caucasus and Turkistan section: Professor von Mende. Do you know him?"

Bräutigam reflected. Mende? Oh, yes—a slight neat man who came from somewhere in the Baltic region; a scholar who lectured on Eastern races.

"Von Mende has never been in the Soviet Union, but he has studied its peoples," Leibbrandt said. "He has personal relations with the exiles from the Causasus and Turkistan, and he is convinced that the peoples of those regions can be organized into new states.

"The section for Russia is still vacant. I can't yet think of anyone who could run it as we would wish. Anyhow, our plans as far as Russia is concerned are not yet settled.

"Thank God, you and I will have nothing to do with police questions. Himmler will take care of that end of things. And economic matters concern us only indirectly. Since a swift victory over England requires that the resources of the East be mobilized as soon as possible, the Führer himself wants to take over the direction of economic exploitation of the area. Our ministry, of course, will also have a kind of department for economic affairs. But Dr. Meyer has worked out an idea that seems to me first-rate. In Göring's Four-Year Plan, Undersecretary Schlotterer is responsible for industry and Undersecretary Riecke for agriculture. Both have by now been assigned corresponding duties for the territories which will lie directly behind the advancing eastern front and will constitute army rear areas under the OKH [Army High Command]. They will now also hold the same leading positions in our organization. In this way, everything will be united in one hand, and we can devote ourselves entirely to nonpolitical and cultural matters."

Bräutigam, too, was not a man of action. But in his many years as a diplomat in foreign countries, he had learned a few things about the reciprocal relationship of politics and economics. How would it be possible to build an independent Ukraine without full power over the economy? And with an independently functioning police force? That was an arrangement acceptable only to inexperienced theorists. Any realist would anticipate trouble.

But Leibbrandt was already rushing on: "Please give my suggestion your consideration. I know how fond you are of the Ukraine and of Ukrainian culture. You simply must participate in a mission that will change the whole aspect of the East forever, that will give the Ukrainians their freedom and Europe security. A favorable decision on your part would be a great relief to Minister Rosenberg and to me, and would carry us a long way forward. Every day we encounter fresh difficulties, if only because of the necessity for secrecy. We must not be caught with insufficient staff when the work starts for us on the East. That would make a terrible impression on the Führer. The Reichskommissars for the Kommissariats into which we will temporarily divide up the Soviet Union have not yet been appointed. The Führer has reserved this decision for himself. Hundreds of lesser posts must be filled under those Reichskommissars who will be responsible for carrying out our orders for the reconstruction of the East. The SA is prepared to help us by providing us with a host of SA leaders. But that may mean that it envisages a complete SA staffing of all presumptive posts—which is certainly not what we want. Then there are the party leadership trainees [Ordensjunker]; but they have no knowledge of languages. Nevertheless, they seem to expect top-ranking positions. We have no real specialists."

He ended with: "In making your decision, I trust you will consider all these facts. . . . Incidentally, a request has already been made in a personal letter to Ribbentrop to have you detailed for detached service in our department."

The "Heinrich," Reichsführer-SS Himmler's private headquarters train, stood on a sidetrack of the Angerburg-Lötzen rail line. The time was some eight weeks later, the morning of July 17, 1941.

Ever since June 22, when the German armies had crossed the Soviet borders, reports of victories had been pouring in unceasingly from the eastern front. Only an hour before, a loudspeaker on the train had announced the capture of the politically and historically important city of Smolensk. Since the German pincers had closed between Bialystok and Minsk no less than 324,000 Soviet soldiers, 3,300 tanks, and nearly 2000 artillery pieces had fallen into German hands, and the defeated Soviet armies were retreating. The hot summer air nurtured among the Germans a feverish certainty of victory.

In the shade of the woods that surrounded the train, Alfred Rosenberg, who had just received his official appointment as Minister for the Occupied Eastern Territories, was taking a walk. As he paced the narrow forest paths, he wore for the first time the uniform that henceforth would identify him and his men. It was not field gray but a yellowish tan, made from existing stocks of Ordensjunker uniform cloth. Rosenberg's adjutant walked on his left, Dr. Otto Bräutigam on his right. With mixed feelings, but also with the resignation of a man accustomed to obey orders and transfers, Bräutigam had accepted the post of chief of the Department of General Policy in the Ministry for the Occupied Eastern Territories, and simultaneously had assumed (as an artillery captain in the reserve) the duties of liaison officer to the Army High Command.

Until Rosenberg's official appointment, Bräutigam had stayed with the Army General Staff in the Mauerwald camp in East Prussia. There he had heard things that caused him to doubt whether Rosenberg, the ministry, and his own department would be able to exert any real influence upon events. Among the first documents that crossed his desk at the end of June was a recent order from the Führer setting forth Göring's extensive powers in the occupied eastern territories. Bräutigam had sent Rosenberg a copy of this document; apparently Hitler himself had not bothered to inform Rosenberg of the order. Bräutigam was further dismayed when, in conversations with Göring's subordinate, Undersecretary Riecke, he learned that neither Hitler nor Göring intended to promote liberation of the Ukrainian peasants in the sense of returning the land the Soviet regime had collectivized. On the contrary, the Soviet kolkhozes were to be retained because they seemed ideally suited to expedite that appropriation of the agricultural wealth of the Ukraine which was already provided for in the Four-Year Plan. Bräutigam sensed unspoken but decisive differences between the plans of Rosenberg and Leibbrandt and the plans of Hitler.

Bräutigam, therefore, had been considerably relieved to hear on July 15 that Rosenberg would be coming to East Prussia the next day, or the day after, in order to "receive from the Führer's hand his final appointment to his historic task." Bräutigam himself had been given instructions to report to Rosenberg, and now was walking at the side of his superior, eager to learn from his lips what the ultimate outlines of his ministry and of the administration in the occupied territories would be. About sixteen hours had passed since Rosenberg had seen Hitler and had a long talk with him before receiving his official assignment. Hitler had been in a euphoric state, ecstatic over the German army's victories.

Rosenberg paced the narrow forest path in silence. Inside the train, the central cars of which belonged to Reich Minister Lammers, the text of Rosenberg's appointment was being worked out; Hitler intended to sign the document this same afternoon in his East Prussian headquarters. Rosenberg stared into space with curiously glazed eyes. The three men had been walking in silence for almost half an hour before he abruptly declared: "The Führer has repeatedly postponed the beginning of our work because he first wanted to have really large areas occupied. Once again he was right in his foresight and in his faith in our victory. But now our work is going to begin. The time of waiting is over. In the course of the next few days, Lithuania will be turned over to us."

Bräutigam asked: "What about the Ukraine? When is that to be handed over?"

"The Führer has decided that conquered Galicia, the western Ukraine, will not be placed under our control. Administratively, Galicia is to be annexed to the Polish government-general and subordinated to Governor-general Frank. Consequently, our work in the Ukraine will not begin for several weeks."

Bräutigam had objections. "But if you want to make an independent territory out of the Ukraine, it cannot possibly be done without the Galician Ukrainians. They have barely two years of bolshevism behind them. Bolshevist government and propaganda has scarcely affected those people as yet. Can we conduct any really affirmative Ukrainian policy if we start out by lopping off so vital an area?"

"The Führer has not yet fully taken in my ideas," Rosenberg said. "He told me we could give the Ukrainians compensation on their eastern border. The Führer is fearful of excessive Ukrainian nationalism and thinks it will be good if the intelligent western Ukrainians are assigned to Frank and do not puff themselves up into masters of their proletarianized brothers in the rest of the Ukraine."

Bräutigam later described his unspoken reactions. Could a government minister really be so naïve? So Hitler was opposed to Ukrainian national-ism? But how could an independent Ukraine arise without it? Did this mean in effect that Hitler had no use for an independent Ukraine?

"Our propagandists will have their work cut out for them," he heard Rosenberg saying. "They will have to make the Ukrainians understand that this temporary renunciation of vital territory is necessary."

His years as a professional diplomat enabled Bräutigam to control himself. He hid his agitation. But he asked: "Isn't it a poor start for the ministry to have to put up with a *fait accompli* on such an important matter?"

"At the moment, the Führer is preoccupied with the swift execution and completion of the campaign. That is the reason for such decisions.

19

THE PROJECTED GREATER GERMAN REICH

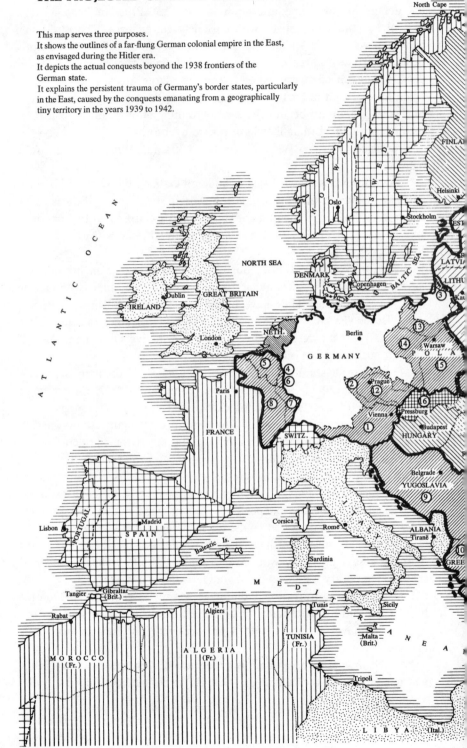

This map serves three purposes.
It shows the outlines of a far-flung German colonial empire in the East,
as envisaged during the Hitler era.
It depicts the actual conquests beyond the 1938 frontiers of the
German state.
It explains the persistent trauma of Germany's border states, particularly
in the East, caused by the conquests emanating from a geographically
tiny territory in the years 1939 to 1942.

North Cape

ATLANTIC OCEAN

NORTH SEA

NORWAY

SWEDEN

BALTIC SEA

FINLA

Helsinki

Oslo

Stockholm

EST

LATVIA

LITHU

DENMARK

Copenhagen

Kat

IRELAND

Dublin

GREAT BRITAIN

London

NETH.

Berlin

GERMANY

POLA

Warsaw

Prague

Vienna

Pressburg

Budapest

HUNGARY

Paris

FRANCE

SWITZ.

Belgrade

YUGOSLAVIA

PORTUGAL

Lisbon

Madrid

SPAIN

Balearic Is.

Corsica

Rome

ITALY

Sardinia

ALBANIA

Tiranë

GREE

Tangier

Gibraltar
(Brit.)

Rabat

Algiers

M E D

Tunis

Sicily

Malta
(Brit.)

T E R R A N E A

TUNISIA
(Fr.)

MOROCCO
(Fr.)

A L G E R I A
(Fr.)

L I B Y A (Ital.)

Tripoli

Farthest limits of the Eastern front
Frontline, Winter, 1941
Germany's frontiers, December 31, 1937
Demarcation line of German-Russian spheres of interest,
September 28, 1939
The "iron core" of the Greater German Reich
Dimensions of the projected Greater German Reich

Archangel

REICHSKOMMISSARIAT

Perm

Kirov   Chelyabinsk

S   O   V
Volkhov   Vologda   I   E   T
ingrad   MOSCOW
                                        Magnitogorsk

Volga River

Moscow   Kuibyshev

MISS.

Bryansk   Voronezh   U   N   I   O   N

REICHSKOMMISSARIAT

Kharkov   Stalingrad

Kiev   Astrakhan
itsa   UKRAINE   Rostov

            REICHSKOMMISS.   CASPIAN SEA

                         Stavropol

            11   CAUCASUS
         CRIMEA   Tiflis   Baku

arest   B L A C K   S E A

A

                    Ankara   K   E   Y   I R A N
         T
      U   R   K   E
                                        Y

                              S Y R I A

      Dodecanese
      (Ital.)   Cyprus   Damascus
                    (Brit.)
                                              TRANSJORDAN
E   A   PALESTINE   Amman
               Jerusalem

         Cairo
E   G   Y   P   T

0   200   400   600   800
                km

Annexed or subjugated:

1 Austria
2 Sudetenland
3 Memelland
4 Eupen-et-Malmedy
5 Belgium with Flanders
   and Wallonia
6 Luxembourg
7 Alsace-Lorraine
8 North and East France
9 Yugoslavia
10 Greece
11 Crimea
   ("Land of the Goths")
12 Protectorate of Bohemia
   and Moravia
13 "Reichsgau" Danzig-
   West Prussia
14 Reichsgau Wartheland
15 Government-
   General of Poland

   Reichskommissariats
   Countries considered
   "ideologically akin"
   Countries to be tied
   closely to the "Greater
   German Reich"
   Satellite states
   Autonomous states
   within National
   Socialist sphere
   of influence
16 Slovakia
   States to come under
   German guidance
   States dependent
   on Germany
   Unassigned border states

For the time being, everything must be done in the interests of victory. Once that is achieved—a matter of a few more weeks—I shall once again make a comprehensive presentation of my plans to the Führer."

"Herr Minister," Bräutigam persisted, "may I ask how the Führer has decided the question of the staffing for the Reichskommissariat for the Ukraine? That is still unsettled."

Rosenberg walked on, alongside the entire length of the train. He spoke only after he had reached the last car: "The personnel question was indeed discussed. The Führer has at last accepted Lohse as Reichskommissar for the Ostland. Over my objections, however, he appointed Koch, the gauleiter of East Prussia, Reichskommissar for the Ukraine. Göring felt someone like that was necessary if we are to take full advantage of the war-production potential of the Ukraine."

This time Bräutigam could not hide his dismay. "Herr Minister," he said, "Koch is famous for brutality. He is said to be a holy terror. He'll do drastic damage to your objective in the Ukraine." Bräutigam pictured the heavy figure of the gauleiter, a former railroad worker from Wuppertal who had fought his way up with cunning, ruthlessness, and hamlike fists. One look at that coarse, empty face was enough: what you saw there was a low craving for power. The man had never so much as set foot in the Ukraine. He knew nothing whatsoever about the region he was supposed to rule.

"I have sent a memorandum to the Führer," Rosenberg said, "explaining that I do not consider Koch suitable because he lacks any philosophical basis and characterological balance. But I must put up with Koch. For the present, military victory takes precedence, and, first of all, appropriation of the Ukrainian harvests and raw materials must be assured in order to guarantee victory. Afterward, I shall once again advise the Führer of my objections. Moreover, Koch has been subordinated to my ministry in his new capacity. He will have to obey my instructions."

"But it's the initial period that is decisive," Bräutigam said.

"I shall give Koch written instructions advising moderation," Rosenberg said. "Koch would have preferred taking over the Ostland Reichskommissariat. Then he would have had an area adjacent to East Prussia. But I managed to block that, at any rate. And in compensation for the appointment of Koch I put across Schickedanz as my candidate for Reichskommissar for the Caucasus. Göring put up strong objections. He insisted on an oil specialist. And the Führer was inclined to accept his views. But I did not yield."

Bräutigam thought of Schickedanz' stooped figure and rather pitiable Mephistophelian appearance. Putting him across was a victory?

"The Führer compromised with me," Rosenberg continued. "Consul General Neubacher will be assigned to Schickedanz as head of his economics section; Neubacher has made quite a name for himself by his management of the Rumanian oil wells. His appointment should be reassuring to Göring, whose primary concern is with economic matters."

There it was again, this ghastly lack of understanding of the indissoluble relationship between the economy and politics. It was clear who the real ruler of the Caucasus would be: Neubacher and not Schickedanz. Bräutigam wanted to point out the incompatibility between naked exploitation and a constructive policy of friendship. He wanted to say that a policy of amity would, within a short time, extract far more treasures from an occupied country than any sort of violent appropriation, which was bound to breed resistance on the other side. He wondered how to present all this to Rosenberg, whose dull, doctrinaire mind was impervious to practical statesmanship.

He had not found the suitable opening when an orderly approached from the direction of the headquarters train. He brought word that the document of appointment had been drawn up and that Reich Minister Lammers was waiting for Rosenberg to come to the Führer, who would then sign it.

Six weeks later, on September 1, 1941, the radios in the former Yugoslav embassy building on Rauchstrasse in Berlin were still announcing continuous advances in the East. The building—a modern structure of highly polished composition stone with an impressive vestibule and big, bright rooms—housed the offices of the new Ministry for the Occupied Eastern Territories.

Late that morning of September 1, Rosenberg sat in his big, pompously appointed room. On July 25 the command of the German army in Lithuania had turned over to Rosenberg the first of the occupied territories. Reichskommissar Lohse, who could barely wait to take over his new zone of power, had reported to Rosenberg, but very briefly. At least he had observed the conventions of courtesy and had let several of Rosenberg's verbose statements wash over him. Then he departed for Kaunas and assumed command of his region.

Since that time, Army Group South had advanced deep into the eastern part of the Ukraine. When a German pincers closed around Umanj, over 600,000 prisoners of war fell into the hands of the Germans.

Now Rosenberg was waiting for Koch, who was also supposed to report to him before assuming his office in the Ukraine. It seemed that Koch knew he had tried to block the gauleiter's appointment as Reichskommissar, and was seizing every opportunity to sneer at his "future boss." Koch kept telling everyone who would listen that the Führer was his boss and no one else. The Führer's door was always open to him, he maintained; he didn't need to take a roundabout route through "that crackpot" Rosenberg.

Before Rosenberg lay the instructions "for a Reichskommissar in the Ukraine," which he had repeatedly revised during the past several weeks. Again and again he reread his own phrases, in order to be prepared for his encounter with Koch: "The primary objective of the work of a German Reichskommissar in the Ukraine is to guarantee the supply of foodstuffs and raw materials for the German Reich, thus promoting the German war effort. . . ."

That was his concession to Hitler and Koch. But he had tried, in a series of elaborations, to tie it in with his own ideas. For example, he had written: "The strengthening of Ukrainian nationalism, however, constitutes one of the possible means for achieving high output, not only by enforcing it with the methods of military power, but, in the course of time, by securing voluntary collaboration on the part of the Ukrainians. . . . Since Germany is seeking a free Ukrainian republic, there can be no objection to announcing this goal at a time yet to be determined. The basis, of course, will have to be defense against Moscow and alliance with the country that has freed the Ukrainians from their oppression: Germany. . . . It follows from this objective that we must immediately . . ."

Rosenberg had cut the word "immediately" and substituted the weaker "as soon as possible." The passage now read: ". . . as soon as possible deal with all questions that can radiate a psychological effect. . . . Ukrainian writers, scholars, and politicians must be enlisted to stimulate historical consciousness of the Ukraine. Along with this educational program, we must introduce legislation to consolidate the political power of the German Reich in the Ukraine, but gradually also to gain the cooperation of the Ukrainians themselves. . . . The founding of a major university in Kiev must be undertaken. We will ask the German universities to provide instructors in the German language for the larger cities of the Ukraine. Ukrainian fiction and political writing must be promoted by all possible means. . . ."

Strange as it may seem, Rosenberg was hoping to convey these pet ideas, obsessions, and plans to the East Prussian gauleiter.

A heavy limousine stopped outside the broad steps leading up to the door of his ministry. The future Reichskommissar for the Ukraine got out. Short, thick-set, thick-necked, with a mustache that did not disguise the vulgarity of his face, Koch paused on the sidewalk for a moment. A bulky seal ring of massive gold glittered on his hand. Then he charged up the steps and bellowed to the receptionist that he was Gauleiter Koch; he would find his own way to Rosenberg's office.

What was discussed between the two men during the next fifteen minutes remained Rosenberg's secret. Probably it was so humiliating that he did not unburden himself even to his most intimate associates. But when the flush-faced Koch left Rosenberg's office and tramped toward the exit, he ran into Cranz, chief of Rosenberg's public relations section, and several other employees of the ministry. The ensuing scene gave a good clue to the nature of their encounter. Cranz innocently offered to shake hands, saying: "May I congratulate you, Herr Reichskommissar, on the interesting and fruitful mission you will now be assuming?"

Koch gave Cranz an appraising look: "What mission do you mean?" he growled.

"I mean the mission of leading such a biologically strong and valuable race as the Ukrainians back to national consciousness," Cranz said.

Koch set his clenched fists on his hips. "My dear sir," he said, "you must have read that in some provincial tabloid. Let me tell you this: the Ukrainians are Slavs through and through. They're going to be governed by makhorka, vodka, and the knout. If you people want to spend your time theorizing about the Slavic soul, that's all right with me. But I'll handle this job my way."

With that he stalked down the hallway. At the head of the staircase he turned around once more.

"I don't need any of your instructions," he called back to them. "And I don't need any funds from your agency either. All I want is an advance. You'll get that back inside of a year, and then we'll be quits."

What We Must Fight For

General Staff Major Heinz Danko Herre went through the severe winter battles of 1941–1942 in the Ukraine, serving as the Ia* of the 49th German Mountain Corps at Stalino. Lean and lithe, looking every inch the excellent rider he was, Herre was just thirty-two years old that winter. He was an intelligent, lively man, quick to enthusiasm and then hard to hold back. He had already been through the campaigns in Poland, France, Yugoslavia, and southern Russia.

The son of an army officer, Herre had early learned from his father a deep love for Russian music and literature. Later, when he was attending military academy in Hanover, he had met the daughter of Count Lambsdorff, former German military attaché in St. Petersburg. A great deal of Russian was spoken in the Lambsdorff household, and this had stirred his ambition to learn Russian himself, which he did in record time. As a young officer he had traveled to Estonia, Karelia, and Bessarabia. He had become so involved with Russia and its plight under Stalin that when he marched into the Ukraine with his corps early in July 1941 it never entered his head that the German armies would be doing anything except liberating the Russian masses from bolshevism, from the ideological statism of the Soviets.

So caught up was Herre in his own point of view that, like many others, he accepted the official Nazi slogans concerning the "annihilation of the Soviet system" and "destruction of the source of bolshevistic world revolution" at face value and failed to recognize them as camouflage for a policy aimed against the Russian peoples.

* General staff officer responsible for operations and leadership, corresponding to the G3 in the NATO forces.

24

There can be no doubt about the ambivalent relationship of the German officer corps toward Hitler. Professional German military men vacillated between dislike and appreciation, contempt and stunned admiration of the Nazi leader. They at once feared him and felt they owed him absolute obedience. Moreover, they lacked the political sophistication to question whether a totalitarian Nazi power apparatus could liberate a nation from a totalitarian Soviet power apparatus. The deeply rooted nationalistic attitudes of the German professional officers made the fascist, nationalist, and military authoritarianism of Hitler far more acceptable to them than a socialist dictatorship. Though they had no love for the Nazi party apparatus, for many of its leaders, and for the SS in particular, they were nevertheless loyal Germans.

Herre had occasionally come upon fellow officers who spoke in general terms about "Russian vermin." But he had given little thought to the implications of that kind of language. Instead, he let his mind dwell on the genuine joy with which large parts of the Russian population received the invading forces, on the greetings they had called out to the German soldiers, and on the throngs who attended the religious services of thanksgiving—the first religious services to be held in twenty years.

Herre had not hesitated to appoint native mayors in the various towns where his corps set up headquarters. On his own initiative, moreover, he had published notices that the peasants could soon expect their land to be returned to them. He had given arms to Russians and Ukrainians who volunteered in large numbers to act as guards for German facilities such as supply dumps, or bridges, or to carry out the duties of ordinary police forces.

The German advance had continued, deeper and deeper into Russia. And everywhere Herre found evidence of how easy it was to secure the helpfulness and even an outright alliance of Russians and Ukrainians "against Stalin." In the area under his supervision he had encountered not a single case of unreliability or of partisan activity. He himself had slept alone in peasant houses among Russian families and discharged Russian soldiers. Many of his hosts had confided to him that they were hoping for a somewhat better life now that the Germans were here. He had also noted the low morale of the Red Army: the greater part of the men fought spiritlessly and were ready to desert at the first opportunity.

Once, after the German army troops had departed from Olginskoye, a small town southwest of Stalino, an SS police squad had taken over in their place and abruptly shot the majority of the men whom Herre had armed as auxiliary police and left behind to keep order. When word of this reached Herre, he assumed, with the curious ambivalence of army men vis-à-vis the SS, that this was the kind of excess the SS people were capable of; he shrugged it off as an unfortunate but isolated incident. From somewhere in the rear echelons, rumors had reached the front that a German civil government under the direction of Erich Koch, gauleiter of East Prussia, had been set up in Rovno, and that Koch had arrived flourishing a riding whip and gabbling about a "coming colonial empire in the East." Again, Herre gave no credence to this sort of story.

The fighting had permitted no pauses for reflection. In spite of all the encirclements and victories, the year 1942 did not see the expected total defeat of the enemy. The first great thrust of the German offensive had come to a standstill outside Moscow. Then winter descended and new Russian armies appeared out of nowhere to besiege the German formations. These new troops seemed to fight without regard for losses. The situation was one in which Herre was kept incessantly busy, endlessly harassed to the point of complete exhaustion.

Probably everybody requires some major, shattering experience if he is to be wrenched away from old prejudices and fixed ways of looking at things.

Herre had this kind of experience on January 26, 1942. For the past week Soviet formations that had pierced the German lines had been occupying the supply lines of the corps, while at the same time fresh Soviet forces were pressing upon the front itself. General Conrad, commanding general of the 49th Mountain Corps, considered a temporary retreat and was trying to mobilize horse sleds in place of the frozen or broken-down motorized supply columns. Herre had sent Captain Geiger back to Stalino to confiscate sleds. Four days later Geiger returned in an overwrought state and reported on "frightful conditions" in the Stalino transit camp for Soviet prisoners of war. That same day Herre asked General Conrad for permission to make a personal inspection of the camp.

On January 26 he drove to Stalino, passing gigantic coal heaps, pitheads, and power plants. His memoirs and diary entries retain a detailed picture of his subsequent experiences. He searched for the camp and finally found it on the outskirts of the city, housed in buildings that had formerly belonged to a Soviet community college. Right at the entrance Herre came upon a row of Russians and Ukrainians who wore armbands identifying them as auxiliary guards. They carried heavy clubs. Either these men came from the scum of humanity that every city in the world can provide, or hunger and despair had driven them to assume their present jobs.

Herre asked to see the camp commandant, who had his office in a doorkeeper's dirty lodge. He turned out to be a nervous, rather frightened, elderly reserve officer. When Herre told him he wished to inspect the camp because he was seeking volunteer sled drivers, the commandant at first refused. Herre needed fifteen minutes to break his resistance. The captain's final argument was that Herre would certainly catch typhus and die an utterly useless death. Finally, he reluctantly gave way and assigned a lieutenant to show Herre around. The lieutenant was fetched from an adjoining room. He reeked of alcohol.

The college consisted of a very large building with many classrooms. It was surrounded by a sizable number of athletic fields in which, at the moment, huge burial pits were being dug. Several elderly German militia men looked on as the auxiliary guards used their clubs to drive to work prisoners who could scarcely stand on their feet.

"You really want to see this menagerie?" the lieutenant asked before Herre stepped outside. "It isn't all that interesting to see the vermin dying. Sooner or later they all croak, there's nothing to be done about it."

Herre turned abruptly to eye the man at his side. "From whom are you getting such orders?" he asked.

The lieutenant dropped his overcasual tone in favor of an aggrieved one. "What are we supposed to do?" he whined. "Nobody here was prepared for such hordes. And the Russkies are right across our supply line. No food is getting through. Your Mountain Corps is already slaughtering its mules for meat. These prisoners are actually half animal, and there are far too many of them. The best thing would be for them to die off as soon as possible."

Herre began to grasp what was going on here, and probably in many other places in occupied Russia. He began to realize that this attitude toward the Russians and Ukrainians was not limited to the SS or the SD (Sicherheitsdienst, the SS secret police force), or to a party man like Koch. It was a kind of contagion that could infect anybody, including enlisted men in the army, including career officers, and certainly including those aging militia men who at home would not have hurt a fly.

Herre snapped out an order: he wanted to see the dormitory of the men "fit for work." It was empty; the "fit" were outside, presumably doing various jobs about the camp. But even without its human contents this dormitory was a hellhole, rundown, filthy, emitting a dreadful stench, and so icy cold that faeces and urine were frozen to the floor. Herre next inspected the quarters of the "conditionally fit." A few militiamen stood at the door. It seemed to Herre that their faces looked stamped out on a gigantic press—incapable of registering any more feeling. There was nothing fanatical about those faces; they were marked by a fatalistic acceptance of a situation they regarded as inescapable.

The lieutenant touched Herre's sleeve. "Enter on your own responsibility, sir," he said. "Anyone who goes in there will either be trampled to death or catch typhus. Most of them already have it. You can't possibly use any of those men. They're done for, no matter what."

Herre ordered the door opened. A terrible reek wafted into his face, taking his breath away. The prisoners were massed so tightly together that no one could stretch out to sleep. Right up against the door there were three bodies, lying huddled on the floor, dying or already dead. The lieutenant gestured to the guards. They seized the three men by the feet and dragged them out into the corridor. Herre set his jaw and stepped forward into the midst of the silent, gray mass of men, from whom only an occasional moan arose. Their faces were livid, their eyes sunken, their beards encrusted with filth.

When Herre spoke his first words of Russian, a movement passed through the ranks of the prisoners. They opened a lane for him. The moans in the background stopped.

The lieutenant clutched Herre's sleeve from behind. "Come back, sir," he repeated several times. "You can't use any of these men. You'll only catch typhus."

Herre said in an icy voice: "You may go. I won't keep you here against your will."

In Russian, Herre asked the prisoners what they were being given to eat, whether there were any doctors for them, whether they had to stand all the time. But he found himself staring into a wall of torpid, burned-out faces. The men were looking only at the lieutenant. It took a long time—Herre was already beginning to wonder how long he could stand the pestilential air—before a voice from the rear replied. The spokesman said that they were receiving nothing but watery soup and mouldy bread; they had no blankets, there were no doctors, and two hundred men were dying every day. Then came another voice: "Gospodin, you too are a mother's son; help us, please help . . ."

Herre was too choked to say a word. He turned and followed the visibly relieved lieutenant back to the door, walking through that lane of gray humanity. When they were outside, one of the militiamen, obviously in a state of funk, slammed the door behind them so hard that the wall shook.

Herre insisted that he be shown the "unfit" also. The lieutenant's alcohol-laden breath puffed into his face. "But, Herr Major," he whined, "you certainly can't use any of those guys. The dead are piled in heaps. I'm not going in there."

"Then I'll go without you."

But the lieutenant followed him, nevertheless. The room Herre was taken to might have been a lecture hall in a German university. But if there could have been any possible intensification of the pestilential air that filled the other halls, this was it. The odor of decaying corpses hung in the air. When the door opened, a Ukrainian auxiliary guard stepped forward. He pounded his club on a table and ordered: "Stand up!"

In the gallery where students had once sat, almost fleshless skulls were raised here and there. They stared at Herre like so many death masks. Herre walked up a flight of steps between the rows of benches. And he saw the dead and dying lying atop of one another between the benches.

He no longer noticed that the lieutenant was still following him, still tugging at his sleeve, and repeating again and again: "Sir, you'll catch typhus. . . ." Herre did not say a word until he had reached the top row and could look down over the circle of death. Then he abruptly shouted: "Are all of you crazy? Don't you think about anything?"

The lieutenant protested in his whimpering voice: "Sir, I object to such . . ."

"Object all you like. You will be hearing from me!"

Herre raced down the steps, ignoring the lieutenant. As he stepped out the door of the building, he came upon a procession of the "fit for work," who hobbled in from the street. Auxiliary guards were at that moment pommelling the huddled body of a prisoner who had collapsed at the entrance. But not only the auxiliaries. One of the militiamen drove his rifle butt into the back of a reeling, emaciated prisoner, knocking him to the ground. Herre rushed at the veteran. He was a man of about fifty, with a round, common face. There seemed no trace of a cruel streak in it.

"You!" Herre bellowed at him. "Aren't you ashamed . . ."

The soldier's mouth gaped as he sought for words, then he snapped to attention and saluted. Finally he brought out: "How else are we supposed to deal with people like this?"

Herre was stunned and at a loss. How could he make this man realize that German prisoners in the same plight would look just the same?

The camp commandant came up to him. "Have you found what you were looking for, Major?" The look in his eyes was a blend of bafflement, self-righteousness, and uneasiness. But Herre looked past him to a group of weeping Russian women who were standing outside the gate; they were vainly trying to throw a few cold potatoes and pieces of bread to the prisoners.

"My God," Herre said to the commandant. "I hope that some day you won't have to pay personally for what you are doing here."

He turned on his heel and strode toward his car.

The commandant came running after him. "You think you're going to find any camp that is run differently? Things here are just too much for us. What else can I do?"

Herre got into his car. The commandant stood beside it, but was not given the chance for another word. Herre drove off. In Chistyakovo, where the headquarters of the 49th Mountain Corps was located, he reported to Conrad. The general looked shocked when he saw his Ia's expression, and heard his report. He promised to do everything in his power to see that the unit assigned to guard the camp in Stalino was relieved and that conditions there were improved. With soothing words, he sent Herre to his quarters.

There Herre sat down and wrote a letter to the chief of the Propaganda Department of the OKW (High Command of the Armed Forces), Colonel von Wedel, who was related to Herre's wife. At this time he knew nothing of the powers that really controlled the OKW. He fully believed he could achieve something by informing Wedel of what he had witnessed. He made the point that this kind of treatment of prisoners of war would destroy the credibility of all the propaganda about liberating the population of the Soviet Union from the communist regime.

On April 21, 1942, three months after his visit to the Stalino camp, Herre received an order to report to the Personnel Department of the Army General Staff. At first this order seemed in no way connected with his experience at the end of January.

Colonel von Wedel had sent a noncommittal reply to his letter. But day after day new and more horrifying reports came to Herre's ears. SS squads, the subsequently notorious Einsatzkommandos, were liquidating all the Soviet political commissars they could lay hands on. In addition, they were recklessly exterminating all "Asiatic or Jewish faces" among the prisoners of war. Moreover, new reports poured in of brutal treatment of the civilian populace by the rear echelon squads. Herre had no conception of the background of these events. But Wedel's reply had given him a lot to think about. He sensed the evasiveness and wondered whether it meant that his relative by marriage was constrained by orders from very high up, which he was not inclined to oppose.

On April 22, 1942, Herre left Chistyakovo and flew to East Prussia. There he learned that because of his knowledge of Russian and his experience at the front he had been assigned to "Foreign Armies East," an intelligence service responsible for evaluating the situation of the enemy on the entire eastern front. A new chief had just been appointed to head it, Lieutenant Colonel Gehlen.

Headquarters of the Army High Command was hidden in the forest near Mauersee, southwest of Angerburg. At the time Herre arrived there it was filled with a hectic animation. The German armies had more or less survived the winter battles. But Hitler's megalomaniac mind was stubbornly insisting on a new offensive to attain the objective that had eluded him in 1941: victory over the Soviet armies.

At the time, Gehlen meant little to Herre. He was a man of forty, of medium height and very lean, with a pale, bony face and a high forehead under hair combed stiffly back. Herre had the impression of a cool, distinctly aloof personality.

Gehlen came from Silesia. He was the son of a onetime artillery officer who had later become a Breslau publisher. Even in his school days Gehlen had a reputation for being a solitary, cool-headed fellow with a passion for figures, formulas, and statistics. Shortly after the end of the First World War he had joined the Reichswehr, the tiny postwar German army, out of nationalistic sentiments. At that time the army had nothing to offer him but the slow, toilsome, and miserably paid career of artillery officer. In 1935 he was still only a captain. The rearmament of Germany that took place then gave him his chance; he became a staff officer and a member of the Operations Division of the Army General Staff. For the first time he had the opportunity to utilize his natural gift for figures, calculations, and the evaluation of facts. After functioning as the general staff officer of an infantry division in Poland, and as liaison officer to the German Sixteenth Army in France, he became chief of the operations division of the Army Group East, responsible for military strategy in the east and the southeast. Ever since, he had continually dealt with the military problems involving the Soviet Union.

He had had a part in the planning of Operation Barbarossa, the name used to camouflage the attack on the Soviet Union, and had solved the problems of supply and the disposition of reserves with such icy perfection that General Halder, chief of the Army General Staff, had heaped praise upon him. But Gehlen had heard little about Hitler's conference with the commanders who were to direct the offensive—in addition to Halder, Field Marshal von Brauchitsch, commander in chief of the Army, and Field Marshals von Leeb, von Bock, and von Rundstedt, the commanders respectively of the Army Groups North, Center, and South in the invasion of the Soviet Union. Gehlen was barely aware of the reservations held by the top command concerning the impending action. They had raised the question of a two-front war and of the vastness of Russia, which had been the doom of Napoleon. But as in the cases of Poland and France, they had finally bowed to Hitler's stronger will and to his theory that the fast-moving German armored division would be able to encircle the Soviet troops in the western part of the Soviet Union and destroy them before they had the chance to retreat into the expanses of Russia. Ultimately von Brauchitsch, Halder, and von Bock became convinced that the "motorized strategy" which had worked so successfully in the West would permit a rapid advance upon Moscow and would seal the defeat of Stalin by occupation of the Soviet capital.

But though he knew nothing of the ideas being considered by the highest military authorities, Gehlen, too, approved of the move against Russia; Germany urgently needed to free herself from a Soviet threat to her rear and assure herself of food supplies and raw materials which would allow her to continue the war on the other fronts. He had argued that military defeat of the Soviet Union was certain if the German offensive concentrated all of its forces on Moscow. He based this conclusion to some extent on what he was told about the sorry state of the Soviet Union's military preparedness. The intelligence estimates had been provided by the General Staff's regional espionage department, Foreign Armies East, headed at the time by Lieutenant Colonel Kienzel. But Gehlen had also been influenced by the nationalistic anticommunist tradition in which he had been reared, which took the destruction of communism as an imperative, although that concept never implied annihilation of the Russian people. Gehlen was vaguely thinking of a regime in Moscow that would be allied to Germany. He also had notions of German participation in the development of Russian industry and agriculture— along with treaties to provide the German population with needed commodities.

Gehlen was unaware of the secret instructions that Hitler had issued on May 17, 1941, three months before the beginning of the assault on Russia, during a conference with the commanders in chief.

The war against Russia cannot be conducted in a chivalrous fashion. This struggle is a struggle of ideologies and racial antagonisms and must be waged with unprecedented, ruthless, merciless harshness. All officers must free themselves from outmoded traditional theories. I know that they cannot make these views their own, but I demand unconditional execution of the orders issued by me.

On May 13 implementing orders were issued by Field Marshal Keitel, chief of the OKW. These provided, among other things, that all captured political commissars of the Red Army were to be shot. Generals von Bock, von Rundstedt, and von Leeb protested to General Brauchitsch about this order; but Brauchitsch replied that he was unable to alter Hitler's decisions. Hitler considered his orders perfectly legal, Brauchitsch added, because the Soviet Union had not adhered to the Hague Convention on the rights of prisoners of war. Von Brauchitsch had contented himself with promulgating new, secret instructions for the army, recommending that it avoid and punish excesses; and the three generals had desisted from further protests.

Finally, Gehlen was ignorant of the establishment of four SS Einsatzgruppen, commando teams that were to follow in the trail of the armies and liquidate all commissars or Russians suspected of being stanch Communists, as well as all Jews.

Gehlen had experienced his revelation and conversion, if such terms are appropriate, during the past winter. At the end of July 1941, Army Chief of Staff Halder had introduced him to Hitler and, like so many others, Gehlen had fallen under the spell of Hitler's "magnetic" personality. Halder's own hopes of swift victory had been shaken that autumn when Hitler had countermanded the plans for a rapid advance on Moscow and insisted on a vast pincers movement in the Ukraine. When the attack on Moscow finally came, it was already too late to be effective, and the disaster that followed destroyed what was left of Halder's hopes. And when Halder, embittered by the misleading information he was receiving from the Foreign Armies East Department, fired its chief, Lieutenant Colonel Kienzel, and turned the department over to Gehlen on April 1, 1942, Gehlen was ripe for conversion. Partly influenced by a number of associates in his new department, Gehlen began changing his whole view of the world.

When Herre first reported to Gehlen, the ensuing dialogue developed— as noted in Herre's memoirs and diary:

Gehlen: "I suppose you were expecting some other assignment."

"Yes, sir."

"Sorry. I want my general staff officers to be young, to have had front-line experience, and to know something about Russia. The number of men who fulfill those requirements can be counted on your fingers. That is why I need you. You've had the opportunity since June of last year to follow the developments of your corps outside as well as inside the area of actual operations. I mean, in regard to German-Russian relations, in regard to German prisoners, and to the civilian population in the occupied territories."

"Yes, sir."

Herre reported on his experiences at Stalino. He spoke of his own policy of reconciliation with the Russians and of how well everything was going in his corps' area.

Gehlen listened in silence.

"You mustn't think we have not heard something about these conditions in certain of the camps. It would be a bad outlook if these conditions were general and deliberately fostered by the army. But the numbers of prisoners have proved too much for us, as have certain commands from the very top that were carried out over our heads. But that is only one problem. There is another. Quite a few army officers have had the same experiences as you with the civilian population and with Russian soldiers. Do you know that by a very rough estimate we already have at least two hundred thousand Russians—prisoners of war, deserters, and civilians—serving in army units at the front and as drivers, guards, workmen, sled coachmen, munition carriers, and so on? Do you know that tens of thousands of these men are wearing German uniforms?"

"I didn't know that," Herre said.

"Officially, the Army High Command doesn't know it either," Gehlen explained, "let alone the OKW. All these Russians—they're generally referred to as Hiwis, from *Hilfsfreiwillige* ["auxiliaries"]—are illegal components of the army. In addition, there are tens of thousands of men like those you've equipped with arms who are serving as guard squads in the rear echelon. Our first task, of course, is to be informed at all times regarding the enemy's situation. But we can already draw certain conclusions. For instance, we can see what a miscalculation it was to imagine that we would be able to defeat Russia by military force. In our department we have come to realize that the only way to eliminate the Soviet system would be to make the masses of the Russian people our allies. What you observed during the advance of your corps has been the general picture throughout the country: a remarkable readiness on the part of the population to welcome us. But all the instructions from the top leadership forbid us to exploit this readiness. Wherever that readiness to fight on our side has been accepted, that has been due to the initiative of the troops."

Herre listened intently. Gehlen concluded: "Everything will depend on whether we can put our point across to Headquarters. Brute power alone will never win us Russia. Perhaps they will realize that this war can be fought to a favorable conclusion only in conjunction with the Russian masses. The best we can hope for is no fantastic notion of a German colony known as Russia, but an independent Russia freed of the Soviet system of government with whom we can live on a friendly footing."

Less than twenty-four hours later, Herre reported to Lieutenant Colonel von Roenne, the chief of Section III. Roenne's section collected all captured documents, Soviet army mail, identity papers, and orders sent in from the eastern front. It evaluated the results of prisoner interrogations. In addition, in the nineteenth-century fortress of Boyen near Lötzen, Roenne maintained a special camp for approximately one hundred Russian prisoners of war who seemed to be sufficiently knowledgeable to provide special information on the situation back of the Soviet lines.

When Herre reported, Roenne had just returned from Lötzen. He had been inspecting the quarters for the prisoners, the library, the movie theater, the kitchen, and the opportunities for walks. From the first he had emphasized that he wanted prisoners under his command to be treated humanely, in spite of wartime conditions.

Herre confronted a man who looked younger than he had expected: tall, lean, with blond hair and the face of an intellectual. Von Roenne had been born in the Baltic region. He spoke Russian fluently, was a deeply religious man, and, like almost all Baltic Germans, rejected the Soviet political system but had an almost mystical affection for the Russians as a people. As Ia of the Twenty-third Division under the command of General Hellmich, he had been through the first few months of fighting in the East at the front. Then a head wound which kept him in perpetual pain disqualified him for front-line duty.

He spoke with a ruthless candor that was quite new to Herre:

"The chief told me you have had some personal experiences with our policy toward the Russians. Every interrogation of new prisoners reveals what is happening. A few months ago the population in the occupied territories still showed curious anticipation, a friendly readiness to welcome us. That attitude has already given way to skepticism, caution, distrust. Soon there will be only hatred and repugnance. Partisans are gathering in the forested areas and attacking our lines of communication.

Granted, some of these have been dropped by Soviet planes. But they are also recruiting reinforcements among the disillusioned populace. They are exerting an increasing pressure on those groups in the population that originally regarded us as liberators and have not yet turned against us. And we are supplying plenty of nourishment for the partisans. We are pretty well informed on recent Soviet history. We know, for instance, that Stalin himself considers the Soviet Union a good deal more vulnerable politically than militarily. The people have paid for the forcible collectivization of agriculture with some ten million dead. The purges by the secret police between 1936 and 1938 throughout the population, the administration, and the army have not been forgotten. Nor have the shipment of some eight to twelve million persons every year to penal camps, labor camps, or death camps. There is scarcely a family which has not borne the brunt of Stalin's transformation of socialism into brutal dictatorship. The entire population lives in terror of the system.

"Stalin had every reason to fear that with our appearance all these suppressed hatreds would be unleashed and would lead to mass defections. You yourself witnessed the beginnings of such a development. All Stalin could do to stem the tide was to issue proclamations. Commands like this one, for instance . . ."

Roenne picked up a sheet of paper from his desk and read:

" 'Not a single kilogram of grain and not a single liter of fuel must be left behind for the enemy. Partisan groups are to be formed in territory occupied by the enemy to harass the enemy units. They must kindle guerrilla war, destroy the communications lines, set fire to forests and depots. Wherever the enemy is to be found, he must be hounded and annihilated. Where cities are under enemy threat, we must set up a national militia and draw all workers into the struggle for their freedom and the honor of their motherland. . . .' "

Roenne laid the sheet aside. "Injunctions of this sort had little effect until well into the winter. Until late autumn we were still having whole regiments desert to us, along with their political commissars. The people in the occupied territories formed defense units to combat the partisans. Everywhere the populace willingly went back to work. I myself drove hundreds of kilometers accompanied only by a chauffeur, and was given a friendly reception everywhere. Neither the nights nor the depths of the forests were frightening or dangerous. But since then, we've provided enemy propaganda with all too much material. Stalin's men don't have to invent anything. From keeping the system of forced collectivization to closing the schools, from the mass deaths of prisoners of war to ruthless stripping of the country, from hunting down and annihilating the intelligentsia to the way our *Herrenmenschen* swagger around—in all our actions, we are providing evidence that speaks for itself. We will end by making Stalin, feared and hated Stalin, the savior and defender of the Russian people. Word-of-mouth propaganda works swiftly, and the reports flying about concerning the treatment of Russian Jews by the Einsatzkommandos are achieving the very opposite of what the program intended. The Russians were supposed to think we were ridding them of the Jewish wire-pullers of bolshevism. Pogroms fit in with Russian history—but our propaganda about Stalin as a puppet of the Jews was plainly ridiculous. The upshot is that instead of fearing Stalin these people are learning to fear us. And anyone who goes around shooting Communist party members without exception should not be surprised to see even the skeptics—and there were plenty of those even in the party—no longer surrendering. Naturally, they prefer to fight for their bare lives under Stalin."

Roenne glanced at an interrogation form lying on the desk in front of him. "I conducted an interrogation in Lötzen today. The man I questioned is a special case; his name is Zhilenkov and he was the secretary of a district party committee in Moscow. When the war began, he became commissar of a Soviet division, later of an army. He's thirty-three years old; in other words, he's typical of the young Soviet citizens who have grown up under the communist system. Last summer he was taken prisoner at Smolensk and slipped unrecognized into one of our anxiliary outfits. Up to three weeks ago, he was driving a munitions truck for us; during the winter he delivered ordnance right up to the positions outside Moscow. By chance, his real past became known. At any rate, he had escaped the wholesale executions of captured commissars last summer and fall. When I received a report on him from Army Group Center, I had him sent to Lötzen because I wanted to make sure he was safe."

Roenne laid his fine hand on the papers in front of him.

"You see, this man owes everything to the party. He was picked up by the Communist party when he was a homeless war orphan, he was raised by the party, sent to study in Moscow, and finally, as a party functionary and the secretary of a Moscow district, was virtually lord and master over several hundred thousand Soviet citizens. At the time of his capture, he was brigade commissar of the Thirty-second Army. In other words, he's a product of the party, and yet he rejects Stalin. All right, you may say, he tells all kinds of stories today because he wants to save his neck, or else he's a spy. It does not prove much that he made a reliable 'Hiwi.' Nor that what he said in an earlier interrogation, a copy of which I have here, pretty much coincides with what I know about him. 'Treat us decently, as equal allies, and you'll have us, you'll have me, you'll have the larger part of the generals and half the party apparatus on your side,' he said. Anyhow, I'm convinced the man is sincere. His reasons for coming over to us would be shared by millions of others, but our top brass won't understand. Among the Russians there is hardly a political individual, no matter what kind of career he's had, who has been able to live the way even Russians want to live: without constant pressure, without everlasting fear of coming under suspicion, fear of being investigated, fear of being charged with having violated one of the ever-changing party rules. As soon as we take over, many of these people feel they've emerged from crushing political pressure. They feel that even under us . . ."

In those last words, "even under us . . .," Roenne revealed that he was well aware of the limited sort of freedom enjoyed by Germans and of how little difference there was between the rule of Hitler and the total despotism of Stalin.

"I am convinced that the majority of the commissars executed by the SS squads, and by members of the regular army who were incited to slaughter them in the prison camps, could have been won over to our side. The opportunists would have come over anyhow, and many others besides. But nothing can be gained by shooting them out of hand, or putting them under pressure again. The only way for us to win here is by showing greater humaneness and by having the courage to trust these people. Zhilenkov sketched out for me a whole program of propaganda which we could follow, and which struck me as highly effective. We would have to pull out of Russia as soon as the fighting was over—and allow a new Russian government to form without Stalin. Of course, nobody can turn back the clock of history and undo things the regime has created: technological development, the educational system, and many other things. We must recognize what has been achieved and combine it with more humanenness toward the individual. That is Zhilenkov's prescription, and it is very close to my own viewpoint."

Von Roenne concluded: "I hope to see you joining our ranks. We are the ones who are closest to the reality of the situation, and we must do our best to persuade the top leadership to perceive this reality. We aren't alone. There are people in the Propaganda Department of the OKW in Berlin who have come to the same view of their own accord. And here in the General Staff we aren't alone either. You will be put in touch with General Wagner, the quartermaster general; you will also be put in touch with the chief of the Department of Military Government, Lieutenant Colonel Schmidt von Altenstadt. You will be put in touch with Major Count Stauffenberg in the Organization Department. . . ."

That same evening Herre met Count Claus von Stauffenberg, major in the General Staff and Group Chief II of the Organization Department. He found the major in his room, his desk cluttered with papers. Stauffenberg was in the midst of an animated telephone conversation. The person on the other end appeared to be his general, but Stauffenberg seemed to be paying little regard to the question of rank. (Here, too, the report follows Herre's memoirs and diary.)

Stauffenberg stepped forward to meet Herre; he was a tall, handsome man, rather carelessly dressed—an unusual thing for an officer. Herre quickly realized that in the swiftness and incisiveness of his thinking, and in technical military knowledge, Stauffenberg stood head and shoulders above almost all the men of his own age, and the majority of older officers as well.

"So you've joined our club," Stauffenberg said abruptly. "Gehlen has asked me to brief you on the state of affairs in my area. A tough assignment, because it's hard to know where the nonsense starts and stops. And my area just happens to include the Russian auxiliaries and volunteers that nobody in the OKW or the Führer's Headquarters wants to know anything about."

He broke off to offer Herre cigarettes, his movement very rapid. "Don't be surprised at the tone you'll hear among some of us here. After a while, you'll be using it yourself. We all need a safety valve. To put it briefly, and at the risk of telling you what you already know, the picture is as follows: the group around the Führer has only one aim—conquest of the Soviet Union and turning it into a source of raw materials for Germany, a reservoir of labor and production. Obviously, none of these global strategists has given a thought to just what form this reservoir is to take. Nor has anyone done any new thinking on the matter, despite the lessons of the past year. We have not yet ascertained whether the Führer himself is the father of this policy and, above all, whether he is kept in ignorance of the facts by his entourage. Right now the Führer's Headquarters is staking everything on a new offensive this year and on winning the final victory. They want to have their hands free for whatever develops after this victory. Consequently, they won't hear of letting the Baltic peoples— the Estonians, Latvians, and Lithuanians—come over to our side. Which they were eager to do, even though we had essentially betrayed them when we gave Stalin carte blanche in there after the partition of Poland. Apparently, the master plan makes no provision for liberating these Baltic countries. Hence, we must not let them collaborate with us, because they might make claims on the basis of such collaboration. The volunteer troop units that sprang up spontaneously after our entry into Estonia and Latvia have been banned. And although some of them are still around, it's only on an undercover basis. Himmler and most of the SS leadership share similar delusions. He has these racial theories about Teutons and Slavs, on the basis of which he has constructed an altogether unspeakable policy. He dreams of a Germanic empire extending to the Urals, with the Slavs being allowed to survive only as labor forces. Rosenberg, meanwhile, has a different slant. He wants to destroy not only bolshevism, but also Russia as a political unit. He and those idiots in the East Ministry are infatuated with the idea of partition on the principle of 'divide and rule.' Aided mostly by exiles, they want to form the Turkistanis, Caucasians, Ukrainians, and White Ruthenians into individual republics. But where this might all happen naturally, where all this stuff about separatism could easily be carried out—in the Baltic countries— they're not ready to lift a finger. There they're obsessed with the old business of the Teutonic Knights and want to turn those countries into parts of the German Reich. As for what should be done with the Russians proper, the East Ministry veers between the idea of driving them beyond the Urals and forming a nebulous Russian state around Moscow.

"I must admit that the various bureau heads in the East Ministry are interested in decent treatment for their pet groups. They're also for liberating the peasants and dissolving the collective farms. But it doesn't even occur to them that their ideas run totally counter to the realities history has shaped, and that such reversals can only be brought about by brute force. On the other hand, all their proposals are empty words because the economic power in the occupied area is in the hands of Göring and Backe, who is the state secretary in the Reich Ministry of Food. And what that means is 'appropriation.' Which comes down to: Why liberate peasants? Let the clods work and deliver the goods! And Himmler with his SS and Gestapo has all the police power in his hands. Which again means force, annihilation of 'racially inferior Slavs.' Even where Rosenberg is theoretically in charge of things, he in fact has nothing to say. The kind of officials the Führer forced on him are people who'll follow a hard line in the occupied territory and won't give a damn about the instructions from their theoretical superior, Rosenberg. I imagine you've heard about Koch and Lohse. Lohse seems to think a dog whip is the only instrument of politics. He stands for exploitation, force, keeping the peasants enslaved, smashing the schools and universities, starvation, and a low birth rate. We've seen how Koch has been acting in the Ukraine up to now—there is nothing more savage than a narrow-minded petty bourgeois turned meglomaniac."

The telephone interrupted Stauffenberg's exposition. While he carried on his conversation, Herre silently studied him. Once more Stauffenberg turned to the matter on hand.

"I beg your pardon," he said. "To continue: now the army comes along and has to prepare the soil for this stupid policy of ours. And I ask you this: Haven't we, the officers of the Wehrmacht, always prided ourselves on our cultural awareness? I'm not yet ready to give up on my fellow officers. I go on hoping that we will be able to reverse course and undo the damage being done by the gauleiters. But a few illusions have already been shattered. Gehlen must have brought you up to date on the larger situation. Over the winter, we've had to revise our notion of our superiority and the certainty of victory. In view of the lack of manpower, the sheer misery here, we've had no choice but to employ Russian prisoners who were ready and willing as drivers or in other auxiliary services, and in critical moments even to put rifles into their hands. And those former Red Army men have fired at the Red Army, at the partisans. Again out of sheer necessity, we've put them into German uniforms to indicate that they're part of the fighting forces. There are divisions that have as many as three or four thousand Russians out of a total strength of twelve to fifteen thousand men. In the rear echelon of Army Group Center, where partisans are cropping up like mushrooms, whole companies and battalions have been formed out of Russian volunteers. In other words, reality has forced on us something inconceivable in terms of the official policy: Russians have become our allies and nobody can get around it because reality is stronger than theory. Do you see the position I'm in, having to sit here and work out new deployments and not allowed to say that the whole picture has changed? Yet I don't intend to go against the current of reality. What I have to do is set up a series of *faits accomplis* that nobody will be able to ignore or undo."

His tone took on an edge of determination.

"And I am not alone in this intention," he said. "Gehlen agrees with me, and so does Roenne. Quartermaster General Wagner and Schmidt von Altenstadt see it my way. The horde of auxiliaries and the Russian units now operating owe their existence to the common sense of the lower ranks, not to any acknowledgment at the top that our policy must undergo a total change. The officers who took the necessary steps in the field, and the staff officers and generals who have tolerated or promoted it, with few exceptions regard the auxiliaries and volunteers as mercenaries, nothing more. They've done no thinking on the subject. They haven't realized that even the most simple-minded of these Russians fighting on the German side has some end in view. His real goal is a new Russian political system. There are very few among our people at the front right now who perceive this. But the so-called mercenaries will sooner or later raise their voices. They will show us that Russians are not what our idiotic propaganda has made them out to be—animals who understand nothing but the knout. Russians have their own nationalism, their own pride. They're ready to go along with us, but they are also formidable fighters. If we want to get rid of Stalin, we must strike up an alliance with their nationalism. Otherwise, the experience of last winter will only be a foretaste of what's awaiting us. The one way to stave off disaster is to muster a mass army of Russians ready to fight for the elimination of Stalin's system, for the building of a new Russian government, for the achievement of a new Russo-German relationship. That mass army must be created under Russian auspices, under leaders whom the Russians will not see as German puppets. We must give them honest aid, but it should be clear to all the world that they are fighting for their own cause."

There had been some surprising statements in Stauffenberg's long monologue, but the next sentence made Herre start.

"Anyone who still believes we can win a military victory in this country is a fool. Dr. Bräutigam, our liaison officer to the East Ministry, whom you will meet shortly, is still dreaming of an independent Ukraine. But he, too, is interested in the idea of finding a Russian personality with leadership qualities who will head up a free anti-Stalinist government and an army of liberation. Of course, he thinks of it in the context of the nebulous Russian republic the East Ministry plans to set up somewhere or other. But the principle is the same. What's wanted is a leader with a well-known name. Not some exile whom nobody in present-day Russia knows, but somebody who'll command the trust of the masses."

Herre was still somewhat staggered by Stauffenberg's openness. "How does the chief of staff feel about these matters?" he asked.

"Halder?" Stauffenberg replied. "Halder thinks only in military terms and always has done so. No, let's have no illusions. We'll get no help from Halder or Keitel on this. But as events take their course, even they may come round. There's nothing like a desperate military situation for helping the cause of common sense." He sounded deadly earnest, but there was a note of fatigue in his last words.

The quartermaster general's barracks were situated in the section of Camp Mauerwald closer to the lake, about a thousand meters from the barracks of the Organization Department. The small building close by was a sauna built specially for General Wagner; the general felt he needed one to keep himself in shape. Though only in his late forties, Wagner was tubby, and his complexion was somewhat too flushed. He was of excitable nature, and when he had had a couple of glasses of red wine, of which he was very fond, he was apt to speak his mind on the subject of Hitler, for whom he had no fondness whatever.

Four days after his conversation with Stauffenberg, Herre reported to Lieutenant Colonel Schmidt von Altenstadt, Wagner's chief of the Department of Military Government. He found a youthful, vigorous cavalryman who came forward to meet him with an elastic step and lively manner. The two men quickly sounded one another out. Then Altenstadt spoke with even more brutal candor than Stauffenberg.

"Either we change our line or we are heading straight for catastrophe," he said. He took the administrator's point of view. "The Russians must be permitted self-government. They may strike us as backward but they are a long way from being 'colonial blacks.' The best thing we can do is let them run their own affairs. At most, we can set quotas for grain and raw materials. If we put in German collectors, we'll ruin everything. They will sow hatred and give a powerful spur to partisan activity. Things are already moving in that direction."

Altenstadt began pacing the room. "We must begin by organizing self-government from the bottom up, on the local level. The district and, finally, county authorities can be established. We thereby turn the occupied areas into an autonomous region, which at the moment, of course, will be expected to perform services for us connected with the war, but which can also be regarded as the nucleus of a new Russia. Then, at the top, a free anti-Moscow administration must come forth, with its own Russian army. Think of the possibilities . . ."

Altenstadt abruptly shifted to another aspect of the obsessive subject. "It's impossible to talk reasonably to our conquistadors," he said. "Besides which, we don't have the time for endless argumentation. Yesterday, Stauffenberg pulled off a masterpiece. He got authorization from the

OKW to set up regiments of Turkistanis. It's what you might call an opening wedge."

He gave Herre a look of ironic complicity. "As it happens, there's a Professor von Mende in the East Ministry whose pet project is creating petty states in the Caucasus and Turkistan—not that Turkistan exists any longer; it's just a historical dream. At any rate, last year he started combing the prison camps for prisoners of war belonging to the races of the Caucasus. He sent in Caucasian and Turkistani exiles to recruit fellow countrymen among the prisoners. One of these exiles was a fellow called Chokai, who claimed to be president of the 'autonomous government of Kokand'; he had fled to France in 1921. The other was a Turkistani living in Germany, Chayum Khan, who had come there in the twenties and studied at the Berlin School of Political Science. But the mission came to a quick end, for there were hardly any Turkistanis in the camps. It seemed that the SS "special squads" had shot most of them because of their Asiatic appearance. Others were on the verge of starvation. In Czestokowo camp in Poland only two thousand Turkistanis were left out of thirty thousand. Chokai himself caught spotted typhus in this camp and died. Still and all, von Mende managed to collect a good ten thousand Turkistanis for his purpose. He was also interested in the northern Caucasians, the Azerbaijanis, the Georgians, the Armenians, and the Volga Tatars. Then came the winter. The dreams of marching to the Urals were over and done with. But the Turkistanis and the Caucasians had been promised liberation. Von Mende insisted on his detachments; Keitel didn't want to hear of it. So the program, such as it was, remained at an impasse. The only way around was sheer deception. You should have heard Stauffenberg buttering up Keitel, persuading him that not only were these Turkistanis archenemies of communism, but that they were of purebred Aryan stock, practically as good as Germans! So now we're to have those legions after all. And just in the nick of time . . ."

Twilight was already falling when Herre left the barracks. But he hardly felt his day was over. The more he learned about the situation, the more the problems seemed to multiply. One thing was clear: the Soviet army, although it had suffered heavy losses, was far from being beaten.

Suddenly he heard his name being called. There was Stauffenberg, standing outside one of the barracks, holding a low-voiced conversation with another officer in the dusk. He motioned to Herre to join them and

44

introduced Dr. Bräutigam, an elderly man in captain's uniform, his thin face dominated by a large nose.

"Let's go into my office," Stauffenberg proposed. "There are some new developments in *Ostpolitik** that you should know about."

The news turned out to be rather significant. As Bräutigam reported it, State Secretary Backe and his assistant Riecke had surprisingly changed their minds on the subject of the collective farms. Previously they had been totally opposed to any modification in the system. Now, however, they were open to the idea of some reforms.

Stauffenberg turned to Bräutigam. "That may sound like a victory for our side. Even our booty collectors are beginning to have doubts about the infinite docility of the peasants. So what are they proposing instead of the kolkhozes? Some kind of agricultural cooperatives, the land to be jointly tilled but ownership to be vested in the peasants? It sounds seductive. But, my dear captain, you told me that the new arrangement will apply to only twenty percent of the kolkhozes. In addition, the lands in question have first to be precisely surveyed. How many years will all this surveying take? Do you think the peasants are going to dance for joy when they hear about this bureaucratic hocus-pocus? Besides, you tell me Koch is already dead set against the scheme. As far as he's concerned, the Ukraine is going to be parcelled out to German settlers. That fathead!"

Stauffenberg slammed his fist down on the table. Then he recovered himself somewhat. "Forgive my fury. But how many Germans does this idiot Koch think will want to leave their country and settle in these wastes? Yet I'm convinced he'll win out on this. Your Minister Rosenberg will always truckle to Koch. The agrarian reform will be a paper reform and the collective farms will continue to exist."

Herre noted later that at the time Stauffenberg's unabashed frankness was still new to him and that he looked around cautiously.

Bräutigam's lips twitched but he made no attempt to defend his superior. Stauffenberg went on undeterred. "As far as Koch is concerned, Minister Rosenberg doesn't exist. He said as much when he took office last September."

Bräutigam made a feeble effort to stand up for Rosenberg. "Don't think my minister is not aware of this. When I was last in Berlin he told me: 'These ruffians don't understand a thing. Their heavy-handed methods will be the ruin of us.' "

* Policy with regard to the East.

"But he won't remove a single one of those ruffians from his post," Stauffenberg retorted. "We could have had the three Baltic countries on our side. If we had promised them their independence, they would have fought beside us and delivered their last stalk of grain. But Reichskommissar Lohse has clamped down on the entire area. Every impulse toward autonomy is to be stifled. Hundreds of German officials have been sent in to the property the Russians expropriated. Lohse's 'Ostland companies' are running the factories that belonged to Estonians, Latvians, or Lithuanians only two years ago. And Lohse is one of Minister Rosenberg's men! He has some notion of an Ostland dukedom and his own son someday wearing the ducal crown. That's the sort of crackpot Rosenberg puts in charge.

"But let's take up the next point. On March 28 the Führer appointed Gauleiter Sauckel commissioner general for labor assignment. And last week Sauckel presented a program for labor assignment which aims chiefly at recruiting Ukrainians, White Russians, Poles, Galicians, and Russians for jobs in German industry. I wouldn't object to that if it were done in a proper way that preserves the dignity of the workers as human beings. It might even contribute to friendly relations between us—we'd get to know a bit about each other. But when I read between the lines I realize what this so-called 'recruiting' is going to mean.

"Bräutigam, you yourself quoted to me Sauckel's remark that the inhabitants of the occupied eastern areas are accustomed to the very worst working conditions, to bare subsistence. You've also mentioned that these labor forces are to be under supervision. The plan calls for every worker's being identified by a cloth badge reading 'East' sewed to his shirt, for all the labor camps to be surrounded by barbed wire, and for the workers being kept in strict segregation, not being allowed to use any means of transportation, and being barred from parks, taverns, or movie houses. Do you see what this adds up to—slave labor, nothing else."

A few weeks later, on the evening of June 6, a car stopped in front of the headquarters of Field Marshal von Kluge at Krasnibor, in the vicinity of Smolensk. The car belonged to General von Schenckendorff, commander of the rear area of Army Group Center. Schenckendorff was coming from Mogilev.

Kluge's special train stood in a wooded ravine surrounded by the barracklike buildings of a former Soviet rest home. Outwardly, the place looked very remote from the battles that were raging along the entire eastern front. The German armies were struggling to patch up the holes that the Soviet formations had driven into their front during the winter battles, and to prepare a springboard in the south for the new grand offensive.

The bitter struggles of the encircled Germans in the Kholm and Deminsk pockets were over. But in the vicinity of Volkhov tenacious fighting involving heavy casualties was going on in swamps and streams as the Germans tried to undo a deep winter penetration by the Second Soviet Assault Army. At Kharkov Marshal Timoshenko, with forty-one new divisions, had been battering the German positions ever since May 12. Sevastopol in the Crimea had to be taken before the new German summer offensive could begin. And sapping at the morale of the Germans was the consciousness of growing enemy resistance, of resistance that was perhaps only now really beginning, and that was fed from reserves of men and armaments out of reach of any attack.

Schenckendorff was a heavy, apoplectic man who suffered from a serious heart condition. Like most of his fellow military specialists, he had invaded the Soviet Union with scarcely any knowledge of Russian problems. But beneath his rough exterior he concealed a good deal of shrewdness. He became aware of a logical discrepancy between the jubilant cheers of the population and the orders "from above" to crack the whip. So, shortly after he took command of the rear area of Army Group Center, he began to seek his own solution to the problem.

We will probably never be able to ascertain when and where in the vast area of the eastern front and during the winter battles the first Soviet soldiers enlisted in the German forces as auxiliaries, when and where the first companies or squadrons of former Red Army soldiers were formed on the German side. The creation of such units was an instinctive act, born of the dire necessity of the Germans and the dire necessity and hopeful willingness of the Russians.

The first signs of such a development had come to Schenckendorff's attention "from below." The headquarters of his field commanders had set up a security police force composed of Russians to combat the initial, and initially unimportant, sabotage attempts by partisans. (These partisans were being organized from the ranks of the Red Army, from NKVD [secret police] men who had been left behind or dropped by parachute, or from the "Asiatics, Jews, and commissars" who had fled into the forests to escape the savagery of the Sicherheitsdienst extermination squads.) In Briansk a major in the reserves named Weiss had on his own initiative set up an entire battalion of Russian volunteers.

Some of Weiss's men had volunteered only as an alternative to imprisonment, whose horrors were by now well known to many of the Russians. In the light of this fact, it must be said that the battalion had fought with amazing tenacity against Soviet partisans parachuted into the rear area. Weiss had collected the weapons for his battalion from abandoned ordnance. The men had to make their own uniforms. There was no budget, no training manual, nothing. Weiss had invented the insignia of rank. By dint of great effort, he had found German noncoms to assume the principal leadership posts. They had no knowledge of Russian and were unfamiliar with the ways of their new subordinates, but were able to count on the traditional respect German military men enjoyed in Russia, a respect that had greatly increased as a consequence of the German army's victories so far in the war.

By now there were a good many *landeseigene* ("native") battalions in Schenkendorff's area. Hard to say who first called them that. Perhaps Schenkendorff's Ia, Major von Kraewel, who, as the operations officer, supported this unusual and semilegal development out of sheer necessity. For the "top brass" still refused to grant any approval to such recruiting among the enemy.

In Mogilev a Russian-led Cossack force called "Detachment 600" had sprung into being. A Cossack named Major Kononov had deserted to the German side with the bulk of his regiment out of genuine hatred for the anti-Cossack Stalinist system. In prison camp he had accidentally made contact with Major von Kraewel and begged for the chance to fight alongside the Germans. Kononov had a tough and self-assured personality. Schenckendorff had promoted him to the rank of lieutenant colonel; and by now Kononov's cavalrymen had become indispensable for guarding the roads and railroad lines.

Something highly unusual had taken place in the vicinity of the small town of Lokoty on the eastern margin of the Bryansk Forest, which had become a hideout of partisans. The mayor of a Russian *rayon*,* a man named Kaminski, was attracting attention there. He had once been arrested by the NKVD and sent to a Siberian penal camp. Later, the punishment had been commuted to permanent banishment to Lokoty.

Kaminski was being noticed because he had established "exemplary conditions" in his district without German intervention. Economic life began to flourish. Delivery quotas were met without the slightest trouble. The school system was functioning again. Russian militia that the mayor

* In the USSR a *rayon* is the lowest administrative district.

had organized on his own initiative and equipped with Red Army weapons saw to security in the *rayon*. In Lokoty there were no partisans. General Schmidt, the commander of the Second Tank Army, summoned Kaminski, placed him in charge of a number of other districts, and without asking permission from "above" created a large Russian area of autonomous administration, the Lokoty Region. All executive authority was handed over to Kaminski. He was appointed "brigadier general" and set up an army of his own in the region. This was given the name RONA (Russian People's Army) and had former Soviet artillery and T-34 tanks at its disposal.

Kaminski founded a political party of his own; it was a mixture of fascism and socialism, although the model for it had not been German National Socialism, of which Kaminski knew nothing. His methods were at once tough and characterized by Russian largeness of spirit. But the people seemed to understand them. In September 1941 General Schmidt summed up the experiences of Lokoty in a memorandum, "On the Possibility of Shattering Bolshevist Resistance from Within." But no one higher up paid any attention to the paper.

Schenckendorff had himself announced to Colonel Henning von Tresckow, Field Marshal von Kluge's Ia.

Tresckow stood as he awaited his visitor in the barracks office—a lean man of medium height with a somewhat spherical, strikingly featured face. He shook his visitor's hand warmly, for they had worked together before. Both had participated in the notable advance of Army Group Center in 1941. They had served first under Field Marshal Fedor von Bock, whom Hitler had dismissed on December 18, 1941, after the failure of the offensive against Moscow, and now under Kluge.

Tresckow knew what Schenckendorff had on his mind, for he himself had seen the alternatives even earlier and had tried, tactfully but persistently, to make the army revise its policy. In October 1941 he and Gersdorff, his Ic,* had wrung permission from Field Marshal von Bock to draw up a plan for organizing a "liberation army" composed of 200,000 Russian volunteers. At the time Tresckow had thought, in fact virtually taken for granted, that this plan would be accepted by the Führer's Headquarters. No other course seemed reasonable, now that hopes of

* General staff officer responsible for analyzing the situation of the enemy; corresponds to G2 in the NATO forces.

rapid military victory had been dashed. A short while earlier, the Russian municipal authorities in Smolensk had presented Bock with Napoleonic cannon and a petition addressed directly to Hitler. They were offering nothing less than to proclaim Smolensk the capital of a new Russian government for all of the liberated areas. This government would serve as a rallying point for all those Russians who were prepared to fight with the German troops against Stalin's regime.

Von Bock took no interest in political matters. His entire energies were bent on persuading Führer's Headquarters that the capture of Moscow was more crucial to the outcome of the war than a pincers movement and encirclement in the Ukraine. Nevertheless, he passed on the petition; but as late as November there had been no response to it. Given the tempestuous pace of events, that did not signify much. It could be a case of sheer oversight. Consequently, Tresckow had gone ahead and drafted his plan for a liberation army. He had left the specifics to the official translator on the staff of the army group, Reserve Captain Wilfried Strik-Strikfeldt, who came from Riga and spoke Russian fluently.

Tresckow knew Strik-Strikfeldt. Of German parentage, he was born in 1896 in the Baltic provinces of the Russian empire, had attended school in St. Petersburg, and had served as a young officer in the tsar's army during the First World War. Later, during the struggles of the Baltic countries for independence, he had served with the British military mission under General Gough and had provided Baltic troops with arms. From 1920 on he had been the representative of a British industrial firm in Riga, Latvia, and in 1939, after the rude reannexation of the Baltic countries by the Soviet Union, he had moved to Posen, where he ran an engineering bureau until the German attack on Poland made that region German once again. He became a soldier once more, this time on the German side, and served as an interpreter. Like Roenne, he hated bolshevism and the Stalinist system but admired the Russian people to the point of idolatry.

During the victorious late summer months of 1941 Strik-Strikfeldt, then on the staff of Army Group Center, had obstinately upheld the view that the Soviet system could be smashed only if the Germans were willing to ally themselves with the Russian people. His ideas about the kind of Russia that would replace Stalin and communism were not of the reactionary monarchist cast, but they certainly were conservative and, in any case, extremely vague.

When, in October 1941, he drew up a plan for Tresckow for a combat-ready Russian "liberation army," he tried to make allowance for a certain nervousness on the part of the German army. His plan provided for the deployment of a German division behind each group of three Russian divisions; and only German aircraft would be permitted to fight in the air. Simultaneously he worked out the plan for an anti-Stalinist government in Smolensk. Tresckow immediately passed the project on to his superiors, first to Bock, and then to Army Commander in Chief Brauchitsch. But the project was still lying on Brauchitsch's desk when something happened that revealed for the first time the state of mind of the Führer's Headquarters.

The city fathers of Smolensk were pressing for a reply to their petition. Army Group Chief of Staff Greiffenberg therefore sent an inquiry to the Führer's Headquarters. In the middle of November a curt note came back from Field Marshal Keitel: "Political affairs are in principle no concern of the Army Group."

Greiffenberg and Strik-Strikfeldt had to inform the Smolensk authorities of this rejection. Although they sweetened the news with a conciliatory gift of medical supplies for the city hospital, they received the significant answer: "If in a decisive moment like this, it takes so long to reply to our offer, the answer must certainly be negative. Obviously, your government has not yet grasped the gravity of its position."

Only a few weeks later, Strik-Strikfeldt's project had found its way back to Tresckow's desk. The margin of the document now bore a comment from Brauchitsch: "I regard this as decisive for the outcome of the war." But there was not a word about Hitler's approval. Evidently Brauchitsch had lacked the courage even to present the project to Hitler. Shortly afterward, in December, Brauchitsch was dismissed; his dismissal was followed by that of von Bock, and the first major effort to create a Russian liberation army had come to nothing.

But Tresckow had not forgotten these events, and he had continued to pursue the idea. However, he had been able to present it to Kluge, Bock's successor, only within strict limits. Kluge was even less interested in political matters than his predecessor. In addition, he had an extremely vacillating character. Grumble though he often did concerning the Führer's Headquarters, he shrank from opposition. At best Tresckow could count on his accepting a *fait accompli*. During the past few months Tresckow had tested him out several times on the key question of using ever-increasing numbers of auxiliaries in the German divisions. The argument that always proved effective with Kluge was the purely military one:

that German reserves had not been sent and it had become sheer necessity to fill the gaps with Russians. Tresckow, of course, had larger aims in view.

Tresckow offered Schenkendorff a chair. "Now what can I do for you, Herr General?" he said.

Schenckendorff: "Can you give me the latest on the military situation?"

Tresckow: "Nothing much is planned for our sector. The Führer has ordered that the new summer offensive is to be carried out by Army Group South, the aim being to conquer the Caucasus on the one hand and thus take away Russia's oil, and on the other hand to reach the Volga at Stalingrad and thus blockade the river. In this way, the Führer hopes to destroy the enemy's defense industries and crush him militarily."

Schenckendorff glanced anxiously at the map. "And what about the northern flank?"

"The Italians, Hungarians, and Rumanians are supposed to hold that. . . . That is why anything we can do to mobilize Russian help is particularly important and urgent."

"To all appearances things are developing well," Schenckendorff said. "The first battalions are stabilizing. Several battalions have fought amazingly well. The demand for replacements is growing from week to week, so that I finally decided to set up an eastern reserve battalion in the Russian barracks at Bobruisk. We'll soon be able to expand that into a regiment. Furthermore, in Orsha we're establishing a preparatory camp where we are first collecting the volunteers from the prisoner-of-war camps and letting them recuperate. The willingness of these people astounds me. In Kossov a convalescent camp for volunteers is being set up, and in Durinichi a rest camp for the wounded and convalescents . . ."

Schenckendorff suddenly pounded the flat of his hand on the table. "But there's the crux of the matter: I'm building on sand. At the moment the Russians are still meeting us halfway. But for how much longer? Officially I'm in command of this show, but whatever I do is shot full of holes by Göring's Four Year Plan specialists and by Himmler's men. And by now, the population has a pretty good idea of what the Reichskommissariat is up to. The worst blow to public confidence is the policy toward labor. People are beginning to hear that those who volunteered for labor in Germany are being kept behind barbed wire. Yesterday three Russians from the Ukraine district arrived in Mogilev; they'd managed to make it to relatives. They had been attending a church service with about forty other people. This was in the vicinity of Rovno. One of Sauckel's commissions descended on the church and rounded up everyone there, packing them off in a cattle car for shipment to Germany. These three escaped during the journey by cutting a hole in the floor of their car and letting themselves drop down between the rails."

"Impossible," Tresckow exclaimed.

"Far from it," Schenckendorff said. "In the so-called 'Russian battalion f.s.d. [for special duty]' in Ossintorf, which is mainly made up of former Red Army officers, there are six men who have heard similar reports concerning members of their family. I don't have to tell you what kind of impression such stories make on men like that. Everything we are attempting here is jeopardized. I cannot expect men to fight on our side when their fellow countrymen or their relatives are being treated the way Negro slaves were treated in the past."

"Have any of Sauckel's recruiting commissions turned up in your area?" Tresckow asked.

"Not so far."

"I'll talk to the field marshal about it. He'll order the arrest of every commission that behaves like that in our area."

Schenckendorff: "Aside from the opportunists, there are a good many Russians who still believe in our good will. They think we are fighting not only against Stalin and his rule, but are willing to help them, the people. But distrust and doubts are rising. 'What do you really mean to do with us?' What answer can we give them? Everything I have been doing is illegal. There are no regulations for my men. No recognized ranks. No uniforms. No official pay. No clothing. No decorations. No German soldier will salute a Russian whom I have chosen to appoint an officer. The German noncoms I've assigned to train or lead my volunteers may very well have fought against these same people only a few weeks ago. So they're apt to have notions about 'bolshevistic criminals' in their heads. In the long run, I cannot subordinate Russian commissioned officers to noncoms. Where the opportunists are concerned, what motivates them is the belief that we are going to win. But the genuine volunteers are not with us for such reasons. How will both groups react when the war goes badly and they realize we are not meeting them halfway, not treating them as real allies? I don't think much of mercenaries. But if we want to fight this war with mercenaries, we have at least to pay them. If they ask me what they're fighting for, I have to tell them something they can accept. And that is not a German victory, but a new Russia. . . . I've seen this coming for a long time. We're going to have to start all over again from the point at which we failed in December. We need a Russian anti-Stalinist

53

government and a Russian of stature to lead it. Such a person would be able to speak of war aims better than we can. . . . Herr General, tomorrow morning I shall fly to Mauerwald."

The Propaganda Department of the High Command of the Armed Forces (OKW) in Berlin, headed by the corpulent Colonel von Wedel, had stumbled virtually unprepared into the war against the Soviet Union. Wedel had maintained from the start that this "campaign" would be over in six weeks.

It was not until April 1941 that two members of the department were instructed to prepare a plan of "psychological warfare" against the Soviet Union. One was Colonel Blau, who was regarded as something of a genius in that branch of propaganda—though his dynamism had long since trickled away. The other was a Sonderführer (specialist officer) who was later promoted to the rank of captain, Nikolaus von Grote. A good-looking man with reddish-blond hair, he was of Baltic birth and as a young man had served in the tsar's army. In peacetime he had been a journalist. Grote had knowledge of the world, an enormous capacity for work, and considerable skill as a negotiator. Above all, he knew something about the Soviet Union and the people who inhabited it.

When he began on his assignment, Grote had taken it for granted that the key point of German policy would have to be the liberation of the peasants: freeing them from the collective farms, giving them back their land. During the First World War he had seen the effectiveness of the Bolshevik slogan: Peace, Bread, Land. Promised the division of the large estates, the Russian soldiers had deserted in droves, and the front had collapsed. For the Russian army was largely composed of peasants and the peasant's hunger for land was the most powerful force in their natures. The peasants still constituted the majority of the Soviet population, and Grote was convinced that their deepest desire was still private ownership of the land.

Within a few days, however, Blau and Wedel had made it clear that Hitler's war aims in the East had nothing to do with any real "liberation." Grote had to ask himself whether there was any point to working under such circumstances. But like so many others, he had hoped that by and by reason and experience would win the day.

On June 16, a few days before the beginning of the war in the East, Grote was assigned an assistant who shared his views: Lieutenant Dürksen, a German who had been born in Russia. As it turned out, this would be all the staff he would get for many months, which meant that he had to carry a fantastic work load. He was responsible for producing leaflets, getting out newspapers, directing radio broadcasts, and providing the texts for loudspeaker appeals at the front. On top of this, he set himself another task—effecting a change in the direction of propaganda.

In March 1942 a special group to deal with "action propaganda" for the East was at last established within the bureau. It was called "WPr IV" (Wehrmachtpropaganda IV), and was headed by Colonel Hans Martin, who had hitherto served as liaison officer between the Propaganda Department of the OKW and the Propaganda Ministry. Writing under the pseudonym of "Nitram," Martin had, before 1933, stirred up something of a sensation with a book on East Prussia. There was no doubt he was temperamentally fitted for "action propaganda." He was anything but a bureaucrat. Thus, when he had a difficult problem to discuss with one of his associates, he would whisk the man off for a drive in the Tiergarten "because we need fresh air for a thing like this." People who did not like him called him "snotty." He was not afraid of taking risks. He did not know a word of Russian, but he would have Grote and Dürksen to lean on.

Two other men important for the further course of events joined this group, one by chance, the other by a somewhat fantastic route. One of them was named Alexander Stepanovich Kazantsev, and one day Dürksen brought him into the office. He was an inconspicuous man with a wrinkled face and shy, intelligent eyes. At this time his German was still fairly poor. He had been born in Russia and during the twenties had made his way to the outside world by way of China, finding a home at last in Belgrade, where a group of Russian émigrés of the younger generation had also settled. He was a member of the inner circle of their organization, the NTS (*Nacionalno Trudovoi Soyus,* or National Labor Union); its leader, Baidalakov, was reaching out for new ideas that might win over the Russian people. Since the beginning of the German campaign in the East, the NTS had infiltrated a great many men into German organizations, from prison camps and administrative offices in the East all the way up to the Ministry for the Occupied Eastern Territories and the Propaganda Ministry.

Dürksen felt that the NTS was the only modern Russian exile organization that could be taken seriously, and therefore hoped for a great deal from Kazantsev. Grote, too, took a liking to Kazantsev and managed to have him hired by the bureau. He would be drafting and checking the contents of propaganda leaflets and propaganda newspapers destined for the eastern front.

The appearance on the scene of the second man was connected with the Action Propaganda group's move to a new building.

Several weeks before the beginning of the attack on Russia the East Department of the Propaganda Ministry, which was located in an old villa in Berlin, Number 10 Viktoriastrasse, gathered together a number of "experts on Eastern languages" and hermetically sealed them off from the outside world. Puny, little Dr. Eberhart Taubert, chief of East Department, who years ago had established the somewhat naïvely managed office known as the Antikomintern,* and had ever since devoted himself heart and soul to combating "Jewish bolshevism," was put in charge of this new group in Viktoriastrasse.

Taubert had camouflaged his "specialists" as employees of a publishing house called "Vineta." They were now put to work preparing propaganda posters, leaflets, pamphlets, and radio addresses in Russian and other languages. The message was: "Hail the German soldiers as liberators from Stalin's yoke." Or: "Kill political commissars, Bolsheviks, party members, and Young Communists (Komsomols)." At its mildest the appeal was: "Rise up against your oppressors. The hour of liberation has come." Deliberately, nothing was said about an alternative, about the fate of the population of the Soviet Union after a German victory.

On June 22, the day the attack on Russia was launched, the monastic seclusion of Viktoriastrasse was broken. The building had become too small; the "Vineta" publishing house looked around for larger quarters. After it moved out, Colonel Martin took over the building that had been shrouded in mystery. In doing so, he also assumed command of a small detention center for prisoners of war housed in a wing above the garage. A few prominent Russian captives were held here. Taubert had had them brought to Berlin so that they could speak on the radio and use their influence to sap the morale of the Russian troops.

When Martin took over in Viktoriastrasse, he found no really prominent Russians. But the presence of the group gave Grote the idea of collecting prisoners of war from all strata of the Soviet political and military leadership and by systematic questioning discovering what approaches would be most effective for propaganda broadcasts on the fighting fronts.

* An organization that existed in Berlin from 1937 to 1941 for propaganda directed against the Communist International.

56

Martin took up the plan. He sent Grote to General Gehlen and got in touch with the intelligence officers of the army groups in the East. He asked them to be on the lookout for prisoners who had special knowledge about the internal material and psychological structure of the Soviet Union. Furthermore, he asked for prisoners, including enlisted men, who were sufficiently intelligent and open-minded to give reliable reports on the effects of German propaganda.

Among the first prisoners to be transported to Berlin under this program was a Major Fyodorov of the Soviet Air Force, who had been captured at Leningrad. He made it perfectly plain that he was a convinced Communist and that he had not the slightest intention of extending the hand of friendship to Germans.

Next came a Major Golovin, chief of staff of a Soviet corps. He declared his willingness to collaborate, but only on the condition that once Stalin was ousted a Russia with greater freedom and no loss of territory could be reconstructed. This demand confronted Martin and Grote with a dilemma. What could they concede; what promises could they make?

After two weeks had passed, fifteen Soviet officers and soldiers were housed in the detention center above the garage. The District Defense Command protested because no barbed wire had been placed around Number 10 Viktoriastrasse and the Russian prisoners of war were being treated with outrageous laxity. The prisoners were sleeping in clean beds. They had tables and writing materials. They received the same rations as German soldiers, also cigarettes and an occasional bottle of vodka. Nor were the prisoners brought to the proper office for questioning. Instead, Martin and Grote called on the men in their own quarters to talk with them on a man-to-man basis. Only in this way, they felt, could they learn answers to the question: What must we do to win over the Soviet population and persuade it to participate wholeheartedly in the struggle against the regime of Stalin?

On April 26, 1942, the first really impressive Russian personality turned up in Viktoriastrasse.

Six days earlier, Lieutenant Colonel von Freytag-Loringhoven, Ic of Army Group South, had telephoned Martin. He had just interrogated a Soviet army commissar who had made a remarkably strong impression upon him and who seemed to be an opponent of Stalin out of conviction.

"His knowledge and intelligence are phenomenal," Freytag reported. "He tossed off an analysis of armaments production that simply knocked me over. His data largely agree with what we know. I would be pleased if you could put him up. That way he would at least be safe from the SS."

Martin did not give the matter long consideration. "I'll take him at once."

On the other end of the line an objection was raised. "I must call your attention to the fact that the man is probably a Jew."

"He'll be safe with me in that respect also."

On April 26 Mileti Aleksandrovich Zykov arrived at Viktoriastrasse still wearing his Red Army uniform. He looked suspiciously around the room into which he was led.

When Dürksen turned up two hours later to interview him, he found him just getting out of the zinc bathtub in which the prisoners did their laundry. He turned his back on Dürksen, dried himself, and dressed quickly, but methodically. Then he turned and scrutinized Dürksen.

Dürksen talked with him for several hours. Every word the man spoke was carefully considered. He wanted to know precisely the purpose for which he had been brought there. To Dürksen he said: "Lieutenant, I am an enemy of Stalin and of the present regime in my country, but I am not prepared to collaborate with you in any way until I am definitely informed what the German side has in mind for the Russian people. I am a socialist and Russian patriot, and I shall do only what helps my country."

Zykov was well informed about the treatment of Russian prisoners of war. It took Dürksen nearly an hour to convince him that such treatment had been either the result of unfortunate circumstances or of orders from a benighted group in the German leadership.

"We, too, are in a quandary," he explained. "We want your assistance in order to strengthen the sensible forces in the German leadership. If you can help us that way, you will be doing a good deal for your own people."

After many hours of discussion Zykov was still wary. "I'll think it over," was all he would say.

Toward the end of the interview, Dürksen said he had learned from Army Group South that Zykov had written an excellent paper on the state of the Soviet armaments industry. Would he be willing to write a detailed account of this for his, Dürksen's, department? Zykov repeated: "I'll think it over."

The following morning he asked for pen, ink, and paper. He thought it over for still another twenty-four hours. Then he set to work. He wrote for thirty-six hours.

Grote found the result the most amazing paper of this sort he had ever read.

Zykov wrote like a specialist, out of what seemed an endless fund of knowledge, about extremely complicated technologies, about the potential production of little-known factories, about the distribution of raw materials and the latest government plans. Grote passed the report on to German experts. They confirmed his impression that this was not mere verbiage but a substantial account, not only based on hard information but also showing a remarkable gift for interpreting facts and seeing implications. Here was a man with a truly powerful mind.

The idea that Zykov might be a spy whose aim was to work his way into some kind of position in Germany naturally occurred to some members of the bureau. But Dürksen kept remembering that Zykov was Jewish. He could not imagine that the Soviet side would be so stupid as to try to send a Jewish agent into Germany.

Next morning Dürksen had his second talk with Zykov. This time Zykov told him a bit about himself.

As a member of the Young Communist League, he had been taken into the "Lenin Guard" after the First World War. He had met Bukharin, Rykov, and Bubnov, the intellectual elite of Russian Marxism, whom Stalin was later to crush, deport, and annihilate. Bubnov had been People's Commissar for Education at the time. His daughter became Zykov's wife. In the course of time, Zykov became Bukharin's associate and later his deputy on the newspaper *Izvestiia*. But he was dislodged by Yeshov, chief of the GPU, as part of the campaign to destroy all the adherents of Lenin. Zykov was arrested and sent to Siberia. He had been allowed to return only the previous year, when the first German offensives had led to acute shortages in manpower. He became political commissar of a battalion, later a division, still later of a corps. And he had waited for his chance to let himself be taken prisoner.

This account of his life explained his antipathy to Stalin. From youth on, he had been an orthodox Marxist. As far as he was concerned, Stalin had perverted Marxism and communism for despotic ends. From Zykov's own carefully considered formulations and thoughtful answers, Dürksen had the impression that the man still guided all his thinking by what he called "scientific socialism."

On May 5 Zykov handed Dürksen another paper. It was entitled "Organizational Plan for the Practical Mobilization of the Russian People against the Stalinist System." It described nothing more nor less than a program for forming a Russian free government and a Russian liberation army subordinate to it, which, in alliance with Germany, would overthrow Stalin.

Zykov proposed that the government and army be headed by some popular Red Army general, a corps or army commander who had won fame by his military achievements and whom the Russian people did not regard as a Stalinist. A good number of such men would come forward, Zykov asserted, as soon as Germany offered a guarantee that the new government would be permitted to reconstruct the Russian republic according to its own lights and within the frontiers of 1938. In return, Germany would be saved endless slaughter, would have peace in the East, and an alliance with a grateful nation. The paper ended with the statement that if Germany were not prepared to take this course, she would lose the war in the East. Any notion of German domination over Russia would prove to be an illusion, Zykov declared.

In the light of history, the situation at this moment was quite grotesque. Here were Martin, Grote, and Dürksen harboring and concealing in their detention center a convinced Jewish Marxist and ex-commissar—the very symbol of German antibolshevist propaganda. Moreover, Zykov was proposing to show them how the Communist dictatorship of Stalin could be replaced by what he called "a genuine Marxist people's regime"—in other words, a regime that was bound to be as much an anathema to Hitler, Himmler, and all who shared Nazi conceptions as the regime of Stalin. In fact, even men like Grote and Dürksen were discomfited by Zykov's ideas. To be sure, they did not entertain the dream of restoring tsarism to Russia, as did many old Russian exiles. People like Roenne were well aware that the social, industrial, and intellectual developments of the past twenty-five years could not be undone. But their own ideas were certainly a great deal more "bourgeois" than Zykov's Marxist structures.

Nevertheless, Zykov's grand intellectual design appealed to them. An anti-Stalinist government under a popular Soviet general, backed by an army of liberation, seemed to them the answer to their search for a political, not just a public-relations, solution.

From May 6 on, all the discussions in the Viktoriastrasse office and detention center centered around the idea of a "liberation army," a "liberation government," and on the individual who could possibly lead both. One of the candidates for the job was Alexander Stepanovich Kazantsev, the more or less secret representative of the NTS. His considerations emerged from a later account:

"The (Russian) exiles held widely divergent views on the circumstances under which a change might take place back home. The Left Wing, represented by the socialist parties, whose leadership, almost without exception, was on the side of the Western powers, tended to hope for evolution in the Soviet political system. It expected Stalin to lead the country reluctantly toward democracy. This viewpoint corresponded to the pro-Soviet illusory notions of the Western powers themselves.

"Another group among the exiles had for long placed its hopes in a Russian Napoleon. They were inclined to see him in every new general who loomed up on the Soviet horizon. For a long while Tukhachevsky was the favorite. After the purge of Tukhachevsky, the exiles' hopes shifted to Marshal Blücher, and later even to Timoshenko. This particular exile group so completely lost all sense of what was absurd that for a while it believed Voroshilov would turn out to be the Russian Napoleon.

"We who had a better understanding of the nature of the Soviet dictatorship rejected the possibility of any evolution. As we formulated it, 'The Soviet system can decay but not evolve.' On the other hand, we did not reject the possibility that a Russian Napoleon might appear. But we had carefully studied the top leadership under Stalin. In the entourage that had surrounded him for many years we had not found so much as a caricature of a Napoleon. We therefore anticipated that the leader of an uprising could only be a corps or army commander who had been unknown up to the war. We even gave him an abstract name: 'Komkor [corps commander] Sidorshuk.' In the hope that our group could offer valuable help to this Sidorshuk, for more than ten years we prepared ourselves to meet him."

On June 4, three days before Tresckow—after his conversation with Schenckendorff—came to Mauerwald and met Gehlen and Roenne, Grote sent Roenne a letter dealing with Zykov's program and his own reactions to it.

Turning German Eastern policy in a direction acceptable to the Russians, he wrote, depended on finding a Soviet personality with leadership qualities who would put himself at the head of an army of liberation. "In all cordiality and urgency," he wrote, "may I ask you to keep watch for any sign of the appearance of such a personality on our side. . . . In the course of weeks of conversations with our Russians here, the names that keep coming up as the type of person needed are Rokossovski, Malinovski, or Vlasov. I think our destiny depends on our finding such a person, or on fate's throwing one our way. But if that happens, not a second must be wasted. . . . I am sure we understand one another."

This letter lay on Roenne's desk when Tresckow came to see him on the morning of June 8. Without a word, Roenne pushed the sheet of paper across the desk to him.

Caucasian Interlude

Cavalry General Ernst Köstring had just passed his sixty-sixth birthday when, on August 10, 1942, he was suddenly ordered to Vinnitsa.

Born in Moscow in 1876, the son of a German bookseller, he had attended school in that city and learned perfect Russian. Around the turn of the century, he had become an army officer in Germany. He had fought in the World War and in 1917, during the separatist movement in the Ukraine, he had been detailed to the German military commission at Skoropadsky. From 1927 to 1930 he had been military attaché of the German Embassy in Moscow, had been dismissed in 1933, but returned to Moscow in the same post in 1935. In the Soviet Union, his prestige was considerable. Communist party leaders and Red Army officers affectionately called him "our last baron."

Köstring had warned his superiors against war with the Soviet Union and cast doubt on the theory that the Soviet Union intended to break the pact of friendship and attack Germany. The Soviet Union had built up her armaments, he reported, but chiefly because she feared the growing power of the German Wehrmacht and was concerned for her own safety. Later, he declared that the German assault had forced the Soviet Union to develop into a military power which, in the foreseeable future, would be more than a match for Germany.

Those remonstrances stuck in Hitler's head. He grudgingly received Köstring when the general returned to Germany in July 1941, by way of Constantinople. But he dropped Köstring for good when the "Russophile" general advised him against prematurely celebrating victories in the East.

Since then, the general had lived in Berlin, doing nothing, not even hoping that he would again be asked for counsel. With growing anxiety, he had watched political developments in the occupied territories of the Soviet Union. Since the beginning of the great summer offensive of 1942 in the southern sector of the eastern front—an offensive that opened on July 1—he had looked on skeptically, gravely, despondently. Consequently, he was totally surprised when, on this August 10, 1942, he received orders to report to the Army High Command and then to the headquarters of Army Group A, which was advancing on the Caucasus.

His official designation was to be "Deputy General for the Caucasus."

Shortly before his departure from Berlin, Köstring learned that the Führer's Headquarters and the Army High Command had been moved to Vinnitsa in the Ukraine. When he arrived there after a thirty-six-hour train journey, he found the OKH established in the university buildings at the western end of the city.

Quartermaster General Wagner was housed in a former mental hospital about a mile beyond the city limits. He shook hands warmly with Köstring, and at once began explaining why he had been sent for.

"We wanted you for this job because the stakes are high. Up to now some terrible idiocies have been committed in the occupied territories. I therefore consider it essential for us to have specialists right on the spot in all future operations in the Caucasian region. Apparently even the Führer regards its population as politically safe. His highness the Minister for the Occupied Eastern Territories also appears to look with favor on the Caucasians. At any rate, it is a remarkable fact that out of all the native formations we have organized so far, only the Turks and the Caucasians have received official blessings. Professor von Mende has a dozen committees of liberation for the Caucasian tribes in his pocket. The prospect of winning over the population down there is at least promising. I'd like to know that we have a man on the spot who is capable of distinguishing sense from nonsense."

Twenty-four hours later, Köstring left in a Headquarters plane. From Poltava he had to continue his journey by automobile. Lieutenant von Herwarth accompanied him as his adjutant. Herwarth, too, had many years of experience as a diplomat in Moscow.

En route, Köstring learned that the operations against the Caucasus had gone well as far as the mountain ridges north of Sukhumi and Tuapse, and as far as the area around Ordzhonikidze, but that the offensive had ground to a halt. Field Marshal List, the commander of Army Group A, had supposedly put an end to the offensive, or else—versions differed—had refused to use his army group to accomplish two aims at once, that is, to reach simultaneously the Black Sea coast at Sukhumi and the shores of the Caspian Sea at Makhachkala. At any rate, by the time Köstring arrived at the headquarters in Stavropol, List had already been relieved of his command. General von Kleist had taken his place. He was a cavalier and cavalryman of the old school and, like most of his fellows, totally lacking in political knowledge or experience.

"I'm delighted to see you here," Kleist said when he received Köstring in his house surrounded by thriving gardens. "These vast spaces depress me. And these vast hordes of people. We're lost if we don't win them over."

"Win them over"—that had by now become a kind of slogan.

About this time, Wagner and Stauffenberg in Vinnitsa were busy trying to plant a second man in Army Group A.

Their object was to send in a representative of the East Ministry who would be provided with sufficient authority to decide political matters independently and thus could become Köstring's political partner. The trick was to launch him in such a way that he would be granted genuine powers. He must be in a position to act without having to consult with Berlin over every minor decision.

They picked on Bräutigam, who could wish for nothing better than to return to the Caucasus and to put an even greater distance between himself and the ministry in Berlin. But he knew it would be no easy matter to obtain the authorization.

And Stauffenberg knew that even better than he did.

"Herr General," Stauffenberg said to Wagner, "as far as Rosenberg is concerned, there are only two men who can even be considered for the Caucasus. One is Professor von Mende. The other is the intended Reichskommissar for the Caucasus, Rosenberg's friend Schickedanz. Herr Schickedanz has been waiting for his chance well over a year. He is said to have assembled some twelve hundred officials to establish his administration in the Caucasus. And he will move heaven and earth to keep anyone else from getting in there first and confronting him with accomplished facts."

Wagner responded decisively, "For the moment, two Reichskommissars are enough for me. I won't permit Herr Schickedanz down there until the Caucasus ceases to be an operational area and we no longer have anything to say. An operational area is a place for solidiers only. And Bräutigam is a captain."

Stauffenberg had guessed rightly in expecting that Schickedanz would put up the biggest fight. Mende was wholly in favor of Bräutigam. He himself wanted to guide affairs from the ivory tower of a folklorist. The elements he hoped to draw on for the renaissance of Caucasian and Turkistanian nationalities lived right in his vicinity in Berlin—headed by Veli Chayum Khan, the leader of the Turkistanian Unity Committee. The other national committees were still in ferment. Among the North Caucasians, representatives of the host of tribal groups and languages were in bitter conflict with one another. Among the Georgians, the aristocrats headed by the old exile Alschibaja battled with the democrats under Colonel Maglakelidse. In the background a new aspirant to leadership, Mischa Khedia, appeared to be rising fast. Similar power conflicts were going on among the Armenians, Azerbaijanis and Volga Tatars.

In this unreal world, where everyone was building on vague hopes for the future, Mende felt at home. He did not want to leave the scene and therefore welcomed the suggestion that Bräutigam be sent to the Caucasus. Schickedanz, however, instantly opposed the appointment. He had been waiting too long, a king without a country, and in order to insure that he would not be passed over, he urged Rosenberg to appoint to Army Group A a man whom he himself had planned to employ in his own Reichskommissariat later on. The ball bounced back and forth between the courts. At last Wagner smashed it right through the net by tempting Hitler into making an approving remark about Bräutigam in the course of a military conference. As so often happened in such cases, Hitler had no idea of the consequences of his remark. But for Rosenberg, Hitler's mere mention sufficed; the Minister for the Occupied Eastern Territories felt obliged to appoint Bräutigam to the post and to give him two assurances. The first was to the effect that no forcible deportations of workers were to take place in the Caucasus region. The second empowered Bräutigam to promise the population the immediate dissolution of all kolkhozes and other collectives. Since Bräutigam was well aware of the dubious value of any assurance from Rosenberg, he obtained additional guarantees by agreements with the ministry's "Labor Bureau" and by checking with its "Nutrition and Agriculture Desk." The latter, however, would only authorize the dissolution of collective farms in the infertile Caucasian mountain regions. In the much more fertile Kuban area, the agreement hedged: "Conditions are to be studied on the local level."

The land that lay beneath the mighty backdrop of the Caucasian mountains, between parched steppe, fruitful fields, and the endless greenery of the mountain forests, had always been a trouble zone for the tsars as well as for the Soviet rulers. Not until 1934 had special Soviet troops overcome the last resistance of the Caucasian tribes. Even now, the urge for independence had not died among the Cossacks, Karachayevs, Kabardians, Balkars, Ossets, and Ingushetes. Wherever German troops marched through their towns and villages, new hopes sprang up among these peoples.

Köstring and Bräutigam were, strictly speaking, a curious team. After all his years in Moscow, Köstring sympathized with Great Russian nationalism and was rather scornful of the backward-looking separatism of the border tribes. Bräutigam, on the other hand, felt quite close to these people. The two men drove all alone on barely traversable roads over the steppes, past fertile fields, into ancient, hidden-away mountain towns. Everywhere they were cordially received. There were no partisans anywhere in this region. Wherever they went, they found the people looking forward to some glad change: either a return to the condition of a free peasantry, which had always prevailed in the Caucasus in contrast to the serfdom in the rest of Russia, or, among some groups, a return to the "free pastoral life."

The Kabardians received Köstring, when he reached their territory in the wake of German troops, in the capital city of Nalchik. Köstring promised the assembled elders of the region that the countryside and the herds of cattle would once more become the property of individuals. Outside the building in which the conference was held, a crowd of Kabardians waited, on foot and on horseback. When Köstring emerged and made the same pledges to them that he had made to the elders, he was seized by enthusiastic hands and tossed repeatedly into the air. As a sign of gratitude, tribesmen were ready to deliver a few thousand wethers and a hundred horses of the famous Kabardian breed to the German army group. The riders of the horses, Köstring was told, wanted to join the fight for liberation on the side of the Germans.

In the Balkarian capital, the celebration of liberation became a religious festival. Dances alternated with displays of horsemanship. When the Balkars produced a gift for Hitler the Liberator, a gold-trimmed bridle, Bräutigam bowed his head for a moment. As he later reported, he felt a pang at realizing how deceived these people were about the supposed author of their "liberation." Nobody seemed to give thought to the possibility that instead of a fine new future the Soviet troops might some day return and take a bloody revenge.

In those late autumn days it seemed as though the advance into the Caucasus had begun moving again as soon as Kleist took over the command. New cheers and new festivities followed when the German troops entered the territory of the Karachayevs. But the "master race" spirit that pervaded the Führer's Headquarters reached even to these distant parts. At the time the Karachayevs invited the Germans to the Bairam festival, representatives of the Four-Year Plan, headed by State Secretary Paul Körner, had already reached the army group. One of them made a speech: "Karachayevs! We have freed you from bolshevism. But that doesn't mean you can do as you like now. Now that you have been freed by our great leader, Adolf Hitler, you must prove yourselves worthy of liberation and work and sacrifice for German victory. Now's the time to really roll up your sleeves. We won't stand for slackers. . . ."

Bräutigam controlled himself and translated: "We are well aware that a noble people lives in the Caucasus, the Karachayevs. We heard that the Bolsheviks had robbed this people of their property and their liberty. Therefore Adolf Hitler has sent his army and liberated you. . . ." Bräutigam's conscience twinged somewhat as he continued: "Henceforth you will be able to live free again in your villages and on your own land." And his conscience hurt even more when the cheering subsided and the spokesman for the Four-Year Plan commission said to his neighbors: "That's the way you have to talk to these fellows. They respond at once to the ring of a master's voice."

On the banks of the Kuban and the Terek, in the gently rolling hill country with its small forests and fertile fields, there followed a succession of celebrations of "liberation" among the Cossacks of the region. Their territories were declared zones of self-government. The Cossacks were empowered to organize their administration and their agriculture as they saw fit. All that was asked of them was that they deliver a certain percentage of the grain raised in their province. Atamans were appointed as Cossack leaders. To show their appreciation, the Cossacks brought vast quantities of gifts to the Germans, whole herds of sheep and horses. Men like Köstring and Bräutigam felt ashamed, for they could feel the storm clouds gathering over the frail structures they were building.

Meanwhile the army group that was supposed to reach the Volga, under Field Marshal von Weichs, was advancing through the territory of other Cossack tribes further north, between the Don and Volga rivers. It occurred to the Ic of this army group, Lieutenant Colonel von Freytag-Loringhoven, to take advantage of the long tradition of hostility between the Cossacks and the Soviet government by setting up Cossack cavalry formations.

Baron von Freytag-Loringhoven had certain doubts about this scheme. He knew that Cossack antagonism to communism was a generational thing. Before the outbreak of the war, Stalin had endeavored to win over the younger generation of Cossacks by setting up new units of Soviet Cossack troops who enjoyed special privileges and who participated in the great May Day parades in Moscow. His wooing had had some effect. Nevertheless, since the beginning of the war, whole groups of Cossacks had gone into hiding to avoid being conscripted. Now they emerged. Ancient, hidden uniforms were dug up, weapons were produced, horses saddled. In no time at all, cavalry units appeared, mostly organized by *stanitsas* (villages), and provided with equipment formerly belonging to the Red Army.

Hetman Kulakov—who, along with General Shkuro, was perhaps the most famous Cossack leader in the struggles between the Whites and the Reds after the First World War—had been reputed dead for some two decades. Now he was fetched out of his hiding place in one of the cliffside villages of Terek Province and driven in a troika, accompanied by roistering Cossacks, to Poltava. During one of the last Cossack battles, both of his legs had been blown off by a shell. For some sixteen years the old man had lived in a shaft some forty feet deep under his own house. During those years of concealment, he had carved himself wooden legs out of beechwood.

The response was so immediate that Freytag-Loringhoven set aside all his reservations. He was further encouraged when Red Army Cossack troops at the front began deserting to the German side, and Cossacks in many German prisoner-of-war camps volunteered.

All the Cossacks who wanted to fight in their own formations on the German side were assembled on the terrain of a Soviet armaments plant in Voyenstroi Seleshchina. That was easily done with those who came from the *stanitsas*. It was more difficult in the prison camps, where thousands pressed forward claiming to be Cossacks in order to escape starvation. Freytag-Loringhoven could think of no other way but to form a commission consisting of trustworthy Cossack officers. They had questionnaires printed which could be answered only by Cossacks because non-Cossacks would not have the necessary knowledge.

This commission went from one prison camp to the next. In the barracks of the German camp command it set up interrogation rooms.

Through these rooms passed the dreary procession of those who had volunteered as Cossacks. The scenes the commission witnessed in the camps were horrible. No straw, no blankets, epidemics and no medicines. The food situation was so bad that those who ultimately were transported to Voyenstroi Seleshchina had to be forcibly prevented from eating more than their weakened physiques could stand.

Meanwhile, many leaders of German security forces in the rear areas of the army group were acting on their own initiative, setting up Cossack squadrons in order to guard the supply lines which, since the offensive against Stalingrad had been launched, seemed to be stretching on into infinity.

Meanwhile also, a Cossack self-government formed and began functioning. At least it brought in the harvests. When the winter of 1942 began, there was no thought among the Cossacks that there might be a German retreat, let alone that they would have to leave their native land.

The farther Army Groups A and B advanced between the Caucasus and Stalingrad in those autumn days of 1942, the wider grew the gap between their offensive spearheads in the Kalmuck Steppe. A single German division, General von Schwerin's Sixteenth Motorized, ultimately was alone in guarding this whole area. Its forces were spread wide and thin, hopelessly isolated in the barren plain, amid the steppe grass and the sand dunes. They had the whole steppe to themselves: a monotonous expanse without fixed points of reference, without settlements, except for Elista, the tiny Kalmuck capital.

In the brilliant sunsets characteristic of the region, when the sky was painted in great bands of orange, purple, and darkest blue, the German soldiers, standing on tiny elevations barely three or four feet high, could look more than sixty miles eastward into nothingness. The only living beings were the remnants of the Kalmuck nation from whom the Soviet government had taken their formerly vast herds in order to force these nomads to a settled way of life.

The Kalmucks now numbered somewhere between sixty and eighty thousand persons. They lived in low tents made of hides and, in winter, in pits that they roofed with reeds. But they had not yet lost their nomadic instincts, nor their wild craving for independence.

The Ic of the Sixteenth German Motorized Division was an industrialist from the Ruhr named Poltermann. He decided to exploit the anti-

Soviet feelings of the Kalmucks by setting up cavalry formations that could protect the unguarded flanks of the division. Lieutenant Colonel von Freytag-Loringhoven in Poltava sent him an interpreter who purported to know how to deal with Kalmucks.

The interpreter's name was Wrba. He had the temperament of an adventurer. Using the alias of "Dr. Doll" he crisscrossed the steppe and managed to set up sixteen Kalmuck squadrons, for whom he obtained German uniforms and captured weapons. These formations lacked Western discipline and order, but they were splendid riders and fighters on their home terrain, and they carried out their task with passion. They took care of the annihilation of remaining Soviet troops in the steppe with such fury that German units occasionally had to intervene to prevent brutalities.

Köstring and Bräutigam were not fully informed about this development among the Don Cossacks and the Kalmucks. Vast spaces lay between their own headquarters and Field Marshal von Weichs' army group.

Köstring, however, was having his own experiences with so-called "legions" that had been formed from prisoners held in camps in Poland. These battalions had been hastily sent to the Caucasus front to participate in the "liberation of their Georgian or Armenian homeland." Köstring found that these forces did not have native commanders. Instead, they had been given German officers, chosen at random, who did not understand a word of the languages spoken by their men. Lacking all knowledge of their subordinates, these Germans were commanding troops of "colonials," and treated them with all the arrogance of neo-imperialists. As for the Georgians and Armenians, they had not been given the slightest smattering of political schooling since being plucked from their prison camps, beyond the standard phrase about fighting against bolshevism. What had kept them in order had been the threat of punishment. At the same time, in Poland they had observed the harsh treatment of the Poles. These impressions had scarcely helped to consolidate their initial willingness to make common cause with the Germans. Their armament consisted only of haphazard captured weapons. They had been told by several of their German superiors that these weapons were good enough for them. Some of the German officers considered themselves downgraded by being given command of these legions.

These battalions now arrived at the headquarters of Army Group A.

By the time Köstring inspected a Georgian battalion and one composed of Ossets, Circassians (Cherkessers), and Karachayevs, the first disaster had already taken place. An Armenian battalion sent to the front had largely deserted. The German regimental commander was outraged. A political innocent, he raged at the "rabble of spies and cowards."

Köstring realized that reports on such incidents could quickly destroy all prospect of "native" troops. He protested urgently to Stauffenberg, demanding an immediate end to the policy of sending such enlisted legions to the front without adequate preparation. He insisted on a thorough review of conditions among the legions that were being raised in Poland. In contrast to the scathing reports from German commanders on the behavior of the first Caucasian battalions at the front, Köstring pointed to the reports coming in at this same period from Captain Theodor Oberländer, the commander of the so-called "Mountaineers" on his experiences with his Caucasian units. Oberländer, it is true, was unhappy because his units were not being used for the purpose he had intended when he created them with so much effort—to combat the partisans behind the German front. In view of the increasing bitterness of the battles in the foothills of the Caucasus and the steady attrition of the German forces, these Mountaineers had been thrown into ordinary front-line duty at the Terek River. But in spite of heavy casualties and third-class equipment, they had fought tenaciously and reliably.

Köstring's appeal to Stauffenberg yielded some results. On September 22 Colonel Ralph von Heygendorff stepped out of one of the furlough trains at the Warsaw railroad station. His train had come from the territory of Army Group Center. While he looked around for some further transport in the direction he was heading, Rembertow, he noticed a train on a siding. There was a large notice on it: "Poles, Jews, and Legionnaires, Last Car."

Thus Heygendorff was given a sidelight on his new task for which, at Stauffenberg's urging, he had been called back from the front. Up to a few days before, Heygendorff had commanded an infantry regiment in Army Group Center. Now he had in his pocket an order appointing him "Commander of the Activation Staff of the Eastern Legions" in Rembertow—in other words, commander of those very legionaries who were being banished to the last car like lepers.

Until this time Heygendorff had heard only sporadically about the activation of various "native formations" in the area of his army group. It was new to him that there were also "native formations" dubbed "Eastern Legions" in Poland. This is not to say that he was in any way vexed at being appointed their commander. Quite the contrary. During the First World War he had learned Russian; in 1930 and 1932 he had accompanied high Soviet officers who came to observe maneuvers in Germany. During the campaign in Poland he had been liaison officer to the Red Army. In conjunction with this task he had become a member of the German-Soviet commission which defined the new boundary partitioning Poland into German and Russian territory. Subsequently, he had become an aide to General Köstring. Stauffenberg could therefore assume that Heygendorff would approach his task with some understanding—which was why he had arranged this new assignment.

On September 23 Heygendorff arrived in Rembertow. Major Meyer-Mader, the first commander there, had left the town as long ago as the beginning of April. In Skierniewice he had activated "Turk Battalion 450" and, at the beginning of May, had personally set out to take his men to Army Group South. Since then the battalion had been under a series of officers.

Four legions had come out of Rembertow: the Turkistanian Legion, the Azerbaijanian Legion, the Georgian Legion, and, finally, the Armenian Legion. The Georgian Legion had been subdivided and a North Caucasian Legion drawn out of it. The Turkistanian Legion consisted of Uzbeks, Kazaks, Kirgizes, Turkmens, Kara-Kalpaks, and Tadzhiks. The Georgian Legion was made up of Georgians, South Ossets, Svanes, Lak, Adzhars, and Karachayevs. Only the Azerbaijanis and the Armenians gave the impression of being a unified group.

The German officers, drawn from a wide variety of units where, in many cases, they were not very well thought of, could not understand why men who had hitherto been regarded as "subhumans" (*Untermenschen*) were suddenly to be fighting on the German side and, in addition, given decent treatment. Most of the German officers and noncoms did not realize that here were people who could possibly possess anything like national pride and self-respect. In the hearing of Turkistanian officers who understood German, German battalion commanders would declare that the purpose of the Turk battalions was to save more valuable German blood. When statements of this sort were made to him, Heygendorff promptly had the commander relieved of his post.

In Kielce, Heygendorff found a convalescent unit for amputated, paralyzed, and blinded legionnaires lodged in a miserable building. Several hundred severely wounded men were under the charge of an SS Sturmbannführer (major) named Geibel. There was no German doctor directing the work, no medical equipment, no therapy room—nothing. A Turkistani doctor showed Heygendorff a letter from the Army Medical Inspection Office. He had written asking for artificial limbs. It read tersely: "Artificial limbs are in short supply and are reserved exclusively for German soldiers." Geibel had then applied for ash wood so that the patients could carve the limbs themselves. The reply was: "Ash is reserved exclusively for the construction of airplanes."

Could not at least a few prostheses have been provided, to show good will? There were no medals, no signs of appreciation. Soldiers who recovered sufficiently to be fit to work had been sent to labor camps, the badge reading *Ostarbeiter* (East-worker) sewn to their jackets.

Heygendorff finally went to Warsaw. There he inspected a hospital for legionnaires and found Georgian and Caucasian physicians whom German corporals had detailed to dirty work like cleaning latrines. The paymaster customarily withheld special rations and cigarettes from wounded legionnaires and was astonished when Heygendorff made a fuss and threatened punishment. The man had simply been doing what he thought was proper.

Heygendorff paid a call on Governor-general Hans Frank. He demanded removal of the signs reading "Poles, Jews, and Legionnaires, Last Car," from the railroad trains.

"But Colonel," one of the officials said, "we cannot have those Asiatics riding in the same car with Germans."

Heygendorff was a man of enormous self-control. But now he exclaimed: "But they're good enough to be put into German uniforms and risk their hides for us."

"Colonel," the man replied, "do you imagine that a native in a British colonial regiment would be allowed to ride in a railroad car with Englishmen?"

Heygendorff repeated his demand that the signs be removed. At last he was given assurances that they would be. He returned to Rembertov firmly determined to do his job thoroughly or resign.

In mid-December 1942, Stauffenberg received an order that at last permitted him to establish an "inspectorate," that is, a supervisory office for the auxiliaries and volunteers, and thus to instill a certain amount of organization into these forces that had so suddenly came into being. Stauffenberg had all along been pushing quietly toward this goal. What had taken longest was obtaining approval from the High Command of the

Armed Forces. When the OKW finally did issue its order, it did so with the proviso that the personnel of the new inspectorate would have only a consultative function. There was also a ban on setting up units larger than battalion size.

The head of the new office would be permitted to bear the title *General der Osttrupen* (General of the East Troops). Roenne at once had objections to this name. The word *Ost* already had an insulting meaning because of its use to designate forced labor, the *Ostarbeiter*. The word *Truppen* sounded like the Russian word *trup,* which means corpse. But it was cause for rejoicing that the office had been approved at all, and Roenne proposed his former divisional commander, General Hellmich, as "General of the East Troops."

At this time Hellmich was commander of a reserve division in Poland. During the struggle to capture Moscow, he had really, or allegedly, failed as commander of the Twenty-third Division and been relieved of his front-line command. Captured by the Russians in the First World War, he had learned to speak Russian halfway decently in the course of his imprisonment. He was a large man with a big head and dark-blond hair heavily sprinkled with gray. His eyes did not seem particularly intelligent, but there was a glint of human kindliness in them. Undoubtedly, he was a solid, experienced soldier, but he had no comprehension whatsoever of politics or diplomacy.

Roenne realized too late that he himself had made a serious error in placing a man who was purely a soldier in a position that called for other than military qualities. What was wanted was an exceptionally skillful negotiator and psychologist, someone above all without military blinkers. The selfsame loyalty complex that, in a sense, had prompted Roenne to propose his old divisional commander led Hellmich in turn to choose former officers of the Twenty-third Division for his new staff. Naturally, they did not speak Russian and brought no special knowledge to their new job. The only one who did have such special knowledge of Russian matters was the first chief of the new staff, Lieutenant Colonel von Freytag-Loringhoven, who, in the middle of December, was detached from Army Group South and sent to Lötzen.

Ever since November 19, General von Kleist's staff had been watching the north with anxious eyes.

Hitler's obstinate determination to conquer Stalingrad had meant a steady withdrawal of men and matériel from Army Group A for the Battle of Stalingrad. Everyone in the intimate group around Kleist knew that the second great effort to win a military victory over the Soviet Union in 1942 had failed. The fronts were stretching out between the Don, the Volga, and the Caucasus. Superior Russian armies had launched a pincers offensive to the northwest and southwest of Stalingrad, and had penetrated the thinly stretched fronts of the Germans and their allies.

Early in December Bräutigam returned from a tour of the Cossack areas and had a brief talk with Kleist. The commanding general told him: "The Sixth Army is encircled in Stalingrad. We will have to think about withdrawing our army group as far as the Don. . . . We will never again return to the Caucasus."

Bräutigam's notes at the time record his preoccupation with the fate of all those Caucasian tribesmen who had hailed the German troops—and him—as liberators and had since then so trustfully begun a new life. Leaving them behind when the army retreated to the west would be equivalent to condemning them to death.

At this time, ill health put Köstring out of action for weeks. Bräutigam was left to handle everything by himself.

On December 29, the orders for the retreat of Army Group A arrived. On the morning of New Year's Day, Field Marshal von Kleist told Bräutigam: "Stalingrad is finished. The Führer forbade the Sixth Army to attempt a breakout. Now it is too late. The Führer has also forbidden us to retreat further than the Don; we are not allowed to cross it but must hold a bridgehead on the Kuban and also hold the city of Rostov. In view of the situation of Turkey, the Führer wants us to maintain a position in the eastern Black Sea area."

"Does that mean that the idea of conquering the Caucasus has not yet been abandoned?" Bräutigam asked.

"The idea is said to be still standing." Kleist's meaning was clear.

"But what will happen to the tribes of the Caucasus who have taken our side? We cannot leave them behind."

"We'll have enough to do without worrying about them," the field marshal answered. "We must start marching to save our own skins."

Bräutigam persisted. "At least we must take along all those who have especially exposed themselves and who want to come with us."

"How could I possibly assume responsibility for that?" Kleist said. "The hordes of civilians would clog the roads and put our own forces in terrible jeopardy."

"Then the civilian columns will have to march without using the roads."

"Do you think that is possible?" Kleist asked.

Bräutigam did not really know whether it would be possible. But he said: "Yes."

"I'll let you know my decision tomorrow," Kleist said.

The following morning Kleist set up a "Caucasus Refugee Staff." General Mierczynski, military government commander of Pyatigorsk, was appointed to head it, with Bräutigam to serve as his deputy. Twenty-four hours later, instructions were issued to all the military government headquarters. Bräutigam must have wished that those autumn days of celebration among the peoples of the Caucasus had never been part of his life and memories.

Within another twenty-four hours, the departure of the Caucasian peoples was already in full swing. No one had time to complain of his individual fate or to curse the Germans. The military government headquarters had explained that this was only a temporary retreat for the winter. Tens of thousands of natives packed their wagons overnight.

Bräutigam did everything in his power to send the columns by relatively secure routes. The Cossacks were supposed to withdraw across the ice of the Sea of Azov to Mariupol. But since the sea had not yet frozen over completely, large groups of Cossacks fell into the hands of the advancing Soviet forces. The Caucasian columns tried to reach the Kuban bridgehead or the Sea of Azov at Azov, where the ice had already hardened.

After some grueling days, Bräutigam himself reached Rostov. There he assembled all the refugees in order to send them on into the Nogai steppe. In Taganrog an order from the East Ministry reached him: he was to return to Berlin at once. The "Caucasian business" was "settled," his instructions informed him. But Bräutigam could not tear himself away from the fate of the people whom he had, he felt, misled. He stayed. He was for letting the Cossacks move into the area of Baranovichi and settling their families there. But Gauleiter Koch threatened to seize the horses of any Cossacks who attempted to pass through the Ukraine. Every day saw new struggles to find a saving route to the West. Finally the march of the Cossacks ended in Tolmezzo in northern Italy. There Bräutigam parted from them.

. . .

During those same weeks, Kalmucks were also pouring westward. Doll, the interpreter, and his assistants assembled the tribes, who at first refused to believe that their trust in the Germans had plunged them into an adventure that might mean the end of their existence as a people. In long columns, including women, children, and herds, they made their way toward the Ukraine. Kalmuck squadrons that reached the eastern Ukraine, where they were at least temporarily safe, were assigned to protecting the railroad lines. They carried out their task to the best of their ability. But the consequences of their transplantation into an alien world soon began to show up. Doll had never tried to convert Kalmucks into soldiers in the Western sense. He knew that it couldn't be done. The result was that they now became an endless nuisance to the German military authorities. Soon one headquarters or another was demanding that they be disarmed. It was mandatory that they separate from their wives and children. The Kalmucks, for their part, reacted as they could not help reacting—like uprooted, homeless, misunderstood, and unjustly attacked individuals. And what the Germans refused to give them they took for themselves.

As the front receded they moved from echelon to echelon further westward, until at last they reached the troop-training area of Neuhammer in Silesia.

On March 1, 1943, Bräutigam, looking worn from his exertions during the great westward trek, called upon General Wagner once more in Mauerwald. The Führer's Headquarters and the OKH had returned to Mauerwald from Vinnitsa after the collapse of the 1942 offensive.

Köstring had been there only a few days earlier. He had now gone to Berlin, but was supposed to return in a few weeks to assume, in Mauerwald, the post of administrator of the Turkic Racial Forces.

"There's no need to report to me," Wagner told Bräutigam. "I know what a fiasco this march on the Caucasians was and that there may be worse to come. We're hopelessly embroiled in the tragedy. If we don't want simply to abandon everything, we have to go on fighting. While you were out there, there have been some new developments here; everything may yet hang on this. . . . "We've found your Russian with leadership qualities."

Vlasov

Nikolaus von Grote had stayed late in his office on Viktoriastrasse on the evening of September 4, 1942. A telephone call came for him from Army High Command in Vinnitsa. Roenne was on the other end of the line, his voice faint but clear.

"Guess whom we've had here for a while," Roenne said.

"Who?"

Roenne paused for a few seconds. Then he said, articulating every word: "The commander in chief of the Soviet army group on the Volkhov."

"Who would that be?" Grote persisted.

"Andrei Andreyevich Vlasov, the defender of Kiev in 1941, the commander in chief of the Twentieth Soviet Army in the winter battle outside Moscow."

Grote needed no further information. Vlasov was not news to people in Viktoriastrasse. For years he had been hailed in Soviet military journals as the reorganizer of the Ninety-ninth Soviet Division. He had served as military adviser to Chiang Kai-shek. After his successes as commander of the Twentieth Soviet Assault Army in the Battle of Moscow he had been lauded by Stalin personally, decorated, and repeatedly mentioned in the press with Zhukov and other prominent Russian generals.

"We would be grateful to you," Roenne was saying, "if you yourself or one of your men could come here. From our talks with Vlasov we have gathered that he is emotionally committed to opposition to Stalin. His experiences in the Volkhov battle have made a lasting impression upon him. But we think you ought to sound him out for yourself. . . ."

Grote proposed that he send Lieutenant Dürksen to Vinnitsa in the Junkers 52 that had been placed at the disposal of his office.

Dürksen landed in Vinnitsa on September 2. He was driven to the hospital buildings in which Foreign Armies East had its headquarters.

Roenne came forward to shake hands. Behind him stood a captain of medium height, around forty-five years old.

"Let me introduce you to Captain Strik-Strikfeldt of my department," Roenne said. "Captain Strik-Strikfeldt has been an interpreter on the staff of Army Group Center until the beginning of this year. He has now been assigned to our department at the request of General Gehlen. Since he conducted the first interviews with General Vlasov, he can give you all necessary information and then let you meet the general."

Strik-Strikfeldt took Dürksen to his office. "If you like, you can talk to Vlasov tomorrow morning," he said. His German had a distinctively Baltic lilt. "And it will be better if you talk to him alone. Vlasov is still very much on his guard. He's more likely to open up with one person than with two. Don't imagine that what I'm going to tell you came out all at once. I had to fight hard to win Vlasov's confidence."

Strik-Strikfeldt handed Dürksen photographs that had been taken, after Vlasov's capture, at Camp Lötzen. They showed a cadaverously thin, hollow-cheeked man of unusual height.

"A Russian in the tradition of Peter the Great," Strik-Strikfeldt said. "Tall and firm as a tree, and yet intelligent and subtle as a vibrating violin string. With a breadth of soul . . ." He broke off, feeling that he was letting himself go in his enthusiasm for Russia. *"Shirokaya natura,"* he said. "You'll see. We won't find another like him. History has simply put him on our doorstep as though to say: Here you are, and now show that you're worthy of this gift."

"He has made a great impression on you," Dürksen said, smiling.

"Let me brief you on the immediate background," Strik-Strikfeldt said. "From what I have been able to piece together, in the spring Stalin personally ordered Vlasov to lead a powerful assault force from the Volkhov front straight through the frozen swamp region up north and relieve Leningrad. With the Second Soviet Assault Army Vlasov drove that sixty-mile wedge into the front of our Eighteenth Army under General Lindemann, but then bogged down. The Second Soviet Army formed a pocket which had only a thin, tubelike connection with the actual Soviet front on the Volkhov. This situation proved disastrous at the beginning of the summer. Once the swamps thawed, supplies could no longer reach the Second Soviet Assault Army through that narrow passage. Meretskov, the former commander in chief, lost his nerve. Vlasov himself took over the command of the encircled army. Lindemann's divisions began slowly squeezing the pocket. The Russian troops were fighting without ammunition and food. Tens of thousands of Vlasov men were dying hopelessly, were turning cannibalistic from hunger, and still they did not receive permission to retreat or to fight their way through to the lines behind the Volkhov. The major from Lindemann's staff who brought Vlasov here told me a few things about it. Do you know the story?"

"Only as much as we have heard from our prisoners."

"It was a graveyard," Strik-Strikfeldt said. "Tens of thousands in the marshes, with swarms of flies and mosquitoes, the stench intolerable. Vlasov saw it all up to the very end. He was one of the few who survived, together with his cook, Marya Voronova, and managed to hide out for a few weeks longer than the rest. But I'll speak of that later. Lindemann's staff assumed that Vlasov had either died or been flown out of the pocket in time. There were a number of false reports. Several times bodies were found that were identified as the general by Russian civilians. Finally on July 12 a message reached the Thirty-eighth Army Corps in the Novgorod area to the effect that Vlasov had been shot by a sentinel the day before, near Yam-Tezero. Captain Schwerdtner, the Ic of the corps, set out to identify the corpse. On the way, he passed through the village of Tukhovechi. The Russian village head informed the interpreter that there was a high Soviet officer hiding in a barn near the village. The man was half-starved, and he had a woman with him. But Schwerdtner first went to see the reported corpse. The dead man was, as it later turned out, Vlasov's chief of staff; Vlasov had covered his dying aide with his own coat. On its return journey, the German group stopped again in Tukhovechi and were reminded of the Russian officer and the woman. The door of the barn was battered in, and there was Vlasov, at the end of his strength, hardly able to stand. He gave up all pretense, saying: "Don't shoot. I am General Vlasov." And he produced papers that he had not destroyed, for a reason I'll explain later. He was immediately taken to Lindemann in Ziverskaya. Lindemann talked with him, treating him like a courageous enemy. Then he sent him to Lötzen, and from there he came to us."

Strik-Strikfeldt rose from his desk. "We ought to go outside. It would be easier to tell you the rest while walking . . . the fact is, I am all worked up about this. Even before the debacle outside Moscow I was looking for such a figure."

They went outside and strolled along orchards that lay peaceful and unharmed in the sunlight, as though worlds were not in turmoil all around.

"If you talk to Vlasov tomorrow," Strik-Strikfeldt resumed, "and if you manage to win his confidence, he may possibly give you further answers to the question of why he remained with his army in the Volkhov pocket, although on Stalin's direct orders the Soviet High Command sent in planes at least four times to take him to Moscow. And you will then ask, as I did, what prompted him not to shoot himself but to surrender and finally to talk with me about things that he has probably never discussed with anyone else."

"The obvious assumption is, of course, that he feared what awaited him," Dürksen suggested. "Maybe he came over to us just to save his skin."

"There's no doubt that he proposed retreat from the bottleneck on the eastern bank of the Volkhov in good time," Strik-Strikfeldt replied. "But Stalin commanded continuation of the offensive toward Leningrad. On March 19 what Vlasov had feared actually happened. Lindemann closed the bottleneck. On March 27 Vlasov succeeded in breaking through once more toward the main Soviet front and forming a connecting line nearly two miles wide. But even then Stalin did not permit the Second Army to abandon the bottleneck. Instead, a woman called on Vlasov, the same Marya Voronova with whom he was taken prisoner. She was his wife's cook in Moscow and a resolute soul. She'd managed to make her way to him, bringing him a secret letter with the outline of his son's hand on the back as a talisman. In the letter itself there were only two words: *Gosti byli,* "Guests have come." I suppose you know what those words meant."

"His home had been searched by the NKVD," Dürksen replied.

"Exactly," Strik-Strikfeldt continued. "From then on, he knew that Stalin's pathological suspiciousness was directed against him. Stalin did not give permission for the army to withdraw from the bottleneck until May 14. But by then it was too late. Vlasov managed only to pluck a few divisions out of the pocket. On May 20 Lindemann broke the connecting tube completely, and Vlasov remained in the pocket with sixteen divisions and brigades. So undoubtedly he knew what to expect as an unlucky loser if he returned to Moscow."

They had reached the steep bank of the Bug River. A vessel was moored down below and was being unloaded by Ukrainian women. Strik-Strikfeldt said: "But that alone doesn't account for his actions. Such an explanation would be too simple for the man. Behind his conduct is a long process of disappointments and of perceptions about Stalin, bolshevism, and what is really good for the Russian people."

Andrei Andreyevich Vlasov was born after the turn of the century in the vicinity of Nizhni Novgorod, the eighth child of a village tailor. He was a charity pupil at the seminary of Nizhni Novgorod. When the Russian Revolution broke out, he fought in the Ukraine and the Crimea as a soldier and later as company commander with the Red Second Don Division in the struggle against the White Russian troops of Generals Denikin and Wrangel. He rose to battalion commander, then became a teacher of tactics in Moscow and, later, commander of the second infantry regiment of a Turkistanian division. In 1933 he married a girl from a village near his birthplace. She had studied medicine and become a doctor.

In 1936 and 1937, as chief of staff of the Seventy-second Soviet Division, he had witnessed Stalin's brutal purge of the Soviet officer corps. Some 30,000 officers were arrested and implicated in Marshal Tukhachevsky's alleged plot to overthrow the government. Three of Russia's five field marshals, thirteen of the nineteen army commanders, and more than half of the 180 generals of divisions were liquidated, some of them with their families. Vlasov's wife, who came from the peasantry and was therefore nonproletarian in origins, could have been a liability to him. The two went through the motions of a divorce.

Vlasov was sent to China, first as an ordinary member, then as chief of staff, of a Soviet mission of military advisers to Chiang Kai-shek. This service kept him out of the firing line. Employing the oddly fateful alias of "Volkhov," he had his first sight of the world outside the Soviet Union and experienced the two faces of Soviet policy, which, on the one hand, was supporting the nationalist Chiang's struggle against the Japanese and, simultaneously, Chiang Kai-shek's internal enemies, the Chinese Communists. The lectures he delivered at the Chinese military academy in Chungking won him honors and decorations from the Chinese Nationalists; these were taken from him when he was ordered to return to Russia.

There the great Tukhachevsky purge was over. The Nonaggression Pact between Stalin and Hitler had gravely shaken the dogma of a deadly enmity between bolshevism and fascism.

On visits to his native village, Vlasov found his father and the friends of his youth living in the same poverty and primitive conditions that had prevailed in his boyhood, in spite of all the promises of the Revolution.

The poor performance of the Soviet armies during the first Winter War against Finland in 1939–1940 underscored the consequences of Stalin's purges of the military. As the newly appointed commander of the Ninety-ninth Soviet Infantry Division, which was notorious for total lack of discipline, Vlasov had shown that he combined tremendous organizational skill with energy and the qualities of a born troop leader. Within a short time he had transformed an anarchic body of men into a crack division. Vlasov himself was decorated by Marshal Timoshenko and singled out for laudatory mention by *Pravda*.

Vlasov had found the constant supervision by political commissars so hindersome that in 1940, after his promotion to the rank of brigadier general, he proposed limiting the jurisdiction of the commissars to non-military matters. He made this suggestion quite publicly, in lectures in Kiev and in an address to high-ranking officers in Moscow. The course of the Winter War in Finland proved him so right that his criticism was accepted and his idea was followed, although rather hesitantly. In January 1941 he was appointed commander of the Fourth Soviet Tank Corps in Lvov and awarded the Order of Lenin. When the German offensive began, the forty-year-old general was appointed commander of the Thirty-seventh Soviet Army and of the fortified region of Kiev. Ordered by Stalin to hold the Dnieper front even after the German pincers had closed around the entire Soviet Southwest Army Group, Vlasov stuck it out on the Dnieper while all around him 600,000 Soviet soldiers were surrendering in total chaos. Finally, with the remainder of his army, he fought his way out to the east to find special squads led by commissars carrying out the "scorched earth" policy, burning down not only factories and military camps but also granaries, supply depots, and whole villages.

The frightful collapse, the refusal on the part of hundreds of thousands of men to fight for their government, made as deep an impression upon him as his earlier visits to his native village. He had time to think, for he was hospitalized in Voronesh in a state of total exhaustion, and old acquaintances kept away from him because they feared he would have fallen into Stalin's bad graces because of the disaster around Kiev. They began seeing him again only after he received a direct order from Stalin, at the beginning of November, to report to the Kremlin on November 10.

At this time Moscow was in a state of panic. German tank formations under Generals Hoth and Guderian were threatening the city from the south and north. In a nocturnal conference, Stalin entrusted Vlasov with command of the Twentieth Assault Army, which possessed all of fifteen tanks and some fresh troops newly arrived from Siberia. Operating in the center of Zhukov's army group, his troops played a major role in the Soviet counteroffensive. Ilya Ehrenburg hailed him in an article in *Krasnaya Zvezda*. After von Bock's army group was thrown back, Vlasov received the Order of the Red Flag.

Early in March 1942 he was once again summoned to see Stalin. He found the dictator in a despondent mood, complaining about the British and Americans who were sending him only second-rate war matériel rather than the whole armies which he had demanded from Churchill as early as September 1941. In the presence of Molotov, Beria, and Voroshilov, Stalin appointed Vlasov commander in chief of the northwest front around Leningrad and told Vlasov he expected him to "put things to rights" there. On March 9, accompanied by Voroshilov, Vlasov arrived at the Volkhov front and took over the command from the hands of Meretskov, who by this time was commander in name only. The next step on Vlasov's road would see him in German prison camp.

Several decades later, Strik-Strikfeldt reconstructed the conversations he had held from the end of July to the beginning of September 1942 with Vlasov. It is possible that the long interval made for a good many shifts in accent, or brought ideas to the fore which could not have been so evident in 1942. But in any case, Strik-Strikfeldt described the inner changes which had brought Vlasov to the point of openly opposing Stalin.

From Strik-Strikfeldt's account it appeared that the weeks before his capture, the weeks spent in the marshes, prepared the general for his subsequent role. His own meteoric career may hitherto have subdued his doubts. Now, doomed by Stalin's irrational order to stand his ground no matter what the price in lives, he recalled all the examples of abuses, cruelty, and injustice he had encountered so often: the fate of his father and of friends of his youth in the countryside; the murderous atmosphere of the Tukhachevsky era; the quiet tragedy of his wife and her parents, whom he had to repudiate because they were "kulaks"; the hopeless battle on the Dnieper under orders not to retreat; Stalin's desperate appeals to the British and Americans whom he had denounced in the most savage terms while his pact with Hitler lasted.

Transferred to Roenne's camp for special prisoners in Vinnitsa, Vlasov met, among other officers, Vladimir Boyarski, commander of the Forty-first Soviet Guards Division, who had been wounded and captured earlier. For the first time in his life, Vlasov found himself talking openly with a colleague without having to worry about being informed on. He found Boyarski a fanatically nationalistic Russian, who vented hatred of Stalin and of bolshevism in the presence of all the other prisoners, and who counted on the help of the Germans to overthrow Stalin and create a free socialist Russia. Boyarski was working on a memorandum in which he argued that there was a good chance of overthrowing Stalin if the Germans would hold back and leave the fighting to a Russian army of war prisoners. All these troops would need were weapons, freedom of action, and the pledge that the Germans would make no territorial demands on Russia. Thus, Vlasov had already given thought to all this when Strik-Strikfeldt tried to win him over. Strik-Strikfeldt writes in his book:

> I told him I and my friends, when the campaign started, believed it to be a war of liberation to free the Russian people from the Bolshevik yoke; but I also told him of the wretched conditions of the prisoners, about which we could do nothing. I told him that the Nazi leaders were obsessed with arrogance and thereby blind. The result was the catastrophic position of the 50–70 million in occupied zones. . . . "But the field-marshals and the senior officers here in the General Staff are doing what they can to modify the war aims, and thus put our relationship with the Russian people on a new footing. Are you willing to collaborate with those who are prepared to fight against Stalin?"
>
> "Against Stalin, yes. But for whom and what? And how? . . . Would the German officers of whom you spoke allow us to raise an army against Stalin? Not an army of mercenaries. It must take its orders from a National Russian Government. It is only an ideal that can justify the taking up of arms against one's own regime."*

There was an implied question here that Strik-Strikfeldt could not answer affirmatively. Instead, he declared that in order to convince the "blind" men around Hitler some proof was necessary of the kind of influence Vlasov and Boyarski might wield within the Soviet ranks. Vlasov must draft a leaflet calling for a struggle against Stalin, without at first mentioning the idea of a Russian anti-Stalinist army. If that leaflet led to unusually large numbers of deserters, it would be time to take the

* Wilfried Strik-Strikfeldt, *Against Stalin and Hitler*. Translated from the German by David Footman (New York: The John Day Company, 1973), pp. 74f.

86

next step and persuade the top German leadership that an anti-Stalinist government and an army of liberation really would be effective weapons.

Vlasov demurred. He refused to issue an appeal to desert. As a soldier he could not incite other soldiers not to do their duty unless a Russian army with a more idealistic mission awaited them, he said. Strik-Strikfeldt and Roenne then decided against this approach. But Vlasov finally was willing to accept another of Strik-Strikfeldt's many different proposals concerning the leaflet. The factor that decisively influenced his change of heart was a remarkable phenomenon Herre had once called attention to: the difference in degree of dictatorial power between the Soviet Union and Germany.

To Vlasov the fact that Strik-Strikfeldt and Roenne could speak frankly with him about plans that ran contrary to Hitler's "line" was staggering. He therefore considerably overestimated the scope of their power. Strik-Strikfeldt comments in his memoirs:

> At that time I, like the other officers, believed that Hitler must ultimately see reason. . . . I told Vlasov this, and, at the same time, asked him never to reproach me if it turned out that I had been mistaken. He gave me his promise, and kept it throughout the time we were together.*

Strik-Strikfeldt could thus allay his conscience in advance. But the truth was that Vlasov was laboring under an illusion when he wrote, with Boyarski's assistance, that first leaflet addressed as a proclamation to the Russians. The text of the leaflet read in part:

> Comrade Commanders! Comrades of the Soviet Intelligentsia!
> I, the undersigned, Major General A. A. Vlasov, am the former commander of the Second Assault Army and deputy commander in chief of the Vokhov front. Today I am Prisoner of War No. 16,901 in Germany.
> Faced with the incalculable sufferings of our people in this war, painfully conscious of our military failures, we naturally ask ourselves: Who is to blame?
> If we look back upon the past twelve to fifteen prewar years, we are forced to the conclusion that the Stalin clique is to blame for all these misfortunes. It ruined the country by the system of collective

*Ibid., p. 80.

farms. It annihilated millions of honest individuals. During 1937 and 1938 it killed the best cadres in the army. By its policy of adventurism that clique has plunged the country into a needless and pointless war for interests that are alien to the people. Now it is leading the country toward defeat, for it has lost the support of the masses, shattered the administrative apparatus, and undermined the economy. After conquering the Crimea and destroying the southwest front, the German armies have advanced as far as the Volga and have occupied the northern Caucasus without encountering any significant resistance. . . .

The predicament of the individual officer at the front is hopeless. The Stalinist clique puts the blame for all failures on him. At the same time his actions are hampered by the commissar, by the Political Department, and by the NKVD, all of whom know nothing about military affairs. . . .

At home we see total chaos and the approach of a collapse worse than anything our country has ever undergone. . . .

The Stalin clique rests its hopes on help from England and America and on the opening of a Second Front. Most of you know quite well what the policy of England and America is—to fight to the last Russian soldier; to let us pull the chestnuts out of the fire for them; to let the Russians exhaust Germany, promising a mythical Second Front in return.

Look back at history. This is not the first time the Russian people have spilled their blood for Anglo-American interests.

How can we escape from this blind alley into which Stalin's clique has led our country? There is only one escape. . . . Those who still love their country, who want to see their nation happy, must dedicate all the energies and means at their disposal to crush the universally hated regime of Stalin. They must strive for the formation of a government opposed to Stalin, for the ending of the criminal war which serves the interests of England and America. They must call for an honorable peace with Germany.

Now it is up to you!

Dürksen was supposed to see Vlasov early in the afternoon on September 7, 1942. He awaited the Russian general in a tiny interrogation room that had formerly served as a sickroom.

When the door opened and Vlasov entered, "it was as though the room had filled up," Dürksen recalled.

General Vlasov stood there, gaunt, still marked by the weeks of hunger at the Volkhov front, wearing a tattered Red Army tunic, leather belt, worn tan trousers, and boots faded by the waters of swamps and melting snow. The man was a giant, six feet five inches tall, with a head whose like Dürksen had never seen before, wholly unique in its lack of symmetry. His forehead was high, his lips full, his cheekbones prominent; with the dark eyes behind horn-rimmed glasses, his face was of an ugliness that fascinated.

Dürksen rose as Vlasov stood in the doorway looking him over. It was as though the Russian was trying to chart his way through a mysterious realm. Dürksen extended his hand and said: *"Sdravstvuitye, Gospodin General!"*

A few days later, after his return to Berlin, Dürksen wrote up a report of the conversation. In the dry language characteristic of such reports he summarized the content of their talk:

> Vlasov stressed that he was a convinced Bolshevist and that he had no complaints about the path that had led him to high rank. But he stressed even more emphatically that he was a man of the common people and that the people's distress could not be hidden from him. The contempt for human life displayed by the military leadership under Stalin had been the crucial shock to him. . . . After the destruction of his army he had roamed around the Volkhov marshes. Over the course of several weeks, he said, he had had time to reexamine his own career and the development of his nation. As he thought about it, a parallel struck him, the parallel to the fate of the Second Russian Army in the initial stage of the First World War. That was the army under the leadership of General Samsonov that was destroyed in the Battle of Tannenberg in East Prussia. Samsonov, he said, had tried to overcome the shame of defeat by shooting himself. . . .

When the highly tentative conversation had reached this point by early in the afternoon of September 7, Dürksen asked: "Quite a few of your fellow officers have followed Samsonov's example, haven't they?"

Vlasov, seated opposite Dürksen on one of the uncomfortable wooden chairs with which the room was furnished but settled down in it with perfect naturalness, remained impassive. *"Za chem?"* ("What for?") he asked. He stared into space for a moment. Then he slowly offered an explanation: "I often held my pistol in my hand. But then I put it away again. Samsonov knew why he shot himself. He believed in the tsar, in honor, and greatness. But I no longer could believe."

Dürksen wrote:

> This to me was the decisive point in the conversation. It was then I realized that Vlasov was not sitting there out of cowardice or opportunism or irresoluteness, but because he had looked carefully into his own motives and ideas.

After this talk Roenne and Gehlen decided to have Vlasov transferred to the Viktoriastrasse in Berlin and to detach Strik-Strikfeldt from his present tasks and appoint him Vlasov's constant companion.

"With the appearance of Vlasov among us it became perfectly clear that . . . if ever a so-called Russian operation consisting in the formation of a Russian National Government or some similar project were to be started, only Vlasov could head it."

Kazantsev wrote this in the Viktoriastrasse in Berlin after Vlasov had arrived there on September 17, 1942, accompanied by Strik-Strikfeldt.

Within two days everyone had gathered around him as people do around a natural center. For some time he listened and spoke little, radiating stability and strength. Of all the prisoners there, the one who became friendliest with him was General Malyshkin, who had come to the Viktoriastrasse from the Wuhlheide camp shortly before. He had been chief of staff of a Siberian military district and had been arrested in conjunction with the Tukhachevsky affair. He had been interrogated for months, and tortured often to the point of his losing consciousness, but he had steadfastly refused to make a confession. After more than a year of imprisonment, he had been released and had become a teacher at the military academy and, in 1941, chief of staff of the Nineteenth Army. The Germans had captured him near Vyasma.

Two sets of reminiscences have been preserved concerning the events of those weeks in the "laboratory" on Viktoriastrasse. One of them was written by Kazantsev.

On September 18 Kazantsev rendezvoused secretly in the Tiergarten with Baidalakov, leader of the Russian émigré organization NTS, and reported: "I think we have the man we have been waiting for."

"*Sidorshuk?*"

Kazantsev explained. The name "Vlasov" meant a good deal to Baidalakov. He instructed Kazantsev henceforth to maintain the closest possible ties with Vlasov, to observe him, and to attempt, when the time was ripe, to influence him in the direction desired by the NTS.

Kazantsev has reported:

> Vlasov came among us like a great silent seeker. . . . When he spoke, he at first told only of his experiences in Russia, of his career, of his conversations with Stalin, and of the events on the Volkhov front. . . . Nevertheless, all that was really no more than the grand backdrop. . . . We did not realize until Vlasov's first leaflet reached us in print that Vlasov had already at least half decided to take up the struggle. From that day on, moreover, he emerged from his reserve, although he never fully abandoned it, and I as an exile needed a long time to win his trust and to make him realize that we had nothing in common with the old tsarist exiles. When, after a number of weeks he said, "You're a funny bunch of exiles—sort of like the Komsomols," the path was open.

Dürksen wrote other accounts of the fateful beginning in the Viktoriastrasse office. Extracts from these reports follow:

> Vlasov's leaflet from Vinnitsa was approved by Wedel and Keitel without more ado, because they thought of it as the usual propagandistic exploitation of a captured general. But when Vlasov arrived among us a bare four days later, we were beginning to receive the first reports on the remarkable effects the leaflets had had on the numbers and attitudes of deserters. Colonel von Uckermann, the Ic of Army Group North, had ordered these leaflets dropped over the Russian lines by plane. He had personally interrogated the deserters. The response to the fact that a Soviet general was speaking out had been extraordinary. Shortly afterward, similar reports came from Army Groups Center and South.
>
> At first there was no retort from Soviet counterpropaganda. . . . But it was obvious that we ought not to lose too much time. As soon as possible, we must make use of Vlasov on a large scale and carry

out Grote's idea of a Smolensk proclamation of a committee and army of liberation. Grote did not rush anything. Although Strik-Strikfeldt, in keeping with his temperament, daily urged immediate action, Grote gave Vlasov enough time to get used to our ways and to form a relationship of mutual trust with the others, especially with Malyshkin, Zykov, and Kazantsev. Only after this was accomplished did he have several long talks with Vlasov and describe his ideas.

Vlasov had been prepared for this by Strik-Strikfeldt. After prolonged discussion he declared his readiness to join with the others in elaborating plans for a Smolensk Committee for the Army of Liberation, and also in preparing their first major proclamation. But he insisted on the reservation that this must not be a propaganda trick, but must represent sincere policy.

Grote replied that he himself had in mind a clear political objective. If the plan were only a propaganda trick, he said, he himself would have had the authority to decide for himself. But because it was a question of the greatest political import, he had to obtain a decision from the highest authorities. In order to urge a favorable decision, he needed from Vlasov a statement that he was prepared, if the decision were affirmative, to head the committee and the army. If his, Grote's, efforts failed, they would have to seek alternative courses.

Today it might very well seem like madness that we assumed at all that our efforts could lead to a result. But at the time our ideas seemed logical. We had found a man to operate against Stalin. In our hands he seemed so certain, so victorious a weapon that in spite of all previous experiences and disillusionments we actually girded ourselves with hope. . . . All through October, Grote and Martin tried, through Wedel, to reach Field Marshal Keitel with their plans. If they could reach Keitel, they thought, they would then certainly reach Hitler. The arguments were so simple and persuasive. . . . As a propaganda man who knew he could not venture beyond the limits of his own field, Grote tried to make the most of what had so far been authorized. He argued that the tactic of using Russians to appeal to Russians would lose its effectiveness if it merely attacked the Stalinist system but offered nothing to replace that system. There would be nothing to which Russians could turn. In the future, propaganda could work only if it was put forth by Russians who could point out that they had formed an anti-Stalinist opposition government and an anti-Stalinist army which was calling upon all Red Army men to join it and help struggle for a new homeland. A man well known in Russia had been found, not an exile, not a reactionary, but a distinguished general whom Stalin had decorated, a defender of Moscow during the winter of 1941–42, who was willing to serve as the leader of a government and an army directed against Stalin. He was now in the Viktoriastrasse. His name was Andrei Andreyevich Vlasov.

Dürksen further reports:

> The number of Grote's memos and proposals increased from week to week. But without exception, all came back rejected. On one of them was written, in violet ink in Field Marshal Keitel's handwriting: "Politics is not our concern." On another: "I know the Führer's attitude toward such ideas. They are out of the question." On still another: "No. Exploit General Vlasov for propaganda to produce deserters as much as you like. But hands off politics!" And finally: "Cease any further proposals of this nature."
> At the beginning of November, Wedel refused to pass on any additional memos.

Of course, it could not be concealed from Vlasov and the other Russians that week after week was passing without any decision. Although Vlasov had been prepared for difficulties, he had no conception of the situation in German domestic politics. The fact that soldiers like Grote and Strik-Strikfeldt spoke so openly against the policies of their government misled him into assuming greater liberty in Germany, and greater influence upon the part of army officers, than actually existed. The more he dealt with the idea of the committee, the more logical and persuasive it came to seem to him, too. And then the decision kept being put off and put off.

It turned out that only Strik-Strikfeldt had enough of a personal relationship with Vlasov to be able to overcome his doubts, wariness, or intention to return to a regular prisoner-of-war camp. Strik-Strikfeldt finally persuaded Vlasov, during this waiting period, to write another leaflet in which he explained the reasons for his change of heart. To cite Dürksen once more:

Strik-Strikfeldt was inexhaustible in devising arguments. Again and again he explained to Vlasov the difficulties that had arisen because of Hitler's rage at the Soviet attitude. And then he read to Vlasov sentences that Hitler had written or spoken which showed that fundamentally Hitler was quite capable of correct insights and that, therefore, success was sure to come sooner or later. Plenty of such quotations from Hitler could be found. For example: "We are attached with boundless love and loyalty to our own racial community. But we respect the national rights of other nationals also because of these very principles. The concept of Germanization is, therefore, something we do not recognize." Or: "Every attempt to extinguish the natural individuality of a nation violates the moral law and is an arbitrary act."

After several pages in this vein, Dürksen continued:

By the middle of November we had to admit to ourselves that we had failed. We had exhausted all our possibilities. The path by way of Keitel was blocked. We held a number of despairing conferences. We had Vlasov's second leaflet printed and dropped on the Russians. . . . In the light of the obvious emotion among the prisoners of war and the general population, not another army in the world would have failed to urge us to hurry.

On November 15 we conferred for fourteen hours at a stretch on what could be done to prevent us from losing this chance to end the war in the east. . . . We were all crushed by a feeling of impotence. . . . Finally Grote said: "If permission is not going to be granted to create the committee and the army of liberation, we shall have to conjure up a movement among the people by spreading a 'fiction' that this committee and this army exist in the occupied areas. The movement will then pose such unequivocal demands for actualization of the committee and the army of liberation that the political leadership will be unable to go on ignoring both the movement and its demands. . . . I'm well aware that when we draw up leaflets to that effect we'll be ordered to drop them only behind the Soviet front. But I imagine there are enough pilots," Grote gave us a meaningful look, "who might have navigational difficulties once in a while."

Grote then turned to Strik-Strikfeldt and pointed out that he had given Vlasov his word that he would *not* use him as a purely propagandistic fiction. But, he said, he saw no other way. Vlasov would have to be informed and give his consent. Strik-Strikfeldt must try to persuade Vlasov that this was the only course.

The following extracts from Kazantsev record the decisive conversation between Strik-Strikfeldt and Vlasov:

In November Captain Strik-Strikfeldt, after a visit "to some of the top brass," returned convinced that no changes could be expected, and went to see Vlasov. "Andrei Andreyevich," he said, "there is still one chance." Vlasov looked inquiringly at him. "Up to now we have been trying to make policy and build up our propaganda on that. What about trying to turn the thing around? Let us couch our propaganda as though the policy already existed. . . . It will then produce reactions. Demands will be made on our army groups and in the occupied areas. Based on these we can then force through a definite policy. . . . I am proposing that we now announce the formation of a 'Russian Committee,' and in its name appeal to the Russian people. The people will want to get in touch with us and clarify the details of a common struggle and of future relations with Germany. On the basis of such requests we here can then insist on concessions. The German army will support us much more resolutely than it is doing now. . . . Here is an action that we can start on at once, because everything involving propaganda inside Russia has already . . . been turned over to us."

Vlasov had objections. "But if it should nevertheless turn out that there is no change in policy on the German side, and when the Russians realize that it was only a propaganda trick, all confidence in me will be gone forever. And then if in the future there really should be a change in policy, any attempt to communicate that will only be regarded as a fresh deception."

Nevertheless, after protracted discussions, Vlasov finally gave his consent.

Aside from this relatively dry dialogue, Kazantsev provided no further glimpses of the struggles that must have preceded this decision on Vlasov's part. Strik-Strikfeldt, for his part, recalled many years later:

. . . Vlasov and his collaborators flatly refused to agree to Grote's proposal. There was, however, one of them who saw in it the possibility of bringing the whole idea of Russian liberation right out into the open. It was Zykov. He supported Grote's scheme of confronting the German leadership with a *fait accompli.* "Let the devil out of the bottle," he said, "and he will do his work himself."

In the end Vlasov also agreed.*

While Strik-Strikfeldt was "wrestling" with Vlasov, Tresckow and his Ic, Gersdorff, in their impatience hit on the idea of establishing a kind of model brigade as a sample of what a Russian liberation army could be. They decided to undertake this on their own responsibility within the territory of Army Group Center. The brigade would be entirely under Russian leadership, would wear altered Russian uniforms, would be provided with Russian weapons, and would have only a small German liaison staff. If this brigade should prove its worth at the front, let alone achieve some spectacular success, that might very well, so they reasoned, exert a decisive effect upon the plans regarding Vlasov.

They secured the approval of Field Marshal von Kluge by promising him, without going into details, reinforcements for his front. Thereafter they proceeded on their own. As the nucleus for this brigade, to which they gave the name "Experimental Formation Center," they selected the remnants of a somewhat mysterious military unit that had been set up in March 1942 by the Abwehr (German Army Counterintelligence). The formation had been housed in a barracks camp formerly belonging to the Soviet peat works of Ossintorf. In conjunction with Abwehr Squad 203 in Smolensk, a number of Russian exile officers, including ex-Colonel Konstantin Kromiadi, Second Lieutenant Igor Zakharov (who had fought in Spain under General Franco), Lieutenant Grigory Lamsdorff (a count), and several others from prison camps had set up a "Russian Brigade for Special Missions." This undertaking was also known as Operation Grayhead.

Its mission was commando operations behind the Soviet front. The strength of the unit at times reached 7000 men, with four battalions and an artillery regiment. Equipment consisted of captured weapons. The uniforms were Russian, but were distinguished by different epaulets and white-blue-red cockades. Kromiadi, who used the alias "Sanin," sometimes gave his formation the romantic-sounding name RNNA, standing for "Russian National People's Army." With it he had carried through a

* *Ibid.,* p. 105.

96

number of significant commando-type successes. But during the summer there had been disputes between Army Group Center and the Abwehr. Thereafter, the latter had lost interest in the formation in Ossintorf.

At this point, Tresckow and Gersdorff took over. They turned to Roenne for suggestions on possible leaders for the new experimental brigade. Roenne recommended General Georgy Nikolayevich Zhilenkov as commander—Zhilenkov, in the meantime, had been transferred from the special camp run by Foreign Armies East to the Viktoriastrasse office in Berlin. Roenne also proposed Colonel Boyarski, who was willing to collaborate wholeheartedly with the Germans so long as they raised no claim to permanent domination of Russian territory. Boyarkski was as straightforward and gruff as Zhilenkov was smooth and pliable.

Roenne accepted Boyarski with a clear conscience after Gersdorff had told him: "I don't want any yes-men here; I want forceful Russians."

Only a week after the beginning of the reorganization work in Ossintorf, suspicious queries began coming in from lower-echelon bureaus. Just what was going on? For word was reaching them of a large formation of Russian prisoners of war dressed in Russian uniforms and headed by a Russian general and a colonel in Russian uniform. Moreover, they had heard from elements of the Russian populace who had had contact with this formation that its officers were strongly critical of the German war aims in the East.

Gersdorff took care that such reports did not reach Field Marshal Kluge, for he was afraid Kluge might be prompted to withdraw his approval. Zhilenkov and Boyarski had no difficulty finding officers, noncoms, and enlisted men for their formation. They could have raised twenty times the needed number. Organization proceeded with amazing rapidity. News of the new brigade spread among the population, and wherever companies or battalions appeared in public, the people waved to them.

At the end of November Zhilenkov and Boyarski handed Gersdorf a memorandum on their formation. One passage from it reads as follows:

> All members of the brigade are united by one idea: liberation of their motherland from the tyranny of Jewish bolshevism; struggle for a bright future for Russia in closest alliance with Germany. . . . The idea of struggle against Stalin, for friendship with Germany and a happier Russia, is one close to the hearts of the people. The populace has been supporting the Russian formation in every re-

spect. It reports on guerillas, furnishes guides in skirmishes, and voluntarily supplies the troops. Many volunteers from the populace are enlisting.

There was some question of what kind of oath the members of the brigade would swear. A compromise was devised on this ticklish matter: in addition to swearing allegiance to Hitler as the leader in the common struggle of liberation, the men also swore allegiance to their country.

By early December the brigade was combat-ready. Zhilenkov was expecting it to be sent to the front. But Tresckow had to wait for the right moment to inform Kluge about the formation and obtain permission to employ it. Squeezed between Zhilenkov's and, especially, Boyarski's mistrustful impatience and Kluge's timorous unpredictability, Tresckow waited until December 16. The army group's front-line divisions were screaming for replacements. The winter was consuming men and whole formations like a Moloch. On the morning of December 16, Tresckow offered the brigade to Kluge, declaring that it was ready for front-line duty. Kluge immediately went to Ossintorf to inspect it. The brigade passed with flying colors. Tresckow and Gersdorff were already beginning to believe that they had navigated all the reefs. Then, as though it were the most natural thing in the world to do, Kluge ordered the brigade broken up, the men distributed among German regiments, and dressed in German uniforms. The sight of Zhilenkov in the uniform of a Russian general had given Kluge a bad fright. Tresckow tried once again to explain to the field marshal how much was at stake. He explained that breaking up the brigade would run directly counter to the objectives for which the brigade had been organized. Inevitably, the men sent to the front would be suffering from the gravest psychological shock.

Kluge did not or would not understand. He insisted on his orders. On December 17 Tresckow once more tried to reason with him. Kluge refused to be swayed. "Can you guarantee that if the brigade is committed as a body it will not attack our own flank and tear a hole in our front? I don't need that formation to endanger our front but to stuff holes in it. We must have troops that are firmly in our hand. With a formation so large, that is impossible."

"I have not the slightest doubt," Tresckow replied, "that left to itself it stands more firmly on our side than all the other native formations because it has a goal of its own, to distinguish itself independently, acting on its own responsibility, and serving as the model for an army. . . .

98

Sooner or later this approach has to be tried. And the commander who tries it will have done a historic service for Germany."

"Or will go out on his ear for taking a crazy risk."

Tresckow knew Field Marshal Kluge well enough to realize that this was the end of it.

Gersdorff went to Ossintorf to prepare Zhilenkov for Kluge's orders. He tried to persuade Zhilenkov not to throw the whole project overboard but to go on working and achieving small successes within the more limited framework. Zhilenkov, the more flexible of the pair, might have come round. But Boyarski was unbending. Enormously disillusioned and embittered, he burst out: "I'd sooner let myself be shot than become a mercenary."

In great haste, Zhilenkov drafted a statement directed to the army group. It read: "The brigade is a part of the future Russian Army and will fight only as such a part. The brigade holds the view that it was organized in order to carry out Russian objectives, the liberation of Russia from bolshevism; and it regards its relationship to the German army as only that of an ally. . . ."

Gersdorff took the statement back with him. It sounded like mutiny. But would silence do them any good whatever? He passed Zhilenkov's statement on through channels. Whatever came of it would have to come.

Kluge, when he received it, blew up. In fury he cried that here was proof of how right he had been to take precautions. Distrust produced more distrust. Rudely bypassing Tresckow as intermediary, he sent an ultimatum to Zhilenkov and Boyarski. They would either obey his orders or they would be arrested and the brigade disarmed.

Before the eyes of the German officers who had brought him the message, Boyarski silently drew a sketch of the position showing what his brigade might do in case of a German attempt to disarm it by force. Gersdorff felt compelled to take some action on his own. Should it come to a fight, what ammunition that would provide for all who opposed the idea of a liberation army! They would forever afterward be able to point to the Zhilenkov brigade as a dreadful warning, and nothing of the sort would ever be tried again. No one would ever ask about the psychological background. The specter of mutiny would henceforth haunt all army staffs and government bureaus.

As luck would have it, on December 17 Field Marshal Kluge was preoccupied with events at the front. Tresckow took command. He asked

Zhilenkov and Boyarski to come to see him, guaranteeing them safe-conduct. A comment by Kazantsev shows how these developments looked to the Russians at this moment of confrontation: "The fact that Zhilenkov and Boyarski were treated relatively decently was probably due to the position of the excellently armed Russian unit at a distance of only twenty miles from the front. A clash with that unit might have led to very dangerous consequences. But the situation was hopeless for the Russians, too."

These words indicate the extent to which distrust prevailed on both sides, for Kazantsev did not have a word to say about Tresckow's efforts to somehow save the project he had himself initiated and nursed along. Tresckow assured Zhilenkov and Boyarski that although the brigade would be divided up, it would keep its Russian officers and not be committed to action at the front but preserved as the nucleus of an "army of liberation" under General Vlasov. After a hasty discussion with Gehlen, he offered Zhilenkov and Boyarski themselves "employment" in the Foreign Armies East department until Field Marshal Kluge's wrath subsided and they could come into the open again.

Both men accepted his offer out of sheer necessity. One of their officers, Major Rily, was appointed colonel and new commander of the brigade. But the atmosphere was dark when Zhilenkov and Boyarski bade the brigade good-by. The following night 300 officers and soldiers went into the woods to fight the Germans as partisans. The rest remained and were employed on security duties in the area around Mogilev. Weeks later Zhilenkov returned to Martin in the Viktoriastrasse office. Boyarski was transferred to a propaganda unit on the northern front.

Early in December, when more and more reports were reaching Berlin concerning the forthcoming disaster at Stalingrad, the Proclamation of the Smolensk Committee was cast in its final form in the Viktoriastrasse office. It read like a medley of truths and falsehoods, of Vlasov's genuine anti-Stalinist convictions and the echo of German propaganda slogans. It was a construct in which the German propaganda about Stalin as a warmonger ran counter to what Vlasov recollected of the beginning of the war. Apparently he had been enough confused by the German version of things to doubt his own previous ideas on the subject. Wishful thinking about a possible transformation of the Germans ran side by side with Strik-Strikfeldt's unrealistic notions of a European community of nations. And the Thirteen Points which the proclamation offered to the Russian people were obviously a muddle of libertarian phrases and Kazantsev's social notions.

Vlasov had resisted, with astonishment, the suggestion that among the Thirteen Points there should be a guarantee of freedom for the various peoples of Russia. When this matter was raised, it was obvious that this was the first time Vlasov had heard of the East Ministry's ideas of dividing up Russia; in fact, he had scarcely known this ministry existed. After long discussions, Strik-Strikfeldt persuaded him that it was essential to pretend agreement with these ideas. Only on this basis would the Committee be approved.

The text of the Proclamation of the Russian Smolensk Committee follows (condensed):

> Friends and brothers!
>
> Bolshevism is the enemy of the Russian people. It has brought incalculable misery upon our country and at last plunged the Russian people into a bloody war for foreign interests. . . . Millions of the Russian people have had to pay with their lives for Stalin's criminal attempts to dominate the world, for the vast profits of the Anglo-American capitalists. Millions have been crippled, will never again be able to earn their bread. Women, old men, and children have died from hunger, cold, or unbearable overwork. Hundreds of Russian towns, thousands of Russian villages, have been destroyed on Stalin's orders, blown up, or burned down.
>
> In this war the Red Army has suffered defeats on a scale hitherto unknown in our history. In spite of the self-sacrifice of our soldiers and officers, in spite of the Russian people's bravery and readiness for sacrifice, one battle after the other has been lost. The blame rests solely on Stalin and his staff.
>
> Stalin and his clique did not know how to organize the defense of the country. They are now trying to prolong their rule at the cost of a bloodbath for the Russian people. . . .
>
> The Russian people have been betrayed by Stalin's allies, the Anglo-American capitalists. These plutocrats are not content with saving their own skins by sacrificing millions of Russians. By supporting Bolshevism they are now stretching out their greedy hands for the riches of our country, and have concluded secret treaties with Stalin.
>
> Germany, on the other hand, is not fighting against the Russian people and our country, but against Bolshevism . . . the mission of

Adolf Hitler's nationalistic Germany is to establish the New Order in Europe without Bolshevists and capitalists; and in this new Europe a place will be assigned to every nation. The position of the Russian people in the European community of nations will depend on the degree of its collaboration in the fight against Bolshevism, for the annihilation of Stalin and his criminal clique is primarily the business of the Russian people. In order to unite and lead the Russian people in the struggle against the hated regime, we—sons of this people and patriots—have formed a Russian Committee for collaboration with Germany and for combating Bolshevism and building the new Europe.

The Russian Committee calls for the reconstruction of Russia on the basis of the following principles:

a. The annihilation of Bolshevism and thus of Stalin and his clique.

b. The securing of an honorable peace with Germany.

c. Creating, in cooperation with Germany and the peoples of the European New Order, a new Russia without Bolshevism and capitalism.

Specifically:

1. Abolition of forced labor. Freedom of the right to work. The guarantee of material welfare to all toilers.

2. Abolition of the collective farms and orderly transfer of the land to private ownership by the peasants.

3. Resuscitation of trade, crafts, and home industry.

4. The intelligentsia is to be allowed to work in a freely creative way for the good of the people.

5. Social justice and protection of all toilers against exploitation.

6. All toilers shall be assured of their right to further education; guarantee of vacations and a secure old age.

7. Elimination of terror and tyranny. Freedom of religion, freedom of conscience, freedom of speech, of assembly, of the press. Inviolability of the individual and the home.

8. Guarantee of racial freedom.

9. Amnesty for political prisoners of Bolshevism. Repatriation from prisons and forced labor camps of all those sentenced in the struggle against Bolshevism.

10. Rebuilding at state expense of the towns and villages destroyed during the war.

11. Rebuilding of the factories and plants belonging to the state and destroyed during the war.

12. Abrogation of the debts incurred under secret treaties concluded by Stalin with the Anglo-American capitalists.

13. Guarantee of a minimum income for all war-caused invalids and their families.

In the firm and sacred conviction that these principles will assure a happy future for the Russian people, the Russian Committee calls upon all Russians both in the liberated areas and in those still occupied by the Bolsheviks, upon all workers and peasants, the intelligentsia, soldiers, and *politruks,** to unite in the struggle for the motherland and against our country's worst enemy, Bolshevism. . . .

The Russian Committee appeals to all soldiers and officers of the Red Army to cross the lines to the Russian Liberation Army, which is fighting on the German side.

The Committee extends protection to all those of the anti-Bolshevist struggle, whatever their former activities may have been or what position they may have held.

The Russian Committee calls upon all Russians to join the struggle against hated Bolshevism, to create anti-Bolshevist partisan units, and to turn their arms against Stalin and his followers.

Russians, friends and brothers! . . .

Rise up and fight for freedom! . . .

A few days after the final draft of the proclamation was completed, Strik-Strikfeldt turned up in Vlasov's sparsely furnished room. He brought with him a civilian suit and a coat. After endless vain efforts to obtain an official requisition slip for a suit, he had by sheer tenacity persuaded a NSV (*Nationalsozialistische Volkswohlfahrt*—the Nazi party charity organization) clerk to let him have an old suit and coat from a winter donation drive. The suit was blue and worn, the trousers too short for Vlasov. And the brown coat was a tight fit about the shoulders.

In spite of his naïve optimism, Strik-Strikfeldt felt ashamed; he was afraid the suit affair might well drag Vlasov abruptly down from his momentary exaltation. How likely that the Russian general might say:

* Political officer of a Soviet troop unit.

"You want to change the plans of the German government and don't even have enough power to obtain a decent suit." He tried to play down this dreary affair by handing Vlasov a pass that permitted him to leave the Viktoriastrasse building when accompanied by Strik-Strikfeldt himself. In the same breath he said that all preparations had been made for him to accompany Vlasov on visits to a number of prison camps for higher Red Army officers, where he would be able to look around for more potential friends of the Committee.

The following morning both men left Berlin for Camp Wuhlheide. The German camp personnel admitted them reluctantly. One of the sergeants who closed the gate behind them had been a guard in a transit camp near Vitebsk. As he slid the bolt, he said: "Would you believe your eyes? Why is this fellow with the Asiatic mug going around with a special pass?"

His companion, an elderly corporal, stared dully into space. He, too, came from a transit camp. He had not yet forgotten the horrors of the past winter.

Vlasov and Strik-Strikfeldt were led to the generals' barrack. The first person to come forward there was Vetlugin, commanding general of a Soviet corps that had been virtually wiped out at Rostov. He was a relatively young man with a haggard, intelligent face.

Vlasov spent two hours alone with him. Strik-Strikfeldt had wanted it that way. If Vlasov were to have any real success, he would have to talk with his fellow Russians without a German at his side. It was essential for him to be as free and unsupervised as possible. Later, when Vlasov returned to the cubicle where Strik-Strikfeldt was waiting, he said: "He was a good prospect. But he cannot forget the camp he was hauled through. He does not believe German promises. He wanted my oath that Hitler has guaranteed to me personally a liberation army and the inviolability of our country's territory. . . . There were a great many things I could tell him, Wilfried Karlovich, but I could not swear that oath." He glowered at "Wilfried Karlovich" Strik-Strikfeldt through his thick glasses. "Could you swear that oath to me?" he asked with a sudden flare-up of doubt and sarcasm. And Strik-Strikfeldt braced himself for the taunt he had been expecting ever since he had provided Vlasov with clothing: "You who can't even obtain a decent suit for me." But Vlasov contented himself with his look of doubt, and went on: "He asked me not to say I had spoken with him. There are terrorists in the camp who would kill anyone who holds out a hand to the Germans."

The next man Vlasov spoke to was General Ponedyelin. The conversation was brief.

"He wanted to spit at my feet," Vlasov said. "In the normal course of things, I would have been insulted. But this fellow is one of those career types whose intelligence is so limited that to the end of their lives all they can do is recite what was once recited to them."

In Wuhlheide Vlasov spoke with five other Red Army generals, the discussions with some of them continuing for three or four hours. They admitted that they would prefer to serve a government that did not constantly keep check on them, watch them, demand daily proofs of solidarity from them, and threaten them with professional, familial, physical, or psychic annihilation. But they all wanted to have the same sort of guarantee that Vetlugin had demanded, assurances that would enable them to trust in the good will of the Germans.

Two days later Vlasov and Strik-Strikfeldt went to Camp Hammelburg in Franconia to have talks with five more generals. They arrived in Hammelburg at mess time and found the generals lining up with the enlisted men for their food. "I don't understand you people," Vlasov said to Strik-Strikfeldt. "I simply don't understand this sort of thing. You claim that you don't want to level everything and everybody like the Communists. Why are you doing this? You can't conquer the world this way."

Vlasov stayed for two days. It may have been some consolation that of all the generals with whom he talked, only one denounced him as a filthy traitor whom he'd gladly see hung. He found four who were prepared in principle to join the committee and to participate in the creation of a liberation army.

These four had been shuttled from camp to camp and had witnessed the Germans' callousness at the deaths of tens of thousands of fellow prisoners. They made the same demand as the six generals in Wuhlheide: a formal German assurance that the territory of their country would remain intact within the borders of 1939, and freedom of action for a provisional government.

The journeys to Wuhlheide and Hammelburg had been a failure.

During the same period in December in which Vlasov was visiting Hammelburg, Rosenberg was receiving the commanders of the rear areas of the northern, central, and southern fronts. The meeting took place in

Berlin at the former Soviet Embassy on Unter den Linden, into whose quarters the East Ministry had moved in September.

Schenckendorff had requested such a conference more than a year ago. What had prompted Rosenberg to hold it at this time, his guests did not know. They had no idea of how helpless Rosenberg was, and did not suspect that he not only could give them no backing but was hoping for backing from them. Three days earlier Erich Koch had once again made him feel his powerlessness. The altercation was over certain plans for schools in the Ukraine which Rosenberg's Cultural Department had been nurturing. As always, Koch had heard about these plans through his own channels. He and his deputy, Paul Dargel, had flown to Berlin and turned up unannounced at the East Ministry. Koch bluntly informed Rosenberg that he was not going to have any nonsense about education in his, Koch's, Reichskommissariat.

While Koch was laying down the law to Rosenberg, Dargel, without knocking, stormed into the office of Anator van der Milwe, deputy chief of the Cultural Department, and informed him that that rubbish about plans for schools would have to be "dropped at once."

Van der Milwe, who kept a diary at this period, entered his reaction: "Would you mind telling me who you are? I have not had the honor of seeing you here before."

"So! You don't even know me! You fellows certainly live in your own dream world. I happen to be Dargel, Reichskommissar Koch's deputy."

"Ah yes, I've heard of you. If I should ever come to see you in Rovno, I would certainly knock on your door. . . ."

"Never mind the courtesies. The subject of the moment is these plans of yours. On top of everything else, they run counter to the Führer's wishes. You want to create an educated class of Ukrainians while we want to annihilate the Ukrainians."

"But you can't annihilate forty million people."

"We'll handle that problem."

"And what is to become of the Ukraine?"

"You people certainly aren't keeping abreast of things. Don't you know that the Führer wants the Ukraine to be settlement land for German farmers?"

"Where are all these settlers going to come from?"

"Are you casting doubt on the Führer's plans?"

"Let's talk in practical terms, not just in slogans. What are you going to do with the Ukrainians?"

"As soon as the victory has been won, we'll set up concentration areas beyond the Volga."

"What would that involve?"

"It wouldn't involve anything. We'll chase them across the river. Those who survive will have to manage as best they can."

"If you really could drive out the Ukrainians you would turn the land into a desert instead of making its wealth useful to Germany. You will not find the millions of Germans necessary to till the soil, nor the additional millions to go into the mines."

"We'll take care of that part of it. We can always keep some Ukrainians around to do the work. But the last thing they need is schools and education. So keep that in mind, from now on. Well, that's all I had to tell you. Good-by."

In the light of this recent defeat, Rosenberg had been prompted to strengthen his ties with the army. Before Bräutigam left for the Caucasus, he had given Rosenberg to understand that the Army General Staff considered the future solidity of the front dependent on safety and peace behind the lines. An alliance with the army and emphasis on the military need for an "affirmative" administration in the Ukraine might, Rosenberg now thought, lend more weight to his voice with Hitler and give him some leverage against Koch.

The meeting with the commanders of the rear areas was in a sense a ghostly session which made only too plain the differences between the army officers, impelled by the needs of the real world, and Rosenberg, the unworldly man of letters. It did not, however, make those differences plain enough for Schenckendorff and the others who were setting foot inside the Ministry for the Occupied Eastern Territories for the first time. At this juncture, they could not see that this *Ostministerium* was totally devoid of any authority.

Rosenberg opened the meeting with a brief speech: "I want to thank all you gentlemen for coming. You are daily grappling with the ambiguity of our policy in the East. I am betraying no secrets when I say that as minister for the occupied territories in the east, I, too, constantly have to fight against those who want to employ brutal methods of administration."

The clash with Koch had left him highly agitated. This was apparent from the stilted language he used. "By now, things have reached a pass which, in the interests of our long-term goals, can no longer be tolerated. The purpose of the present conference is to provide me with material so that I shall be able to achieve a change in Eastern policy on the part of the top leadership. I have asked you gentlemen in particular to attend this conference because I hold that the military viewpoint should take precedence as long as Germany is at war. May I ask you, therefore, to outline the military requirements in the light of our Eastern policy."

Rosenberg did not have to ask twice. Plenty of tinder had by now accumulated in men like Schenckendorff. He began with a few courteous flourishes toward Rosenberg. Then he took over leadership of the debate and held it from then on to the end of the session, which came around one o'clock in the afternoon.

Occasionally seconded by the commanders in the northern and southern rear areas, Schenckendorff drew an unsparing picture of the effects of the mad-dog policy practiced by the Reichskomissariats and by the economic staffs and the SD (Sicherheitsdienst). He presented an equally unsparing picture of partisan activity and of the conflict into which the native formations were being driven month by month.

So dire was his picture of the progressive weakening of German military power that Rosenberg became extremely alarmed. This was the first time he had talked with leading generals. Up to now, he had received his information about military developments through official channels. Consequently, he had never doubted that sooner or later victory in the East would be achieved. During this session he began to have an inkling, for the first time, that his whole dream-world of a New Order in the East was seriously threatened not only by men like Koch, but also by sheer military defeat. He suddenly saw the possibility that it might be swept away entirely.

But Schenckendorff was equally ill-informed on the reality of power, as his concluding statement proved. "I cannot imagine," he said, "that the Führer has any clear picture of these conditions. I therefore request you, Herr Minister, to give the Führer the necessary explanations in person and as quickly as possible."

Flustered, Rosenberg answered: "I shall try to secure an interview with the Führer immediately. I hope I can bring about a fundamental change in our Eastern policy."

On December 22 Rosenberg actually managed to see Hitler, but the encounter ended in a fresh humiliation. With his usual timidity, he tried to shift responsibility for what he was about to say to the shoulders of the generals. "In regard to our Eastern policy, the generals believe . . ."

That was enough to send Hitler into a rage. Let the generals attend to their business of waging war, he rapped out. It was not for them to concern themselves with policy.

Three days later—while Vlasov was returning, silent and pensive, from Hammelburg to Berlin—Gehlen in Mauerwald dispatched Herre to Angerburg to interrogate Krupyennikov, the commander in chief of the Third Soviet Guards Army. The general had been captured in Stalingrad and had just arrived at Camp Lötzen.

Herre had assumed that he would be back in Mauerwald by evening. In fact, he spent three full days on the interrogation. Since he treated Krupyennikov with courtesy, by the second day he was on fairly good terms with this outwardly rough but shrewd-minded man. Krupyennikov—who long before the Battle of Stalingrad had held a prominent position in the administration of the Red Army—spoke of one thing and another that he had experienced under Stalin, sometimes with a note of contempt in his voice. Herre pricked up his ears. Nevertheless, he was surprised when, on the afternoon of the third day, Krupyennikov suddenly asked: "Why haven't you Germans called on the prisoners of war to fight against the Red Army?"

Herre—as is clear from his notes—had been meaning to touch cautiously on the subject of Vlasov toward the end of the interrogation. It made it easier that Krupyennikov of his own accord brought up the delicate subject. "Would you, General," he asked, "be prepared to offer your services in such a struggle?"

"I might prefer to return to Russia but no longer to Soviet Russia," Krupyennikov answered.

An hour later, Herre had to break off the conversation. He had already run over his time in Lötzen by two days. But he was able to note: "Krupyennikov estimates that seventy percent of the Russian officers in German captivity would be prepared to fight against the system of Stalin because about this percentage has either suffered personally or through family members under Stalin's rule. Germany, he said, had wretched allies in Rumania, Italy, and Hungary. Germany needed allies who were capable of fighting. The crucial precondition would be a well-formulated program under the slogan of 'Fight until Bolshevism is destroyed.' With such a program, the prisoners of war would volunteer by the thousands. Krupyennikov suggests that we begin by selecting officers and noncoms from groups that have been especially penalized under communism. For

109

pilots he would at first pick only soldiers whose families are in occupied areas on this side of the front."

Gehlen passed this report on to Berlin. He himself arrived back in the Viktoriastrasse headquarters four days after Vlasov's return from his unsuccessful mission. Since his return, Vlasov had shut himself away from everyone. Strik-Strikfeldt looked for an opportunity to break through Vlasov's wall of silence. When Herre's report came in, he hurried with it to Vlasov's room. The room was already dark with evening and at the desk the giant Russian was sitting motionless, like a great figure carved of wood. Years later, Strik-Strikfeldt described the scene as follows.

"What is it, Wilfried Karlovich?" Vlasov asked.

Strik-Strikfeldt read the report slowly and with great emphasis. Vlasov only shook his head.

"Krupyennikov, too, will not take action without a guarantee," he said. "Give him the strongest possible guarantee, Wilfried Karlovich! Give him a document signed by Adolf Hitler. Unless you can furnish that, I wouldn't bother to ask him. . . . Men like Krupyennikov need even more," he went on. "They might also need a scrap of paper from Stalin saying they'll be taken back into favor if things go wrong. . . . The Krupyennikovs are corrupted by twenty years of fear. . . . All of us are corrupted." He propped his head in his hand. "But does that surprise you?" He looked down at his comically short trousers, and then it came, the remark Strik-Strikfeldt had been expecting for days: "You can't even give me a decent suit and you ask for trust." But then he added in a resigned tone: "Don't take offense, please, Wilfried Karlovich. Besides, none of this really changes things for me. All these days I have been pondering the matter. . . . For me there is no turning back. Anyone who crosses a certain line cannot go back."

"Someone must always take the lead when a road is still dark," Strik-Strikfeldt said. "The weaker ones will follow after it grows lighter." He spoke insistently: "Andrei Andreyevich, you must sign the proclamation of the Smolensk Committee alone. Perhaps Malyshkin, as deputy and secretary, could add his name. And perhaps the mayor and the town fathers of Smolensk. It is too early to despair. I beg of you: sign the proclamation."

A few hours later Vlasov and Malyshkin put their names to the document.

The next morning, Martin and Grote began their struggle to get permission from the OKW to publish the proclamation as a leaflet. They argued that previous propaganda had proved its ineffectiveness; something new had to be tried. When this argument proved insufficient, they fell back on another approach, using terms like "propagandistic trick" and "a fiction." They can be said to have played their game without a scruple, utilizing all the cunning and sleights they could think of. They exploited the shadows of Stalingrad. Even so, it took them ten days before they achieved a partial success. At last, permission arrived from the Propaganda Department of the OKW, along with instructions that had obviously been added by Keitel. These instructions stipulated that none of the leaflets could be dropped on the German side of the Soviet front. front.

What happened next is described in Dürksen's report (condensed):

All the preparations had already been made, so that we were able to begin printing millions of leaflets as early as January 12. Most of the leaflets were dropped behind the Soviet front by the planes provided. But copies began disappearing even before they had been shipped from the Smolensk print shop, and seemed to be distributed throughout the city. Planes lost their bearings and dropped the leaflets in the rear occupied areas.

Then we waited in great suspense to see the effect. The Soviet propaganda apparatus continued to keep perfect silence. It had evidently decided not to make the name of Vlasov even better known than it already was. But our intelligence officers reported a sudden increase in the number of deserters. Some of the armies reported as many as a thousand in a single night. Every single deserter asked about Vlasov and the Russian liberation army. The commanders in the rear areas, headed by Schenckendorff, reported a "wave of hopeful excitement" passing through the population in their areas. A sudden change in mood among the Russians seemed to be impending. Similar excitement was registered in the volunteer formations. Everywhere the soldiers wanted to see Vlasov and to hear details about the Committee from him personally. Although the disaster at Stalingrad made plain the irrevocable reversal in the balance of military power, the partisan situation changed remarkably during the last weeks of January and the first weeks of February. Obviously the uncertainty and dissatisfaction among the populace, which had given a spur to the partisan movement, had been somewhat allayed.

Our own spirits rose from day to day. It seemed to us that only one thing mattered: the movement that had been kindled by propaganda must not be allowed to subside. The flames must be fed so that the political consequences would follow and the "fiction" would become a reality.

The next steps . . . resulted from the daily more urgent demands raised in the rear areas of Army Groups Center and North that Vlasov be sent there to speak in person to the population and to the volunteers. Partisan propaganda was now calling our entire operation sheer bluff and trickery. Such allegations had to be refuted by letting Vlasov show himself.

Strik-Strikfeldt insisted with his characteristic passion. With the consent of Grote and Martin he had a highly imaginative uniform made for Vlasov, a brown tunic and cap, black trousers with a red general's stripe, and a brown coat with red lapels.

Meanwhile, Martin and Grote were wrestling with a difficult decision. So much now depended on Vlasov's appearing that hesitation and protracted consultation with the authorities back home would be fatal. They would have to go ahead on their own, calling whatever they did "propaganda." It was decided to send Vlasov to Smolensk by way of Lötzen on February 25. Schenckendorff's Ic, Lieutenant Colonel Schubuth, who spoke Russian fluently, was to meet Vlasov in Lötzen and accompany him. During the journey through the area that was governed by the Reichskommissars and their civil administration, Vlasov would (as a precaution) not leave the train.

There are numerous reports on Vlasov's journey. At his departure, Lieutenant Colonel Schubuth was waiting for him at the small station in Lötzen. Vlasov appeared in his new uniform. There was a note of reserve in his whole manner. Schubuth assumed that Vlasov regarded him also as a guard.

Together they took their seats, in a compartment that had been reserved for Vlasov, in the furlough train that made regular runs between Lötzen and Smolensk. Vlasov stepped out of the train onto the platform just once, in Minsk. Amid the swarm of uniforms he did not attract attention. During the long ride Schubuth told him about Schenckendorff's efforts to improve the conditions for prisoners of war, of his struggle for Russian self-government, of his solicitude for the volunteers. Gradually, Vlasov thawed.

They arrived in Smolensk on the evening of February 26.

It was intensely cold. A biting wind swept through the streets. A few officers of the Smolensk Propaganda Department were waiting for them. For the first time since he had left Moscow, Vlasov stood facing cameras, a person of importance. He talked with Schubuth and the officers of the Propaganda Department until the wee hours of the morning. And in the course of this conversation he forgot how subordinate and powerless these Russian-speaking officers were, and his spirits rose.

Next morning a car was waiting to take him and his companion to Field Marshal Kluge in the "forest camp" on the outskirts of Smolensk.

Brigadier General Gersdorff greeted them in a lively, frank, cordial manner and brought them in to Kluge. The field marshal was reticent and careful in his choice of words. But Gersdorff had expected no more. At any rate, Kluge was the first German field marshal to shake hands with Vlasov and welcome him to his command.

They drove to Mogilev to see Schenckendorff. He proved to be the first German general who received Vlasov with real cordiality and shook hands with him with utter naturalness. Schenckendorff invited him to dine. He toasted Vlasov. Here there were no reservations, no resentments. Schubuth watched Vlasov's reaction closely.

As the car was driving back toward Smolensk, Vlasov for the first time since the beginning of the journey looked around the endless expanse of level land with his eyes bright.

"Zamechatelny chelovek (a grand fellow)," he said.

When they reached Smolensk, the news of Vlasov's presence had spread by the same mysterious channels that had already circulated the contents of his leaflet. The people, wavering between incredulity and hope, between the Soviet counterpropaganda claim that it was all a "German bluff" and the thought that Vlasov might exist after all, wanted to see the general. They wanted to convince themselves with their own eyes that he was alive. Groups stood around in the streets, and what they had suffered could be read in their faces. Hunger, poverty, the alternation between fear, hope, and disappointment, between belief and doubt, between propaganda and brutal reality, between the cruelties of the past and the cruelties of the present—a precarious existence between forces that hurtled them back and forth.

Vlasov asked the driver to stop the car. Then he went into the street among the people. The crowd swelled. Women kissed his coat and his hands. He existed. The Germans had not lied.

Vlasov drove to the cathedral and looked down at the destruction, which for once had not been wrought by the Germans but by NKVD troops, who before their retreat had rolled burning barrels of gasoline down the sloping streets into the residential quarter. The wooden houses had caught fire like tinder. The theater was one of the few buildings that had survived the conflagration. The Propaganda Department had announced a public meeting there that evening. The hall was dimly lighted and unheated, and it was only half full.

As Vlasov stepped toward the speaker's lecturn, he said softly: "They're afraid. They're afraid the way everybody is afraid. Out in the streets they are not so closely watched. But whoever enters this hall will be noted. And after all that has happened, how do they know what the future will bring?"

When Vlasov began to speak, there was absolute silence.

He told his own story, and the story of his change of heart. Then he said: "Now tell me your story. Tell me what troubles you and what you have experienced. I'll answer. And don't be afraid to say everything that is on your minds. I want to help you. And these Germans here with me are friends who want the same thing."

At first there was great hesitancy. Then Nikitin, the deputy district head of Smolensk, broke the ice.

"General," he said, "we have hoped for a great deal and received very little. We know that you are a famous general of our country. For that very reason, you must advise us. Most of us did not believe that you had really gone over to the side of the Germans. The propaganda that has trickled through from Moscow, and the partisans who come into the city, say this is only another piece of German trickery. But we now see that you really are here. Our questions are simple. Do you believe that Germany wants to make our country into a colony and that the Germans regard us merely as labor slaves? Many people say they would rather live in a bad Bolshevik Russia than under the German whip. Are they right? And our other question is this: We're always being told we have to fight against Stalin and bolshevism. All very well, but we're never told what we would be fighting for. Why has no German authority and why has the Germans' leader never explained what is to become of our country? The Germans have been here more than a year. But they have asked us to set up only the very lowest administrative bodies. And even these are allowed

114

to function only under German supervision. If the Germans really mean to liberate us, they could have long ago let us create a government of our own for the whole country. We want to know why that has not been done. We want to know whether there are reasons for it that we can understand. Will you answer those questions, General?"

Vlasov answered: "At the present time we are still in the midst of the fighting. The Germans are fighting against Stalin and bolshevism, which last winter showed that it is not yet dead. Millions and tens of millions of our people go on fighting in the service of Stalin, either because they must or because the Germans' mistakes have made them fear German occupation. For the same reasons many of you fought against the Germans. As a result, the Germans have assumed that the masses of the Russians support bolshevism. They cannot help distrusting us, and convincing them that they are wrong is your as well as my business. As a result of this distrust, the Germans have made mistakes. But I have spoken with good Germans and I know that they fully realize the nature of these mistakes and want to make up for them. But in order to do so, they must fight against the profound suspicions that have sprung up in their own country. And it is our responsibility to assist them in that . . . to show the Germans that we really do not love bolshevism and are sincerely ready to fight against it. . . . All the Germans with whom I have talked have sincerely told me that it is a monstrous notion and an impossibility to convert a nation of 190 millions like ours into a colony. The Russian Committee, which I shall head, has the task of concluding treaties with Germany which will lead to honest coexistence of the peoples of Russia and Germany. I have become acquainted with a world that is freer and, nevertheless, better organized and that has greater wealth than we have. Until this war, we ourselves never had enough strength to rise up against bolshevism. We need help from outside. And in return for this help, we must be prepared to make sacrifices. We have always been a generous nation. We are people who do not only take, but who have always been proud if we can give generously in return for aid. That is what we must do now. Don't be confused by the propaganda that comes from across the lines. You all know what twists bolshevist propaganda has always used. Now I am here and will speak up on your behalf among the Germans. Help me, and don't let anyone call you a traitor to your nation. If the masses of our people reject Stalin and bolshevism, it is not treason to fight against Stalin and bolshevism and to accept help from the only people who can back us in this struggle. . . . That is what I have to say to you. I myself fought for Stalin for a long time. I fought to keep the Germans from our capital. And I have now changed course. No German has compelled me; I am acting of my own free will. But if I am to realize my goal, which is our people's goal, I need your trust and your help."

The first applause began even before his resonant voice had faded. Those Germans who could follow the speech recognized that here stood a man who was more than an army general. Here was a natural leader, with a gift for analysis and a talent for simple and persuasive argument.

In Berlin, Mauerwald, and Lötzen, meanwhile, the backers of Vlasov had not been idle. After discussions with Gehlen and Hellmich, the decision was taken to place the small special camp in the Viktoriastrasse on a broader basis and to create a "planning center" for Vlasov and the group around him, in which the outlines of his future government and army could be developed.

Outwardly, the project was camouflaged as a training camp for propaganda units which would visit the prison camps and carry out "propagandistic ideological training of the volunteer formations." Once again Grote's idea was to establish realities under the banner of "propaganda." Strik-Strikfeldt was given the assignment of setting up this camp.

Strik-Strikfeldt had already taken steps in this direction. He had decided that Vlasov must have a halfway decent "residence" in keeping with his role as leader of a liberation army and an anti-Stalinist Russian government.

He had located an empty house on Kiebitzweg in the Dahlem section of Berlin, and proceeded to negotiate with bureaucracy to get hold of it. Ostensibly, he wanted the house for the Propaganda Department of the OKW. At this point, the idea for the "planning center" was born—and Strik-Strikfeldt began looking around for suitable quarters for the forthcoming operation. Again, a camouflage was needed. Very well—the new outfit was to be known as the East Propaganda Department for Special Purposes. Early plans called for a staff of about forty, but Strik-Strikfeldt had visions of an immensely larger operation. In Dabendorf, south of Berlin, on the rail line to Zossen, was a camp formerly occupied by French prisoners of war. Strik-Strikfeldt decided that he would put his Russians there.

For the present, he thought he would satisfy Hellmich by setting up a sort of propaganda school for the "volunteers." But beyond that he could already see a free "academy of the liberation movement" under Russian leadership.

116

Once more Strik-Strikfeldt began to pick his way between the powers. He took advantage of the fact that four different authorities were responsible for his camp. Theoretically, he received his instructions from Colonel Martin; his orders in regard to troops came from Major General Hellmich; Wehrkreis III was the agency for administration; and finally, General Gehlen in Foreign Armies East was still Strik-Strikfeldt's direct superior, although this relationship, in fact, existed only on paper.

With the aid of Roenne, Altenstadt, and Stauffenberg, Strik-Strikfeldt managed to make room, within the Army High Command budget, for no less than eight Russian generals, sixty staff officers, and several hundred subaltern officers at Dabendorf; only twenty-three officer posts would be manned by Germans. And he was going to install them only twenty miles from Berlin, practically under the eyes of the OKW, the Propaganda Ministry, and the Ministry for the Occupied Eastern Territories.

First of all, he transferred to Dabendorf the inmates of the Victoriastrasse building, including Zykov. Zykov and his assistant, the Ukrainian Kovalchuk, were to begin building a propagandistic base for the liberation army. They started issuing the magazines *Dobrovolets* ("The Volunteer") and *Zarya* ("Dawn") for the Russian prisoner-of-war camps. Ultimately, these periodicals attained editions of from 100,000 to 120,000 (and illegally disseminated the text of the Smolensk Proclamation.) They also contained German translations of the Russian texts so that the German personnel of the volunteer regiments could familiarize themselves with the problems of the Russian volunteers. But all that was only the tip of the iceberg.

A Baltic German "training officer,"* Lieutenant Georg von der Ropp, was brought in to conceal the true nature of the operation. Actual "ideological training" was assigned to General Blagoveshchensky. He had served in the Soviet Marines and had been captured in 1941 on the Baltic coast. He was a taciturn but intelligent man, rather unstable in his moods because of a liver complaint. Ostensibly, his task was to carry on legitimate antibolshevistic and anti-Stalinist propaganda among the volunteers and prisoners of war. In reality, however, he functioned as a supervisor, training and indoctrinating the officers who came to Dabendorf from units and camps. Once back with their men, these officers were to fight for humane standards for the prisoners of war and to report on conditions in the camps. But they were also to prepare their fellows for subsequent

---

* *Schulungsleiter*—an officer responsible for indoctrination in Nazi party ideology; virtually the Nazi equivalent of the Communist political commissar.

induction into the liberation army, and to keep up their morale until that army could become an actuality.

Still burrowing from within, Strik-Strikfeldt managed to create a new position in the table of organization of the German divisions to which volunteer units were attached. This post was to be filled by a Russian officer who had passed through the "academy" in Dabendorf. The effect of this was to create a shadow officers' corps which would be ready to assume command of the liberation army as soon as the hour had struck. Strik-Strikfeldt felt that this hour was significantly advanced when he came upon Major General Fedor Ivanovich Trukhin in the Wustrau special prison camp. An older man who had begun his military career in the tsarist army, Trukhin was painfully conscious of the coarsening effect of living under bolshevism. He himself had received a good bourgeois education, but it was noticeably overlaid by the plebeian manners which were standard in the Red Army. Thus, he unabashedly picked his nose during his interview with Strik-Strikfeldt. But little habits of this sort did not make him less valuable to his interlocutor.

At the time of Trukhin's capture in 1941, he had been chief of staff in the Baltic Military District. He had been held for a while in Camp Hammelburg and had here joined a so-called Russian Social People's Party organized by another prisoner, a military lawyer named Maltzev. The new party had a rather freakish character, for it derived its program from what Nazi writings happened to be available to it. To be sure, there had once been a Russian fascist party; it had sprung up in the thirties in Kharbin. Maltzev was either reviving its principles, or he had stumbled on them of his own accord. There was also a Gestapo agent in Hammelburg who may have had something to do with the whole affair. In any case, the Gestapo agent tried to utilize the new party as an instrument for purging the 6000 Russian officers "of Jews and bolshevists."

At this point, Trukhin broke with the "new" party. In Wustrau, he instead approached the NTS. With this ideological history, Trukhin seemed the very person Strik-Strikfeldt was looking for, the Russian who would run the more or less secret "academy" operation in Dabendorf. For Strik-Strikfeldt was already envisaging the training of a close-knit corps of higher officers for the liberation army. There would also be the business of formulating an ultimate ideology for a socialist but not bolshevistic new Russia, and training a body of technical experts who would form the staff of a liberation government.

Strik-Strikfeldt took it for granted that the precise nature of this new ideology was a matter for the Russians themselves to settle. He gave

Trukhin an assistant who could fulfill the function of "chief ideologist," or "instructor"—a Soviet sociologist who had also fallen into German hands and whom Strik-Strikfeldt had dug up in Wustrau. The man's name was Alexander Nikolayevich Zaitsev. He, too, had moved close to the NTS and was seeking a new course between liberalism and moderate state control. In his exuberance, Strik-Strikfeldt also selected the rest of the German staff, from Camp Commandants Elben and Peterson to the representatives of the German political education team and the German counterintelligence officer, Peter von Kleist, mostly from Russian-speaking fellow Balts or friends. He rightly assumed they would watch the Russians closely but would not be overbearing. And he made it clear that they were to protect the Russians from outside interference and to provide them with whatever literary materials they might need "in order to find their own way between National Socialism and bolshevism."

Unfortunately, in this approach he was moving steadily away from all realities. He should have realized this the day that General Hellmich came to the camp for initial ceremonies. Alongside the swastika there waved above the camp a flag that had been designed, in tough discussions and negotiations, as the emblem of the future liberation army. It showed a blue St. Andrew's cross on a white field with a narrow red border. This flag had been approved by the OKW, the Propaganda Ministry, and the East Ministry because a flag seemed indispensable for propaganda pictures. On the other hand, it was considered that the Russian national colors were "sufficiently recessive," as compared with the large amount of white.

General Hellmich addressed the volunteers, greeting them forthrightly as "honorable comrades in arms in the fight for Germany's future." With great presence of mind the German interpreter translated the last phrase as "in the fight for the future of the Russian people."

But Hellmich himself was quite incapable of such shades of expression.

On March 10, 1943, Vlasov arrived back in Berlin. After that memorable evening in Smolensk he had traveled by way of Mogilev and Berezino to Bobruisk. From there he had gone to Veretsy near Osipovichi and then back by way of Mogilev to Orsha. He had called on the Russian mayors in Mogilev, Bobruisk, and Borisov, and entered into discussions with the men of Cossack Detachment 600, Volunteer Regiments on Special Service 700 and 701, and East Battalions 601, 602, and 605. He had seen appalling and incomprehensible sights. But he had also witnessed the enormous trust that most of the Russians felt for him—with the exception of some émigré officers and certain groups of Cossacks who were afraid of losing their independence.

The inspection of a replacement battalion in Bobruisk had been the high point of the journey, and the memory of it still buoyed him up. This battalion, which had purely Russian leadership and was supported by only a few German administration officers, had made the best impression of all. And the battalion's cheers had shown him that the men were waiting for him to lead them. He needed only one thing: the go-ahead from the decision-makers among the Germans.

The night after his return Vlasov dictated a report on his experiences:

The Russian people has always been distinguished by its patriotism. For twenty-five years the Bolsheviks tried to stamp out its qualities. The struggle took a heavy toll of the Russian people, both in spiritual and physical terms. . . .

Consequently, the masses of the people hailed the German troops at the beginning of the war. With German aid they hoped to liberate themselves from an oppressive regime. That was two years ago. The mood of the population has changed because of various events. . . .

The majority of the Russian population—especially the educated classes—now regard this war as a German war of conquest. . . . German propaganda offers . . . no affirmative program to counteract this view. It speaks only of the ugly aspects of the Bolshevik regime. But hatred for Bolshevism is not sufficient to mobilize the Russian people today. The population wants to know what . . . it is being asked to fight and shed its blood for. . . .

No Russian administration exists, for the local Russian authorities have no power and are entirely dependent on the German interpreters assigned to them, people who frequently bear only illwill for Russia. Without control over the local police and the economy, these native authorities are impotent. The best representatives of the educated classes therefore do not volunteer for administrative posts, because they do not want to work against their own people. The ranks of the local police forces are filled with opportunists, agents of Stalin, and, in general, the scum of the population. These men fawn upon the German authorities and put on a great show of zeal. The German commandants, who do not understand the mentality or the language of the people, frequently place confidence in just such types. But the people hate them and the net result of their conduct is suspicion of the Germans.

The levies for labor service in Germany have done especial harm to the morale of the population. The local police picked people up wherever they found them, often in bed at night or at the movies, and carried them off for shipment. Permission to bid good-by to relatives was refused; without clothing and often without shoes, they were locked into the cars. Such actions have produced hatred, terror, and anguish. Many went over to the bandits or committed suicide. Only the sick come back from Germany. No healthy man has been permitted home leave.

To add to this there is the advance of the Red Army this winter. The partisans spread news of the Russian victories. Hope of a German victory is vanishing.

All this has produced a radical change in the attitude of the populace toward Germany.

The critical turning point has come. It is essential to alter completely the policy toward the Russian people. . . . The populace is impatiently awaiting a declaration by Adolf Hitler on these questions. The populace, especially the peasants, hope for a good Russian administration and a settlement of the land question at long last. . . . The peasants observe that the local police are not able to protect the yield of their labors. They see that the partisans are constantly growing in number. And finally they see the police and other officials taking their own families into the cities—where they will be under the protection of the German troops. All this gives the peasant the impression that the situation is not stable and fills him with fears for the future, all of which prompts him to seek contact with the bandits.

The Russian volunteer formations in the German Army have been recruited almost exclusively from former Red Army men.

I could feel in my contacts with every soldier and every officer that these men lack sustaining ideals. The strong and honest are waiting and hoping. But the weak are already vacillating. In these forces, too, the advance of the Red Army is undermining faith in a German victory. The idea is gaining ground that the Bolshevik system is improving. . . . The majority of the honest captive officers and soldiers, like the majority of the decent populace, cannot yet decide. They await a statement by the leader of the German people, Adolf Hitler. Today they can still be won over for the great struggle. Tomorrow it will be too late.

On April 10, four weeks after Vlasov's first journey, Strik-Strikfeldt was waiting on a platform of the Schlesischer Bahnhof in Berlin for the furlough train from Riga.

Since Vlasov's visit in the rear areas of Army Group Center had left such an impression behind, Field Marshal Küchler and General Lindemann had asked the Propaganda Department of OKW to send Vlasov to their own rear areas of Army Group North. Primarily they were hoping to quiet the population, to limit partisan activity, and to raise the morale of the "native anxiliaries." They, too, had made this request on their own responsibility.

As the train pulled in, Strik-Strikfeldt spied Vlasov's tall figure in his brown coat at one of the windows. Beside him stood Captain Antonov, his adjutant, who had deserted at Stalingrad after reading one of Vlasov's leaflets.

Vlasov's expression was one of deep gravity.

"Andrei Andreyevich," Strik-Strikfeldt said, "it was a triumph. I've heard."

Vlasov's face showed his emotion. "Yes," he said, "they are waiting for us."

Strik-Strikfeldt gripped his arm. "I have a surprise for you. We've taken another step forward. You'll see." Strik-Strikfeldt spoke with his characteristic intensity.

They passed through the platform barrier and went out to the car.

Vlasov had spoken in Riga, Pskov, Luga, Volosovo, Plyussa, Pliskov, and Gatchina. The interest of both the population at large and the volunteers had been even greater than in the rear areas of Army Group Center. The Russian newspaper *Pravda* that was being published in Riga had hailed him as a hero of the antibolshevist struggle for liberation. There had, it is true, been a few marginal protests by the Latvians who feared that Vlasov's moment might adversely affect their own goal of regaining their national autonomy. But otherwise his tour had obviously been successful. Although the Smolensk Proclamation had not sufficed to win over the OKW and Hitler, this new success in the north certainly could not be ignored. That seemed inconceivable, impossible.

The chauffeured car rolled out toward Dahlem. When it stopped in front of the small house on Kiebitzweg, Vlasov looked around in wary surprise. But then the door opened and he saw Malyshkin.

"Welcome, Andrei Andreyevich," Malyshkin said. "This is our home now."

To satisfy the OKW's demand that there be at least formal supervision of Vlasov after his move to Kiebitzweg, Strik-Strikfeldt had looked around for a kind of "majordomo" whom Vlasov could not consider a guard. On March 8 he found him: the Baltic German Sergei Fröhlich. Fröhlich had come to Germany in the course of the 1940 resettlement of Baltic Germans, and at the beginning of the war against Russia had joined Operation Zeppelin, a counterintelligence and sabotage organization of the Sicherheitsdienst (SD) in the East. There he had heard of Vlasov and had come to Berlin several times to see him. But he had not been admitted to the Viktoriastrasse center because nobody there knew him, until at last he recognized Strik-Strikfeldt as an old acquaintance. At first Strik-Strikfeldt had distrusted the man. What motives, he wondered, had prompted Fröhlich to try to make contact with Vlasov on his own initiative? Was he acting as an SD agent? For a while he had had him watched, until he was convinced that Fröhlich really was acting out of personal interest. Then he introduced Fröhlich to Malyshkin, with the idea that Malyshkin was to consider him for the post of "majordomo." Malyshkin, not a German, was to introduce him to Vlasov.

At the time Fröhlich first entered the house on Kiebitzweg, April 14, Vlasov had been installed there for three days. He was still full of the impressions of his recent trip, and he hit it off with Fröhlich almost at once, without much talk.

The house was simply furnished. Vlasov's study was on the ground floor, with the window looking out on the garden. In it was a plain desk, a few chairs, a radio. On the walls hung maps of Russia with the changing positions of the front marked. The second room on the ground floor, which looked out on the street, served as his living room. Upstairs was Vlasov's bedroom, beside it Malyshkin's room, and another room occupied by two adjutants. The kitchen was in the cellar. There the cook lived, and the orderlies whom Strik-Strikfeldt had detached from Dabendorf.

As yet the house was unguarded. Strik-Strikfeldt soon had a guard driven over from Dabendorf to patrol the entrance. The unit was placed under Fröhlich's command, and Fröhlich was instructed to admit no one into the house who could not produce a written order from OKW/WPr. It was much more difficult to guard Vlasov personally. In spite of all his customary wariness, he had suddenly developed a carelessness for which there seemed no explanation. He did not want to go out with an armed escort, although he attracted attention everywhere because of his height. Either he would go alone or he would prefer to stay in his garden, he said. Similarly, he preferred to ride the subway or the suburban rail line (the Berlin S-Bahn) instead of using the car Strik-Strikfeldt placed at his disposal. Partly this conduct was an expression of his dislike for any kind of supervision; partly he wanted to be able to observe daily life in Berlin; partly he wanted to enjoy the feeling of independence, of freedom, irrational though that might be.

Through the many channels of communication that flowed between Russians in Germany, Vlasov's whereabouts in Kiebitzweg soon became widely known. Russian émigrés, volunteers on furlough, and *Ostarbeiter* turned up at the house wanting to talk to Vlasov and refer their problems to him. Sometimes Fröhlich rebuffed them, but Vlasov himself came to the door and invited them in. He wanted to hear the truth from his fellow countrymen directly.

The guard would return to Dabendorf in the evening. Then only a single pistol was left in the entire house. A few armed agents could easily have eliminated Vlasov and Malyshkin.

There were no weapons available at OKW/WPr, and there were no superfluous guns in Dabendorf either. Fröhlich, therefore, did some procurement on his own. Sturmbannführer (Major) Kleinert, a member of the SD whom Fröhlich had met in the course of Operation Zeppelin, obtained a submachine gun with two belts of ammunition for him. Then Fröhlich made a trip to Riga and through various connections managed to come by six Russian submachine guns that had been taken from partisans, as well as some Soviet hand grenades. Only then did he feel that his wards were safe.

The quantities of mail addressed to Vlasov forced the military post office to give him an army postal number of his own and to set up a secretariat. The secretariat consisted of four Russian students who later took over some of the guard duties as well. Major Kalugin became their chief. All the inmates of the house received ordinary ration cards. A courier went back and forth daily between Dabendorf and the Kiebitzweg house and brought the soup that was cooked in the field kitchen at Dabendorf. Fröhlich, moreover, exploited his connections in Riga to obtain vodka, bacon, and cigarettes. These provisions enabled Vlasov to act the host toward his countrymen occasionally. The whole thing remained on a very modest level. But it was a crucial fact that the general was in a position to "give" anything at all.

Thus life in the Kiebitzweg villa began with great hopes. No one there had the faintest inkling that a storm was brewing which might dash those hopes.

At first, it was just a matter of some rumors that reached Grote. It seemed that there were some unpleasant repercussions from Vlasov's visit to Army Group North. The general had been invited to dine with a German headquarters staff there, in the neighborhood of Gatchina. On this occasion speeches had been made about friendship between Germany and Russia. Vlasov had supposedly looked in the direction of Leningrad and declared that in the not too distant future he would take pleasure in having German officers there as his guests, so that he could return their hospitality. This remark, apparently, had reached the ears of Himmler, who had gone to Hitler in high indignation. Had things come to such a point, he was quoted as saying, that a Bolshevik from nowhere had the nerve to invite German generals to be his guests, and that such a man had the arrogance to think he could play the ally?

On April 17 the first bad news arrived. Field Marshal Keitel sent General Wedel a note demanding to know how it was possible that Vlasov should have made political remarks against the explicit wishes of the Führer. Keitel wanted the exact text of Vlasov's statement, and threatened dire measures if Vlasov had in fact put himself forward as the "future leader of Russia."

Colonel Martin sent for Strik-Strikfeldt, who arrived in happy innocence. At Martin's first words, Strik-Strikfeldt's heart sank. He himself could not have said what his feelings were at this moment. Outrage that a harmless social formula should have been given such an interpretation? A dawning recognition that his entire scheme was going to turn out mere self-deception and illusion?

Martin ordered him to check on the exact wording of Vlasov's speech. Strik-Strikfeldt drove out to Dahlem. When he drew up to the house, Vlasov was also just arriving; he had been for a drive. "Wilfried Karlovich," he said, with utmost friendliness, "I've just been watching your peasants at work. Incredible. They remove every pebble. . . ."

This was the Peter-the-Great-type Russian to whom Strik-Strikfeldt responded so warmly. He could not bring himself to raise the unpleasant issue right away. As they entered the house, they had to push their way through a group waiting to see Vlasov. In Vlasov's study Malyshkin sat over a huge pile of letters addressed to "Commander of the Russian Liberation Army A.A. Vlasov."

By roundabout means Strik-Strikfeldt found out what he needed to know. Guilelessly, Vlasov repeated the words he had spoken in Gatchina: ". . . The war will come to an end. We will free ourselves from Bolshevism. And then, in our own Leningrad, to which we will restore its proper historical name, we will also receive the Germans as our welcome guests."

Later that afternoon Strik-Strikfeldt was back with Colonel Martin. Throughout the ride his conscience had been plaguing him. The innocence with which Vlasov had quoted this sentence seemed to him proof of how little ill will and how much faith in a common future were implicit in it. Was he, Strik-Strikfeldt, to falsify its text? That would not help, because undoubtedly it had been reported more or less accurately by others.

Martin listened in silence. Then he said: "It is the Führer's will that Leningrad be leveled to the ground for all times to come, or at best provide the soil on which a German city will be built, a mart for the trade with Russia. . . . Don't you know that?"

"I hadn't heard of it," Strik-Strikfeldt said, "but it seems totally fantastic."

"That isn't what matters," Martin retorted. "Vlasov should have had a better escort assigned to him. This natural but superfluous remark may just possibly mean our losing everything."

"Sooner or later our leaders must make the acquaintance of Vlasov as he really is," Strik-Strikfeldt said stubbornly. "We can't carry the whole thing off by trickery. What have we achieved so far, with our clever calculations? We're still at the starting line."

Martin kept cool.

"Our only safety lies in subterfuge. We must play this very carefully," he said.

A few hours later Martin received a memorandum from Field Marshal Keitel addressed to all bureaus and agencies that could possibly be involved, including the headquarters of the commanders of army groups and armies. It stated icily: "In view of the outrageous, impudent remarks made by the captive Russian general Vlasov on a visit to Army Group North, which was carried out without the Führer's knowledge and without my knowledge, it is ordered that the Russian general Vlasov be transferred immediately under special guard back to a prisoner-of-war camp. . . . The Führer no longer wishes to hear the name Vlasov in any context except for pure propaganda activities which may require the name but certainly not the person of General Vlasov. If General Vlasov should come forward personally once more, he must be turned over to the Gestapo and rendered harmless."

Gehlen received the memorandum at the same time. Although he had been expecting some setbacks, this order struck at the core of his far-reaching plans. It hit him all the more painfully because it burst like a shell squarely in the midst of the preparations he had been engaged in ever since Vlasov's visit to Army Group Center. What he had in mind was an attempt on the largest scale to induce Red Army men to desert. This was to be coordinated with the German summer offensive planned for the beginning of May 1943 to start on the Kursk front and extend to the entire eastern front.

The details and goals of the planning are evident from the notes that Herre kept conscientiously along with his regular work. Under the date of April 15, for example, he set down:

> Our preparations for the deserter campaign, which is being given the name Operation Silver Lining, have been completed. They proceed from the assumption that such an operation cannot fail if it is started in conjunction with a successful German offensive. The second requirement is a set of guarantees to the Red Army men who are willing to desert. The very least is the promise of preferential treatment and the provision of quarters in first-class camps. These promises make up the message of Leaflet No. 13, the text of which was drafted yesterday after intensive discussions with Grote. But the decisive factor will be the simultaneous emergence of the Smolensk Committee, Vlasov, and the Liberation Army. This must be signalled by the dropping of millions of the "Vlasov and Smolensk" leaflets that were already approved in January. OKW will raise objections, but that will be after the fact. . . .
>
> We expect a successful large-scale operation and vast numbers of deserters to give the final jolt to our plan. Preparations have been made to establish decent reception camps. In addition, every German division participating in the offensive, as well as a large number of other divisions on the entire eastern front, will be assigned a Russian caretaker unit to welcome the deserters, talk to them in a friendly, humane fashion, inform them about Vlasov and the planned Liberation Army, and suggest that they enlist in this army.

On the basis of arrangements with Grote and Strik-Strikfeldt, these caretaker units would be given crash training courses during the next two weeks in Camp Dabendorf, so that they could join their divisions on May 5. Gehlen has decided to sign Leaflet No. 13 himself, thus avoiding the bother of finding some other important German military man to sign it.

Under the date of April 17 Herre entered in his diary:

> We are waiting for the most favorable moment for Gehlen to extort the order for Operation Silver Lining from Chief of Staff Zeitzler. Unless some bombshell comes in at the last moment from the OKW or the Führer's Headquarters, the plan is bound to succeed. But such a bombshell seems highly unlikely, since we have spoken to the OKW only about Leaflet No. 13 and said nothing about Vlasov's older leaflets. . . .
>
> This evening Gehlen informed me that I have been picked for the new chief on Hellmich's staff. Hellmich is a fine soldier, said Gehlen, but needs an assistant who will guide him politically in regard to the hoped-for change in the status of the volunteer formations. Hellmich's staff must be changed, Gehlen says. . . .

The bombshell that Herre thought unlikely was already on its way. Herre's diary entry for the fateful day, April 18, read: "An incomprehensible counterstroke against all our efforts has come from the very highest authority." There is no diary entry for April 19 and 20. Herre did not find the strength or the time to resume his entries until April 21. Late at night on that date he wrote:

> Impossible to describe the last few days. Setback upon setback. . . . Bitterness and furious indignation. Strong measures against Vlasov. . . . With difficulty obtained permission for Vlasov to remain in the Kiebitzweg house "under guard." The consequences for Silver Lining are incalculable. . . .
>
> In the present situation Zeitzler will never sign the orders for the operation. There remains only Leaflet No. 13. This means discarding the crucial political concept. All that is left is an appeal to petty human instincts, which in view of the consolidation of the Soviet front and the setback at Stalingrad, can only have a slight effect. . . .

Extensive conversations with Altenstadt. Also with Gersdorff at Army Group Center. Both determined not to take this blow from the Führer's Headquarters lying down. Gersdorff wildly excited, suggests starting Vlasov off in the Army Group Center territory on his, Gersdorff's, own initiative. He will seize some favorable moment to persuade Field Marshal Kluge to take the responsibility. Once Kluge has said yes, he won't be able to back out.

Herre's next diary entry is dated April 24. It reads:

Silver Lining is going through. The Chief of Staff has signed Gehlen's proposals. But there is no mention of Vlasov. . . .

More elaborate discussions with Gehlen, Altenstadt, Grote, Strik-Strikfeldt, Gersdorff. General determination that now we must either act on our own initiative and . . . present *faits accomplis* or force joint action with Rosenberg to reach the Führer. Military channels now blocked by Keitel. Must enlist political spokesman. Rosenberg.

Again a few days passed without significant entries. At last, on May 4, Herre wrote: "Eighteen million leaflets readied. From the Black Sea to the North Sea . . . And underneath it all, inner doubts of whether this vast enterprise makes any sense." On May 5: "A report has just come that deprives the whole Silver Lining operation of its last real chances. The offensive at Kursk is not beginning on May 6, but has been postponed indefinitely. The Führer has redirected sizable forces to Kharkhov." And a week later, on May 13, Herre's entry reads: "Failure of the operation, which had to be started on the night of May 6, without an offensive and without Vlasov. A few thousand deserters. It turned out as might have been expected."

The next entry is dated May 14, 1:20 P.M.—a time of day at which ordinarily Herre never wrote in his diary. Now he noted:

Conference in Mauerwald: Schenckendorff, Tresckow, Gehlen, Gersdorff, Altenstadt. Resolve not to accept the Führer's Headquarters' decision against Vlasov. . . . Altenstadt brings up his old idea: establishing Vlasov as head of the Russian self-governing administration that will be built up from below. Once Vlasov holds the reins of government—even if for the time being this is limited to the rear areas of Army Group Center—everything else will shortly follow of its own accord. . . . Enlist Kluge in view of the military situation. Am almost sure that in spite of the setbacks I must take

129

over the position under Hellmich. Freytag advises me to do so only if I am given absolute authority to act on my own, especially in replacing the personnel of Hellmich's staff.

On May 16, finally, Herre wrote:

> General Wagner is intervening. Today, through Dr. Bräutigam as liaison man, he delivered an ultimatum to Rosenberg and the Political Department of the East Ministry. He wants to call a meeting between representatives of the General Staff and fully empowered representatives of the Ministry, which will issue a joint appeal directly to the Führer. Its contents: the demand for introducing Russian self-government, placing Vlasov at its head, and reversing present occupation policy. . . . Threat to act independently in the rear areas of Army Group Center.

In the midst of this tense situation Herre, on May 21, 1943, assumed his new position as chief of staff under General Hellmich. Several members of the staff, who seemed to Herre totally unfit for their future role, were relieved. In their place, Herre brought in Lieutenant Ungermann, who was already an expert on the Russian question from working with the volunteers.

In the meantime, Second Lieutenant Urban, the first adjutant, was engaged on a propect of his own: obtaining some kind of survey of the volunteers and auxiliaries in the German forces. He had to assure the responsible officers in the various army groups that they would not get into trouble if they provided him with truthful data on their own "native" auxiliaries, reporting on the existence of units they had hitherto concealed.

For the time being, Herre retained Lieutenant Michel as the Ic of the staff, although he felt an instinctive distrust for this man, of so different a breed from himself. He had, however, a linguistically gifted lieutenant named Ofzcarek in mind as a successor to Michel.

While these changes were taking place, a reply arrived from the East Ministry in response to Wagner's ultimatum of May 16.

From the text it was apparent that Rosenberg was writhing in agony. The demand that he throw his support behind, of all persons, a Pan-Russian like Vlasov ran so counter to his dreams and ideas that he found it almost intolerable. On the other hand, he did not dare give these high-ranking army officers an unequivocal refusal, for by so doing he would lose the only possible allies who could come to his aid in his frequent tangles with Reichskommissar Koch. And still less did he want to admit that, in actuality, he had no influence at all upon Hitler.

Therefore he temporized, insisting that the conference take place in his ministry. Wagner replied that all the necessary documents were in Mauerwald and that it would scarcely be possible to ship them to Berlin. Rosenberg then promised to send representatives of his ministry to Mauerwald.

These representatives arrived punctually. But they were headed only by Dr. Bräutigam. Leibbrandt and Meyer had found pretexts for remaining in Berlin.

Bräutigam reported that Rosenberg might be prepared to present Hitler with the new Vlasov plans, provided that this was done conjointly with one of the prominent leaders of the armed forces, say Field Marshal Keitel or General Jodl. But the request for such a presentation must come from Hitler, and it was up to the army to persuade Hitler to look into the matter.

To Wagner and Gehlen, who were trying to work through Rosenberg precisely because they no longer saw any way of having their protests or their proposals communicated to Hitler through military channels, this reply was equivalent to the failure of their effort. Altenstadt was so desperate that he again thought of acting on his own initiative. Wagner, however, saw quite clearly that at most they would be supported in such a step by Tresckow and a few others (who a year later, on the occasion of the attempted assassination of Hitler, showed that they, like Altenstadt and Wagner, were capable of revolutionary acts of violence and of transcending fixed ideas about an officer's honor and duty to obey). But as soon as he thought about Gehlen's attachment to those same traditional ideas, despite his resolute character and general clearheadedness, Wagner realized that a small group would not have a chance. Nor were the principal figures in the drama, Vlasov and his followers, ripe for any such extreme undertaking. It bordered on the grotesque to think of Kluge as cooperating. And among the masses of unsuspecting, still unprepared German soldiers, no one would understand what this group of crackpot generals was up to. The idea of taking independent action as a means of alerting Hitler to the problem was a thoroughly desperate, confused illusion. . . . So there was nothing to do but to persuade Rosenberg after all, or to apply pressure to him.

The conference began on May 26 in the oblong assembly room of Wagner's barrack headquarters. Bräutigam and two associates found themselves confronting sixteen additional army officers besides Wagner, Hellmich, Gehlen, Altenstadt, and Herre.

In front of Wagner was piled a heap of papers containing demands, complaints, and pleas from army groups and armies. On top was a long letter from Army Group Center that had been written by Gersdorff and Tresckow. Tresckow had actually extracted a signature to it from the eternally vacillating Field Marshal Kluge. The letter contained everything that Wagner or Gehlen would themselves have been able to say. It pointed out that Russian self-government in Kluge's rear area had been making enormous progress. The time had come, however, to turn the administrative apparatus over to native leadership. The time had come to formulate a political program for Russia and to activate Russian military formations. He was, therefore, putting in an urgent plea for "making the Vlasov factor function as quickly as possible." Victory could not be achieved without Russian help.

General Wagner read this letter aloud. It seemed almost too good to be true that it bore Field Marshal Kluge's signature; and it was really an open question whether that waverer, who so shied away from any contact with "political" problems, knew what he had signed.

"Gentlemen of the *Ostministerium*," Wagner continued, "I would rather not read you this whole heap of petitions and protests against our present policy in the East. They are all in the same tenor as Field Marshal von Kluge's letter. The officers present here are convinced that Vlasov has fallen into our laps like a gift from heaven. . . . If we are not to be allowed to form a genuine Russian liberation army under Vlasov, at least we must try to install Vlasov as head of a native administration. None of us here is a born politician, but we have a fairly clear idea of what will happen behind our own lines and especially behind the Red Army's lines if Vlasov were to promise to restore to the Russian peasants their own land. A deadline should be declared, within which everyone who has a claim to land must come forward. It takes the grossest blindness not to perceive how this would rally the people around Vlasov. Once Vlasov is made head of a Russian government, we could soon afterward begin at least preparing plans for a liberation army. What matters now is the first step. And everything depends on whether or not that first step is taken. I can tell you in dead earnest that any hope of winning the war in the East with our present military power is an illusion. This action must be carried out on the political plane. That is the reason for our appeal to you, gentlemen."

As a diplomat Dr. Bräutigam, as appears from his notes, tried to blur the fact that he had practically no power to negotiate on his own. Instead, he pointed out that the army representatives were proceeding from military arguments, in spite of all they were saying, and that therefore the first step was up to them. Moreover, he declared, they were the ones with the most forceful arguments. Only considerations of military defeat or victory really affected Hitler. After his rebuff in December Minister Rosenberg could not once more approach Hitler on the question.

Herre scribbled on his note pad: "Tug-of-war, the slogan being: 'You first!' "

"As the East Ministry's liaison officer to the Army General Staff, you ought not to be saying these things," Wagner told Bräutigam sternly. "You know very well that we have tried more than once to take the first steps and that we would do so again if we could. But it has clearly proved hopeless to obtain a hearing from Hitler through our channels. And although we as soldiers proceed from military arguments, the thing itself remains a political matter. The impetus must come from a side that has hitherto not raised a finger for Vlasov. It should not be hard for you to find political arguments—if you want to."

"I didn't say that Minister Rosenberg won't act," Bräutigam replied. "But recently he has so often tried in vain merely to see the Führer that he considers it out of the question that the Führer will receive him in the Vlasov affair even if he were to ask. Any step he could take would have a chance only if this step had already been initiated by the military side."

"And why by the military side?" Wagner demanded. And he went on to reveal his own ignorance of the political power-relationships around Hitler. "Rosenberg is one of the oldest of the Führer's Old Fighters."

"The Minister for the Occupied Eastern Territories has no direct representative who is in the Führer's entourage all the time," Bräutigam explained, by way of glossing over Rosenberg's lack of status. "The top men of the armed forces and the chief of staff see the Führer daily. That means they always have the opportunity to talk to him, whereas my minister has to request an audience."

General Wagner slammed his fist down on the table. "Let's not beat about the bush, gentlemen. You have evidently come here without any power whatsoever and with the assignment to save your minister . . . from taking any initiative. That seems to me symptomatic of the political situation in which we find ourselves, and for which we soldiers are risking

133

our necks. We have tried everything, while your ministry has done nothing. And if I tell you once more that the army alone cannot win this war in the East without political assistance, your ministry must consider itself responsible for all that is going to happen, if only because it has carried out its own emasculation."

At that moment Bräutigam was called to the telephone. It was a call from Berlin. Leibbrandt was on the phone, his voice excited and nervous. "I hope you've made no concessions at all," he blurted out "The minister instructs you to refuse all assurances to the army. Dr. Köppen had just passed on to us from the Führer's Headquarters some new and devastating remarks of the Führer concerning Vlasov. It is absolutely out of the question that the minister can undertake anything at all. . . ."

Bräutigam returned to the conference room.

"Gentlemen," he said, "when I return to Berlin I shall explain to the minister the full gravity of the situation. I firmly promise you that I shall . . . attempt to influence him toward your point of view. . . . I shall also seek political arguments. But from my knowledge of the situation I can tell you that my minister will insist on linking any thrust from me with a new thrust from the military side."

The other members of the conference rose in silence. Altenstadt approached Bräutigam slowly. "Whom the gods wish to destroy," said he, "they first strike blind."

Two days later Bräutigam was back in Berlin. Before going in to see Rosenberg, he wrote a report on the conference in Mauerwald. "The representatives of the various departments of the Army General Staff were unanimous in their view that the war in the East is lost unless there is a fundamental change in the direction and new support from the political side," he concluded.

He personally presented the report to Rosenberg and made the point that the army in the East considered the minister its last hope. Rosenberg's reaction was gloomy. It would be hard to say what most depressed him at the moment: the thought that he, of all people, was being asked to promote the Pan-Russian ideas of Vlasov, which he abhorred, or that he would have to have an interview with Hitler which would surely bring him fresh humiliations.

After a long silence he said that he would write to Standartenführer (Colonel) Köppen and ask him to get in touch with Field Marshal Keitel or General Jodl. Then the General Staff could not reproach him for not having taken the initiative. With an air of almost relief he added: "But the discussion would have to take place before June 3. I cannot postpone my visit to the Ukraine on that account."

And, in fact, he received no answer. On June 3 he entered his special train for a new journey through a portion of the eastern empire that to all intents and purposes lay outside his domain.

Five days later, on the evening of June 8, 1943, Keitel, Chief of Staff Zeitzler, Hitler's adjutant Schmundt, and Colonel Scherff were gathered around Hitler at the Berghof for a military conference. This was one of the minor military conferences for which there was no special pretext aside from the generally black picture on the eastern front. Keitel was the only man present who knew how it would end.

Keitel had been informed two days earlier of all that had happened at the meeting in Mauerwald. He was aware of the letter signed by Kluge that had been read aloud there, and he knew also of the attempt to enlist Rosenberg as the spearhead of a campaign for Vlasov. This open disregard of his anti-Vlasov order of April 12, which he had issued without bothering Hitler about the affair, had sent Keitel into a fury. He was the last man who could be persuaded to commit himself personally on a matter that he knew ran counter to Hitler's ingrained ideas. In keeping with his servile temperament, his total lack of any large perspective, and his utter incapacity to think for himself, he now decided to obtain a direct "Führer's order" which would once and for all "get Vlasov off his back."

The military conference at the Berghof was a perfect occasion for this. A copy of Gehlen's Leaflet No. 13 had fallen into his hands. It was innocent enough in itself and did not mention Vlasov. But in one passage it used the phrase "liberation army." Keitel showed Hitler the leaflet and remarked that he had learned that commanders on the eastern front, including even Field Marshal Kluge, were drawing wrong conclusions from what was meant as pure propaganda and were counting on the levying of such an army.

This was enough to send Hitler off on a long, excited monologue. Amid a host of irrelevant flashbacks to the First World War and to Ludendorff's disappointments with Polish legions, Hitler declared: ". . . I can tell Kluge and all these other officers just one thing: I will never build up a Russian army. That is a first-class fantasy. I don't want anybody harboring the notion that all we have to do is to establish a Ukrainian state and everything will be all right, it will give us a million soldiers. We won't get anything, not a single man. But we would be committing an act of sheer madness. We would throw away our war aim, which has nothing to do with a Ukrainian republic. . . .

"We cannot go making promises of liberation and independent republics, promises that are irreconcilable with our aims. There is the chief danger. We must not allow any wrong ideas to arise among us on that score. This is something I must personally get across to the generals and field marshals. . . .

"Outside the front we can cook up as much propaganda as we like. We can do anything and say anything. But in our own rear areas we must not allow anything to be done that might lead to a situation like that of 1916. Under no circumstances can that be permitted. And we must never be so stupid as to hand over existing forces to any third party, to any Russian, who will then have them in his hand and tell them: 'Today you'll cooperate but not tomorrow.' That would lead to something like strike demands. That would lead to blackmail. . . ."

None of those present dared to make the slightest objection to the misleading comparison between 1943 and 1916. Instead, Keitel hastened to turn Hitler's rantings into a firm order: "Then I shall announce that by your decision no practical effects of the temporary Vlasov propaganda are intended and that Vlasov shall continue to be forbidden any activity in Russian territory." He concluded fawningly: "I saw that the whole thing was a minor self-deception. They're hoping for some relief out there and don't realize what kind of trouble they're courting."

At this time Rosenberg's special train was already deep in the Ukraine. He had gone first to Rovno by way of Brest Litovsk, taking with him only a few officials from his ministry. These included Undersecretary Kinkelin, Wilhelm von Allwörden, and Undersecretary Joseph Zimmermann, the chief of his press department. There were, however, several outsiders in the train, and in particular two gauleiters: Dr. Siegfried Ueberreiter, gauleiter of Styria, and Dr. Otto Hellmuth, gauleiter of Mainfranken—a colorless mediocrity whom Rosenberg liked because of his antipathy to the Christian churches.

During the ride, Rosenberg had been working out his plan for announcing to the Ukrainians new regulations regarding ownership of property.

Gauleiter and Reichskommissar Erich Koch awaited Rosenberg in Rovno surrounded by his entire staff. As Undersecretary Kinkelin, accompanied by Undersecretary Zimmermann, entered the waiting car behind Rosenberg and Koch, his glance fell upon the back of Rosenberg's frail neck and the solid, bull-like neck of Koch. He whispered to Zimmermann: "Compare those two! How is this going to end?"

That first evening in Rovno, Koch cut Rosenberg down to size. He forbade the proclamation of any kind of new order, whether it concerned property or anything else. If Rosenberg were going to foul things up by introducing his harebrained theories, he, Koch, would at once have the Führer put a stop to it.

Rosenberg yielded to the obviously stronger man.

The trip through the Ukraine began next day. It took Rosenberg and his companions to Kiev, to Poltava, to Krivoi Rog, to the Zaporozhye power plant, which was by now half rebuilt, to Dnepropetrovsk, and to Nikolaev, then on to the Crimea, to Simferopol, to devastated Sevastopol, and on to the palace of the khans in Bakhchisarai. Finally they went to the palace of the tsars in Yalta and to Simeis, where Rosenberg once had lived with his first wife—she had come there in hopes of being cured of her pulmonary disease. Rosenberg had tears in his eyes when he arrived in Simeis; but perhaps these tears were not entirely due to memories of those far-off days.

Koch forebore to accompany him. He did not want it to seem that he was Rosenberg's subordinate. Here and there he turned up briefly, but did not shake hands with Rosenberg and put on a show of brusqueness. It was obvious, however, that Koch was roundly hated by his own people. The local German commissioners went to some trouble to introduce Rosenberg to Ukrainians and let him say a few words to the "natives." But whenever a Ukrainian delegation appeared to offer Rosenberg bread and salt, Koch interfered.

A ceremony had been arranged in the marketplace of Melitopol, in front of a monument erected by the Ukrainians for the German soldiers who had fallen during the Civil War, 1918–19, in the struggle for the Ukraine. When Rosenberg and his entourage, surrounded by Ukrainians, paid their respects to the dead, Koch suddenly appeared and in the solemn silence said loudly: "No German soldier is going to die for this pack of niggers."

At a dinner in Kiev Rosenberg expressed the wish to meet a few Ukrainian scientists and have them dine with him. As Zimmermann reported, Koch threw him a scornful look. "If I find a Ukrainian who is worth sitting at the same table with me," he said, "I would have to have him shot." Rosenberg was too dismayed to take issue.

He likewise flubbed his chance when he and Koch were visiting Field Marshal von Kleist in the latter's headquarters near Dnepropetrovsk. Kleist, ignorant of Rosenberg's character, had been waiting for this moment to appeal to the minister. "Herr Minister," he said, turning to Rosenberg, "I am most grateful for this chance to speak to you personally. There is one matter that concerns us soldiers deeply. Unfortunately, we have been forced to recognize, by bitter experience, that we are all in hopeless positions unless there is a revision of policy in the Ukraine and toward the Ukrainians. . . ."

Koch quickly put an end to Kleist's petition.

"It is well known, Herr Feldmarschall," he said, "that you regard the situation with an extremely dangerous degree of pessimism. I have long had the impression that you lack faith in the Führer, as well as the confidence essential for a soldier, and without which he is probably in the wrong place. I have been informed by the Führer personally that the real situation is rather different from your view of it."

Like Rosenberg, Kleist was incapable of using the language of brute force, the only language to which Koch was accessible. However, he was more forceful than Rosenberg. "I would only wish, Herr Gauleiter," he said, "that your optimism might prove of some practical comfort to us here."

Rosenberg stood by in silence. As he was leaving Kleist's headquarters, he heard Koch's growl ringing in his ears: "There's another one who's just about due."

Returning to Berlin and his quiet office, Rosenberg was flooded with a sense of relief. Here, at least, he felt safe. But the very first day back inflicted another blow. On his desk he found a teletype message from Field Marshal Keitel: "At the military conference on June 8, 1943, the Führer raised the question of the Vlasov affair. He categorically forbade any further use of Vlasov in the occupied eastern territories. Furthermore, he ruled out any thought of acting on the promises made to Vlasov. Therefore there is no further need for submitting the proposed joint report to the Führer by Reich Minister Rosenberg accompanied by General Jodl or me."

A few days later Herre noted: "We have lost. What for a long time we were unwilling to believe seems irrevocably true: that it is the Führer himself who rejects the obvious rational course. Our efforts are wasted. What remains?"

Candies: The Long Wait

Who was it at the Steinmetz barracks in Lötzen who coined the phrase "candy time"? That remains a mystery. But it was an apt term for the period that began about the middle of June 1943.

At any rate, the word "candy" ("bonbon") already appears in Herre's journal under the date June 28, 1943:

> If I were to give up hope that the military situation will force the top leadership to come to its senses after all, I would be questioning the existence of reason itself. . . .
>
> I tell Hellmich: Since we cannot offer the grand political goal we had in mind, at least we must be able with a clear conscience to tell the volunteers: "You are fighting with us against the Soviet regime. In this struggle you stand as the equals of German soldiers." Of course, what we can give them are no more than candies, but this is all we can do in our present quandary.

Herre's notes indicate that he had recovered quite quickly from his profound disillusionment and was once more beginning to "hope against hope." Hellmich actually seemed happier. He was just as glad to have retreated from the alien ground of politics and thought he would be able to carry out his task entirely on the "field service" level. He was to learn otherwise.

Lieutenant Joachim Urban had determined by laborious statistical studies that at least 600,000 auxiliaries were engaged on the eastern front in June 1943, and that these Russians, Ukrainians, etc. were scattered among the German front-line troops. Another 200,000 "volunteers" were serving in their own formations as fighting soldiers, but these formations were likewise scattered over the entire front.

The confusion had about reached the limit of tolerance. Auxiliaries who were accustomed to being treated in one army as equal allies were still treated like slaves in the territory of another army. In the one, they were eligible for furloughs; in the other, that was out of the question. In the one, commanders gave them medals; in the other, the medals were taken from them.

Since the auxiliaries had nothing to do with the volunteers, who were isolated in their own formations, Herre's predecessor, Colonel von Frey-tag-Loringhoven, had begun trying to straighten things out with the "Hiwis" (auxiliaries). In their case he thought he could most likely assume assent from "on high." He had drawn up an army manual for the auxiliaries, which was referred to as "Manual 5000." In the battle to get it approved, General Zeitzler, who had succeeded Halder as chief of staff, for the first time came to the fore.

Zeitzler had last been chief of staff to the commander in chief on the western front. He had a reputation for vigor, and was, therefore, in favor with Hitler. Short, chubby, bald, he bore the nickname "Ball of Lightning" because he put on a remarkable display of lightning-fast activity wherever purely military matters had to be settled. On the other hand, he was apt to shy away from political problems. His attitude toward the problem of the auxiliaries was grudging and ambivalent. He realized that no army in the East could get along without them any longer. But it was only under the influence of Stauffenberg, who skillfully managed to keep him out of trouble with the Führer's Headquarters, that Zeitzler signed his name to "Regulation 5000" and thus made it valid for the eastern theater of war.

The regulation provided:

> Auxiliaries are volunteers drawn from peoples of Russian territory who are incorporated into existing German troop formations and who after a solemn swearing-in henceforth belong permanently to such formations.

> The oath for the auxiliaries from the old Soviet areas runs as follows:

> "As a loyal son of my native land I voluntarily enter the ranks of the Russian (or Ukrainian) Liberation Army and solemnly swear that I will fight sincerely against Bolshevism and for the welfare of

my people. In this struggle, which is being waged on the side of the German and allied armies against the common foe, I pledge Adolf Hitler as Leader and Commander in Chief of the Liberation Armies fidelity and unconditional obedience. I am prepared at all times to risk my life for this oath."

Toward the auxiliaries every German soldier will conduct himself: As a superior strictly, correctly, justly (no humiliating punishments), and with the same concern that he would show toward fellow Germans. In living with the auxiliaries the German soldier will be helpful both on and off duty (no indifference or contempt), and will maintain German dignity (no criticism, no griping in front of auxiliaries).

The auxiliary may choose a wife from among his own people. Such marriages are to be considered valid.

Within the operational territory of the army group, auxiliaries are to be allowed to visit their families.

The auxiliaries will receive pay comparable to the army pay scale.

Members of the families of auxiliaries whose homes lie outside the general districts of Lithuania, Latvia, and Estonia are to receive dependency benefits.

That document was the work of Freytag-Loringhoven.

Now Hellmich was trying to coordinate the medley of volunteer formations into a single military organization and thus "bring some German order into the mess." Although Herre laid more importance on political matters, he was far too normal a General Staff officer not to sympathize with what Hellmich was trying to do.

A new designation was created among the officer ranks of all the army groups and armies in the East: Kommandeur der Osttruppen z.b.V.—"Commander of the Eastern Troops f.s.d. (for special duty)." In filling their staffs, these commanders had no choice but to accept whatever officers the Army Personnel Office supplied. They had to be grateful if among these were at least a few people who did not approach their task with traditional notions, regarding the auxiliaries and the volunteers as mercenaries.

Commander of the Eastern Troops f.s.d. in the Eighteenth Army was Colonel (later Brigadier General) W. von Henning; in the Third Tank

Army, it was Colonel (later Brigadier General) Ullmer; in Army Group A, Colonel (later Brigadier General) Fritz Freitag, and so on.

At the same time, Hellmich encouraged the establishment of leadership training schools for the "native soldiers." In Mariampol in Lithuania a "School for Native Officers, Officer Candidates, and Interpreters" was set up. On Herre's insistence its commander was "even" a Russian, the captive Colonel (and later General) Assberg.

There was progress on other matters.

Stauffenberg, who was still striving toward the goal of raising sizable volunteer contingents, could report a single success. The soldiers involved were Cossacks. Because of the setbacks on the eastern fronts various Cossack formations were drifting about. By oblique means, Stauffenberg managed to get permission to gather them into a cavalry division. Colonel Hellmuth von Pannwitz became its commander.

Pannwitz, a stocky man with a broad, Slavic-looking face, spoke only a little Polish aside from German, but he had a certain feeling for the particular nature of Eastern Europeans. Moreover, he had qualities that made him a predestined Cossack commander. He was an enthusiastic horseman, and his men regarded him more as a father than as a strict commander; the word was that he had a "truly great heart."

Entrusted with his new assignment, he could scarcely wait until the scattered Cossacks from Army Groups Center and South arrived from northern Italy at the training center in Mielau, East Prussia.

Pannwitz had only a few interpreters at his disposal. The German training officers sent him by the Army Personnel Office were, as usual, people without the slightest appreciation of what their new task called for. The experiment would have failed within a short time if Pannwitz had not ridden roughshod over rules and regulations. He started at once to learn Russian, and very quickly talked to the Cossacks in a "daring Russian." He had speeches translated into Russian, and written out phonetically in Latin script. In this way he addressed the Cossacks; and this effort by a German general to use their language made a great impression on them. He drank with the Cossacks, spent time in their quarters, held riding contests with them, and organized a bugle corps in Cossack uniform. And he paid not the slightest attention to the condescending looks of other German generals who happened to be staying in Mielau.

During the few months allotted to him for organizing the division, Pannwitz had no time to sift through his German skeleton staff. Its defects remained glaring for a long time: ignorance of the Russian mentality, of Russian habits of fighting, and total ignorance of the customs and historical traditions of the Cossacks.

On the other hand, the Cossack corps of officers at first consisted of a random lot of émigré Cossack officers of the old tsarist army, Cossacks who had served as officers in the Red Army, and men whom the Germans had arbitrarily named as officers in the earliest Cossack formations. There were fearless fire-eaters; there were men with a highly-developed sense of honor, and men who were completely indifferent to all concepts of honor. Tensions existed between the older émigrés and the freed prisoners of war; at times, hatreds reached murderous intensity.

To form some kind of unity out of all this variety seemed a feat beyond human strength. Nevertheless, it was accomplished because Pannwitz put his whole heart into it.

During those same months, hundreds of miles away, still another formation was developing. Since the middle of 1942, certain White Russian émigrés, who after the Bolshevik Revolution in 1920 had fled to Serbia by way of Gallipoli, had been petitioning the German commander in Serbia to let them become soldiers again. Most of them were former officers or the sons of officers. Many of them wanted—like the recent Russian émigrés of the Kazantsev type—to break with their eternal grieving over the past and "fight for the homeland in new ways."

After many referrals to Berlin and to the headquarters in East Prussia, the German commander—harassed by partisans—granted them their wish, although under the typical condition that émigré formations might only be employed to fight in Serbia.

The "Russian Defense Corps of Serbia" soon reached a strength of 15,000 men. It was commanded by a Russian, General Staifon. He organized five regiments. Although the only Germans were liaison officers, Staifon soon made his corps into an instrument that fought successfully against the partisans.

Thus, there was a degree of progress. But the organizing of commanders of Eastern troops, like the raising of the Cossack division, necessarily remained without real substance as long as no specific directives existed for the volunteer formations. Working out suitable regulations presented no difficulty. Getting them approved was the real problem. And putting them into practice even harder. Herre wrote:

> In order to understand the sort of difficulties we were running into with our "bonbons," we might take the question of marriages. Before a marriage was officially approved, it had to be reviewed by the following authorities: Personnel Office of the Army High Command, Ministry for the Occupied Eastern Territories, Reich State Security Office, and Commissioner General for Labor Assignment, within whose province many of the prospective brides were working, and finally the Office of Racial Policy.
>
> The Commissioner General for Labor Assignment stated: "If we allow these people to marry, your damned volunteers will make the female Eastern workers pregnant and we will lose that part of our labor forces."
>
> The Office of Racial Policy put up the strongest opposition, attempting several times to bring Hitler into the matter, by getting to him through Bormann. Evidently, only pure chance forestalled this. We found ourselves faced with sheer insanity. . . .
>
> Our efforts to introduce German uniforms and German insignia came up against resistance from a wide variety of camps. . . . The feeling was that "Russians could not be worthy of the German uniform."
>
> During these months, I fortunately made the acquaintance of a young General Staff officer in the Armed Forces Operations, Major Rohrbeck. He was a veritable gift from heaven, an ally who kept me constantly informed whenever attention "up there" happened to be directed our way and new thunderclouds could be spotted in the sky. Another fortunate turn was that Major Klamroth took the place of Stauffenberg, who in a sudden impulse of disgust volunteered for front-line service. Major Klamroth fully accepted Stauffenberg's ideas. . . . That proved especially important when the question of awarding decorations came up. Since the commanders at the front were not permitted to give the volunteers German decorations, they had created decorations for "members of the Eastern peoples" on their own initiative. But when the German soldiers began . . . smiling at these decorations, they ceased to be honors and became instead . . . something of an insult.
>
> We managed to get the Personnel Office to agree to the volunteers' being eligible for the German Assault Badge and then the

German Wound Badge. When we had come so far, we fought for the Iron Cross. But since we had to negotiate these matters with a man who was distinctly committed to the Führer's Headquarters, General Burgdorf, we kept running into a blank wall. . . . We always had to be careful that our demands were not phrased in so sharp a manner that Burgdorf would refer the matter to Hitler.

By 1943 we had at last obtained the regulations we were demanding. . . . But by that time the effects of German policy in the occupied areas and at home had produced new crises. The problem that had become evident in 1942—the wretched treatment of the *Ostarbeiter*—was now becoming acute.

No one in the top leadership gave any thought to the probable feelings of a volunteer on furlough when he walked in the streets of Germany with a woman worker who wore the word *Ost* [East] on her blouse. He himself could now go into movie houses or taverns or take the streetcar. But the woman worker with her identifying *Ost* was turned away everywhere. Hellmich thundered against the arguments of the State Security Office that there had to be special controls on these Eastern workers to curb their criminal instincts.

Hellmich thundered, but found himself helplessly entangled in the thicket of political bureaus that had to be hacked through. . . . More and more often he went off on inspection trips . . . at the front. He left the fight . . . to his staff.

I shall never forget how we tried to put our point across to Gauleiter Sauckel's people. . . . They took shelter behind the Führer's assignment to Sauckel to ensure the needed supply of labor from the East. The quota must not be endangered, not by anything. These people could not comprehend that trust and decent treatment from the start would have brought in much larger numbers of workers and much higher production.

[There was] . . . a circular letter sent out by the chairwoman of the Women's League of Berlin-Charlottenburg. She advised women not to offer a bed to domestic servants from the East. They were accustomed to sleeping on the ground, the letter said. . . . A letter from the leader of Munich Women's League waxed indignant at German women who allowed their Russian maids to eat at the family table. "How can they let such a creature from the sinister East, a creature that can only in a limited way be considered human, sit at table with them and eat from the same bowl as their own children!"

. . . When autumn came and the psychological crisis at the front grew more and more urgent, we were still confronting a wall of incomprehension. . . . Vlasov, meanwhile, had also followed a course that ended up against this frightful wall. . . .

Decades were to pass before Strik-Strikfeldt could talk about the June day on which he drove out to the house on Kiebitzweg to tell Vlasov that all his efforts had come to nothing. He described how Gehlen had informed him of the decisive conference with Hitler at the Berghof. Gehlen then asked: "Does General Vlasov know about this conference with the Führer? Does he know that a fundamental and possibly final decision has been taken? It would not be fair to keep him in the dark. The Führer apparently doesn't need Vlasov, but the rest of us are going to need him badly. Tell him that."

These dry and rather enigmatic words indicated the job Gehlen was expecting Strik-Strikfeldt to do, namely to "keep Vlasov on tap." But Gehlen's outlook, that of a master strategist's, which was so different from Vlasov's complicated and emotional one, made this task no easier.

Strik-Strikfeldt continued his report:

I told Vlasov that all the officers' efforts to bring about a change of policy on the Liberation Movement had come to nothing. . . . Our talk took place in the presence of Malyshkin. . . . My news was the severest blow Vlasov had suffered since he had staked his hopes for his nation on the German card. . . .

"I have always," Vlasov said, "respected the German officer. . . . But these men are flinching when faced with brute force; they accept moral annihilation so as to avoid physical annihilation. I have done that myself. We have here what we have in my country—moral values trampled down by force. . . . I can foresee Germany's defeat and collapse when the *Untermenschen* from prison camps and workers' camps will rise up and take revenge for all that the Germans have done to them. . . . I know there will be varying verdicts on our struggle. We have been playing for big stakes. A man who has once heard the call of freedom must needs ever follow it, come what may. If your Führer imagines I could serve as a tool for his plans of conquest, he is wrong. I shall go back to a prison camp, back to my countrymen. . . ."

I tried to tell him this was not necessarily the end of all things, and repeated Gehlen's parting words to me. . . . Malyshkin turned the conversation to the Decembrists, and quoted the words of one of them under sentence of death: "Our guilt lies only in our demand for freedom." . . . I cannot describe the aura of gloom hanging over our little circle. In the end we agreed to . . . think it all over in quiet. . . . [Zykov said:] "If you let go the reins, shady opportunists will take over. And that would be the end of the Russian fight for freedom." . . . Trukhin said: "Hitler has shown his true face. The Russian Liberation Movement must now stand on its own, together with the few German friends who remain by our side. The movement lives, though it may not come to full fruition until after we are gone."*

It is hard to say how accurately Strik-Strikfeldt's later recollections preserve the actual events and Vlasov's psychological state during those June days of 1943. In any case, it partially explains why Vlasov did not follow his first emotional reaction, throwing the whole thing up and returning to a prison camp. No doubt the truth for Vlasov, for his Russian and his German followers, and for Strik-Strikfeldt himself, lay somewhere between ideals and the primitive human instinct for self-preservation. The human being goes on hoping because life without hope is impossible. All of them, including Vlasov and Strik-Strikfeldt, within a few days began patching together their naïve hopes and justifications. They were incapable of abandoning their dreams; and in this sense Vlasov's statement that it is impossible to ignore the call of freedom struck to the heart of the matter, in the midst of all their relative and daily threatened real freedoms.

Hope naturally alternated with resignation; the reaction to an encouraging rumor would be a plunge into deepest pessimism. On the side of the Russians, the effort to understand gave way to hatred of the Germans, assumed indifference to an avidity for news, feverish conversations, and attempts to forget.

Malyshkin took refuge in music and poetry. Vlasov resorted more and more often to vodka, and to the card game called *Préférence*. Or he found forgetfulness in the arms of women who in mysterious ways flocked to him at the Kiebitzweg house—German women as well as Russians. He used them, then thrust them aside, apparently not caring whether the woman of the moment was an *Ostarbeiterin* or a blonde—or one rather

* Strik-Strikfeldt, *op. cit.,* pp. 147ff.

plump, and none too bright German named Ilse whom he had picked up on some half-forbidden, half-permitted drive. She had fallen in love with the giant Russian and would sit about the house for days on end, although Vlasov sometimes mocked: "Look at her, Catherine the Great!" His sarcasm grew more and more biting. During a dinner with several German officers whom Strik-Strikfeldt had brought with him, the Russian cook who waited on table once let the door slam loudly behind her. "I beg your pardon, gentlemen," Vlasov blurted out in his broken German. *"Untermensch!"*

The monotony and hopelessness of the waiting affected everyone's nerves. Strik-Strikfeldt saw he had to do something to interrupt the dreary succession of hope, disappointment, resignation, and self-laceration, or else his own dream would be irrevocably shattered. He made an effort to restore Vlasov's vitality and faith in himself by introducing him to new people, by conversations, and by travel. In this effort he was assisted by Lieutenant Michel of Hellmich's staff. Among Michel's acquaintances was Günter Kaufmann, the editor in chief of the leading Hitler Youth magazine, *Wille und Macht*. Kaufmann was a close friend of Baldur von Schirach, who had been the first leader of the Hitler Youth movement, and was now gauleiter of Vienna. Michel arranged a meeting between Kaufmann and Strik-Strikfeldt.

Several Hitler Youth leaders, who while serving as reserve officers on the eastern front had become aware of the gulf between official policy, their own ideological persuasion, and reality, had tried as early as 1942 to preach "reason" after their own fashion. They had established a "village of German-Russian friendship" behind the northern front, in the territory of the Sixteenth Army, and brought together Russian civilians, German soldiers, Russian mayors, and auxiliaries for a few weeks of joint rest and recuperation. In this village Kaufmann, too, had undergone a sudden conversion, at least in regard to the party's colonialist plans in the East.

When, in 1943, Michel showed Kaufmann Vlasov's leaflets and told him that these were supposed to be used for propaganda only on the Russian side of the front, Kaufmann decided to publish Vlasov's statements in *Wille und Macht,* and to bring out a special issue attacking the official doctrines. As his assistant in the preparation of this issue, he obtained the services of the writer Edwin Erich Dwinger.

Dwinger was well known; his books *Armee hinter Stacheldraht* and *Zwischen Weiss und Rot,* in which he described his experiences as a prisoner of war in Russia during the First World War and the Russian

148

Revolution, had been world-wide successes. He had written many other books whose antibolshevistic and nationalistic viewpoint fitted well into the broad spectrum of National Socialism. His enemies maintained that success and vanity had gone to his head and led him to accept a good many seamy honors, including a rank in the SS. For him, undoubtedly, the decisive factor was that the antibolshevistic spirit that pervaded his work was also one of the principal points in the Nazi program. Like so many others, he fastened on the one aspect of the program that corresponded to his prejudices, ignoring the remaining ones.

In 1941 Heinrich Himmler had considered making Dwinger his consultant on Eastern questions. In the course of their initial conversations, however, he had realized that there was an enormous difference between his ideas of a Germanic colonization of Russia and Dwinger's antibolshevist obsession. Dwinger, rather like Strik-Strikfeldt, was an "admirer of the Russian soul" who dreamed of a Russia without bolshevism. Apparently he had dreams of a Russo-German alliance which would put an end to the Bolshevik era. These ideas, romantic rather than thought out, took no account of the realities. At any rate, the destruction of Russia, and the transformation of large parts of the country into German colonial territory, were not part of his program.

Dwinger had entered Russia with a tank division as a war correspondent. What he encountered there had prompted him to send letters and memoranda to Himmler, their thesis similar to that of the Germans who were promoting Vlasov—calling for a radical change in policy. Dwinger's more decorative than active membership in the SS shielded him against any punitive action, but he was pulled out of the war zone and sent back to "Hedwigshof" in the Allgäu, the estate he had bought with the proceeds from his books, and told to limit himself to "creative" writing.

Now Dwinger contributed an essay to Kaufmann's special issue, which came out in June 1943. It was entitled "The Russian People—The Way to Overcome Bolshevism." In it he stated: "All the sacrifice of our soldiers' lives will some day turn out to be pointless if . . . ill-digested ideas without any deeper understanding are allowed to wreck everything in the rear areas. Only men who can serve as models can be used successfully in those areas. At any rate, crude insistence on the viewpoint of a lord and master is always wrong. . . ."

Kaufmann had no doubt that Dwinger's essay and the publication of Vlasov's proclamation would create a sensation and provoke counteraction. He had prepared himself accordingly by obtaining assurances of protection from Baldur von Schirach.

As a romantic intellectual who had a higher regard for books than for realities, Schirach was somewhat of an alien among the gauleiters. In a spirit of youthful idealism, he had been the spokesman for the fascist idea of national rebirth, and with his particular kind of unworldliness had recognized too late that he was ushering the young men of Germany into a training course for militaristic conquest. At the outbreak of the war he had withdrawn from leadership of the youth, and had fallen prey to grave inner conflicts with regard to Hitler, whom he had hitherto worshipped. He lacked strength and opportunity to go beyond ineffective letters and take the course of genuine opposition; but when Kaufmann was planning his special issue, Schirach pledged his support.

When Himmler and Rosenberg heard about the special issue, it was already too late to stop its publication. They did succeed in having Goebbels send out orders to all German dailies forbidding any reprinting of articles from *Wille und Macht*. But the issue existed, and Strik-Strikfeldt used it to build up Vlasov's morale.

Three weeks later, a small squad of guards from the Grossdeutschland Division, which was at von Schirach's disposal, welcomed to Vienna an unusually tall man in a brown tunic. He was accompanied by Strik-Strikfeldt and Dwinger.

Propaganda Minister Goebbels' action against *Wille und Macht* had provoked Schirach to forsake his usual reticence and to object, at least rhetorically, against the policies being pursued in the East. Schirach informed Kaufmann: "I don't think I can open the way for a Russian such as Vlasov to see the Führer. But I can show Vlasov that not all of our leaders approve the actions in Russia."

Dwinger surprised Strik-Strikfeldt with the news that Schirach was prepared to receive Vlasov on an official visit to Vienna. This was to be the first sizable tour that Vlasov was undertaking in Germany. His thirst for knowledge was boundless. He was interested in everything—in the way this or that piece of agricultural machinery worked, in every town and every area, in the position and importance of the gauleiter of Vienna. Time and again he raised the question of how was it possible for a high but still subordinate state functionary to receive him if Hitler personally would have nothing to do with him. To Vlasov this was once more a sign of the relative freedom in Germany, which from the beginning had astonished and tempted him. But he could not entirely forget what things were like back home, with the result that he suspected Schirach might,

150

after all, be acting on orders from the chief of state, if only to test him, Vlasov.

Schirach gave a dinner for him. Vlasov stayed in the Hotel Bristol as a guest of honor. Schirach's car was at his disposal, so that he could be shown the beauties of Vienna and its most modern factories. Vlasov went on a veritable voyage of discovery. He visited St. Stephan's Cathedral, the opera, a horse race, and the Spanish Riding School. A small group of Viennese had assembled there to greet the mysterious stranger. Colonel Podhajsky, the commander of the school, displayed his Lippizaner stallions in the *haute école*. Afterward, Podhajsky invited Vlasov to lunch. Dwinger had prepared him, and Podhajsky expressed a great deal of cordiality in his welcoming words.

After Vlasov had drunk a few glasses, he stood up to reply to Podhajsky. This was going to be his first impromptu speech to an official German group.

"I wish to thank you," Vlasov said. "I am an infantryman and, if you will, a simple son of Russian peasants. I know nothing about horses and the *haute école*. It would be hypocritical of me if I were to praise your achievements; and what would my praise mean to you? But it is always possible to express gratitude. What I saw today moved me very deeply." His words up to this point seemed to be more or less conventional. But he did not miss his opportunity. He continued: "If the Germans would treat the Russian people and their prisoners of war with as much affection as you, gentlemen, bestow on your horses, you would not have a Russian problem at all, and this wretched war would be over and done with."

There was an embarrassed silence. Strik-Strikfeldt had some reason to fear that this remark would lead to a renewed uproar such as Vlasov's toast in Army Group North had stirred. But Vlasov merely replied to his strictures: "So what? Isn't it the truth? What more can happen to me?"

In fact, Schirach seemed not to be greatly upset by the speech, for on the following day he received Vlasov and his companions at the Ballhausplatz. It was apparent from Vlasov's expression that he was feeling a certain amount of hope for the first time in a long while, more hope than distrust and doubt. At the end of the leave-taking ceremonies, Schirach had a photograph taken of himself and Vlasov together. Then Schirach took Strik-Strikfeldt aside and said: "I'll do my best to see that this matter is straightened out and handled properly from now on. I'll report to the Führer. . . ."

Strik-Strikfeldt had the impression that Schirach really would act. He recalled having heard that Schirach was regarded as Hitler's crown prince; but Strik-Strikfeldt knew nothing about the recent clouding of the relationship or about Schirach's lack of consistency in political thinking.

When Dwinger invited Vlasov to pay a visit to him at "Hedwigshof," he traveled with the Russian to Allgäu and was delighted with the way his companion responded to the landscape, the villages and farms. Vlasov especially marveled over the latter; how could it be, he wondered, that in the midst of war the farms contained more "riches" than was conceivable in a Russian village. Russian prisoners of war who were working in this area provided a memorable experience for Vlasov; the prisoners reported that they were being treated well: "Now we have our own people in Berlin to look after us—Vlasov and the others." Then they recognized him, and Vlasov had one of his happiest and most relaxed hours in a long time.

But soon after their return to Berlin the memories faded; the visit to Schirach seemed to have produced no lasting result. All that happened was that a rumor reached the house on Kiebitzweg, to the effect that Schirach had kept his word and written to Hitler, but had received no reply.

Strik-Strikfeldt would have preferred to take Vlasov on more tours of Germany and, if possible, also of France. But General Wedel shirked the responsibility. He was afraid that some chance report by a Gestapo office might bring on a sudden storm that would overwhelm Vlasov, Strik-Strikfeldt, and all their friends for good and all. In lieu of travel, therefore, Strik-Strikfeldt looked for ways to introduce Vlasov to those in Berlin whom he hoped might have some influence on Hitler or Himmler. He seized every helping hand that was offered, including that of a woman named Melitta Wiedemann.

She was in her mid-thirties, with a sturdy little figure, a broad but pretty face, blond hair, lively blue eyes. At one time she had been a secretary on the Nazi newspaper *Der Angriff;* eventually she had moved up to become editor of the anti-Comintern magazine *Aktion.* She had already reached the point of thinking along the lines of a pro-Russian policy in the East. Immediately after the appearance of Vlasov she had tried to get in touch with him, and finally managed to meet him through Dürksen. She offered to use her ties with leading Nazis in Vlasov's behalf.

Melitta Wiedemann arranged to have Vlasov meet the governor of Galicia, SS Gruppenführer Dr. Otto Wächter, who was well regarded by everyone in the "pro-Russian" group because of his relatively moderate policy in Galicia. As another guest for the evening she invited SS Ober-gruppenführer Maximilian von Herff, head of the SS Personnel Office. He had been Field Marshal Rommel's chief of staff, and had moved over to the SS from the army. The little affair took place in the apartment of Melitta Wiedemann's parents, and Melitta pulled all the stops of the wide Russian emotional range. She offered Russian hospitality, with zakuska and vodka. After the evening with Dr. Wächter, a pleasant-mannered Austrian, Vlasov commented: "So that man is part of the SS, too." The fact that Himmler's organization was only seemingly monolithic had presented Vlasov with a new riddle, but also led him to overestimate differences of nuance only.

Actually, this meeting produced no results. Strik-Strikfeldt still knew nothing about the power relationships inside the SS. He did not know that Wächter was regarded as "too soft" and Herff as an outsider whom the more "orthodox" SS people hated. When an opportunity came to intro-duce Vlasov to Robert Ley, Nazi Party Organization Leader and chief of the Labor Front, Strik-Strikfeldt seized on the idea. An old schoolmate of his, Paul Walter, served as interpreter. But the encounter proved a ghastly fiasco. Ley gave short shrift to Vlasov's demands for better treatment of the *Ostarbeiter*. Such matters were out of his sphere; they were the business of Rosenberg, Koch, and Sauckel. "That's what the Führer has appointed them for. And the Führer is a genius. Knows what he wants. . . . Anyhow, we have the Ukraine, and let Stalin try and take it back from us." He refused to give any credence to Vlasov's explanation for his turning against Stalin. Slightly drunk, he babbled, "If, General, you had just told me you hated Jews and were fighting Stalin because of the Jews all round him, I would have understood."

Vlasov stalked out of the building. "Joseph Visarianovich [Stalin] can wish for no better allies," he said.*

In hot June, a surprise visitor arrived at the house on Kiebitzweg: an emissary from the colony of old Russian émigrés in Paris, whose numbers ran into the thousands. Yury Sergeyevich Sherebkov, a descendant of the tsar's former adjutant-general, came in person to invite Vlasov to speak at a public meeting of the Russians in Paris. He had been one of the first émigrés in France to take up the cause of Vlasov and his Liberation Army, despite the bitter opposition of many loyal tsarists. Strik-Strikfeldt

* Strik-Strikfeldt, *op. cit.,* pp. 163f.

regarded the invitation as a new opportunity to bring Vlasov out of the "prison" of Kiebitzweg. He dashed to Viktoriastrasse and pleaded with Martin and Grote to fix things so that Vlasov could go to Paris. By now Strik-Strikfeldt had become so committed to his protegé's cause that Vlasov himself called him "my starets" (my saint). In his enthusiasm, Strik-Strikfeldt failed to see that Hitler and Himmler would regard such a trip as an outrageous provocation, so that if it were carried off it might well seal the fate of Vlasov.

Martin finally decided that quiet Malyshkin would go; but that he should proceed with restraint and caution. On July 24, 1943, Malyshkin arrived in Paris. That evening he spoke in the Salle Wagram to some 6000 Russians, with newspaper correspondents from neutral countries on hand. He was given several ovations lasting for minutes. After all, he was the first former Soviet general to appear in France and seek to establish a link between the old émigrés and their native land. He spoke in his prudent, sensible manner, but ultimately a statement of principle was inescapable, and he made it: "We are for a *zelostnaya rossya*—a united Russia." His audience cheered and wept.

No more than twenty-four hours passed before Grote received an inquiry from the State Security Office (Reichssicherheitshauptamt) asking whether it was true that in Paris Malyshkin had spoken of the resurrection of a united Russian republic. The Viktoriastrasse staff telephoned Vlasov's German adjutant, Fröhlich, who hastened to the railroad station to meet Malyshkin and take him to the Viktoriastrasse at once. They took Bus Number 12, and on the way, in the deserted upper floor of the bus, Fröhlich told Malyshkin what had happened. He implored him to say whether or not he had used that phrase about a united Russia. Would it be possible to contend that the Gestapo was misinformed?

Malyshkin merely answered, "Did your Beria hear it himself?"

"No," Fröhlich said, "some German agent took down the phrase."

"So, what do you think?" Malyshkin said. "Maybe he took it down wrong, eh?"

Then he fell silent and said nothing more until they arrived at the Viktoriastrasse headquarters. But Fröhlich knew Malyshkin well enough to realize that these words were a secret avowal. And Malyshkin answered Strik-Strikfeldt's and Martin's questions in the same way. At last he said slyly: "Let us give them the shorthand record of the speech."

"Do you have . . ."

"No," Malyshkin replied, even more sly. "But tomorrow . . ."

Frölich brought the shorthand record over next day. He had no doubt that it had been produced in the course of the night.

The deception succeeded. But the incident was a warning.

Among the men whom Strik-Strikfeldt invited to the Kiebitzweg house in order to cultivate Vlasov's ties with "good Germans," and keep the flames of hope alive, was Theodor Krause, one of Strik-Strikfeldt's closest friends among Baltic Germans. During those months in which he was conducting endless conversations with the waiting Russian, Strik-Strikfeldt wrote:

> Vlasov has come to us from the government founded upon a strict, dogmatic philosophical system, that of dialectical materialism. Vlasov, himself, has been so strictly trained in this philosophy that his thinking is inevitably influenced by it even though he has inwardly moved away from its doctrines. Vlasov came to us from this world of a dogmatic system as a seeker, a seeker for a more ethical, more human, more life-affirming system. He imagined that the Germans would have it because of their demonstrated military and organizational achievements. . . .
>
> Instead, he has come up against the German governmental apparatus, founded on such murky conceptions as blood and soil, race, racial community—ideas which seem utterly meaningless to him. Moreover, these ideas have generated a stream of actions which cannot help appearing surpassingly idiotic to him. . . .
>
> Were it not for a small circle that at least in theory corresponds to this seeker's image of the future of Russia and Europe, he would find nothing in Germany but naked, undisguised colonialist brutality directed by political and cultural illiterates. Theirs is the only real power and theirs is the responsibility for all the sins, betrayals, and destruction visited upon the masses in the East.
>
> As a realistic thinker and seeker, Vlasov could only be shocked by the realities of power politics, the bitter experiences and discoveries to which he is constantly exposed. . . .
>
> Influenced by several Russians who have long despaired of Germany, Vlasov has begun to look beyond Germany to the other great nations of the West, America and England. He is trying to arrive at some conception of these countries.

Alexander Stepanovich Kazantsev continued, whenever his work in Viktoriastrasse permitted, to go out to Dabendorf to see Trukhin or Zykov.

One early autumn day Baidalakov and Kasantsev met at noon at an out-of-the-way bench in the Berlin Tiergarten for a sensitive conversation.

"The matter is this," Baidalakov said. "For the first time we have an opportunity to build a bridge to the West. An acquaintance of ours, a Swiss, will shortly be arriving in Berlin. He has connections with Americans who are active in Switzerland. I'd like to know whether you are in a position to talk with Andrei Andreyevich about this matter. We should like to ask him whether we may attempt in his name to establish ties with the British and Americans and to make arrangements for the future struggle."

"I have already cautiously broached the subject with him," Kazantsev said. "You know that. And I notice he has begun to read up on England and America. I'll talk to him again."

"Then do so today," Baidalakov said. "It would strengthen our hand if we could say that we already have the leader for the coming struggle, namely Andrei Andreyevich. We are risking our necks in any case. But we can only risk Andrei Andreyevich's if he is ready to go along on this. This Swiss is reliable."

That evening Kazantsev went out to Dahlem. What follows we know from testimonies of Kazantsev, Fröhlich, and others.

Vlasov was sitting over vodka playing *Préférence* with Malyshkin and Konstantin Kromiadi, the first commander of the former Russian Battalion f.s.d. ("for special duty") in Ossintorf. In the dim light Kazantsev could see the mounds of papers and books heaped on Vlasov's desk— Russian translations of German, American, and British writings and articles which the secretariat was producing for him. He was apparently reading the translation of an American book on Churchill. Kazantsev observed this with satisfaction. Strik-Strikfeldt and the other Germans were not providing all this reading matter. Some of the books from "the still more western West" had come from "somewhere" on Kazantsev's orders, so that Vlasov might have a chance to learn and understand what was happening outside Germany. By such means Kazantsev hoped to thaw Vlasov's frozen will to action.

"There you are," Vlasov said. "Sit here, Alexander Stepanovich. . . ." He waved his hand. "Marya, bring another glass."

Kazantsev looked around. He had heard the names of a good many women out here, and seen quite a few, but the name "Marya" was new.

She came from the cellar, a Russian, perhaps in her late twenties, possessing some charm but distinctly unkempt.

"This is Marya Ignatievna Voronova," Vlasov said, going on with his game, "my faithful cook, who was with me on the Volkhov to the last. She was separated from me when the Germans caught up. I always kept saying, 'Find me Marya and then our kitchen will have something to offer guests.' And what do you think? Sergei found her. Up in Riga, and he brought her here. And now she's cooking for us and helping us wait. . . ."

The woman reached over Kazantsev's shoulder and placed the glass in front of him. "Yes, wait," she said crossly, "it's always waiting. For what?" Vlasov waved her away. "Back to the kitchen," he said. "This is not your concern."

When the door slammed behind her, Vlasov gave Kazantsev one of his ambiguous looks. "You know what?" he said. "She ran away from the Germans. Joined the partisans. And she was given the assignment to poison me. She has confessed it all to me. But she can't bring herself to it." He shrugged. "She simply cannot. . . . She hates the Germans, but she thinks a lot of things are good, very good. That's how it is."

He drained his glass at one gulp.

Kazantsev looked in the direction of the papers and books. "Andrei Andreyevich," he said, "you're reading about Churchill. Do you know what England and America are like?"

"I'm not through with the Germans yet," Vlasov said. "I should be hating them more from week to week. Their leaders are stupid, conceited, a pack of unimaginative bourgeois. But they caught me twice. Once on the Volkhov. And again whenever I go out of this place and see the houses of ordinary people and the peasants. The peasants . . ."

He fell silent and gazed thoughtfully at the wall.

"Have you thought about the Americans?" Kazantsev asked. "There the agricultural, industrial, and scientific development is even more advanced than among the Germans. And there is generosity and all the things we still don't have."

"Are you starting that again?" Vlasov said. "I've read about the English and your Churchill. He's said to be the greatest antibolshevist in the West. But what does he know? He knows even less about our country and about Stalin than Hitler does. And Roosevelt—he doesn't even know what bolshevism is."

"It's lovely outside," Kazantsev said. "Andrei Andreyevich, you shouldn't be sitting here. You should be out enjoying the evening."

Malyshkin swept the cards aside. "Alexander Stepanovich is right."

Vlasov filled his glass once more while Malyshkin stood up, then left the room. Vlasov drank and sat for a while in silence.

"There's something you want to tell me, I suppose," he said finally.

Kazantsev nodded. "Yes, from our 'senior.' "

They left the dim room and walked through the vestibule, where one of the men from the secretariat was keeping guard. Then they began walking back and forth along the narrow garden paths. Kazantsev explained why he had come. Vlasov finally answered: "I thank your 'senior' for the proposal. But I must reject it. You will ask me why. . . ."

It is possible that Kazantsev's memory expanded Vlasov's answer or complemented it from hindsight, but since Vlasov reacted in similar fashion to Fröhlich and Krause, the substance of his answer is not in doubt.

Vlasov continued: "I don't know whether it is possible at all to conduct negotiations. But let us assume that you actually could make contact with the British or the Americans. What have we got to offer them? And what would they ask of us? We might tell them that in Germany and in the German-occupied areas there are so and so many Russian antibolshevists who are waiting for permission to fight for a new homeland. No more. And what does that amount to? You see, I've been reading. And I've been listening to what goes on in the outside world.
. . . Wilfried Karlovich and the others pretend not to notice. And by now I hear more than the Germans are permitted to hear. And what have I found out about the British and Americans? They adore Stalin. They eat up everything Stalin's clever men tell them. They believe our country is changing into what they call democracy, or maybe even back to tsarism because the Little Father in Moscow is digging out the old uniforms and the old national heroes, giving the priests a little leeway, and proclaiming a Great Patriotic War. . . . Alexander Stepanovich, do you think it ever even occurs to them that one day Stalin might be their enemy and that therefore it might be a good idea to form an alliance with us today? I don't believe it. For nine whole months Little Father in Moscow kept the lid on any mention of my name. And just a few weeks ago, Little Father finally took a position and told everybody at home that I'm a traitor by nature and was often a traitor before, but they foolishly forgave me. Before in China, with Tukhachevsky . . . What rubbish it all is. But your people in the West eat it up. For your Churchill and the rest of them we're nothing but traitors, bought by the Germans."

"Don't you think they only mean the Caucasians and the Turkestanis and all those who really have become German mercenaries?"

"You think too much in terms of theory," Vlasov retorted. "Real life is different. How many of them wanted to become mercenaries and traitors? They believed in the Germans—just like me. And then it all took a different turn. But what does it matter whether people just seem to be traitors or really are? How does that change your actions? It doesn't, not a bit. It only makes everything more hopeless than it already is. The British and Americans will put you down as traitors also, and either not listen to you or arrest you."

"Andrei Andreyevich," Kazantsev said urgently, "all that will be changing. They'll realize who and what their allies are just as soon as the Red Army advances as far as Central Europe and, for instance, takes all of Poland. After all, it was for the freedom of Poland that the British and the Americans entered the war. They need our country to defeat Germany. And that is why they're putting up with a bad alliance, just the way you're putting up with a bad alliance with Hitler. In reality Roosevelt and Churchill know that this friendship is only an expedient."

Vlasov shook his head. "What about Yugoslavia?" he asked. "Your British wanted to fight for Yugoslavia's freedom, didn't they? But they betrayed General Michailovich because he was more against communism than against the Germans. They supported Tito and are supporting him right now, although he will make Yugoslavia communistic. Don't you see what that means? You have a theory, but it isn't a good one today. Today your British and Americans have only a single goal: to destroy Hitler and Germany. And they would be interested in us only if we could help them with that. Can we? We would be doomed even before we started. No, Alexander Stepanovich, you people certainly are more learned than I. But sometimes you think like the scholar in his study. You imagine the Bolsheviks and the Germans will tear each other to pieces, and then we'll come along and the British and Americans will help us. But even if they did, once the Germans are beaten—what would we have to offer unless our German friends in the meantime had managed to give us our Russian army? You hate the Germans, and you're right; we have reason to hate them for all they have done to our country, for all the things I didn't know about when I came to the Germans. You think you'll find more friends in London or in America. I don't think so. And even if you do, they're too far away to give us anything tangible. What we need, what everything else depends on, is a government and an army. And right now, nobody can give us either except the Germans. There is no other way, Alexander Stepanovich."

"But what happens when the army exists?" Kazantsev asked. "When it is ready . . ."

"First we have to have it. That is what I am waiting for. What we are all waiting for. Maybe we are waiting in vain, and maybe some day we will really become deceived and deceivers. But at least we'll have made a try. By now I understand what the Germans are all about. I was looking for an idea. At least socialism is an idea; nationalism is just the pursuit of power. These Germans have organization, technology, and order, so I thought there had to be a higher principle somewhere. But there isn't; there are nothing but individuals and groups who have power or don't. That's our opportunity, because those who have power will lose it out of stupidity. Should I hate Hitler? I can only despise him because he's stupid. And so are the others. But they will turn to us when they lose their stupid arrogance and are up against the wall. Then they'll give us the government and the army we want."

"But when will that be?"

"I've told you: when they're up against the wall. And then you and I can talk over this matter once more. Maybe . . . You know, it's not a good idea to change sides too often or too fast."

Vlasov began walking slowly toward the house.

"Maybe you want to laugh," he said. "Maybe you think, Vlasov is a peasant, a stubborn donkey. But I've changed sides once. It costs a lot. . . ."

A new blow against Vlasov's hopes was already in the making. After many delays, Hitler had finally ordered troop movements aimed at creating a gigantic pocket at Kursk. By September 14, 1943, it became clear that this strategy was hopeless. The night military conference in the Wolfsschanze, the underground Führer's Headquarters near Rastenburg, East Prussia, was held under the impact of the bad news. Hitler was deathly pale. His entourage was expecting one of his outbursts of despairing rage.

In this tense atmosphere, Himmler undertook to deflect attention from the real cause of the failed offensive, the deterioration of the German striking force. He may well have been trying to deceive himself also, and to give vent to his hatred for the Slavs.

"My Führer," he said, "I have just learned that the Russian successes against the southern army of Army Group Center are due to treachery by Russian volunteers who were committed there contrary to the ban on their use at the front. I was always against putting Russians into German uniforms and giving them weapons. Here you have the consequences of the madness of certain army circles."

Hitler, bent over the map table, straightened up abruptly. His face changed from chalky pallor to a faint purple.

"Keitel," he called out, "do you know anything about this?" And then, before the startled field marshal could think of what to reply: "I suppose you cannot deny that it's true. This wouldn't be the first time I've received better, faster, and more reliable information from outside the Wehrmacht."

Keitel hastened to answer the charge. "My Führer, it is true that the commander of one of the armies down south has reported that the volunteer formations employed in his sector proved unreliable. But there is no evidence that this has any connection with the Russian penetrations of the front. . . ."

Hitler had already found what he was probably subconsciously seeking: the scapegoats. He did not allow Keitel to continue.

"I suppose the commander is one of those who was ready to organize an entire Russian army," he said. "So now he doesn't want to admit the kind of criminal idiocy he was advocating. The report of their unreliability at this perilous hour is enough for me. Now at last we're finding out who is for us and who is against us. I've had enough. I've always been too lenient. . . ." Suddenly his voice rose to a shout: "Now this boil is going to be lanced!"

He began pacing the underground room with long strides, hands behind his back. "Keitel, you make this clear to the members of the General Staff. We're going to make an example. I hereby order you to have all Russian formations dissolved at once. As a first installment, 80,000 men. They are to be immediately disarmed, and the whole crew sent to the French mines to grub coal. . . . I don't need any Russian traitors stabbing us in the back. I need miners. Put the lazy bastards to work. This comes just at the right moment. It's like a sign from Providence."

Keitel said: "My Führer, I must call your attention to the fact that the army will need sizable forces to carry out this disarmament."

"Magnificent! Magnificent!" Hitler jeered. "Have those officers on the General Staff succeeded in creating a power so strong that we can no longer disarm it? The Army General Staff had better find the forces wherever it can. Herr Himmler will lend his aid. In forty-eight hours I shall expect a report that my order has been carried out. I hope I have made myself clear. I warned them often enough. Now let the generals who cooked up this mess see what they can do about it. Tell that to Zeitzler. I repeat, I want to hear within forty-eight hours that this order has been carried out. Otherwise I shall instruct Himmler to undertake this police action, and then it will go fast. . . ."

Early on the morning of September 15 Brigadier General Hellmich was routed out of bed and summoned to Mauerwald. Chief of Staff Zeitzler informed him of Hitler's order. "I've had enough trouble because of your damned volunteers. I'm sick of the whole business. Within six hours you'll bring me a set of instructions for the front-line troops on how to carry out the disarmament."

"It can't be done," Hellmich objected.

Zeitzler shook his head. "It's the Führer's order. There is no doubt that the volunteer troops on the southern wing of Army Group Center have failed. They deserted. They caused gaps in the front. The Führer's command is going to be carried out. I tell you once more. I am not going to be bawled out repeatedly because of these Russians."

"But the volunteers couldn't have cracked that way," Hellmich insisted. "I am kept constantly up to date on the volunteer formations' degree of reliability. As far as I've heard, unreliability has nowhere amounted to more than 1.5 percent—including the southern wing of Army Group Center. I should like to know who has spread reports to the contrary."

"The Führer has been informed directly. The commander in chief of the Army has so reported. Besides, that is no longer to the point."

"I beg your pardon," Hellmich said. "Even if the reports were accurate, the people at the Führer's Headquarters do not seem to be aware of what disarming means and what consequences it will have."

"I have to obey the Führer's order. If I don't carry it out, Himmler will. That might be a good deal more unpleasant. I must ask you to draw up instructions for implementation of the order within the deadline I've set and let me have it."

When Hellmich arrived back in Lötzen, he found Major Röpke in Herre's place. Herre was not expected back until about noon.

"Herr General," Röpke said, "if this order is carried out, it means the end of all our work. How are we to disarm 80,000 men? Does anybody up there imagine that the volunteers will take it tamely? It will mean demoralization and revolts; whole battalions will go over to the partisans."

"I told them all that long ago," Hellmich replied.

"I'm convinced that the information the Führer has received is either false or exaggerated. I suggest giving the counterintelligence officer an assignment to determine the actual situation in all the army groups. In any case, drawing up such instructions within six hours is quite impossible. The chief of staff must realize that."

"I doubt it."

"Sir . . ." Röpke fought to break through Hellmich's phlegmatic resignation. "We must ask for more time. Everything depends on it. At least have the Abwehr officer consult by phone with the army groups and armies."

"All right," Hellmich said. "Try it."

When Herre returned toward noon, the atmosphere in Hellmich's headquarters was turbulent. For the past two hours, a series of telephone talks had been held with the staffs of the army groups and their armies. Uniformly, no signs of diminishing reliability among the Eastern volunteers were reported. One after another, the corps of Army Group South had nothing alarming to report. On the contrary, several of the Russian units had proved particularly staunch under trying conditions. Army Group Center was still to be heard from.

Communications were not exactly smooth and swift. Herre and Röpke kept after the communications officers, conscious that they were in a race with time. In the meantime, Hellmich had departed for Mauerwald to plead for an extension in time before producing the plans. He had not yet returned.

At last the intelligence officer of Army Group Center answered the telephone. He was somewhat surprised at all the agitation in Lötzen. Didn't they have anything else to worry about back there in the rear echelon? His Eastern troops? Nothing unusual to report. Unexpectedly good, as a matter of fact. "But what about those reports the Führer has referred to?" Herre asked.

Reports? They might have something to do with a Cossack unit on the army group's southern wing, which had deserted; also some men in a construction battalion. A few German supervising personnel had been killed. But both these Eastern formations had been given inadequate equipment and had faced insuperable tasks. As far as the Ic could judge, these incidents must have been reported right after they happened in some alarmist communique which may have found its way into SS channels. Certainly, there could be no question of general unreliability. Of course, the hardships of defeats and retreats were tremendous, and nobody could predict how the situation would develop. But at the moment, there was certainly no reason for the slightest concern.

In spite of this reassurance, Herre insisted that every individual army in the army group be questioned. This process again took time. But the reports were all alike: hard defensive battles, withdrawals, large numbers of soldiers reported missing among the Germans as well as the Russians, but no indication of defection. Finally the report from the affected army itself arrived. But even its Ic judged the situation calmly. He declared that his commander had already reassessed the incidents and regretted his hasty step. As he put it: "Our old man got ants in his pants again. On the other hand, there's no saying how the units will react if the only way we move is backwards, the way we've been doing. But to draw conclusions now is downright silly."

By the time Lieutenant Schareck, the Abwehr officer, hung up for the last time, the six hours were nearly up. It was hopeless to try to draw up the requisite papers in time. And Hellmich was not back yet.

It was another hour before Hellmich arrived. He brought the welcome news that he had secured a postponement of twenty-four hours. He had paid a call on Gehlen. Everywhere, he said, the view prevailed that they must play for time until Hitler's rage over the defeats had subsided. All reports suggested that disarming the volunteers was bound to have catastrophic effects upon the millions of Eastern workers in Germany—to such an extent that the security forces of the home front probably would be unable to handle the crisis.

Next morning more phone calls were put through to the army groups and armies. The situation remained unchanged.

Toward noon Herre brought Hellmich the final results of his survey. The general glared at him gloomily and recommended that Herre himself should try his luck with the General Staff.

When Herre left for Mauerwald, he brought with him proofs that a total of 1,300 volunteers and auxiliaries had defected. This amounted to no more than 1.5 percent of the total strength of the volunteers and auxiliaries.

Zeitzler's waiting room was jammed as always. When the small group of officers who had been admitted just before Herre filed back through the waiting room, Herre overheard the rather dashing phrase: "What a mood he's in, old Ball of Lightning."

Herre, as he himself described the scene, strode swiftly across the office and presented himself at the big desk where the chief of staff sat, his head bowed over papers. "Well," Zeitzler said without looking up: "Grubbing coal; that's the subject for discussion. Sit down, but make it short."

The bright lamps over the desk radiated so much heat that Herre's forehead became beaded with sweat.

"The Führer has calmed down somewhat by now," Zeitzler growled. "Probably it won't be necessary to break up all your—formations. But the Führer wants at least 50,000 of your Russkies for the mines. And that's that."

"General," Herre said, "anything like that would be a disaster."

Zeitzler frowned. "I thought you'd be giving me that line. On what do you base such a judgment?"

"The volunteers have a sense of military honor just as our own soldiers have. Taking away their weapons would be a dishonor to them, and being sent to the mines a double dishonor. Perhaps the idea is to deliver a fatal blow to the entire volunteer movement; but its effect on the entire German armaments industry should not be overlooked. News of a large-scale action like that will spread like wildfire among the millions of Eastern workers. What happens if the six million *Ostarbeiter* start throwing sand into German machines?"

Zeitzler looked up angrily: "Oh, you're exaggerating."

Herre refused to give way. "Sir, I am not exaggerating. Experience tells me that that is exactly what will happen. General Hellmich is supposed to advise the Army chief of staff on all matters concerning the volunteers. Conscious of this responsibility, in the name of my general, I must urgently warn against execution of the measures proposed by the Führer."

"It's not a question of proposing measures—the Führer has given an order."

It seemed to Herre that his protest was going to be in vain. But at this point Zeitzler began to waver. "We must be responsive to the Führer to the utmost limit of what is possible. Where does this limit lie?"

"During the past twenty-four hours," Herre said, "we have been checking on the reliability of all the volunteeer formations. Here are the documents. Please look them over yourself, sir."

Zeitzler hesitated. Then he skimmed through the reports. "Why, this is impossible," he growled. "One and a half percent! These have been doctored!"

"No, sir," Herre said. "This is the truth, and the question remains who gave the false information to the Führer. The commander of the army in whose area the defections occurred now discounts the whole thing. Our percentage is based on the total number of Eastern volunteers. In other words, only a few small formations have failed. Such formations can be dissolved and disarmed without stirring up the masses of the volunteers."

"But how do you conceive of this?" Zeitzler's small eyes expressed his uneasiness at having already made some concessions. "How many thousand men will that amount to?"

"It might be as few as 300 who are at fault. 5000 at the most."

"Five thousand instead of the 50,000 or the 70,000 the Führer demands? Do you seriously think the Führer will put up with that?"

"The Führer will have to put up with it. The Führer must be made to realize, on the basis of this evidence, that there is no other way to handle the problem."

Zeitzler was obviously wavering between recognition of objective facts and his personal horror of controversy over matters outside his own immediate sphere. Finally he said: "We can't waste too much time on this. By tomorrow morning give us your list of formations which in your view can be disarmed and broken up without causing any fundamental damage. Inform my adjutant of your final figures on the coal grubbers I can place at the Führer's disposal. . . . That is all."

The decision came three days later. Hitler agreed to have the punitive action limited to the formations Hellmich and Herre had specified. But simultaneously an unofficial report came from the Führer's Headquarters that all Eastern troops were going to be withdrawn from the eastern front and shifted to the western theaters of war, to remove the danger of their "deserting to their Slavic comrades."

The same afternoon that Herre got wind of this, he called Major Rohrbeck of the Armed Forces Operations Staff and asked him to visit.

Rohrbeck arrived at eight o'clock that evening. The decision to transfer the Eastern troops to the West had arisen in the course of a conversation between Hitler and General Jodl, he said. It was the answer to a number of different problems. In the first place, there was Hitler's desire to be rid of the Eastern formations. In the second place, it had finally entered peoples' heads that the troops couldn't be disarmed without serious consequences. In the third place, there was the fact that the front-line troops in the western theaters, but also in the southeast, the south, and the north, had suffered great losses in strength; there were enormous gaps, and further shifts of troops from these theaters to the immediately menaced eastern front would be possible only if replacements could be brought in. Rumor had it that Keitel had finally come up with the idea which seemed to settle everything: removing all the Eastern troops from Russia and transferring them to western theaters, thereby filling existing gaps, and freeing other troops for commitment on the eastern front. Once the Russian troops had been shifted to the West, moreover, the formations would be so carved up and taken so firmly under German control that they "could no longer become dangerous."

"Is this authentic information?" Herre asked.

Rohrbeck nodded.

Herre asked himself why nobody had seen the fatal flaw in this new plan. Most of the volunteers were simply keeping in readiness for the time when their own goals would be recognized and they would be given an army and their own leaders. They had waited in vain for a long time. But at any rate they had been fighting on their own soil, for their own future. What would they be doing in France or Denmark, Italy and Norway? What sense could they possibly find in fighting against Englishmen and Americans?

"Don't you see," Herre said, "it would nullify, once and for all, any sensible plan. It would mean the final ruin of the Eastern formations."

"Colonel," Rohrbeck said, with the prudent deliberation that sat rather oddly on so young a man, "the eastern front is continuing to recede. All right, it has turned out that the reports on the failure of the volunteer formations were exaggerated. But if our retreats go on—and they will—don't you think that the strain on the Russian troops will prove to be too strong in the long run? Fresh reports are coming in about deserters, assassinated German cadres, conspiracies with partisans, and I'm afraid such cases will now begin increasing. Any day now, we're going to be ordered to dissolve the troops and send them to the mines. But shifting the troops to the West will, on the contrary, have the result that those formations will remain intact and won't be wiped out because of some new conflict with the Führer."

Herre replied: "What good is all that? We'll be saving the substance, but the content will be lost once and for all."

"Colonel, this is a case of choosing the lesser evil. Granted, transfer of those troops to the West will only save the substance. But in the East even this substance would be lost. Who knows how things will develop. If there are further setbacks, the Führer will be left with no choice; he'll have to come around. Then, if we still have some substance, we'll be in business."

Herre returned to Hellmich.

"What are we going to tell the men? What possible pretext can we give them for fighting in the West, without destroying their last illusions?"

Hellmich replied:

"The chief of staff wants to see me tomorrow morning. He will inform me of the Führer's new decision. Then we'll see . . ."

"The initial orders for transfer of the Eastern troops are already drawn up," Zeitzler said. "The Cossack division that has just been organized in Mielau will not be committed on the eastern front at all. It is going to be transported to Yugoslavia immediately. The Eastern Legions will be the first to be transferred to France. All the other volunteer formations will follow, step by step. Those that have been little affected by the fighting during the withdrawals are to be shifted directly. If recuperation and replacements are needed, they will be sent through the Mielau troop training camp. The organization of Commanders of the Eastern Troops will be dissolved."

Hellmich acknowledged receipt of this information.

"Well," Zeitzler said, "from now on the OKW itself will have to deal with your volunteers. If in exchange I receive troops from the West, it isn't a bad swap. But the arrangement may also be a godsend for your men, too. Apparently the Eastern troops cannot stand up to the hardships of planned withdrawals. You should be glad the Führer's decisions were taken before these reports reached us."

"If the volunteers go completely to pieces because of this, nobody ought to be surprised," Hellmich said.

Zeitzler made a gesture as if to wipe away the whole complex of problems.

"I can't do anything about it," he said. "I have other worries. Let me know what suggestions you have about how to arrange the transfers."

"And what are we to tell these volunteers to explain their sudden removal from the battle area where they enlisted to serve?"

Zeitzler countered: "They ought to be glad they're out of the mess. Perhaps you can put that across to them."

So began the transfer of an "army of 800,000"—split into a great many individual formations but still, on a higher plane, a psychologically coherent entity.

There was little time for Hellmich's staff to confer on the possibilities for "motivation propaganda." The only formula they could find was to inform the volunteers of a "temporary crisis" on the German eastern front; the troops were being shifted to quiet sectors in order to prepare for a decisive German counteroffensive on the eastern front in 1944. After the heavy fighting they had been in, the Eastern troops would have a chance for rest, recuperation, and reequipment, the ultimate aim being to prepare themselves to serve in the Liberation Army. All concerned knew that they would be handing out a lie; there was only one way to soothe their consciences—to whip up fresh hope in themselves that Hitler would change his mind. But they had barely arrived at their desperate propaganda story when new complications arose.

"General Jodl," Rohrbeck told Herre, "has just bethought himself of Vlasov. He thinks that Vlasov, who was set at liberty for propaganda purposes and has since been guarded like a raw egg, is at last in a position to prove whether he really has all that influence on the Russians he's supposed to have. So now Jodl wants Vlasov to write an open letter explaining to the formations that the transfer to the West is necessary and that it doesn't matter where they fight."

Herre hurried to Berlin to discuss the matter with Strik-Strikfeldt. He found the captain in a state approaching nervous collapse. Strik-Strikfeldt had just been to see Vlasov, and had found him in a roaring fury over the transfers, which were already taking place. The new action, Vlasov said, was a shameless admission that the Germans had never wanted the Russians for anything else but mercenaries. In impotent rage, he had threatened to brand this fresh betrayal for what it was. The Germans would find out, he said bitterly, that even without the help of a propaganda apparatus his statement would spread among all the Russian soldiers and workers, would travel rapidly by word of mouth and crush out their last spark of faith in the tricksters. Strik-Strikfeldt had not ventured to contradict him.

Herre tried to reassure him. He explained how the new decisions had

169

come about, and described the alternatives as they now appeared to him. Either there would be increasing disintegration of the Russian forces on the eastern front, fresh alarms about deserters, and rabid orders for total disbandment from Hitler, or something of the substance could be saved. At the bottom of his heart Strik-Strikfeldt also wanted to believe, in order to prolong his own dreams; and so Herre at last succeeded in persuading the captain that his "substance" theory had merit. Strik-Strikfeldt then agreed to go to Vlasov with it. But as for Jodl's request, he refused even to attempt to influence Vlasov.

Herre returned to Lötzen with nothing accomplished. There more bad news awaited him. The German officers of the Russian formations that were on their way to the West reported rebelliousness, loss of confidence, deep suspicion of the official story, refusals to fight against the Americans or British. They wanted to hear what Vlasov had to say about it. They would believe what Vlasov told them, but nobody else.

During the last weeks in October, the men in the Viktoriastrasse offices drew up the text of an Open Letter from General Vlasov. It emphasized the theme of a period for rest and recuperation as a prelude to the troops' unification in a Liberation Army. The Open Letter also added a new twist: that the Americans and English were allies of Stalin. If the troops should find themselves engaged in fighting in the West, every volunteer would be fighting Stalin here, too, and would therefore be still faithful to his own aims.

This text was presented to General Jodl and accepted by him. It was then turned over to Strik-Strikfeldt who was to persuade Vlasov to accept and sign it.

Strik-Strikfeldt could not have been assigned such a task at a more unfavorable moment.

On October 4, 1943, Heinrich Himmler had delivered an address to high-ranking officers of the Waffen-SS and the regular army in Posen, and on October 14 in Bad Schachen. On both occasions he had spoken of German objectives in the East. On October 4 he declared: "I am absolutely indifferent to the condition of the Russians and the Czechs. Whatever good blood of our kind is present in those nations we will bring over to ourselves, if necessary by kidnapping their children and raising them among us. Whether other nations live in prosperity or croak from starvation interests us only to the extent that we need them as slaves for our civilization. . . . Whether in building a tank trap ten thousand Russian women collapse from exhaustion interests me only to the extent that the tank trap is finished for Germany. . . . If somebody comes to me and says: 'I cannot build the tank trap with children or women, it's inhuman, they die as a result,' then I must say: 'You are a murderer of your own blood, for if that tank trap is not built German soldiers will die, and they are the sons of German mothers. They are our blood. . . . ! Most of you know what it means when a hundred corpses lie piled up . . . or a thousand lie there. To have stuck it out and . . . to have remained decent, that is what has made us hard. This is a page of glory in our history which has never been written and is never to be written. . . . If the SS in conjunction with the peasants . . . will undertake the settlement in the East, on a generous scale, with no inhibitions . . . then in twenty years we shall have pushed the racial boundary fifteen hundred kilometers eastward."

In the second speech in Schachen he had first elaborated on his theories of Teutons and Slavs. Then he had spoken out on the subject of Vlasov.

Here let me quite candidly mention the name of General Vlasov. Some of us placed great hopes in this General Vlasov. The hopes were not so well-founded as they seemed. I think that in taking such a view we were proceeding from a misjudgment of the Slavs. If we make a Slav or a Russian general talk by appealing to his vanity, every single one will begin to chatter away in a manner that strikes us Germans as a veritable wonder. . . . General Vlasov—and this is what so tremendously amazed me—engaged in propaganda even in Germany itself and . . . delivered lectures to us Germans in a sometimes thoroughly grotesque manner. I regarded this as extremely harmful. Toward the outside we can make propaganda and use whatever methods we please. . . . Any method that brings these wild peoples to heel and that leads to a Russian's dying instead of a German is right. That is right before God and man, and we can take the responsibility for it. But in this case something happened without our desiring it: Herr Vlasov, with the arrogance peculiar to Russians, to Slavs, began to tell stories. He told one story that Germany has never been able to defeat Russia, that Russia can be defeated only by Russians.

I tell you this, gentlemen, such a remark is dangerous. . . . The morning, noon, and evening prayer of the German army must be: We are superior to the enemy; we, the German infantry, are superior to any foe in this world. When some Russian comes along, some

Russian from nowhere—perhaps a butcher's boy the day before yesterday and made a general by Stalin yesterday—comes along and delivers lectures with the arrogance of the Slavs and then slips in the remark that Russia can be defeated only by Russians, then I must say: With that one remark the man shows what a swine he is. . . .

Everything we are going to have to suffer during the coming winter, during which we will certainly have to kill and slaughter two or three million more Russians—all such things are only passing phases.

We will win through, both through the phase that is immediately impending and all the other phases still to come, without ever asking how much longer the war is going to go on. . . .

It took Frederick the Great ten years before Prussia won confirmation as a European power. For us the end of this war means an open road to the Orient, the creation of a Teutonic Empire, and in one way or another—we cannot yet specify the details—the bringing in of thirty million people of our blood, so that even in our lifetimes we will become a people of 120 million of Germanic stock. . . .

That, gentlemen, is what peace means; that is what the end of this war means; that is the wonderful future on which we should fix our thoughts.

At this time Strik-Strikfeldt could only hope that the text of this monstrous sermon would not reach Vlasov. But the grapevine operated as efficiently as ever. When he arrived at the house on Kiebitzweg, he found Vlasov in possession of the entire text of Himmler's speech in Schachen, already translated into Russian.

Vlasov was sitting with Malyshkin, Zhilenkov, Trukhin, Zykov, and Kazantsev; it was obvious that a violent dispute was in progress. Evidently, the subject was only partially Himmler's statements, which were so utterly crude and brutal that, according to Trukhin, they contained not the slightest element of surprise. Himmler was pouring out his familiar ideas in a wild jumble as a way of countering his hidden fear of military defeat. Trukhin explained the intensified irrationality as a consequence of "the objective situation"—because for Himmler, as for Hitler, there were no longer any rational possibilities of victory. Zykov, who for days had been rushing back and forth between Dabendorf, Dahlem, and the Viktoriastrasse, agreed. To him, Himmler's denunciation was a clear sign that the Germans would soon be abandoning their own arrogance and "reaching for Vlasov as their last straw." Therefore, at this moment above all, Vlasov should not give up, should not be provoked into any defiant reactions, certainly should not voluntarily return to a prisoner-of-war camp.

Malyshkin was the calmest of all, as always. Coolly, he interjected that the propaganda argument about "saving the substance" was, of course, a filthy lie. Nevertheless, for friends like Martin, Grote, Herre, and some others it was a white lie. In practice it might turn out to be the truth, provided the volunteers did not get involved in fighting with the British and Americans.

Zhilenkov agreed with him. Everything depended on whether increasing pressure against the Germans on the eastern front, more violent setbacks there, brought them to their senses before the Americans and British landed in France. In that case, they might let Vlasov quickly unite the troops, which were now being collected in a relatively small area, and lead them back to the East.

Kazantsev held an entirely different view. The NTS had already written off any prospect for German help in the struggle for liberation. Baidalakov was evidently worried that commitment of Russian volunteers on the western front would put an end to all hope of collaboration with the British and Americans. Kazantsev begged Vlasov to wait no longer, to enter at once into negotiations with the Western powers. If fighting actually developed between volunteers and Americans or Englishmen, everything would be lost; the credibility of the whole liberation movement would be blasted, as far as the Western powers were concerned. Every day, every hour that Vlasov hesitated meant diminishing the last chances. He must send a message to the Western powers calling the Germans' betrayal exactly that and offering the Allies cooperation: he would call on Russian troops not to fight, but to attack the Germans in the rear and desert to the Allied side in case of an Allied invasion.

The vodka bottles circled the room and heated the general mood. Vlasov, too, drank—nevertheless, his resignation or studied calm made him seem like a lighthouse tower in the surf. No one seemed bothered by Strik-Strikfeldt's listening to Kazantsev's proposals for negotiations with the Western powers. They were sure Strik-Strikfeldt would even understand that, would, in fact, become their ally if it proved necessary. "Well, Wilfried Karlovich," Vlasov said, "what new bad news have you brought?"

In silence, he read the draft version of the Open Letter. Then he regarded Strik-Strikfeldt with one of those indescribable looks that cut the German captain more deeply than any accusing words could do, and passed the text on to Malyshkin. Then the dispute erupted anew. The passage suggesting that a struggle against the British and Americans would also be a struggle against bolshevism prompted Kazantsev to exclaim that this was the very height of shamelessness. Trukhin covered his face with his hands as if he were weeping.

Then something quite unexpected happened. Zykov, who had been sitting staring vacantly into space, suddenly said: "We must consider this text very carefully and look at it from every side. There's one side to it that those German blockheads haven't appreciated." He turned to Strik-Strikfeldt: "It is true, Wilfried Karlovich, that General Jodl has approved the text?"

"He has," Strik-Strikfeldt said.

"In that case," Zykov continued, "he is thereby recognizing the proposition that the troops are only to receive rest and recuperation in the West and then are to be united in the Liberation Army." He turned to Vlasov, his eyes flashing with the conviction that he had found the perfect legalistic exit from the trap. "You can sign this Open Letter if they will agree to have those troops placed under your command, Andrei Andreyevich, within a definite time—let's say, a few months. The Germans urgently need your signature, so let's take them at their word."

His theory sounded so appealing that Strik-Strikfeldt also succumbed to it. Three decades later he could still write: "But, I thought, supposing Jodl did confirm the draft, then he would have to keep his word. He could not back out."* His wishful thinking led him to accept Zykov's arguments.

But Vlasov was not ready to commit himself. Strik-Strikfeldt waited tensely for his decision. No profound psychological insight was needed to recognize that the Russian was going through the gravest crisis he had suffered since Strik-Strikfeldt had first met him. But after a few days it became apparent that he, too, could not give up his aims and his dreams; he stepped upon the bridge built of wishes that Zykov's tricky intelligence had devised. He sensed that Kazantsev's ideas would lead nowhere as long as he had no authentic power—"a genuine army"—and that only the Germans could provide him with such an army. He decided to continue to count on the Germans' changing their minds, and to play for time. Accordingly, he made a few revisions in the text of the Open Letter,

* Strik-Strikfeldt, *op. cit.,* p. 178.

modifying the unequivocal tone of the statements, and consented to sign the letter on condition that the Armed Forces Operations Staff would guarantee to place all native formations in the West under his command within a period still to be determined.

Relieved at hearing what would look like a success, and what was perhaps a solution to the dilemma, Strik-Strikfeldt set out for OKW headquarters. But at Viktoriastrasse a fresh shock was awaiting him. He learned that there was no longer anything to sign. Jodl, without waiting for Vlasov's answer, had, on November 5, ordered the existing text printed with a facsimile of Vlasov's signature, and distributed to the troops. The operation was already in full swing. Strik-Strikfeldt returned to Kiebitzweg once more to bring this piece of news to Vlasov. Vlasov at first did not react at all. Then, after a gloomy pause, he cried out: "What am I? What am I? What have you made of me?"

Not until the following day was Strik-Strikfeldt able to have a calmer conversation with him. The German captain himself, who was always in flight from one set of vague hopes to another set of still vaguer hopes, tried a new tack to save whatever was still salvageable of Vlasov's self-respect. He pleaded with him: "Andrei Andreyevich . . . don't reject the troops because they have become . . . mercenaries. You must go to the western front and speak to them yourself. . . . Even if you recognize the transfer to the West only in formal terms, you can tell the units what you really think about it. . . ."

So the ever pertinacious Strik-Strikfeldt set about obtaining permission for Vlasov to visit the western front. But events quickly outran his efforts. General Trukhin, on his own initiative, sent propagandists and advisers from Dabendorf to the new locations of the Russian troops, just as he had regularly sent them to the eastern front. These officers undertook to provide interpretations of the Open Letter, declaring that the troops' new mission would consist solely in preparing for union in the Liberation Army, not in fighting against Englishmen or Americans, whereupon, the officers were arrested or sent back to Dabendorf. Trukhin, Malyshkin, and Zhilenkov then went in person to the western front and to Italy, where some of the Russian troops had also been transferred. For Vlasov's peace of mind, Strik-Strikfeldt set out for France. He accompanied Zykov, who would have been in too great danger had he traveled alone. The generals and Zykov gave the same explanations, and Trukhin on the southern front managed to get as far as an interview with Field Marshal Kesselring. Then they, too, were ordered back to Germany.

On the margin of Strik-Strikfeldt's request that Vlasov be permitted to visit the front, General Jodl penned his answer: "No. Purpose met by Open Letter. I do not intend to repeat the mistake with the Dabendorf propagandists to the hundredth power. Dabendorf is a nest of anti-Germans. It ought to be disbanded."

Meanwhile, in the course of the major troop transfers to the West, a dramatic situation had developed in the Mielau transit camp. Major Walther Hansen has described it:

> When I returned from the eastern front in the middle of November and reported to Lötzen, I was met with the surprising order to report to Mielau as the Ia in order to arrange the reorganization of the formations that were to be sent to the West. The situation I found on arrival in Mielau on November 21, 1943 was not exactly pleasant.
>
> The struggle for quarters flared up all along the line. We had to accommodate to the fact that we were dealing with "home-front authorities" who knew virtually nothing about Russian troops. The men arrived from the forested regions of the eastern front in a gruesome condition. I do not mean this only in regard to their equipment. Their morale, too, had suffered badly. Those Eastern formations had been welded together by common struggles. But the unclarified background of the impending transfer to the West aroused unrest and uncertainty, which their situation in the transit camp only increased. The camp command was hostile to us. We were constantly having unpleasant arguments with the home-front officials.
>
> On December 2, 1943, General Hellmich arrived for a visit. He brought news that the first sizable contingents could be expected shortly. . . . In addition, arrangements had to be made to settle somewhere the hundreds . . . of wives and children who had been accompanying these troops, since they got in the way of the training program. In any case, the rations for these family members were scarcely adequate. Once again, this was the fault of the home-front officials, who could not conceive that these family members might merit the same kind of treatment as German civilians. . . .

176

The conditions were untenable. Every night there was a great rush of the Russian soldiers to the women's camp. We found ourselves compelled to seal off the women's camp and to place guards in front of it. Some of the guards were overpowered, so that with heavy hearts we were compelled to authorize them to fire their weapons if necessary.

It required endless efforts before we succeeded . . . in obtaining clothing. Our requests for uniforms for Russians struck many of the home-front officials as quite incomprehensible. We even ran into enormous difficulties obtaining Christmas furlough ration stamps for our troops. Nobody wanted to issue such stamps for Russians. On December 11, 1943, the camp headquarters announced that because of the arrival of German tanks there were only six barrack areas available for approximately 5000 men and 1500 horses. All protests were in vain. Then, on December 12, the "destination points" for the transfers arrived. It was truly in the nick of time.

Toward the end of September, before Hansen's arrival in Mielau, General von Pannwitz's First Cossack Cavalry Division had started its march away from Mielau.

A few days before its departure, Pannwitz had invited General Pyotr Nikolayevich Krasnov, an émigré and former Cossack leader, to inspect the division. He had informed him of the impending commitment of these troops in the Balkans and asked him to address the Cossacks and explain that their employment in the Balkans was no whit less important than fighting in the East would be.

The younger generation of Cossacks no longer had any historical associations with the name of General Krasnov. Only the older Cossacks knew him personally. Nevertheless, the dignity of Krasnov's appearance made his visit in Mielau a great triumph. The bugle corps glittered. Pannwitz greeted Krasnov at the camp gate. The old man, wearing a German general's cap, reviewed the men drawn up in parade order and made a speech. He spoke with fire, though perhaps no longer with conviction: "The common struggle against bolshevism is at stake. It does not matter at all where you happen to be thrown into this struggle." It was partly because of his speech that the departure of the Cossacks a few days later went off without a hitch.

The transport trains rolled past Warsaw, through Czechoslovakia and

Hungary. At Esseg, the Cossacks reached Yugoslav soil. The division was unloaded in the vicinity of Osijek-Ruma and promptly sent in against Tito's partisans in the Fruska Gora. This fighting continued until the beginning of November. Then the division was shifted further west to the region around Brod on the Sava River.

The areas the Cossacks were sent to secure were soon cleared of partisans. The Cossacks' tradition of tricky fighting, combined with their ability to move in the most difficult terrains, were the secret of their success.

In the spring of 1944, the division was transferred to the vicinity of Agram. The guerrilla warfare in Yugoslavia became what was well-nigh a private war between Pannwitz and his Cossacks on the one side and Tito and his partisans on the other. In the summer of 1944, the Cossacks were at last shifted down the Sava to the region around and north of Sisak. Here they remained until the beginning of the year 1945.

In the autumn of 1943, the Kaminski Brigade, the successful "experiment" of the Second German Tank Army in Lokoty, was also rudely wrenched from the region in which it had struck roots.

On September 29, 1943, Major Keiling, commander of East Artillery Battery 621, was guarding the important bridge at Peritorgi on the Desna River against partisan attack. The sky was cloudy; there were intermittent showers of rain. An endless line of German troops marched across the bridge, heading westward.

At three o'clock in the afternoon an officer appeared, his uniform half German, half Soviet, with shoulder patches such as Keiling had never seen before. The Russian requested Keiling to inform his *komandyr* how he and his men could cross the bridge.

Keiling asked who the *komandyr* was.

"Brigadier General Kaminski," the Russian said.

Then Keiling remembered Lokoty and the Second Tank Army's experiments.

An hour later Mieczylav Kaminski himself appeared. He wore his blue vizored cap, blue riding breeches, and gymnast's tunic. He held out to Keiling an old, typewritten notice of appointment, signed by General Schmidt, and said in broken German: "I Brigadier General Kaminski."

Kaminski, with a total of some 30,000 persons, was headed for the district of Lepel. Almost the entire civilian population of Lokoty was going with him. Some had been squeezed into railroad cars. The rest, about 15,000 men, were now waiting beyond the Desna in order to cross the Peritorgi bridge.

An hour later Kaminski's men marched across the river. Kaminski and his officers were in the van, followed by the main body of the troops in their parti-colored uniforms, with Russian equipment. Heavy artillery, T-34 tanks, and anti-tank guns drawn by horses moved between columns of infantry. After them came long lines of wagons with women and children, and herds of cattle.

It took Kaminski a week to reach Lepel. Thrown into a region completely dominated by the partisans, in which the sins of the German administration had left behind an ineradicable blight, Kaminski suffered his first setbacks. He tried to operate as he had in Lokoty, distributing his troops among strongpoints. But here in Lepel the partisans were already masters of the situation. And they held a tremendous propaganda advantage, for they could point to one crucial fact: the German retreat.

Several of Kaminski's regiments mutinied and threatened to join forces with the partisans. Kaminski wheedled a "Stork" light plane. Without escort, he landed in front of the staff headquarters of one of his rebellious regimental commanders. He seized the man by the throat and strangled him in front of his own men. He had several officers shot. Then he flew to the other strongpoints and acted in the same manner. By evening he reported: "Situation restored to normal."

From that moment on, his star began rising once more. Nevertheless, Kaminski was never able to subdue the partisans completely. They hid in the woods. Kaminski's troops were constantly being drawn out of their garrison area in Lepel. They were committed, as part of larger operations, against the partisan brigades that were active between Minsk and Lepel. Once again Kaminski's method of infiltration won successes. But whatever he now undertook lacked the political roots he had had in Lokoty. His final plunge into a purely mercenary function began when Curt von Gottberg, the SS group leader in White Ruthenia, who was making every effort to keep his territory under control, approached Kaminski and offered to assimilate his entire force into the Waffen-SS (the SS-in-Arms, the military branch of the SS). He promised to provide uniforms and arms comparable to his own troops, and to confer on Kaminski himself the uniform and rank of an SS brigade leader. Kaminski agreed on condition that he would not have to leave his civilian following behind in Lepel unprotected. Gottberg promised that all the civilians would be settled in Dyatlovo, in the formerly Polish territory between Warsaw and Minsk. So a new trek began.

By the beginning of 1944 the majority of the Russian formations transferred to the Atlantic front had reached their destinations. This front was tense in the expectation of an invasion by the Western powers. Brigadier General von Wartenberg assumed, in Paris, "command of the volunteer formations under the commander in chief in the West."

In 1940 Wartenberg had been a regimental commander and a member of the supervisory commission for unoccupied France. When the staffs of the commanders of the Eastern Troops were being formed for the armies in the East, the Army Personnel Office had appointed him a commander of Eastern Troop 703, although he, like most of the other such commanders, had no special qualifications for the job.

It could not be denied that Wartenberg had made a certain impression on the Russians—he was a man accustomed to command and enormously tall. But no one could possibly have claimed that he had intellectually grasped the complex political problems of the Russian volunteers—although he soon ceased saying things like: "The Russian soldier needs no rations. He can live on bark and roots." He had, in fact, made such remarks in the beginning.

Since Wartenberg loved public display and travel, the real work of his staff rested on the shoulders of his Ia, the same Major Hansen who had been detailed from Mielau to Paris.

When Hansen began his labors, the situation of the volunteers in France was totally confused. Wartenberg was traveling. The staff was more or less paralyzed. Hansen had no personal contact at all with Field Marshal von Rundstedt, the commander in chief in the West. But he did meet with a degree of understanding from Rundstedt's chief of staff, General Blumentritt. This was all the more important because the majority of the Eastern Troop commanders on the Atlantic coast regarded the Russian units with distaste and skepticism. Some of them had never heard of Russian battalions.

While Hansen was still working his way into his new assignment, a new order arrived from the High Command of the Armed Forces. The Russian divisions on the western front were not to be employed as independent units within their own divisions. All battalions were to be incorporated into German regiments as third or fourth battalions in order "to diminish their dangerousness." If the volunteers had believed the new propaganda line and Vlasov's Open Letter—that their transfer to the West was only a temporary measure which would lead to their organization in the Liberation Army—this new order was bound to shatter their faith. Formations were arbitrarily torn apart. Within a matter of days, German regimental commanders who had never dealt with Russian volunteers destroyed the fruits of years of toilsome labor. Yet the thinned-out German divisions needed these volunteer formations like their daily bread, for, without the Russians, whole segments of the coastline could not be manned.

As late as May, stragglers from the great movement from East to West kept arriving in France. In France remnants of the Eastern legions were gathered together into a volunteer parent division into which Russian replacement units were also taken. The officers' school for native formations, which had long been stationed in the Lithuanian town of Mariampol, was transferred to Conflans in France. Finally, Wartenberg was replaced by General Oskar von Niedermeyer, who for a time had commanded an entire division consisting of men from Turkistan and Azerbaijan.

But the discrepancy between the propagandistic somersaults, the delaying tactics, the promises, the deceptions, and the real facts, remained too obvious. How would the volunteer formations behave if they were called upon to battle an invasion?

The situation grew even more confused toward the end of December, when General Hellmich at last came to doubt the validity of his assignment.

Hellmich longed to be back at a post in which he could issue orders and make arrangements without engaging in difficult negotiations. He told Herre: "I'm not suited for all this stuff. I've failed all along the line."

Herre and the other officers of his staff could hardly contradict. Nor could Stauffenberg, who had just returned to the Army High Command after being severely wounded in Africa, where he lost a hand and an eye. General Olbricht, the chief of the Allgemeine Heeresamt (the office in the War Ministry charged with directing the entire army), had brought him to Berlin as his chief of staff; there Stauffenberg heard little about the disputes that had been raging for the past several weeks over the Russian volunteer formations. But when he learned of Hellmich's request for another assignment, he used his influence on the Army Personnel Office to see to it that Hellmich's plea was granted as quickly as possible. He urged that Hellmich be replaced by Köstring. The objection was raised that Köstring was too old and that his inclination to favor Pan-Russian tendencies could scarcely be the right medicine for the separatistic volunteer troops. Moreover, it was argued, Köstring was inclined to view matters from the lofty vantage point of age, which enabled him to see them rightly as often as not, but also inclined him to give up too easily and fall back on sarcasms. Köstring himself objected. He was convinced that all efforts would prove vain in the end. But when Stauffenberg succeeded in pushing the appointment through, Köstring was ready to take it on.

Transfer of the post took place in Lötzen. Hellmich sounded a note of deep bitterness, and his last words—"Perhaps I shall follow my two sons"—seemed to express a premonition of death. At this time, he knew he would be taking over a division on the Atlantic front in France. And there he was, in fact, killed in an air raid.

In his function as "Inspector of the Turkic Formations" Köstring had been staying for some time in a sportsmen's resort, Hotel Jägerhöhe, between Angerburg and Lötzen. He stayed there even after assuming his new post. That was one example of the obstinacy of age. Silently, he watched the bustle and made a point of knocking off work as early as possible, which meant that he tried to sign documents early in the day. Those who had spoken of his growing attitude of fatalism had not been entirely wrong.

Köstring and his staff reaped some of the crops as well as some of the weeds that Hellmich had sown.

Köstring's authority was broadened. He now was permitted to exert influence upon those volunteers who were in the Air Force and the Navy.

Twenty new clearing stations and military hospitals for volunteers were created. A "native nurses' corps" in Russian dress was established; the "native medical corps" was made independent. Russian, Ukrainian, Turkistani, and other doctors were permitted to participate in German medical training courses.

At the infantry school in Posen a special Inspectorate for "native" officers was established. Rest homes sprang up, likewise homes for wounded veterans, retraining camps, field libraries. German movies were supplied with Russian texts. Germans were required to salute Russian superior officers. German commanders were allowed to confer the Iron Cross on Russians. Permissions for marriage at last became a reality. The military penal code was revised with the volunteers in mind.

Henceforth, native associate justices had to be present at courts-martial of volunteers. Putting across this point involved tenacious negotiating with the Reichssicherheitshauptamt (primarily a task for Herre) and was bitterly opposed by the SS leadership.

But if all these gains were viewed from a lofty vantage point, they remained a matter of placating soldiers who since their transfer from the eastern front were more and more becoming mercenaries who had been cheated out of their political aims. Herre always called himself a manufacturer of "bonbons." Since the bitter struggles of the winter months no one was any longer trying to effect a change of viewpoint in the German top leadership. Vlasov seemed finally condemned to helpless inactivity. Everything was frozen; in the black clouds massed on the horizon there was no sign of a silver lining.

In April Herre finally became totally discouraged. Toward the end of the month he told Köstring he would prefer to be sent back to the front. He explained that since April of 1942 he had not had a command at the front and was suffering from a "desk complex." Köstring knew this was merely a pretext. But he wearily consented, his only condition being that Herre train a successor.

Two days before Herre's departure for the Italian front in July 1944, his counterintelligence officer, Lieutenant Schareck, asked him for a personal interview. He had apparently hesitated for a long time before taking this step. But now he said: "I understand your motives, Colonel Herre. But in my view—based on certain special knowledge—there is another possibility that nobody here recognizes."

Herre gave him an incredulous stare. "What on earth might that be?"

Schareck replied: "You will surely say: 'After all that has happened, your idea is impossible and absurd.' And yet it's a good bet. I am referring to the SS."

Herre actually did say: "Schareck, at the moment I am in no mood for jokes. Have you forgotten about the 'subhumans' or Himmler's speech in Schachen? Have you forgotten the fact that Himmler instigated the whole transfer to the West? And the attitude of the State Security Office?"

But Schareck persisted. "Of course, I have not forgotten any of that," he said. "But the SS is not the coherent, united organization permeated by a single idea and a single will that it pretends to be. There is hardly another organization which contains more divergent currents, groups, and power struggles than the SS. And there is nobody more vacillating and uncertain than Himmler himself."

"All that may be true. But what does that mean for us?"

"Since 1940 certain changes have been noticeable in the SS leadership. They seem to have been initiated by Dr. Franz Riedweg, the Swiss military doctor who entered the Waffen-SS. He translated the vague SS notions about Teutonism and the Germanic domination of Europe into practice. He created the non-German Teutonic SS divisions composed of Dutchmen, Flemings, Norwegians, Danes, and Swiss with which we are familiar. At first, these were just tolerated by Gottlob Berger, chief of the SS Hauptamt [Home Office] and by Himmler. But by now the groups have long since become regular components of the Waffen-SS. After that, the people around Riedweg took a further step which represented a clean break with the whole notion of Teutonic Supremacy. They created the Walloon SS Degrelle Brigade. Then followed French SS formations. Riedweg's men cleverly obtained Himmler's consent to this sort of thing by feeding him romantic historical notions about Burgundy as part of the Holy Roman Empire. They made the French formations palatable by presenting them under the name of 'Charlemagne.'

"Behind all this, of course, there is no change in the SS elite's concepts of power politics. On the contrary. They have merely recognized that the course of the war is endangering them. They know that a military victory which would give Germany dominion over Europe is now out of the question. And they also know that the Waffen-SS needs more forces than they can recruit from the so-called 'Germanic area.' For that reason they are toying with the idea of a European SS empire which will not only offer new potential sources for recruits but also a way out of the military impasse. Ever since the withdrawal movements on the eastern front began—which made even these people realize that the official doctrine of a Teutonic Empire in the East is nothing but a chimera—they have extended to the East their idea of a vast European area under the control of the SS elite. The policy began with their taking the Estonian and Latvian volunteer formations into the Waffen-SS. The first such SS divisions and brigades even have a Latvian inspector, General Bangerski. Berger and Himmler were won over by citing the rule of the Teutonic Knights in the Baltic region. But that step was a first breach in the anti-Slavic doctrine.

"SS Standartenführer [Colonel] Sparmann took Riedweg's place. Other Waffen-SS men from the earlier Youth Movement gathered around Sparmann, and they have by now reached the point of repudiating the whole 'Slav as subhuman' concept. Sparmann has gone ahead and organized a Galician SS division. He means to do the same with the White

Ruthenians and the Turkic peoples. He is counting on establishing an 'Eastern Desk' which will rank right alongside the Germanic Desk and the European Germanization Bureau. The idea is to develop a vast antibolshevist region of 'equal nations,' of which the Russians will be part. The unifying factor will no longer be a Germanic SS elite but an international SS."

Herre had listened to all this as quietly as his nervous temperament allowed. But now he interrupted: "But that is a political and military monstrosity."

"Of course, it is," Schareck said. "But so was the theory of Germanic domination. And given the military situation, not much will ever come of it. But desperation is driving the SS people to push this plan with every means at their command. Not that that means anything definite with a man like Berger at the top, for you can put across practically anything with Berger, only nothing sticks. But in this case, he has been persuaded to install a specialist as head of the 'Eastern Desk.' The fellow's name is Dr. Fritz Rudolf Arlt; he comes from the SS and is still in his thirties—a specialist in the nationalities of the Soviet Union. Serving in the Polish government and in a Waffen-SS division, he gained practical experience of real conditions in the East. He has already been reaching out for Ukrainians and is planning Ukrainian SS divisions. Unquestionably he will be approaching Vlasov as soon as the situation within the split SS leadership allows." Schareck paused a moment. Then he made his final statement: "Sir, in my opinion, we can't let him take over all we've built with so much toil and trouble."

The conversation ended there.

Two days later, on July 10, 1944, Herre strode down the long corridor of the Lötzen headquarters barrack. Tucked under his arm was the final report on his fourteen months of work. He was going to pay his respects to Köstring before leaving.

"Do sit down, Herre," the old officer said. He glanced at the fat volume Herre was carrying. "I suppose that is your last will and testament?"

"It is, sir," Herre replied. "I want to turn this testament over to you. But may I also make a comment on it?"

"By all means. Get it all off your chest," Köstring said.

"Probably it is too late," Herre said. "But possibly there still is a way to salvage our project."

"And what would that be?"

"Cooperating with the SS, sir."

"The SS? You can't be serious?"

Herre passed on the information Schareck had given him. "I've thought about it day and night," he concluded, "and I believe that this may be a last desperate chance. The question is only whether and to what extent the cause justifies a pact with the devil."

Unlikely Change

Waffen-SS Sturmbannführer Dr. Fritz Rudolf Arlt was thirty-two years old in the spring of 1944. One thing which set him apart from the intellectuals and pseudo-intellectuals of the SS was the fact that he could not be termed an "uprooted bourgeois," like so many of the others. He had been born in 1912 in Niederkumersdorf, where his family had long been landowners. At the University of Leipzig he had explored the fields of sociology, theology, genetics, and statistics, and had spent considerable time studying in Poland, Czechoslovakia, Austria, and Hungary. In 1936 he became an instructor at Breslau University.

In 1937–1938 he got into some difficulties over his scholarly work. He was prevented from publishing his dissertation because it did not entirely conform to the dogmas of the Office of Racial Politics. Nevertheless, in 1939 he was appointed to a professorship in population statistics at Breslau. He then took part in the war against Poland and was detailed to the staff of General Blaskowitz, the military commander in Poland. From there he was coopted into the administration of Hans Frank, governor-general of Poland.

He did not always operate according to the policies of Frank and, behind him, of Himmler's Reichssicherheitshauptamt regarding the treatment of the Poles. Making use of that small margin of freedom which existed, though precariously, behind the superficial totality of the Nazi state, Arlt created central organs for representing the populace of the "government-general," as Poland was officially called. These bodies were to represent the interests of the different nationalities within Poland. Thus, he formed a Polish Special Committee, a Ukrainian and a Jewish Auxiliary Committee.

187

Oddly enough, all this was tacitly tolerated by his superior. Frank was beginning to see that the policy of naked force would not in the long run yield the best results.

Frank, therefore, held on to Arlt in spite of the objections of the State Security Office. And Arlt had begun to extend the sphere of his concern beyond the boundaries of the government-general of Poland. He had taken an interest in the Ukrainians, the White Ruthenians, and the Russian and Georgian émigrés in Poland, and in particular had studied the difficult predicament of the West Ukrainians, caught as they were between the Russians and the Poles.

When the campaign against the Soviet Union was about to be launched, Arlt intensified his relations with the Ukrainians in particular. He had a hand in the matter when the German Abwehr set up smallish Ukrainian fighting units, known as "Roland" and "Nightingale." He had furthered the establishment of Ukrainian youth and labor camps. He maintained secret links with Melnik, Bandera, and other Ukrainian leaders. In 1943, consequently, he was the only man in Frank's circle who understood the internal situation in the Ukrainian independence movement, insofar as it was possible for an outsider to do so.

The fact that Arlt became a member of the Waffen-SS at the very time the Reichssicherheitshauptamt regarded him as unreliable is one of those paradoxes that were so common in SS affairs. SS Obergruppenführer (Lieutenant General) Reinhard Heydrich (who was killed in 1942) told himself that it was useful to have Arlt in the SS and therefore under closer supervision, since Frank had become too dependent on his expertise to let him go. Later, this problem was resolved by Arlt's transfer to the eastern front.

At the beginning of 1944 Arlt had been severely wounded while serving with the Reich Division, and was returned to Germany for medical treatment. In the hospital an inquiry from Sparmann had reached him: would he be willing to help give the Eastern policy of the SS Hauptamt (headquarters) "a new direction."

On May 25, 1944, Arlt reported to the SS Hauptamt in Berlin.

He had frequently heard of Berger as chief of this, the central office of the SS, but had never met him. Nor did he know that since 1943 Berger had additionally held a post in the East Ministry. Desperately searching for some way to increase the influence of his impotent ministry, Rosenberg had dropped Undersecretary Leibbrandt and obtained Berger, as a supposedly strong man, to replace him. Rosenberg had not been aware that Berger, a former Swabian schoolmaster who had miraculously soared to undreamed-of heights in his SS career, was himself a feeble reed swaying with every ideological and power-political wind. Instead of bringing new élan to Rosenberg's ministry, Berger had soon turned back entirely to his duties in the SS. His chief contribution was the dash of peasant's slyness with which he "informed" Himmler of the new course.

He received Arlt with a pretense of jovial innocence: "So you're the guy who knows all about that there Eastern stuff." Their conversation was fairly brief. Berger told Arlt of the plans afoot in the SS Hauptamt and asked him whether he would take charge of the raising and organizing of SS volunteer formations composed of Eastern nationals.

"I would do that," Arlt said, "if I were authorized to concede national autonomy to those formations, just as much for the outlying nationalities as for the Russians. Anything else is pointless. Unless we do it that way, there's no sense even starting."

"We'll put that over," Berger commented somewhat oracularly.

Nevertheless, it was not until July that Arlt was entrusted with the task of heading up the "Eastern Volunteers Desk" in the SS Hauptamt. In the early part of July he moved into a building on Fehrbelliner Platz in Berlin. Arlt divided his staff into a number of separate bureaus for the Ukraine, White Ruthenia, the Caucasus countries, Latvia, Estonia, Lithuania, and Russia. He thus made it clear that he intended to take in the "Russian nucleus" as well as the outlying nationalities, not in any "Great Russian" sense, but rather as parts of a "national structuring of the East." Thus, Arlt pursued a different line from Rosenberg in wanting to grant the "nations," including the Baltic nations, much greater liberty, and also in intending that Russia would survive as an independent state.

Arlt was aware that there were far too few officers in the Waffen-SS who were well disposed toward the "nationalities of the East." But he was certain that plenty of army officers would be glad to cooperate, the more so if he could assure them the freedom of action which Köstring would never have been able to win for them.

Köstring, who was still trying to gain basic rights for his volunteers on a par with those enjoyed by German soldiers, was extremely surprised—in spite of Herre's preparing the ground—when Arlt approached him and spoke to him of his plans. This sudden change inside the SS struck

Köstring as uncanny; he was extremely wary. However, one thing was clear: that the volunteers might get a better deal with the aid of the SS. He felt he did not have the moral right to block this chance. The result was the beginnings of cooperation between Köstring and Arlt.

The strange alliance also included Rosenberg. Arlt was advocating the remote goal of a breakup of Russia into nationalities in consonance with the new ideological line of the SS, which was strong on racial organization. Rosenberg, on the other hand, saw in such ideas only the fulfillment of his old concept of "divide and rule." Hence he was ready to join forces with Arlt, who, he thought, would help him put across his own ideas.

Word of Arlt's endeavors soon got around among all those committees and national representatives who had previously attached themselves to Rosenberg. Automatically, they now sought help from the young man at Fehrbelliner Platz.

The first problem Arlt attacked was that of the Ukrainians. He appointed as head of his Ukrainian Desk Obersturmbannführer (Lieutenant Colonel) Ludwig Wolff, a German native of Poland. He had been a kreisleiter (local chief) in Lodz but had been dismissed because of his opposition to the strictly Germany-centered policies.

Both Arlt and Wolff realized that they could do nothing effective until they had reshaped the Ukrainian organizations, which were rife with dissension. Above all, the groups needed some leadership which would be acceptable to all the factions.

Neither Bandera nor Melnik would fit the bill. Arlt made contact with the UNR, a five-man Ukrainian directorate which had emigrated to Poland under the leadership of Colonel Simon Petlyura after the collapse in 1921 of the first Ukrainian struggle for independence. As a nonpartisan "government in exile" the group had continued to exist in Poland, but had had no direct connection with the underground Ukrainian organizations. After Petlyura's assassination, a man named Levicki had assumed the leadership. Since 1939 the UNR had continued its quiet existence in the vicinity of Lodz, closely watched by the Sicherheitsdienst. Arlt now asked Levicki for advice. Levicki proposed former General Shandruk as the suitable leader of all the Ukrainians.

Pavlo Shandruk had been born in Kremenets in Volhynia in 1889. In 1917, as a Russian lieutenant colonel, he had led one of the early tank detachments, and in 1920 had commanded a Ukrainian brigade in the Ukrainian struggle for liberation. In 1921 he had fled to Poland where Pilsudski gave him an appointment in the Polish army.

190

Levicki explained to Arlt that most of the Ukrainian officers in the Polish army were regarded by Ukrainian nationalists as collaborators with Poland. But Shandruk, he said, was an exception. In his dealings with Poles Shandruk had always advocated an independent Ukrainian nation-state. In 1939 he had led a Polish regiment. He had been taken prisoner by the Germans, and held in a prison camp near Breslau, but was finally released with permission to live in Skierniewice. There he was working at a humble job in a movie theater.

Up to this time, Arlt had never heard of Shandruk. Levicki not only gave him all this background material but also arranged for him to meet the general. Shandruk was invited to Berlin. Arlt met a man who was prepared for any sacrifice for the sake of the Ukrainian cause, but who had been schooled in mistrust by the disappointments of many years.

"This change in the SS is certainly surprising," Shandruk said.

Arlt tried to defend the SS: "Don't forget the Ukrainian division."

"To this day it is not called 'Ukrainian Division.' It is called 'the Galician Division,' and I know only too well that you organized it merely in order to have mercenaries. That's its only reason for being."

"That, too, isn't quite correct," Arlt said defensively. "At least, not as far as the governor of Galicia and I are concerned."

"To this day, the division is commanded by German officers and a German general. Its equipment is poor, and no Ukrainian has any say on where it is to be committed and for what purposes."

"If so, I am offering you the opportunity to have that say," Arlt said. "In all these matters, we have had to fight our own old ideologists. It was good strategy to choose the name 'Galician' and accomplish something under that name. If we had tried to set up a Ukrainian division, we would have been turned down immediately by our superiors. We've made progress, and if you are willing to take hold, we'll make a good deal more progress in a few months."

Shandruk remained aloof. Finally he laid down conditions. They were: Native command for the Galician or Ukrainian Division and for all other existing Ukrainian formations and those still to be raised. Liberation of Bandera and all other Ukrainian nationalists from the concentration camps. Freedom of assembly, of organization, of the press. Formation of a provisional Ukrainian government. Renunciation by Germany of all territorial claims in the Ukraine.

"Under these conditions," Shandruk said, "we can be allies. The Ukrainian troops would come over to our side, and not as mercenaries but as liberators. What would the battle lines look like if this had been allowed in 1941? . . ."

There was no need for Arlt to answer this lament, because it was, if belatedly, his own.

"General," he said, "if you are willing to shake hands on it, I'll do my damnedest to obtain consent to those conditions. I cannot on my own initiative make binding promises on all your points. But I can give you a piece of advice. Don't insist on conditions, but get in on a developing situation. That way you will achieve everything you want to achieve." Cautiously, he added: "Even if Germany comes through the war in fair shape, she will no longer have the strength to reject your conditions once you are involved. And once you take over the military leadership of the Ukrainian troops, you are no longer an outsider; you yourself will have the rank of an SS Gruppenführer [Group Leader] and will enjoy an equal voice in our affairs, just as all the non-German officers in the Germanic SS units have long had."

Shandruk twisted his lips contemptuously: "An SS leader?" he said. "Never!"

Arlt pleaded for a more flexible approach. "That is only a form, you know. To achieve our goal we must sometimes put on forms that don't suit us." But meeting unswerving resistance, he finally declared: "I hope I will be able to spare you the form, if you have the courage to shake hands with me."

Shandruk asked for time to think it over. Arlt heard that he was consulting with various officers of the Galician Division. The following week, he said he was ready to take command.

Arlt enjoyed his quickest success with the Latvians. Bangerski and his chief of staff, Colonel Silgeilis, were eager to take over leadership of the Latvian Waffen-SS formations. Bangerski had no scruples about forms. He did not care one way or another whether he was an SS Gruppenführer or not. He regarded himself as nothing but a soldier.

The Estonians posed a more difficult problem. The Estonian SS brigade could pride itself on having seven wearers of the Knight's Cross. It was regarded as one of the toughest formations in the Waffen-SS, but it still had no higher officers who had the makings of national leaders.

Arlt also had success with Professor Ostrovsky and the White Ruthenian police forces. These were assembled into a White Ruthenian SS division of volunteers. But here, too, suitable leaders were lacking for the higher command posts. For the time being, therefore, a German, Ober-sturmbannführer Hans Sigling, had to take command of the division.

Arlt also initiated friendly relations with Chayum Khan. He discussed rounding up the Turkistani formations scattered throughout the army into a Turkistani SS division. Khan saw this as the opportunity to combine his National Committee with a military fighting force and to unite his dispersed fellow-countrymen. He began negotiations with General Köstring and Lieutenant Colonel Voelkel, Herre's successor under Köstring, with a view to obtaining the release of the Turkistani formations. But he had no success.

Arlt managed to establish an especially good relationship with Misha Khedia, the cunning head of the Georgians.

At the time Arlt took office there was a Caucasian SS battalion being organized in Denmark. Simultaneously, an SS Standartenführer was busy in Paluzza, north of Tolmezzo, Italy, setting up an SS Caucasian cavalry formation. This, together with a Caucasian National Committee still to be formed, might serve as the rallying point for a Caucasian division or a liberation army.

In the middle of July General von Pannwitz unexpectedly turned up for a conference with Arlt. He had an offer to make. In expanding his Cossack division into a corps, Pannwitz had run into increasing obstacles with the army. He had observed that the Waffen-SS had far greater supplies and funds at its disposal when it set about organizing its non-German formations. In principle, he declared, he was willing to have his Cossack corps subordinated to the Waffen-SS if in return he received material help. Arlt promised him that non-SS officers would be appointed to command the Cossack corps. Consequently, Arlt added a "Cossack Desk" to his growing organization. The time had come to attack the central problem of the Russians head-on.

Since 1943 Arlt had been closely watching developments in conjunction with Vlasov. He knew that Vlasov was a Pan-Russian, and he doubted that Vlasov would be able to relinquish his Pan-Russian attitudes. But he pushed that question aside for the present. He had first to determine whether Vlasov would be prepared to cooperate with the Eastern Desk.

On July 10 Arlt discussed the Vlasov problem as he saw it with Berger. Berger made a sour face.

"You can put across all sorts of things with the chief [Himmler] these days," he said. "But Vlasov is like a red flag to him. After those speeches he made, he's way out on a limb."

"All the same, it should be tried," Arlt said.

On July 12 he went to see Berger again to talk about his Vlasov plans. He had to wait in the anteroom for a while, and while waiting met an SS Oberführer (a rank between colonel and brigadier general) who introduced himself as Dr. Erhard Kroeger. They fell into conversation and Arlt spoke about his plans.

"That interests me," Dr. Kroeger said. "At the moment I am head of recruiting in Denmark. But your Russian Desk would have a great deal more attraction for me. Is the post already filled?"

"Not yet."

Kroeger reiterated: "I'm serious. That is a slot where I could be highly effective. I'm a Balt and speak fluent Russian."

"A Balt?" Arlt said. "In my student days I had a lot to do with members of the Baltic Brotherhood. . . ."

Kroeger replied: "I belonged to the Baltic Jungmannschaft [Nazi party cadet organization]."

Arlt recalled that the people he had met in the Baltic Brotherhood had been without exception of the kind whom his circles referred to as "decent characters." And SS officers who spoke Russian were not so common that he could afford to do without such a man.

Shortly afterward, he was called in by Berger and learned that Hitler showed scant inclination to use Vlasov inside the SS in any way. Berger added, however, that there was always hope and that the matter could be brought up again at some favorable occasion.

Arlt briefly mentioned his encounter with Kroeger. Berger made a note of the name.

As Arlt watched Berger's fleshy fingers scribbling Kroeger's name, he could not foresee how tremendously this seemingly casual event was going to influence his own future. Nor did he know that at the same moment a more powerful SS man was at work trying to draw Vlasov out of the obscurity into which he had sunk. The man was Gunter d'Alquen, commander of the SS war correspondents' regiment "Kurt Eggers." Above all, d'Alquen was a man very close to Heinrich Himmler.

Gunter d'Alquen belonged to that peculiar intellectual, or pseudointellectual, contingent who lurked behind the outwardly brutal coherence of the SS facade. His father had been a wool merchant in Essen whose heart was set on providing his eldest son, born in 1910, with a top-notch middle-class education. But young d'Alquen, impelled by restlessness and eagerness for action, had early broken out of the middle-class fold. The social tensions in the Ruhr area during the twenties had helped to radicalize him. At sixteen he had joined the SA. During the summer holidays, he took a factory job in one of the Krupp plants, and then worked as a hauler in a mine. Injured in a clash at a Communist party meeting, he came home to be greeted by his father with the words: "Go back to the swine you've just come from." After that, his road in life was pretty well marked out.

Despite his youthful social idealism, he did not end up with the Communists or Socialists largely because he could not overcome the German nationalist and middle-class character of his origins. After several years of journalistic work in Munich and Berlin, he founded, along with a group of extremely variegated intellectuals, the SS magazine *Das Schwarze Korps*.

Even before the war the editorial offices of *Das Schwarze Korps* were a laboratory in which all sorts of ideas were experimented with, not all of which fitted precisely into so-called SS ideology. Many ideas were tolerated because the ideology was still in a state of development—from which it never emerged to the end of its days.

D'Alquen underwent voluntary training in the army, and during the first phase of the war completed his officer's training in Berlin-Lichterfelde. Himmler then entrusted him with the task of organizing an SS company of war correspondents. He was given ample funds and a free hand in picking the best men for the job. D'Alquen recruited capable journalists and photographers, whether or not they had any connection with the SS. The first units were sent to the front in May 1940, during the campaign in the West.

D'Alquen's front-line propaganda units displayed the same undeniable bravery that was characteristic of most SS divisions. Like these, they paid for mistakes in leadership with heavy casualties. But they did better than the Army's propaganda units because they were freer, more mobile, and better equipped. It was characteristic of d'Alquen and his circle that he promptly and enthusiastically took up the new concept of a "Germanic SS." D'Alquen's company of war correspondents, which in 1941 expanded to a regiment, became a model of "Germanic" cooperation. Men of the most widely varied nationalities served in it, not as hirelings but out of belief in its underlying doctrine. They had been captivated by muddled, unrealistic notions of a "Germanic sphere of influence" and the "essential battle against bolshevism." These nationals of other countries were treated as equals among equals and attained leading positions. They greatly enhanced the effectiveness of d'Alquen's propaganda, far beyond the former borders of Germany. For d'Alquen had at his disposal Britons,

Danes, Norwegians, Icelanders, Finns, Swedes, Swiss, Dutch, Flemings, and others.

The idea of a "European SS," which came next, was just as unrealistic and abstruse as the idea of the Germanic sphere of influence—but d'Alquen's regiment gave it a warm welcome. His supposedly "Germanic" force was now joined by Frenchmen, Walloons, Spaniards, Croats, and Serbs. Inevitably, the day came when d'Alquen and his men would have to view the problems of the Russian "territory" in a different light.

These men had entered the campaign against the Soviet Union with the assumptions that were current in the SS: Jewish bolshevism, Slavic inferiority—in brief, a country full of *Untermenschen*. But d'Alquen had learned a few things and undergone a psychological transformation. From 1942 on, he played a mediating part in the internal struggle between front-line veterans and the ideology of the leadership. Moreover, he had done so with skill, never challenging Himmler directly, but cleverly waiting for the proper moments to intrude his novel ideas.

The first of such moments had come in 1943, when d'Alquen found Waffen-SS leaders placing increasing stress on the discrepancy between reality and ideology. In particular, SS General Felix Steiner had vigorously attacked "all that bunk of Himmler's about the Germanic Empire in the East." For the first time, Waffen-SS men had declared that they were ashamed to wear the same uniforms as the SD squads who by preference dealt with the annihilation of Soviet commissars, Slav intellectuals, Russian Jews, and "subhuman" Slavs and bolshevists in general. Threatening defeats brought about some remarkable changes of heart.

It was pure chance that led to d'Alquen's having a virtually private interview with Himmler in September 1943, the first in a long time.

Himmler invited d'Alquen to fly to Siverskaya with him in order to visit the Fifth SS Mountain Division at the Arctic Ocean front near Kiestinki. In the course of the flight Himmler took a newly published pamphlet from his pocket and showed it to d'Alquen. Its title was *Der Untermensch* ("The Subhuman"). D'Alquen had just come from the eastern front. D'Alquen's ears were still ringing with General Steiner's recent complaints and demands. And here was this pamphlet—produced after two years of fighting in Russia and more unrealistic and bestial, more stupid and backward, than the propaganda pamphlets that his own units had turned out in preparation for the war against the Soviet Union.

He held his tongue until Himmler asked cheerfully: "You don't say anything. How does it strike you?"

D'Alquen said slowly: "Reichsführer, do you want to hear my candid opinion?"

"As always."

"Then I must say that this pamphlet will lay an egg with the units of the Waffen-SS that I am familiar with."

Himmler smiled naïvely and retorted with a jocular air: "I suppose you don't like the thing because you didn't write it."

"No, Reichsführer," d'Alquen said, "that isn't it. But if I can be perfectly frank, our men out there are getting the shit knocked out of them by those 'subhumans.' When our men see this pamphlet, they'll ask: Are you trying to tell us that those fellows who are giving us such a hard time and have better tanks than ours and are pretty damn good in tactics and strategy—are you trying to tell us they're all subhuman?"

Himmler's jocularity evaporated. "What sort of tone is this?" he said.

"Reichsführer," d'Alquen said, "that's the tone I've heard among our men on all the fighting fronts. After two years of war with the Russians, we can't go on operating with such theories any longer. Those two years have taught our men what we didn't know at the start. This enemy can't be written off so cheaply."

Himmler displayed the icy silence that was typical of him when his theories ran into conflict with reality. "Enough of this subject," he said. And for two days he did not address a word to d'Alquen.

After forty-eight hours had passed, however, he summoned d'Alquen again. "A few days ago you dropped some hints," he said. "I mean hints about my commanders in the Waffen-SS. I should like to hear more about their attitudes."

"I would be glad to give you a report," d'Alquen said. "But perhaps it would be well for you to talk to Steiner yourself, or better yet, visit him at the front."

"I have no time for that," Himmler said. "I'll send for the commanders myself. But perhaps you can give me some preparation—what is the nature of the ideological change these people seem to have undergone?"

D'Alquen knew Himmler well enough to understand that he assumed a mask of harsh superiority whenever his inner insecurity reached a peak. And d'Alquen decided to play on that insecurity.

He gave an elaborate description of what he had seen, experienced, and heard at the front. And he summed it all up in these words: "In the field of political warfare we have totally failed. The bravest men have come to

197

the conclusion that we cannot win the war in the East militarily. I'll be perfectly frank with you: they gave me a message, and it went like this: Tell the Reichsführer when you have the chance that all these theories about the racial inferiority of the Russians and the Germanization of Russia are so much drivel. We cannot kill all the Russians. What we've done with these theories is drive them into Stalin's arms and made fighters of them. If we went about it the right way, we could have some of those fighters on our side."

"I thought your earlier remarks were a joke," Himmler said crossly. "I can hardly imagine that temporary difficulties would induce my soldiers to stray from the goal of our fighting—the Greater Germanic Empire. I thought my commanders would have read my speeches more carefully."

"Reichsführer," d'Alquen said, "your commanders are as loyal to you as they ever were, but they see the reality every day, a reality that you cannot see here, Reichsführer."

"I'll deal with those gentlemen myself," Himmler went on. "Inform them that the moment we betray our principles and our goal, we are lost."

D'Alquen knew from experience that this was the end of the matter for the time being. The more he talked, the more Himmler would wall himself in behind the bastion of his theories.

Himmler did not turn to d'Alquen again until they were on the return flight to East Prussia. "You told me," he said, "that our political warfare is in a bad way. Very well, the army may have failed in the East. But your regiment is there to fight the battle on another plane. I give you carte blanche. Promise the Russians anything you like, so long as it will further our vital mission. Come up with some new ideas. The main thing is results."

"Reichsführer," d'Alquen replied, "the way we have acted there, there's hardly any line that could bring the Russians over to our side."

"That is enough of such defeatist remarks," Himmler snapped. "You've done very effective work up to now. You have only to exert yourself. I want your outfit to prove that we are way in front of all others in psychological warfare. . . . What area do you want to be sent to?"

D'Alquen thought of General Steiner. "Into the Oranienburg pocket," he said.

"Good. And what do you need aside from your own men?"

"Perhaps a few propaganda units from the army."

"From the army?"

"Yes. There are some competent people there, people with experience . . . I think I can use them to good advantage. . . ."

In November d'Alquen began his propaganda experiment in the Oranienburg pocket, the area held by Steiner's corps. He set up headquarters in Gubanitzi. His operation bore the code name *Wintermärchen* (Winter's Tale). He had orthodox priests say masses from sound-trucks and Russian women deliver nostalgic talks about home—especially at night. He dropped leaflets recommending various methods for self-mutilation to escape further service at the front. He conducted experiments with sexual propaganda.

The religious propaganda was almost useless; the sexual propaganda did not work at all. Not that the number of deserters was so very low in absolute terms; but relatively, such numbers were insignificant. Members of the army propaganda units told him he might as well save himself the trouble. There was only one effective method left, they maintained: recruiting for a Vlasov Liberation Army. But as he well knew, they had been forbidden to use this method.

D'Alquen thereupon took it upon himself to conduct an additional experiment. His calls for deserters to enlist in General Vlasov's Liberation Army, which was now allegedly being organized and would shortly be ready for fighting, immediately sent the tally of deserters shooting up to remarkable heights.

D'Alquen made up his mind to use his operation to prove the need to abandon the SS's dreams of Germanic colonization and to switch to Vlasov. He had questionnaires prepared with no less than 140 questions. All prisoners and deserters were carefully interviewed. D'Alquen sent his men into transit camps for special interrogations.

From November 1943 to February 1944 he conducted 8000 individual interrogations. He had the results evaluated and used them week after week to prepare impressive reports full of graphic summaries. The graphs dramatized the enormous attraction exerted by the name "Vlasov."

D'Alquen knew that both Himmler and Hitler had a weakness for graphs. He hoped that all this material would influence Himmler and prepare him for another talk. Instead, early in March, out of a clear sky, he received orders to go to Italy and try out his "action propaganda" on the Polish troops who had been reequipped in England and were fighting on the Allied side under General Anders. So that was his reward for a successful operation! Along with a spasm of total frustration, he had the impulse to laugh.

In the process of organizing a new propaganda operation code-named *Südstern* (Southern Star), d'Alquen learned a good deal about technical methodology. But it all seemed trivial compared with the complex problems of the East. After a few months in Italy he was ordered to report to Berlin.

"The situation on the eastern front has deteriorated," Himmler told him. "We need intensified operational propaganda. Winter's Tale must be repeated on a much larger scale."

D'Alquen was instantly on the alert. "May I conclude, then, that you are in agreement with the deductions deriving from Operation Winter's Tale and that I can start the new operation on the eastern front in accord with those deductions?"

"What deductions do you mean?"

D'Alquen had a briefcase of material with him. He brought out his folder on the winter of 1943–1944, presented it to Himmler, and read aloud from its summary which dwelt on the profit to be had from organizing and making propaganda for a Russian liberation army.

"Are you starting that again?" Himmler said, with a quaver of both uncertainty and anger in his voice. "The Führer flatly rejects Vlasov and everything connected with him. You are not the only one who keeps after me about this fellow. The best commanders of the Waffen-SS are taking on as though there were no other way to win the victory except by using that Russian. I clearly expressed my opinion on that subject in Schachen. I didn't send for you so I could hear the name of Vlasov again."

"Then the new operation will fail," d'Alquen said.

Himmler flew into a temper. "All right, promise the Russians whatever you like. Promise them a monster of a liberation army. Who's going to make us keep the promises we make to deserters?"

"The wish for success," d'Alquen retorted. "It's surprising how quickly deception becomes known on the other side of the front."

Himmler's voice grew shrill. "Then find another Bolshevik general for a liberation army. But I forbid Vlasov. Do you understand me clearly? I forbid him!"

That same afternoon d'Alquen went to see Grote; they had met in the course of Operation Winter's Tale. He reported: "I am now in a position to reach the goal, which is yours also. Only I cannot use Vlasov. Can you recommend some other Russian whom I can take to the Ukraine? Everything else will come later. Leave it to me."

Grote reflected. "There's Trukhin and Zhilenkov," he said. "But Trukhin is doubtful. I believe that he is very closely watched by your own SD. Perhaps you have the means . . ."

"The means, yes," d'Alquen answered. "But at the moment I want to avoid creating any internal stir at all. I had better be very discreet for the time being."

"Then I suggest Zhilenkov."

"And how would you rate the other politically experienced Russians who might collaborate?"

"If you want the smartest, I suggest Zykov. But then, he is very likely a Jew. Probably he is also being watched by the SD."

D'Alquen considered. The most stubborn prejudices might shift, given time and the specter of defeat. "Do you really think he's the best man?"

"Absolutely."

"Then the other thing doesn't matter. Can you arrange for me to see the Russians tomorrow evening?"

Twenty-four hours later d'Alquen had his meeting with Zhilenkov, Zykov, and Strik-Strikfeldt. The latter acted as interpreter. This was the first time his path had crossed that of the SS man.

As was his way, d'Alquen took a rather challenging tone. "You're well aware that I'm from the SS," he said, "and my superior has described your General Vlasov as a butcher's boy. I know that up to now you've been tricked, kicked, and licked. I can't promise I'll be able to undo what's been done. But I give you my word that if you'll pitch in, I'll do my damnedest to help you."

Strik-Strikfeldt remained wary. After a long pause, Zhilenkov was the first to stand up and extend his hand to d'Alquen. "Do we have any other choice?" he said. Zykov was more restrained. He, too, made it clear that he was accepting the offer because it was their last chance. He posed a number of keenly phrased questions. Then he said: "Good."

It was agreed that in two days Zhilenkov and Zykov would fly with d'Alquen to the headquarters of Army Group South in the Ukraine. There, in the territory of Field Marshal Model, who was known to give a warm welcome to propagandists, the new operation would be launched.

The next day in Dabendorf, Zykov prepared for departure. He turned the editorial direction of *Zarya* (*Dawn*) over to one of his associates, Kovalchuk. Then he took his leave and, accompanied by a young Russian who served as a kind of adjutant, he went out to Rüdersdorf-Kalkberge, where he had a small apartment.

He had just sat down to his supper when a messenger came over from the house next door to say that Zykov was wanted on the telephone. That was nothing unusual. The only telephone in the vicinity was in this house next door, where a bakery was located. Zykov and his adjutant left the apartment and were never seen again.

Witnesses later declared that the two men had been stopped by two civilians. There had been a brief, excited conversation. Then the civilians ushered Zykov and his adjutant into a large car that bore a Wehrmacht license plate. The car started off in the direction of Berlin. That was the last anyone knew of them.

At first there were only theories about what had become of Zykov. The most common of these was that Zykov had been liquidated by the SD. Many years later this version was corroborated. Behind the multiple façades of the SS, one arm had killed a man at the very moment that another had recruited him to play a part in an SS operation.

D'Alquen reported to Field Marshal Model on June 26, 1944. Model's headquarters at this time was in the vicinity of Lvov. D'Alquen set up his headquarters in Symna Woda, southwest of Lvov. Zhilenkov, and several others who were intended to replace Zykov, were quartered in a forester's house; Zhilenkov was treated like a general. The front was fairly quiet at this time. Model welcomed all support. Under these relatively favorable circumstances, d'Alquen's new operation was launched. It was given the code name *Skorpion* (Scorpion).

In order to allay Himmler's suspicions, d'Alquen at first tried a host of other propaganda approaches, couching his appeals in religious, humane, sexual, and other terms. But the core of the operation remained the announcement that the "Russian Liberation Army" was at last in process of being built up and Russian soldiers were being invited to fight in its ranks. D'Alquen asked Zhilenkov to write proclamations and leaflets along these lines, and to sign them as, so to speak, Vlasov's deputy.

After they had worked smoothly together for some two weeks, it occurred to him simply to replace Vlasov with Zhilenkov and in this way avoid any run-in with Himmler. He called on Zhilenkov in the forester's house. But when he made this proposal, Zhilenkov brusquely refused. All attempts to appeal to his ambition failed. Zhilenkov knew only too well that the Vlasov legend had been steadily growing and was now too essential to be discarded.

The results were fantastic. The number of deserters before the beginning of Operation Scorpion had amounted to little more than three hundred a month in the whole territory of Army Group South, Ukraine. Within a few weeks the figure rose to 4500. But the genuine Liberation Army did not exist, and Vlasov was not there. Before very long the credulity of the Russian troops would be exhausted.

On July 11 the great Russian summer offensive of 1944 was launched against Army Groups Center and South. By then it was plain to d'Alquen that the game was up unless he could manage to bring Vlasov personally into the fray.

The very first day of the offensive saw the destruction of all the planes at his disposal. He used the pretext of trying to find replacements to hitch a flight to Warsaw. He knew perfectly well that there were no planes available in Warsaw, but from there he would be able to communicate by telephone with Himmler, who was in Salzburg. As it happened, an air raid on Munich had destroyed the telephone lines. D'Alquen was well aware of the tactlessness of turning up unannounced in the presence of Himmler at a moment when a great battle was raging at the front. Nevertheless, he decided to fly on to Salzburg.

He arrived in the evening just as Himmler was leaving his headquarters surrounded by a cordon of generals. Himmler recognized him at once. "What are you doing here?" he snapped. "A major offensive began on your front yesterday."

D'Alquen had already prepared his lines. "I've come to make an urgent report."

"Why? Where's the fire?"

"Fire is no longer the right word for it. Reichsführer, when can I talk to you?"

"I have no time now," Himmler replied irritably. "We're leaving for East Prussia tonight. You can come along. Then we'll see."

By four o'clock the following afternoon Himmler's train was in the vicinity of Breslau. Here Himmler sent for d'Alquen.

"All right, what do you want?" he asked.

"Reichsführer, we have been doing splendidly," d'Alquen said. "But we have come to the end of our resources. Now we are inescapably confronted with the problem of Vlasov. Further success depends on our doing more than merely talking about a liberation army and Vlasov. We need the man himself. Otherwise, the Russians will not believe us any more. We need him—the new Russian offensive is rolling on. . . ."

"It's enough to drive a man mad," Himmler expostulated. "I've known you too long to suspect you of being Russophile like these army bastards. They're soft in that direction. But that's out of the question with you. What in the devil's name has got into you?"

"Reichsführer," d'Alquen said, "please believe me when I say I've thought the matter over very carefully. This Vlasov must be a bona fide personality. I have never set eyes on him, but I've sensed his authority everywhere. I've tried to get around him and make Zhilenkov play his part. It was no use."

He briefly explained his efforts, then continued insistently: "Propaganda is all very well, but the successes we have had so far are only a pale shadow of what we could do. If we could bring Vlasov on the scene as the enemy of Stalin and the leader of a Russian liberation movement, there would soon be a mighty force ready to follow him."

Himmler broke in: "Have you considered how that would affect our whole ideological and political conception?"

"Reichsführer, in our present situation victory or defeat is the issue. We can consider the ideological consequences later on."

Obviously, Himmler had the dangerous question, "Do you doubt the Führer and his victory?" on the tip of his tongue. But he said only: "With whom have you discussed this matter?"

"With nobody," d'Alquen replied.

"Would you sketch me a picture of just how we would cooperate with these Russians?"

"I couldn't give you any details at this point—I don't know enough. But the men around Vlasov have some specific ideas." He continued, with a flash of inspiration: "Reichsführer, you ought to talk with Vlasov yourself."

Himmler stared at him speechless. "Do you fully realize what you are proposing?" he exclaimed.

"Yes," d'Alquen replied. "I am convinced, Reichsführer, that you are the only one who can effect a decisive turnabout in the campaign in the East."

As he later stressed in his report, he sensed that he had made a telling point. There were doubts covered up by Himmler's ostentatious belief in victory.

They talked for more than an hour. Finally Himmler said: "Very good,

204

get in touch with Vlasov. But I'll discuss the matter with the Führer once more."

That same evening d'Alquen flew back to the eastern front to fetch Zhilenkov, whom he needed as an intermediary with Vlasov. At the front he heard that, in spite of the successful Soviet offensive, there were still a great many deserters who came to the German lines during the night.

On July 15 he arrived in Berlin with Zhilenkov. Zhilenkov went out to Dahlem to talk with Vlasov. Twenty-four hours later Vlasov, accompanied by Zhilenkov and his adjutant Zakharov, called on d'Alquen in Zehlendorf.

Like so many others before him, d'Alquen was instantly impressed by this giant of a man. Vlasov had had a night and half a day to prepare himself for this interview. Nevertheless, he showed the tremendous inner tension that had gripped him at the thought of dealing with a representative of Himmler.

It took a while for Vlasov to thaw. Clearly, he was probing to discover whether d'Alquen should be taken seriously, whether he had power behind him or was just another of those well-meaning subordinates who had proved their ineffectuality. When d'Alquen, acting again on a sudden inspiration as in his conversation with Himmler, frankly admitted that he had vainly tried to fill Vlasov's place with Zhilenkov, he could see that this mark of candor improved his standing with Vlasov.

The main purpose of their meeting, d'Alquen said, was to discuss the conditions for a conference between Vlasov and Himmler. At this moment Vlasov no doubt thought of Himmler's speech in Schachen, of his words about the *Untermensch*. Why should he be eager to oblige these people who not too long ago assumed that he was "subhuman." Nevertheless, he said that for his part nothing stood in the way of such a conference provided Himmler were at last a person who embodied power and could make decisions. It was late but not yet too late. If Himmler developed confidence in him and could make it possible for him to set up a regime opposed to Stalin and an army of adequate strength, there were still good prospects for success even after all this time. The greater part of the occupied territories in the East had already been lost, it was true, which meant the loss of the mass of the population on whom he could have relied as little as six months ago. But there were still millions of his countrymen who were prisoners of war, and, in addition, six million

Russian workers in Germany. If there was to be any action at all, there was no time to lose. All the units that had been formed of soldiers from his country, which since 1943 had been scattered here, there, and everywhere in Europe, would have to be gathered together at once and placed under his command. The Allied invasion of France was threatening to shatter the volunteer formations that had been transferred there the previous year. Also, there must be an end to the splintering of antibolshevist forces by the establishment of so many different national committees. What had once been broached in Smolensk must be carried out at last: the formation of a political and intellectual center with a clear program directed against the Stalinist system.

All he was asking of Germany, Vlasov said, was military aid until the overthrow of Stalin and freedom to rebuild a new, independent Russia that would, however, be allied with Germany.

D'Alquen was no profound political thinker who could perceive all the implications. Primarily, he was judging the Russian's propagandistic effectiveness.

On July 17 he went to Rastenburg. Himmler listened in silence to his distinctly enthusiastic report. Then he said that in the interval he had talked with Hitler, and that Hitler had given his consent to use Vlasov for purposes of propaganda.

"I'll expect Vlasov here on July 21. See to it that he arrives punctually." And then, taking an enormous leap, he said: "What do you think of our appointing Vlasov Marshal of the Liberation Army? The title would be effective."

D'Alquen went on to Berlin, where he went straight to the Kiebitzweg house. He had had no dealings with Vlasov during the period of hopeless waiting, and therefore could not be aware of the recent change in atmosphere at the Vlasov headquarters. In fact, he did not realize that he was the bearer of overwhelming news until the moment he stood facing Vlasov and delivered his message. Vlasov drew him to his huge chest and kissed him. There is nothing in his reports, however, about the vast discrepancy between his propagandistic project's and Vlasov's hopes.

D'Alquen flew back to his units with the Army Group South Ukraine to inform them of the new developments and prepare them for future operations. It was there, during the retreat from Lvov to Cracow, that the first news reached him of the attempt on Hitler's life on July 20. Next morning a radio message reached him: "The conference set for July 21 must be postponed. A later date will be set. You will be informed by radio. Himmler."

So even in the agitation of the July 20 events, Himmler had not forgotten his appointment with Vlasov. He was really giving it high priority, d'Alquen told himself.

Strik-Strikfeldt had not been in Berlin on July 20. But in the preceding days he had frequently visited the house on Kiebitzweg to discuss the sudden rapprochement of the SS with Vlasov. For the "subhuman" and "butcher boy" phrases stuck in his head and he continued to fear that behind the new cordiality on the part of the SS there might be nothing more than the desire, born of the desperation of the moment, to exploit Vlasov for propaganda purposes, and to deceive him.

It became evident to Strik-Strikfeldt that the Russian, too, had forgotten nothing. But like a hungry man who does not ask who is giving him bread, Vlasov did not want to ask who could provide him with an army.

On the morning of July 21, when Strik-Strikfeldt heard the first clear reports on the events and participants of July 20, he decided to go out to Dabendorf. The fact that Freytag-Loringhoven had been in on the plot made him fear the worst. If it were true that Tresckow as well as Stauffenberg were involved, it was impossible to foresee what might happen in the next few days. The investigators might discover that the conspiracy included members of Vlasov's and the Dabendorf circle. For they would already have known that some of those whose names figured on the lists of plotters wanted to make peace in the West and then fight on in the East, with the help of Vlasov's army.

When Strik-Strikfeldt reached Dabendorf, the first person he met was Trukhin. Trukhin's first words were: "What does this mean? New hope?" that threw Strik-Strikfeldt into more confusion. Had the men in Dabendorf known more than he himself knew?

But he found Dabendorf untouched. Obviously, the Gestapo had more important business at the moment. Strik-Strikfeldt stayed until afternoon and had long discussions with Trukhin, Boyarski, and several others. He found no signs that there had been any communication between Trukhin and the conspirators. The talk revolved around the question of whether the conference between Vlasov and Himmler would take place in view of the new situation.

Late in the afternoon Strik-Strikfeldt returned to Berlin. Throughout the ride he kept fearing that when he reached Kiebitzweg he would find a Gestapo squad there.

But his fears were needless. Vlasov and Malyshkin were sitting about as usual and Vlasov threw his arms around Strik-Strikfeldt. The Russian leader had been drinking.

"Today was the day we had pinned our hopes on," he said. "Another few hours and this day will be over."

Strik-Strikfeldt threw a questioning look at him. "Andrei Andreyevich," he said, "the man you were going to see today is among the victors, and is now busy wiping out those who intended to kill him, too. His power has only increased. Yesterday and today we lost many friends who helped you during the hard years. Stauffenberg is dead."

Vlasov stared into space.

"Stauffenberg?" he said slowly. "I don't know anybody by that name."

Strik-Strikfeldt straightened up abruptly. "But Andrei Andreyevich," he said, "you certainly do know Stauffenberg, that splendid German colonel who worked so hard in your behalf."

Vlasov's face remained rigid. "No," he said, "you must be mistaken."

Malyshkin left the room. Vlasov listened to his footsteps receding down the corridor; only then did he look squarely at Strik-Strikfeldt. As slowly as before, he said: "One does not talk about such dead friends."

He stressed the word "such." "One doesn't know them. Please recall, I have passed through the Soviet school. Never admit that such men were friends. Never trust anybody. Even in Malyshkin's presence there are certain things I should not hear and should not say; I may not even trust Zhilenkov, not even my brother."

Strik-Strikfeldt understood. This was part and parcel of the giant's psychological training. And since yesterday, since public purges and liquidations had become commonplace in Germany, too, these lessons had once again come to the fore.

There was a stir in the outer hallway. An SS car had driven up outside the house. The Russian guards did not know what it meant and whether or not they ought to shoot. But it turned out to be only a courier. In his pedantic way, Himmler was taking care of every item in his appointment book.

The courier delivered to Vlasov personally word that Himmler would set a new date for their meeting as soon as events permitted. He suggested that Vlasov use the interval to go to South Germany for a rest. He, Himmler, was placing an SS convalescent home in Ruhpolding, a small Bavarian village, at the general's disposal. It would be well if he could prepare for the coming task, and be in a position to make specific proposals to the Reichsführer at their eventual meeting. That should be taking place in three weeks or so.

Vlasov, who had listened in silence, asked the courier—an SS officer—to wait until he made his decision. As soon as the door closed behind the officer, he went up to Strik-Strikfeldt and put his hands on the captain's shoulders.

"He didn't forget it," he said. Then he paced in silence for a while. Abruptly he said: "We will go, and you will accompany me. You and Sergei. I must have you with me while I plan. Don't say no."

The thought passed through Strik-Strikfeldt's mind that Himmler's generous offer might be a trick to get Vlasov away from Berlin and keep him under closer supervision in Ruhpolding, perhaps even arrest him there, where he would be far from his men.

"Of course, I'll go with you," Strik-Strikfeldt said.

On July 27 Vlasov, accompanied by Strik-Strikfeldt and Sergei Fröhlich, arrived in Ruhpolding. The Russian wore civilian clothes. Nevertheless, this huge man with his alien face created a considerable stir on the day of his arrival. But most Germans would not have known who General Vlasov was, even if he had been identified, and the mysterious stranger quickly vanished with his two companions into the old monastery in the vicinity of the Taubensee about two miles north of Ruhpolding. And here once again a long wait began—much longer than the three weeks Himmler had mentioned in his message.

Perhaps it was a kindness of fate that during this period Vlasov met a woman who meant more to him than all his previous casual acquaintances. Her name was Heidi Bielenberg; she was the widow of a doctor who had been killed in the fighting. She had converted the monastery into a hospice for needy family members of soldiers killed in the war, and had just about completed furnishing and equipping the place when SS Headquarters expropriated it as a convalescent center for members of the Waffen-SS. Heidi Bielenberg had utilized a private connection with General Steiner in the attempt to regain control of her convalescent home. But her efforts had been in vain. Sixty gravely wounded members of the SS had arrived, and she could not very well refuse to admit them. The last of the sixty were well enough to be on the verge of discharge when Vlasov and his companions appeared at her door.

Heidi Bielenberg was a trim-looking woman, well-groomed, blond, intelligent. She played the piano and accordion and had a good, if small, voice.

Soon after Vlasov's arrival it became a custom for her to play and sing for the general, Strik-Strikfeldt, and Sergei Fröhlich. Since Vlasov loved music, there was an immediate rapport between them. Undoubtedly, there were crasser motives operating also. Heidi Bielenberg had frequently mentioned that she had personal connections with leading groups in the SS. When she became more familiar with Vlasov's personality and situation, she spoke of asking her friends to remind Himmler of the appointment, which he might have forgotten.

Heidi Bielenberg was a woman with ambition. Perhaps Vlasov attracted her at first less as a man than as a chance to move into an unusual role. She had learned enough about Vlasov and his potentialities for her lively imagination to picture him as head of a new Russia, and perhaps she herself at his side.

Heidi Bielenberg did not speak a word of Russian. But Vlasov proved to have learned more German than Strik-Strikfeldt and Sergei Fröhlich had suspected. Strik-Strikfeldt looked on in silence; he could not have foreseen that the affair would lead to engagement and marriage—although the marriage took place only after Vlasov's hopes were finally crushed and he had heard, in response to his questions about the fate of his family in the Soviet Union: "Hanged long ago." For the moment Strik-Strikfeldt was pleased by this diversion which kept Vlasov occupied and helped him through those weeks of waiting, which stretched on into the autumn.

It was not until September 9 that a telephoned message came: Vlasov was to return to Berlin at once; Reichsführer SS Heinrich Himmler would expect him at his headquarters in Rastenburg on September 16.

The regular courier train in which Vlasov left Berlin for Rastenburg on September 15 departed from Berlin at 8 P.M. Accompanying him in the train, in addition to Strik-Strikfeldt and d'Alquen, was the Dr. Kroeger whom Arlt had recommended to Obergruppenführer Berger many weeks before. His presence was a great surprise. It seemed that Berger had actually taken him under his wing. Now he was to serve as interpreter.

Vlasov kept Strik-Strikfeldt and d'Alquen close to him. During the night he stood for a long time in the corridor of the railroad car. He could not conceal the tremendous suspense that filled him. Again and again he asked d'Alquen what Himmler had said, how he was to address Himmler. He kept saying that he regarded d'Alquen as his ally in tomorrow's negotiations; d'Alquen must help him.

D'Alquen replied: "My own prestige is involved in the outcome of these negotiations. Of course, I will help you. But I must ask you to be diplomatic, to let bygones be bygones, and not to demand the impossible at this first meeting. Remember that Himmler has increased his power a great deal in the interval. He now is also the commander of the Reserve Army and can therefore provide everything you need to organize your Liberation Army."

D'Alquen did not know that Himmler had meanwhile spoken with Hitler again, partly from insecurity that never quite left him. This time he had spoken of organizing Vlasov divisions, but presented them merely as a necessary evil for the sake of improving propaganda in the East, not as genuine beginnings of a Russian Army. He had also spoken of the propagandistic necessity for forming a Russian anti-Stalinist government, but had added that such things, of course, did not impose any obligations.

Hitler had approved these moves, but with the clear proviso that the whole operation was solely for purposes of propaganda. Neither the recent retreats and defeats on the eastern front, nor the successful Allied invasion of France, nor the attempted assassination of July 20 had changed his attitude. He would have balked even now if the suggestion of a Vlasov action were coming from anyone but Himmler—the SS chief whom he trusted more than ever after July 20 and on whom he had heaped additional powers.

Incomprehensibly, he had added the instruction: "But in this matter keep in touch with the Foreign Office."

Himmler had passed these words along to the SS Hauptamt, taking them to mean that in the future the East Ministry no longer had a voice in matters concerning Vlasov. At most, the Foreign Office would have to be consulted. D'Alquen did not yet know anything about these developments.

At nine o'clock in the morning on September 16 Vlasov and his companions reached the complex of bunkers (some twenty-five miles from Hitler's "Wolf's Lair" headquarters) in the center of which Himmler's special train was waiting on a siding. At ten o'clock Vlasov was taken to the Labor Service barrack in which Himmler's office was now located. Himmler awaited him standing; beside him were Obergruppenführer Berger and a Gestapo officer. Dr. Kroeger had posted himself in front of the door and let all pass except Strik-Strikfeldt. He blocked his way and said coldly: "The Reichsführer wishes to speak with General Vlasov alone." Since Vlasov's adjutant Zakharov had already entered the room, Strik-Strikfeldt stared at Kroeger in astonishment.

Vlasov took a step backward. "Wilfried Karlovich, what does this mean?" he said. "I won't go without you."

But Strik-Strikfeldt hastily shook hands with him and urged him on: "Go alone if that is how it must be. . . . Too much is at stake."

He turned away and left the barracks to wait outside.

It fell to d'Alquen to introduce Vlasov to Heinrich Himmler. He observed in amazement with what perfect dignity Vlasov conducted himself. And he could see that Himmler, too, was surprised by his first personal impression of Vlasov.

Himmler opened the conversation, addressing Vlasov as "Herr General." He said: "I shall be candid enough to tell you how much I regret today that this conference is taking place so late. But I am convinced that it is not too late. I am not the man to make hasty decisions. But once I have made a decision, it is firm."

He threw a rather uncomfortable look at d'Alquen, then went on quickly: "I know the kind of reputation I have. That does not affect me. People say a great deal that is not true, but such stories increase their respect for me. That is why I don't trouble to deny these things, although they are not true."

He spoke emphatically, like someone who knows quite well that, for good reasons, he will hardly be believed and therefore takes some pains to strengthen his credibility.

"Many mistakes have been made," he continued. "I am aware of the mistakes committed in our treatment of you. And I am prepared to discuss them with you quite frankly."

D'Alquen felt a certain admiration for the agility with which Himmler set about bridging the gulf between himself and Vlasov. But that was the way he could be when he wanted to; he had that plausibility and seemingly honest manner. "Unfortunately," Himmler went on, "our meeting has been repeatedly postponed. This was due to events with which you are familiar, and to difficulties that arose for me personally because of new duties."

Vlasov had listened to the words that Dr. Kroeger translated with a frozen face, as though to indicate that he had not forgotten previous insults. Was this Himmler the Terrible? This was the first man from the uppermost level of the hierarchy with whom he was at last face to face!

"Herr Minister," Vlasov said in reply, "I wish to thank you for your invitation to come here. And I am happy at last to meet one of the real

212

leaders of Germany and have the opportunity to present my ideas to him."

He manifested a keen instinct for Himmler's vanity, but also his own self-assurance. "You, Herr Minister," he continued, "are today the strongest man in Germany's top leadership. I, General Vlasov, am the first general in this war who defeated a German army outside Moscow. Is there not an implicit program in the fact that these two men are meeting?"

He watched Himmler carefully to see the effect of his remark about the defeat of the Germans outside Moscow. But Himmler kept himself in hand.

Vlasov sat up straighter and said with a note of solemnity: "Herr Minister, before I can present my program to you I must tell you this: I hate the system that gave me a great career. But I consider it of the utmost importance to make clear that I am a Russian. I am the son of a simple peasant. Therefore, I love my native soil as the son of a German peasant loves his. I am convinced that it is not too late if you, Herr Minister, will find within yourself the readiness to lend us real support in the quickest way. Even now Stalin's system is doomed to death if it can be struck at its most sensitive places. But I must state it as a prerequisite for success that our cooperation has to take place on the basis of complete equality. Hence, I will have to speak as frankly as you have done, Herr Minister."

"Please do so," Himmler countered.

Vlasov kept his unbending posture. "Unfortunately," he said, "there have been many things that you and I must get out of the way, Herr Minister. I was most pained by your pamphlet, *Der Untermensch. I* would like to hear your present thoughts about this pamphlet."

Himmler dodged this delicate question. "You are right to bring up this subject," he said. "I suppose it is part of the long period of maturation that we have learned to discard generalizations and to drop prejudices. The pamphlet you mention was intended to show a human type produced by the bolshevist system, a type that threatens Germany just as much as it does your country. There are subhumans in every nation. The difference between our country and yours is only that there the *Untermenschen* hold power, whereas in Germany I have put them behind bars. It would ultimately be your task to carry out this reversal of the situation in Russia also."

He looked at Vlasov as if to determine whether this grotesquely twisted version of the *Untermensch* theories was acceptable to the Russian. He

213

went on rapidly: "I should like to hear your thoughts on the question of whether the Russian people would still support you today in such an attempt to turn the power-relationships upside down, whether they would still regard you as a liberator."

Vlasov was still far from satisfied with what he later called "the *Untermensch* blasphemy," but he overcame himself, adopted a diplomatic tone, and said: "My answer to that question would be 'yes.' It would depend, however, on certain prerequisites."

With that preamble he began to range far afield, as was his habit. D'Alquen noted some of his arguments: "You invaded my country on the grounds that we were prepared to stab you in the back. That is not so. In 1941 Stalin did not intend to attack Germany. Instead, he was planning for February 1942 an incursion into southeastern Europe, in the direction of Rumania, Bulgaria, Greece, and the Dardanelles. To be sure, he did not put too much faith in the pact with Germany and was expecting a German attack when England was defeated. But he feared the direct military confrontation with Germany and hoped to be able to seize the decisive centers of power in the Southeast unchallenged, since Germany was then involved in the struggle with England. He thought that if he held these key positions he would be able to exert enough pressure upon Germany to make a German attack unlikely. That was the reason we had assembled so many assault armies in the southern part of my country. I must say that your attack profited enormously from the element of surprise. That is the explanation for your great initial successes. I cannot help acknowledging the high level of performance of your troops. Nevertheless, it has been evident from the beginning that the war as it is being waged by you could not be won. I am aware, Herr Minister, that this viewpoint of mine has been reported to you, and that it earlier prompted you to refuse to see me."

In saying this, Vlasov was alluding to the Schachen speech. He did so in the manner of a person who has suffered too long to be able to dissimulate his suffering.

Vlasov continued: "I do not want to say anything more about this aspect of the past. But permit me to explain to you, Herr Minister, why I decided as early as 1941 that Germany was pursuing the wrong strategy. For great military successes to have been won at all, the entire strength of your forces would have had to be concentrated upon Moscow and Leningrad. Then we would have had to give up the south without a fight. But even such operations would hardly have been decisive. Stalin himself never believed that the German leadership was counting on military force alone to bring it victory. He expected political warfare. In the spring of 1941 Stalin called a conference of army commanders at which he crowed over the political failures of the German leadership. He said with total openness that his greatest concern was not the temporary German military penetrations. His greatest concern was that the Germans would bring with them a program of national liberation. He knew, he said, that the peoples of the Soviet Union had not yet overcome their past national feelings. Moreover, the Bolshevik Revolution had not yet been carried to completion. Bourgeois instincts were still widespread among the masses, and fascism was shot through with bourgeois elements. In his talk to the commanders, Stalin for the first time put forward the ideas which were soon to be embodied in the propaganda line of the 'Great Patriotic War.' He spoke, for instance, of national heroes in our Russian history. Stalin's postulates were so unusual that those present accepted them with the greatest hesitation. Germany had immense political opportunities in our country, and threw them away. But even so it is not yet too late."

D'Alquen was concerned. How often Himmler had spoken of Slavic arrogance? How long would he tolerate Vlasov's didactic tone?

Yet Himmler's face showed no signs of anger, at least while Vlasov's words were being translated. With a gesture, he invited the Russian to continue.

"Herr Minister," Vlasov declared, "I think that even at this late date I can still end the war against Stalin. If I had at my disposal a large force of shock troops consisting of men from my country, and if I could advance as far as Moscow with it, I could end this war over the telephone by talking to my comrades who are fighting on the other side. A German army—that is another matter. But with the exception of the profiteers from bolshevism, the majority of the Russian people are still antibolshevistic.

"Herr Minister," he pleaded, "believe me, I do possess the authority to lead this army and with this army to win over the people of my country. I am not just any unknown émigré. I became your prisoner in a hopeless situation. In the solitude of the Volkhov pocket I began to see the real plight of my country. That was the sole reason I accepted the German offers of collaboration at the time, even at the risk of being considered a traitor. I could not have suspected then that I would have had to wait so long for the meeting that is taking place today. But in spite of all disappointments, I clung fast to the conviction that collaboration with Germany is the only road to salvation. Perhaps fate has brought about Stalin's successes in order to pave the way for this meeting. Herr Minister,

I do not come to you with empty hands. For in this salvation and liberation of my country from Stalin, Germany, too, will be saved."

Had anyone up to this moment ever dared to speak to Himmler of Germany's being saved by Slavs? But all Himmler said was: "General, would you give me your view of the military situation?"

Vlasov glanced around as if he were looking for a map. Then he said: "I am in a position to predict the next steps of the Soviet Army. I have guessed right ever since I was taken prisoner. But nobody has come to me for my predictions. Every rigid system has its weaknesses, and that is also true of the Soviet system. It is always sensitive to the unforeseen. And in all its calculations and plans the Soviet leadership has to this day not yet taken into consideration one factor. That is the actual existence of a Russian Liberation Army."

D'Alquen observed with admiration the skill with which Vlasov avoided a protracted discussion of military matters and turned straight back to his goal.

"Herr Minister," he said, "give me the necessary Russian forces. I made many protests when battalions of my countrymen were sent to the German western front in France in 1943. Now they have been plunged into the Anglo-American invasion. They have been forced to fight in the wrong place, a fight whose purpose they do not understand. They have been scattered, beaten. But it is not yet too late. In Germany, Herr Minister, there is sufficient Russian human material for an army of more than a million soldiers. Not only in the prison camps, but also wherever my countrymen are working in Germany, some six million of them. There is the foundation for an army that could produce the decisive turning point in your war in the East. I am not worried about raising enough soldiers if only I am given the freedom to appeal to them. But only a Russian can appeal to them, not a German, for they attribute their sufferings to the Germans. Unfortunately, most of the war matériel belonging to the scattered Russian units has been lost in France. I saw that coming. So I must now ask you, Herr Minister, to give me weapons— weapons!"

D'Alquen held his breath. But Himmler answered smoothly:

"Herr General," he said, "I have spoken with the Führer. From today on you can regard yourself as commander in chief of an army with the rank of a full general. You will receive the authority to appoint officers up to the rank of colonel at your own discretion."

He hesitated for a moment, as if he were embarrassed by the admission he was about to make.

"I am personally strongly in favor of your project. But my means as commander of the Reserve Army are limited at the moment. It may be that there is an ample supply of human material. But you must not forget that the people who will join your army will then be missed as workers in our factories. We cannot afford to jeopardize our production. I will, therefore, authorize you to raise two divisions, with the understanding that further divisions will follow later. It would be unfair of me to make you extravagant promises. Does my proposal seem satisfactory to you? If so, I shall issue the necessary orders."

The excitement that Vlasov had worked up while he spoke had drained away. His disappointment could be read on his face. But he quickly regained control of his feelings.

"Herr Minister," he declared, "I can appreciate the difficulties you mention. But I would assume that the raising of these two first divisions was really only a beginning, for so small a force could not possibly bring about the turn of events that is to your interest and ours."

"Of course," Himmler said. "Our weapons situation is strained at the moment only because of the need to relocate our armaments production. That situation will soon change, especially as regards the manufacture of new weapons, of which you have certainly heard; they will undoubtedly have a decisive impact upon the war, but I cannot give you any specific details as yet."

This last remark sounded odd indeed coming from Himmler. Either he was implying that he himself did not believe all that strongly in the "secret weapons," concerning which there were so many rumors—for if he did put his trust in them this conversation with Vlasov would have been quite unnecessary—he wanted Vlasov to understand that Germany was not dependent on him. But Vlasov did not react. He concentrated wholly on his immediate goal. "Good," he said. "Until that time there are urgent things to do. Although the greater part of the Eastern units in France have been more or less dispersed, I should like to point out the need for immediately collecting all such units and remnants and placing them under my command."

"Of course," said Himmler.

Vlasov continued: "There is another important matter I must raise with you. If I am to have any success in opposing Stalin, it cannot be achieved by having the existing forces broken up into many splinters as has hitherto been done under the aegis of the German East Ministry and other agencies and bureaus. If I am to create a freer Russia, such an intention, of course, involves my giving the people of Russia the chance to decide whether they wish to form nations of their own or continue to remain members of the great Russian community. I, myself, believe they will choose the second course and that the separatist forces that are being fostered by the East Ministry and other German agencies will not find popular support. But, in any case, we must first of all join forces to fight Stalin."

Vlasov had reached this point when, to d'Alquen's complete surprise, he took a tack that revealed how carefully he had prepared for this meeting. "I know that you, Herr Minister, have been pursuing a wider, European goal, and that your SS troops are composed of nationals from other European peoples. They are fighting together. They are fighting above all against Stalinism and bolshevism, which are the archenemies of this New Order in Europe. But this future order can be created only if the battle is won. If with your aid I am able to defeat Stalin, I know that I shall have to make sacrifices for this future. And, perhaps, someday we will face the problem of throwing overboard all the old frontiers and creating entirely new geographical entities. Perhaps, then, the Ukraine or some other part of my former country would become not a separatist part of Russia but a part of this New Order. That is something that can be discussed on the basis of equality after we have won our victory. But for the moment only common action can help."

Berger had tried to signal Himmler. But Himmler paid no attention. It did not matter whether Vlasov was speaking from conviction or from calculation. In any case, in a few words he had hinted at a way to bridge the gap between Himmler's conception of "Germanic cultivation of the East" and his own call for a Pan-Russian approach.

Berger, too, was taken by surprise. Meanwhile, Vlasov was presenting a new request.

"Herr Minister, we cannot proceed further unless I am allowed to deal directly with representatives of my country's so-called nationalities. So far this has been banned. Similarly I need to be in direct touch with authority, real authority."

Without reflection Himmler said that he quite understood the need for this. "These two gentlemen with me can serve as liaison between us. Gruppenführer Berger and Dr. Kroeger will henceforth be at your disposal."

"Thank you, Herr Minister," Vlasov replied. "I had all but given up hope that this moment would ever come. Forgive me if I raise a few more points. There is the question of my countrymen who are working in Germany. You were afraid that incorporating a large number of these people in our army would be a blow to the German armaments industry."

"So it would," Himmler said. "Besides, I have long been highly dubious of these people." He smoothly sailed past the reef of the *Ostarbeiter* question. "By now I must admit that we have had unexpectedly good experiences with them. Cases of sabotage are far more uncommon than I originally feared."

"Herr Minister," Vlasov interjected, "there will be no sabotage at all if my countrymen know that they are not working for a foreign country but for themselves, for a new and better homeland. Success against Stalin requires not only the Liberation Army but also a political center that can proclaim a program for the new order in my country."

"The requests along these lines have, of course, already been communicated to me," Himmler said; by now he was more and more recklessly making large gestures. "I approve them in principle, just as I do the raising of the Liberation Army. I assume that you wish to be the chief of this political center."

Vlasov beckoned to his adjutant to open his briefcase. "We have had leisure enough to draw up our proposals for the . . . the government which, for the present, we wish to call a 'Committee.'"

Himmler showed some surprise. However, he accepted the sheaf of papers with perfect civility. "We will have your proposals examined," he said.

Vlasov gave the hint of a bow. "In connection with the Committee," he said, "I should like to return to the question of my countrymen now working in Germany. I should like to propose that all of them, as Russian citizens, be placed under the jurisdiction of the Committee. For my part I would guarantee that the enlisting of some of my countrymen in the Liberation Army would not adversely affect armaments production. I would guarantee that the remaining workers would make up for any drop in production by an increase in their own efforts."

Himmler was evasive. "I quite agree that we must concern ourselves with the political activation of all these fellow-countrymen of yours. But placing them under your jurisdiction would involve you in some unpleasant duties. For example, you would have to decree punishments. Such negative use of force might well be a burden to you. I have a bad reputation anyhow. You, on the other hand, should be responsible for the brighter side of things. But all these matters can be settled later. Once the Army and the Committee have been formed, I will be able to present you as their leader within the framework of an official state ceremony. Then, perhaps, we can sign an alliance."

Whenever Himmler began to talk of vague ceremonial matters, he was indicating that the conversation was reaching its end. Himmler rose. Vlasov did likewise.

The meeting had lasted all of six hours. After Vlasov took his leave, Himmler ordered d'Alquen to stay. For a while he paced in silence in front of the windows. Then he said: "You are right. The man is an effective personality. But—" all his old prejudices returned at once, with a rush—"you must never forget that he is a Slav, in spite of everything. You are to keep your eyes open and to report to me anything that goes beyond the framework necessary for propaganda. I must be prepared to cover myself at all times, where the Führer is concerned. . . ."

In saying this Himmler betrayed the real content of his arrangement with Hitler. In conclusion he said: "I was much impressed by what Vlasov had to say regarding future possibilities. Possibly more can be achieved with him than just propaganda. Still, he is a Slav. He remains a Slav. . . ."

On September 17, one day after this meeting, Lieutenant Colonel Hansen, Ia to the commander of the volunteer formations under the commander in chief, West, reached Simmern, northeast of Koblenz, after the precipitous retreat from France. Hansen wrote in his diary:

> Here is all we know about the fate of our formations. Of the volunteer parent division, remnants of the Second Regiment with a hundred men are west of Belfort. Cossack Unit 403, Cossack Unit 454, and North Caucasian Battalion 836 with 600 to 700 men are near Belfort. The First Regiment of the North Caucasian Legion with 375 men, north of Kaiserstuhl. Remnants of the Armenian Legion, 300 men, north of Kaiserstuhl.
>
> Matters could scarcely be worse. Our hands completely tied. The situation at the front goes steadily downhill and the confusion reaches desperate proportions.

On the day of his conversation with Himmler, Vlasov did not yet know the full extent of this tragedy, which had begun on the morning of June 6 when the first Eastern troops, Battalions 439, 441, and 642, were caught up in the invasion battle.

Extracts from Hansen's journal during those days of collapse follow:

June 6: All communications are cut. What is more, we still have no commander. Wartenberg's successor has not yet arrived.

June 9: Since we can get no news of our battalions in the invasion area, a staff officer has been assigned to make his way forward as far as possible. A telephone call from Army High Command informs us that Battalion 441 has fought with distinction.

June 11: Our battalions are not mentioned in the Armed Forces communiqué, but there is mention of Grenadier Regiment 736, to which East Battalion 642 belongs. Disturbing news that there has been a kind of mutiny in Georgian Battalion 797. . . . Our Russian staff officer, Major Molchanov, is sent to the front to maintain communications with newly committed battalions.

June 15: The new commander has just arrived. Major General Ritter von Niedermeyer, hitherto commander of the 162nd Turkic Infantry Division in Italy. He is an old "Russian" who regards only Russian units as real fighters. . . . He takes reports on Georgian Battalion 797, which had to be disarmed, as bearing out his point of view.

June 22: Not much sense in keeping journal, since we are without communications. The reports that do arrive, however, indicate that a large number of battalions, including 439, 635, 642, and 441, have fought with astonishing bravery in spite of their wretched equipment. Only 200 men left of Battalion 441.

June 24: Major General Niedermeyer decides to go to the battle areas. Many of our formations are in the "fortresses" that have been left behind on the coast. There are reports of American and British sound-truck propaganda calling on our battalions to desert and promising speedy repatriation to all who do. Obviously, the enemy knows nothing of the psychological state of the volunteers and of conditions in their homeland.

July 6: Major General Niedermeyer has returned from his visit to the front. . . . With the general's approval, an attempt has been made at the invasion front to unite Russian battalions in larger battle formations. The author of this idea is a Russian, Colonel Bunyachenko, who had previously exercised sole command over a Russian battalion on the eastern front. A troublesome but remarkably competent officer, Bunyachenko. Made a career in the Red Army, at the end chief of staff to Marshal Timoshenko. Deserted by flying over the German lines and landing his plane in our rear. From the first tried to join up with the Vlasov movement. . . . Hence, regarded as troublesome and unreliable. Now has again pressed for the creation of solidly Russian units. But failed halfway to his goal. The two battalions under his command retained their German supervisory staff. Armament and training inadequate for an attack. The use of two languages created greater difficulties than normally. But Bunyachenko with his tenacious determination forced commitment to the attack. It failed. Up to seventy percent casualties. But no deserters.

July 8: Bunyachenko arrives at our headquarters. Forty, of medium height, stocky, round head shaved bare. The son of small farmers from the vicinity of Kharkov. Joined the Communist Party as early as 1919. Three years of General Staff training. In 1939 dispatched to Vladivostok as commander of the Far East Division. His numerous family sentenced to death as retaliation for his fighting on our side. Bunyachenko reports to us on the battle and points out the reasons that led to the failure of his battalions: miserable armament, shortage of munitions, inadequate training. . . .

Major General Niedermeyer agrees with Bunyachenko's criticism. But at the present stage it is quite impossible to undertake major reorganizations.

July 10: General Malyshkin has arrived from Berlin to investigate the fate of the Russian formations in the invasion battle. Group around Vlasov lacks all information. Malyshkin is worried that all the volunteer formations intended to be the backbone of Vlasov's plans may be lost in the West.

Malyshkin points out that the Russians have proved their will to fight. Inadequate arms, training, and leadership impose limits. But the decisive factors are the psychological ones. All the wounded men he has visited in the hospitals ask the same questions, he says. The Russians think they are being used as cannon fodder in the present situation. They invariably ask: When is the real Russian Army coming? Where is Vlasov?

Malyshkin says it is becoming more difficult for him, too, to convince the soldiers that what they are doing in the West has any point. A year ago everyone was saying: "Things are moving. A Russian Liberation Army will be formed." But now this promise looks increasingly empty. The only way to restore some credibility, Malyshkin insists, is to set up really large Russian formations under Russian leadership. Either the Germans must be generous and trust the Russians, or else the whole thing should not have been started.

At this point Major Molchanov puts in: "It would help a great deal if the German supervisory and liaison staffs were better selected. Some of them still look upon Russians as half animal. Some of the Germans are also prepared to shirk and send the Russian troops on ahead. The only thing we can do at the moment is to send our supplies to the places where we guess the volunteer formations to be. It's grotesque that while we are desperately hunting for our units, reports are pouring in from all parts of the army of unusual numbers of auxiliaries who need supplies. These reports may be correct, although they don't agree with earlier reports. But they may also represent attempts on the part of German formations to improve their own supply situation."

August 4: Colonel Bunyachenko is dispatched to Berlin. As a battalion commander he is part of a delegation that will call on Minister Rosenberg. . . .

August 6: The few telephone calls that come through request interpreters and propagandists for the battalions engaged in battle. . . . On the other hand, German divisions reject Russian propagandists from Dabendorf. Dabendorf is like a red flag.

August 10: Major General Niedermeyer back from his visit to the front. Recognized that further commitment of our battalions on the major front is pointless.

It is obvious that in the long run battalions cannot stand up in a major battle with strong antagonists whom only extreme sophism can make out as their enemy. . . . Moreover, faith in German superiority is crucial to these battalions. While they were in the East that faith could be at least halfway sustained; here it is crumbling from week to week.

The Volga Tatar Legion and Armenian Legion have had to be disarmed. . . .

August 17: No more news at all from the invasion front. Signs of dissolution among the German troops.

Hansen was now involved in the retreat from Paris, as his diary notes indicate:

Command to leave Paris with staff of commander in chief, West. Departure in the evening. Command, West, transferring to Metz. No specific orders for us. Major General Niedermeyer sends me ahead to Verdun. . . .

August 25: General German retreat. . . .

August 27: Volunteer parent division on the march northward. Leader of the Georgian Guard Company from Paris reports. He withdrew from Paris on August 23, has had casualties of 40 men. Discipline among the rest completely shattered. Assigned to construction tasks. Americans report number of captured volunteers at 20,000.

August 28: Major General Niedermeyer arrives in Verdun. . . . Objectively considered, it is amazing that any of the volunteer formations are still fighting. Undoubtedly, fear that the British or Americans will turn them over to the Soviets plays a part. . . .

September 1: Retreat in the Koblenz area. On German soil in Simmern. Incredible scenes on the roads. Chaotic flight. . . .

September 4: Reestablished communication with Headquarters Commander in Chief, West. First news of Thirtieth SS Sigling Division composed of Russians and sent into battle at Belfort for the first time only a few days ago. Held for three days. Then caught up in the general wave of retreat.

September 6: This SS division, which we had never heard of before, turns out to be a formation of White Ruthenians. Inadequately armed. Amazing fighting spirit in the face of the general collapse.

Commandant's headquarters of the encircled fortress of Brest reports: 203 deserters from North Caucasian Battalion 800, 53 deserters from Battalion 633. . . .

A few hours later staff of commander in chief, West, orders the disbanding of all volunteer formations. To be disarmed and used for fortification labor.

If we are to salvage anything out of this miserable business, only the general of the volunteers can help. General Köstring promises to be in Simmern on September 12.

September 12: General Köstring arrives. The old man faces the ruins of his work. But is composed, as though he expected this outcome. After two days of conferences with the chief of staff, General Westphal, the following agreement is reached: all volunteers who return either in units or as stragglers will be assigned to fortification work. They will retain their arms. After the work is completed, all formations will be sent to their replacement units in Germany. . . .

September 20: More and more formations report in, their numbers down to burned-out remnants. The adjutant of Volga Tatar Battalion 627 arrives. After hearing his report I am not surprised at the dissolution of the battalion. It was continuously employed on fortifications in the main battle line. The divisions to which the battalion was attached were relieved, but the battalion itself never. There were no medals awarded. Medical and sanitary conditions were terrible because the departing divisions thought of the Volga Tatars last. All things are avenged on this earth.

September 21: Difficulties with General Westphal, who does not want to be bothered by anything concerning Russians. . . . New demands keep coming in from German units that desperately need auxiliaries. The slow stabilization of the new front so plainly reveals the inequity of the sides even General Westphal begins to take another attitude toward our Russians. It's maddening!

September 27: Major General Niedermeyer shows growing bitterness.

September 28: Major General Niedermeyer is summoned to the chief advocate general under the commander in chief, West. In the evening we hear that he has been denounced for his criticisms.

September 30: Major General Niedermeyer taken to Berlin to answer charges there.

October 2 (morning): Official communication from the paymaster's office of the Torgau Army Prison that Major General Niedermeyer has been delivered there. . . .

October 2 (evening): Like hot coals of mockery comes word from the prop-slot of commander in chief, West, that in the case of Vlasov the propaganda line has changed one hundred percent. Pact between Himmler and Vlasov. First Pan-Russian units under Russian command to be organized soon. . . . Can I possibly grasp this?

Late evening of September 22, 1944 had provided Dr. Bräutigam in Berlin with a considerable surprise. He had just got home from work when he received a visit from Embassy Secretary Hilger. Hilger had been attached to the German Embassy in the Soviet Union until 1941. He was one of the foremost German experts on Russia—although Hitler no longer wished to hear his advice after June 1941.

He had only come, Hilger explained, to bring Dr. Bräutigam to State Secretary Steengracht, who urgently wanted to see him. Steengracht had already gone to bed. "Forgive my informal attire," he said. "I really could not wait to see you."

He quickly came to the point. Would Bräutigam be prepared to work on the Vlasov affair for the Foreign Office's Eastern Desk?

"I beg your pardon," Bräutigam said. "I don't understand the context. Up to now I've always thought the Foreign Office was deliberately keeping out of all developments concerning Vlasov."

"Of course," Steengracht replied. This rather colorless man of fifty who had succeeded State Secretary von Weizsäcker in the Foreign Office was considerably cleverer than he appeared. "We have never given up hope that after all we might still be called on for some kind of peace negotiations with the Soviet government we have recognized. Had we identified ourselves with the Vlasov project, that would have been an obstacle."

Bräutigam looked puzzled. This made Steengracht's proposal even more incomprehensible.

"However, much has changed in the past few days," Steengracht continued. "On September 16 Himmler received Vlasov and has, as it were, assumed a protectorate over the Vlasov movement. Obviously, he is acting with the Führer's consent, for the Führer has given Himmler instructions to keep in touch with the Foreign Office. The Führer's directive has been passed on to us. I don't as yet understand the purpose of it all. But it is a directive, so we have to act on it. And we thought of you immediately."

"I'd first have to be released from the East Ministry and officially reinstated here," Bräutigam said. "But I myself can see some of the implications."

"Please clarify them."

"I can only think," Bräutigam went on, "that Himmler made this decision without realizing its full import. The existing national committees have been recognized by the East Ministry for a long time. If we backed Vlasov, we never did so with the idea that he was to form a Pan-Russian liberation army. Vlasov was supposed to represent only the historically Russian area and the Russians themselves, just as Shandruk represented the Ukrainians or Chayum Khan the Turkistanis. This new arrangement will upset the applecart. None of the national committees will voluntarily submit. And Rosenberg will be backing them in their resistance."

"All this seems frightfully parochial," Steengracht said. "For me the question at the moment is whether you are willing to take over this assignment."

226

Bräutigam replied cautiously, "Perhaps I might be able to do something and work in the direction of compromise. But I simply do not understand what part Gruppenführer Berger is playing in this affair. For a year he has been my chief at the East Ministry. He knows where things stand. He supported the independence of the national committees. The Volunteers Desk of the SS is subordinate to Berger's office, and that desk is supposed to represent the interests of volunteers of different nationalities within the SS formations. I cannot imagine that Berger has so completely changed course overnight."

Steengracht shrugged. "How has your relationship with Berger been?"

"Smooth, on the whole."

"Good," Steengracht said. "We'll simply ask for you to be sent back to us."

Bräutigam spent a sleepless night. But by the morning the decision was out of his hands. Hilger informed him that he, Hilger, had been chosen to deal with the Vlasov question in the Foreign Office. Berger had objected to Bräutigam.

"May I ask why?" Bräutigam said.

"Gruppenführer Berger thinks it highly questionable whether, in view of your long association with the East Ministry and your well-known preference for the breakup of the Soviet Union, you would be the right man to work for subordination of all the volunteer formations to Vlasov."

The following week, on October 2, General Köstring was summoned to Himmler.

Himmler was at the western front where fierce battles were raging. As a result of his increase of power since July 20, he now held the post of army commander, although he lacked all military experience.

Himmler received the old general in his parlor car. In light of Stauffenberg's recent attempt to assassinate Hitler, the general's briefcase was taken from him. Himmler began by proclaiming his faith in the final victory of Germany. He supported this by curious information to the effect that Stalin had taken several million Chinese into the Red Army. This he interpreted as a sign of incipient Russian exhaustion.

He then moved on to the subject of Vlasov: "Herr General, you are aware that I have decided to raise a Russian liberation army under General Vlasov. We shall employ it to accelerate the Soviet exhaustion. That is why I have asked you to come here."

Köstring listened.

Himmler went on: "The most obvious and best way to organize a Russian liberation army is probably by assembling the Russian battalions which are, after all, in your charge. How many of these Russians are there?"

Köstring replied: "The volunteers are only partly Russians. The rest are Ukrainians, Caucasians, Cossacks, and so on. Do you mean all *en bloc,* or only the Russians?"

Himmler ran his hand through his thin hair.

"All that is totally irrelevant," he said. "If one of these White Ruthenians or Ukrainians belongs to a regiment of his own kind, he's nevertheless a Russian. Otherwise, he'd be like some German emigrant who came from Bavaria or Baden and went around saying he wasn't a German but a Bavarian or Badener and fighting for the freedom of Bavaria or Baden. That's sheer nonsense. Those are fantasies concocted by that idiot Rosenberg. What I want to know is the number of all Russians."

"In the air force and the navy alone," Köstring replied, "up to the time of the invasion, there were approximately 100,000 Eastern volunteers and auxiliaries. But the majority are in the army. All in all, between 900,000 and 1,000,000."

With a jerky movement Himmler set down the teacup from which he had been about to drink. "Why, that's impossible," he exclaimed. "That can't be possible."

"Those are my figures," Köstring said slowly.

"This is the first time I've heard of it. Nobody ever told me this before. That would amount to two army groups. It's positively frightening."

His face twitched, and Köstring thought: Out of what bottomless ignorance and thoughtlessness has this man made his decision about Vlasov?

"It seems to me," Köstring said, "that this large number indicates how eager these men used to be to join us."

"And how many of the so-called genuine Russians are among them?" Himmler asked, still with a tone of distaste in his voice.

"Hard to say. The boundaries are fluid. I, myself, don't think much of the separatists. The pure Russian units, volunteers and auxiliaries, constitute at least half of them."

"In other words more than 400,000 men."

"Approximately," Köstring said. "But they are scattered among hundreds of German units. And at the moment, the situation in the West is totally opaque. We can't find out how many of them have been killed in the invasion or have been captured by the Anglo-American forces, and how many of them are reassembling here or back home."

Himmler could not conceal his alarm, his uncertainty, and his fear of this field into which he had ventured unawares. Finally he said, as if in an effort to save face: "I should like to begin with the organization of one division. That division could be ready by the beginning of next year. But first it would have to prove itself. Then we might raise a second division. But I will have to have another talk with the Führer about it."

Köstring quickly took him up on that. "Under these circumstances, I would propose as a first step that the widely scattered Russian units be nominally placed under Vlasov's command without actually taking them out of their German formations. That would give them a sense of belonging until the divisions are ready."

Himmler nodded. "I'll consider that."

Two days later Köstring went to Army High Command (OKH), and then to the High Command of the Armed Forces (OKW), to find out what was known about these surprising plans of Himmler. He met with General Guderian, who, since July 20, had become chief of staff. But Guderian was thinking only of ways to bolster the eastern front. He was crying out for divisions, no matter where they came from. "Two divisions?" he said hastily to Köstring. "Organize them, organize as many as you can!" He obviously knew nothing about the background.

Then Köstring met Field Marshal Keitel and General Jodl. He tried to discover whether there had been a change on Hitler's part which would explain the remarkable change in Himmler. After he had reported on the plan to organize the Russian divisions, he repeated his suggestion that all volunteers be placed under Vlasov's nominal command, not only those in the army but those in the navy and air force as well. Jodl replied coldly: "We don't intend to arm our own executioners." And Keitel said: "I won't lift a finger for Vlasov; the Führer has given me hell too many times about this matter."

By the time Köstring left the OKW, he knew that Hitler was not standing behind Himmler's project. This meant that everything depended on who won the upper hand in the internal struggles for power that were evidently going on behind the scenes.

At the time Köstring was going to see Himmler, Vlasov at the Kiebitz-weg house, in Camp Dabendorf, and in the hidden headquarters of the NTS, was drawing up plans. Knowing nothing of the ramifications of the

SS apparatus, its multiple strata, rival power groups and personalities, ignorant of the sudden "conversion" some of its members had undergone with a view to saving their own necks in the impending military defeat, Vlasov had the impression during the first few weeks that Himmler and the SS were at last displaying "genuine activity" in behalf of his cause.

Oberführer Kroeger was appointed chief of a permanent liaison staff to Vlasov. Though Vlasov never developed a personal relationship with him, he nevertheless regarded Kroeger as an energetic man who backed him up. Even more promising was the organization of a Special Command, East (*Sonderkommando Ost*) as a staff to maintain liaison with Himmler's Reich Security Office, especially with the SD. Vlasov did not know that d'Alquen, after his talk with Himmler, had undertaken in his informal, easygoing way to inform the other powerful men at the head of the SS of Himmler's "conversion" and suggest how useful their own conversion might be.

Such intimations on the part of d'Alquen had made not the slightest dent on Heinrich Müller, the Gestapo chief. His limited policeman's mind was not capable of abandoning, or even modifying, the notion of the Slavic "subhuman" who was to be annihilated. Müller was prepared to obey any orders Himmler issued, but not out of conviction. In this attitude he differed from the head of the Reich Security Office, SS Obergruppenführer Kaltenbrunner, who told d'Alquen: "When I listen to you talk this way, I could almost share your optimism." Or: "Things are starting to look different to me. You know, that will have enormous consequences." Remarks of this sort seemed grotesque because Kaltenbrunner was among the group who most adamantly fought any proposal for making the lives of the Russian workers easier. But he, too, seemed to have experienced a "conversion." He was hunting for ways out of the present impasse. The same was true for SS Brigadeführer Ohlendorf, head of the Interior Department of the SD, who during the first twelve months of the war in the Soviet Union had headed the commando squad D (*Einsatzgruppe Süd*) which liquidated at least 90,000 "Asiatics," commissars, and Soviet Jews. Later he had opposed Koch's methods of governing the Ukraine, but only because he understood that "too much" brutality was impractical and produced more partisans than the most effective Soviet propaganda could have done. He, too, was trembling with fear of the impending defeat.

At the beginning of November 1944, d'Alquen was involuntarily removed from participation in the further course of events. A severe case of scarlet fever sent him to Berlin's university hospital, the Charité. During a heavy air raid he was trapped for some time in a shelter under the bombed-out children's clinic. Rescued, he was taken at the end of February 1945 to the SS hospital in Berlin.

Kaltenbrunner and Ohlendorf henceforth competed for the best contact with the Special Command, East. This was headed by SS Sturmbannführer Dr. Burchardt, a Russian-speaking Balt who for the past few years had run the Political Intelligence Desk for Eastern Races in the SD. In the course of this work he had become aware of the attraction the name "Vlasov" exerted, and had finally come around to the view that a liberation movement led by Vlasov could develop a dynamic impetus of its own and might help to stabilize the almost hopeless struggle on the eastern front.

No one could doubt that something was afoot. Dabendorf—for so long barely sustained, suspiciously watched by the Gestapo and the SD, constantly threatened with losing its funds—Dabendorf suddenly received SS emissaries and money to build new dormitories and offices and to attract new staff from volunteer units or camps. To some extent in Dabendorf, to some extent in Dahlem, beginnings were made on organizing the Committee for the Liberation of the Peoples of Russia. It was dubbed KONR and was divided into four main departments.

The first was the organization department, headed by Malyshkin, who also functioned as Vlasov's deputy. The second, the civilian department, was placed under General Sakutny. It was to deal for the time being with questions relating to the Russian workers and prisoners of war. A third, the propaganda department, was entrusted to Zhilenkov. The fourth department, contained the staff of the Liberation Army, also known as the KONR Troops. It was headed by Trukhin, whose deputy was General Boyarski.

Aided by the SS, Russian workers rebuilt ruins in Dahlem with breakneck speed. Trukhin's army staff moved into a five-story building on Thielallee. Within a short time an administration and a planning apparatus consisting of nearly 700 Russians had been assembled. That was possible only because the Dabendorf "reservoir" had been planning for such an eventuality for so many years and knew precisely where generals, officers, scientists, or specific Soviet officials were to be found.

These preparations naturally engendered a kind of euphoria in Vlasov and his entourage—even though during the very first week there were clashes between friends and associates of the presumably dead Zykov and other Dabendorf personnel, or between the old German staff of Dabendorf and the new SS men. At one point, Kroeger even threatened to arrest Strik-Strikfeldt.

It began to dawn on Vlasov that complications were far from over when he began trying to persuade the numerous national committees to join his one National Committee in a program aimed at achieving liberation for the peoples of Russia. Early in October all the "national representatives" assembled in Berlin, conferred at the East Ministry, composed protest manifestos directed against Vlasov, and sent emissaries to their still existing volunteer formations in Denmark, Holland, on the western front, in Italy, and in the Balkans, in order to obtain the backing of these forces.

A typical protest manifesto was that of the Caucasians, which was signed by Misha Khedia, Kantemir, Alibegov, and Chamalyan. Its text read, somewhat condensed:

Hatred for the Bolshevist intruders and traditional friendship with Germany were among the reasons that the majority of Caucasians, both those who had forcibly been mobilized into the Red Army and those who were in exile abroad, went over to the side of the Germans after the declaration of war between the Soviet Union and Germany, and flung themselves into the common struggle for the liberation of their homeland, the restoration of their independence, and the New Order in Europe.

The number of Caucasians who are bearing arms on the German side is as follows:

1. In legions and reinforcement battalions:		
Armenians	11,000	
Azerbaijanis	13,600	
Georgians	14,000	
North Caucasians	10,000	48,600 men
2. In construction and supply units:		
Armenians	7,000	
Azerbaijanis	4,795	
Georgians	6,800	
North Caucasians	3,000	21,595 men
3. In German units		25,000 men
4. In the Waffen-SS and Luftwaffe		7,000 men
	total	102,195 men

In 1942 almost all the battalions were committed to front-line service. In spite of errors and abuses, they served well and frequently earned recognition from the highest German command headquarters.

There are engaged in battle in Croatia at the present time: I. Georgian Mountaineers Battalion. II. North Caucasian Mountaineers Battalion and North Caucasian Battalions 842 and 843. The above-mentioned units participated in the difficult withdrawals from Greece. In Italy there are the Azerbaijanian regiment of the 162nd Infantry Division, Georgian Battalion II/198, and the Caucasian SS cavalry formation presently being organized. The total losses of the Caucasian volunteers amount to some 50,000 men. Nevertheless, their fighting spirit has never flagged.

In view of this situation, the Caucasians can only regard with the greatest amazement the powers that have been accorded Russian General Vlasov. The Caucasians are quite prepared to accept a liberation movement headed by General Vlasov as a partner in the struggle against Bolshevism, provided that movement is limited to Russia; but they will never accept General Vlasov as a supreme head to whom they are supposed to submit. . . .

An outraged Rosenberg comforted the national leaders with promises, collected their petitions, and passed these on to Keitel and Bormann with the plea that they be presented to Hitler. He himself no longer dared ask for a conference with Hitler, but he asked Bormann to explain to Hitler that "revolutionary movements aiming at setting up a Pan-Russian dictatorship" with the support of Heinrich Himmler were forming. He also had copies of all the protests and manifestos sent to Himmler. It would have gladdened his heart had he learned that Hitler, alerted by Bormann, had indeed questioned Himmler about his "Vlasov operations." Himmler replied with some embarrassment that merely propaganda operations on a very large scale were involved, nothing more. Afterward, he let Berger know of his misgivings, commenting that it might be best to drop the whole thing. Rosenberg, however, received no reply. The only SS leader he was able to see was Fritz Arlt. But Arlt was only a fellow sufferer.

At the time Vlasov came into the open, Arlt had already achieved some measure of success in his own efforts. He had pushed through a reorganization of the Galician Division which, as a result of miserable

German leadership, had been shattered at Lvov. The name "Galician" disappeared, to be replaced by "First Ukrainian Division." The Ukrainian national anthem became the divisional song. Ukrainian flags were introduced. Uniforms were quietly changed. Instead of the usual oath of allegiance to Hitler, Arlt introduced a Ukrainian oath. This was facilitated by the fact that the temporary German divisional commander, General Freitag, understood no more Ukrainian than the interpreters, who spoke only Russian.

The First Ukrainian Division was on the march into Slovakia. Shandruk himself was busy organizing a second Ukrainian division; it was to be composed of eastern Ukrainians and commanded by Ukrainian Colonel Diachenko. In addition, preparations were going forward for the formation of a Ukrainian national committee. Efforts to obtain the consent of such radical Ukrainian leaders as Bandera, Melnik, and Hrinyokh, seemed promising. On Arlt's insistence Stefan Bandera had just been released from the concentration camp where he had been since 1941 and "turned over" to Arlt.

Like Rosenberg, Arlt suddenly found himself pressed by all the nationalist leaders with whom he had been dealing in recent months. They, too, were seeking support against Vlasov. Arlt hoped to enlist Kroeger as a mediator. But Kroeger coldly turned him down, informing him that he shared Vlasov's viewpoint: success in the East could be achieved only by uniting, not by splintering, the various forces.

Even as the nationalist leaders were feeling encouraged, Vlasov resisted the advice of his friends in Dabendorf who, in the euphoria of the moment, urged him not to bother negotiating with the "separatistic traitors." Vlasov insisted on the prudent stand he had outlined to Himmler: to appeal for joint action in the struggle against Stalin. Only after the struggle had been won should the Ukrainians, Caucasians, or White Ruthenians decide what relationship they wished to have toward "Little Mother Russia." In other words, Vlasov was prepared to negotiate. But every effort to bring about a frank discussion seemed doomed to failure. There were nationalist leaders, such as Misha Khedia, who considered Vlasov worse than Stalin.

The period at the end of October was filled with preparations for the first meeting of the Committee for the Liberation of the Peoples of Russia and for the proclamation of a manifesto. Vlasov insisted that this manifesto must not be issued from Potsdam—as Kaltenbrunner, who lacked

234

all instinct for the whole matter, had promised. It must be promulgated on Slavic soil, Vlasov said, and he selected Prague as the proper site. Karl Hermann Frank, deputy protector of Bohemia and Moravia, protested because he feared unrest among the Czech population. But Kaltenbrunner pushed the matter through.

Vlasov himself and the whole intellectual "brain trust" of Dabendorf threw all their energy into drafting a strong manifesto. The authors of the first version were Kovalchuk, a surviving friend and associate of Zykov, Professor A. N. Zaitsev, and N. Nareikis. All agreed on the purpose of the manifesto. It must reach the rest of the world, and the Western powers in particular, not just Germany and the Soviet Union. And it must make clear that here a man and a movement "were opposing Stalin and his brutal form of Bolshevism not as mercenaries, not as participants in Hitler's war, but as a spiritually independent force." The manifesto must irrevocably state that Vlasov's conception of a new Russia "had nothing to do with the Fascist regime of Hitler and was not shaped in its image." It must "make clear that the National Committee was also not influenced by the reactionary spirit of Tsarist émigré circles." It must make "indisputably clear that it was linking up with the Russian Revolution of 1917. Once Stalin was overthrown, it would promulgate a social and democratic popular government with guarantees of individual freedoms—and that in the midst of a country dominated by the dictator Adolf Hitler."

The text and the fourteen points of the program were the fruit of the discussions and studies that had been carried on all the while in Strik-Strikfeldt's Dabendorf "academy." The term "National Socialist" was not used even once in the manifesto. There was mention of accepting German armed assistance, which would not offend Russian honor or independence. There was also mention of concluding an honorable peace with Germany—which presumably ruled out the idea that Germany would be treating Russia in any sense as a colony. No mention was made of the future frontier between the two countries; but in Dabendorf there was general agreement that the new Russia would be content with its borders of September 1, 1939 and make no claims upon Poland, the Baltic States, or Finland—in order to underline to the whole world Vlasov's conception of a peaceful country living in freedom.

The fourteen points of the government program might be characterized as "progressive Social Democratic." Only a single point remained controversial up to the very last moment. That was Point 7, which announced the restoration of free economic relations. The former Soviet economists who were now working in Dabendorf were all for continuing the existing

Soviet monopoly on foreign trade. They feared that the underdeveloped Russian economy would be at the mercy of "foreign capitalists." But Vlasov himself in the end decided—apparently under Strik-Strikfeldt's influence—that the clause about "free economic relations" must stand. He did not want Russia to be once again condemned as bolshevist by Englishmen, Frenchmen, and Americans because it barred private initiative.

When the text of the manifesto was complete and had been translated into German, Kroeger had to present it to Himmler and obtain his approval. During the second half of October the Russians and Germans alike in Dahlem and Dabendorf waited for the response. The manifesto was so bold and frank that even in the face of Himmler's "new attitude" it would have taken something of a miracle for Kroeger to return with the Reichsführer's approval. And, in fact, Himmler turned down the manifesto. His chief complaint was that it nowhere mentioned "Jewish bolshevism" and that there was no point in the program about the "fight against world Judaism." Moreover, Vlasov refused to include the shibboleth about the "Jewish nature of bolshevism" in the manifesto, nor make room for anti-Semitism in his policy statement. Kroeger implored him to throw Himmler at least one bone—at least in one passage to mention the alliance of England and America with Stalin.

That was a difficult concession for Vlasov to make, especially when he thought of Kazantsev, the NTS, England, and America. But after a protracted struggle he gave way, in order not to lose all that he believed he had already achieved. Kroeger went back to Himmler and this time actually received his approval. But Himmler cautiously warned him that Hitler had heard about the manifesto through the Foreign Office. Now Hitler would have to pass on the document: without his say-so, nothing could be done.

By now somewhat suspicious of Himmler's actual powers, but still trusting, Vlasov went on with the preparations "for Prague." It began to look as though the proclamation of the manifesto would actually become an official event in the presence of representatives of the German government and the few neutral and allied diplomats still accredited in Germany. The neutrals were considered particularly important. It was hoped that they would inform the Western Allies concerning Vlasov's real plans and ideas.

Himmler had commissioned his assistant, State Secretary Stuckart of the Ministry of the Interior, to go to Prague as representative of the Reich

Government. State Secretary Steengracht was to represent the Foreign Office and State Secretary Hayler the Ministry of Economics.

Then Vlasov received confidential word that none of the announced government officials would be coming to Prague. That was a fresh blow. Hitler, it was said, had approved the text of the manifesto but forbidden any official participation by the German government. The scene in Prague must be kept as inconspicuous as was possible for a propaganda operation.

Malyshkin tried to put a less discouraging interpretation upon these words of Hitler's. After all, he was referring to the Prague operation, not the whole plan for the liberation movement and liberation army. And, in fact, did not the Prague proclamation have a propagandistic purpose? But Vlasov sensed that even Himmler had not made a genuine decision in his favor, that behind all that had been said and promised were only fresh disappointments, half-truths, or lies.

At the end of October Captain Strik-Strikfeldt had his last meeting with Vlasov for some time.

Strik-Strikfeldt had not relinquished his suspicion of the SS leadership. He who had been so hopeful all through the years, who had repeatedly done his best to instill hope in Vlasov contrary to all reason, now abandoned hope. In several talks with Vlasov, he warned his friend not to trust the SS and to be wary of its selfish motives. As he afterward recounted the story, he said: "You, Andrei Andreyevich, must go and issue the manifesto. Then, when the whole free world will have heard of you, when the Prague ceremony is over, you must retire, explaining that the Nazi government has failed to keep the promises made you. Only thus can you lay a foundation for what comes after the Nazis."*

Vlasov remained silent for some time. Then he said: "There is no turning back. What you ask is impossible; we need the army. It doesn't matter who gives it to us. Haven't you always said yourself that the end would justify any means. . . ."

Strik-Strikfeldt asked Vlasov to think over the problem for another twenty-four hours before giving him an answer. If Vlasov insisted on his present decision, he, Strik-Strikfeldt, would regard himself as no longer attached to the Vlasov cause. They would have come to a parting of ways.

* Strik-Strikfeldt, *op. cit.,* p. 215.

Twenty-four hours later Vlasov, with tormented expression, told him that he could not change his mind.

"Wilfried Karlovich," he said, "I cannot desert all those who now place their hopes in me more than ever. I simply cannot do that."

Whom the Gods Wish to Destroy...

The assignment to make arrangements for the issuance of the manifesto in Prague was given to Dr. Heinrich Kurtz, who had played some part in the "Vineta" organization during the early years of the war in the East.

On October 16 he set out for Prague. There Sturmbannführer (Major) Walter Jacobi of the SD met him and informed him that they were to work together. After lengthy discussions it was settled that Vlasov would be received with honors by a military company. Then he would have a ceremonial breakfast with Deputy Reich Protector of Bohemia-Moravia Frank. Afterward, the proclamation of the manifesto could proceed at the Prague Citadel.

Frank had chosen the Czernin Palace in the citadel as the proper setting for the breakfast and a dinner. Vlasov and his entourage would stay at the Hotel Alcron. The rooms chosen were checked for hidden microphones and then watched over by SS guards. For a "late evening get-together" at the end of the day the Film Club was chosen; it was conveniently situated diagonally across from the Hotel Alcron.

Drawing up the guest lists for the breakfast and the dinner created unusual problems. When Kurtz read through the list of those who were suddenly eager to see Vlasov and sit in his presence, he was overcome by a feeling of disgust.

He had similar feelings in regard to the make-up of the special train which was to take the Berlin participants to Prague. First the plans called merely for attaching two cars to the train. These two cars eventually became an entire train because the number of those who wanted to "show their colors" increased from day to day. The opportunists came in droves from every government ministry that could possibly have anything to do with the matter. The "delegates of the peoples of Russia," who were supposed to be the principal persons at what was already being grandiloquently called "the manifestation," were overlooked during the initial distribution of seats on the train. There seemed no end to shortsightedness and arrogance.

In the early part of November Kurtz had to go to Prague once more in order to make sure personally that thirty Russian delegates would have hotel rooms. At last, on November 9, Kurtz informed Berlin that the preparations were complete and that the Prague manifestation could take place as planned on November 14.

During those weeks of November, the 232nd German Infantry Division was involved in fierce defensive battles on the Italian front, on both sides of Abetone Pass. On November 6, 1944, during the worst of the fighting, Colonel Herre, who was serving as Ia of this division, suddenly received an order to report to the staff of General Köstring, who was in Potsdam. No reason was given.

On November 8 Herre arrived in Berlin and went on to the barracks at the rear of Sanssouci Park in Potsdam. Köstring was waiting for him. He reminded Herre of the time he had referred to the possibility of SS interest in the Vlasov movement. "The time has come," he said.

He informed Herre of the orders for the organization of two Russian divisions at the troop-training sites in Württemberg, Münsingen, and Heuberg. Those orders had come from the SS leadership, he said. In the course of the preliminary negotiations he, Köstring, had insisted that Herre be brought in to raise the two divisions.

With a twitch of sarcasm in his face, the old general looked out the window at the barren square. "The time has come," he repeated slowly. "Now that we are scarcely in a position to equip our own divisions." Then he added: "On November 14 a Committee for the Liberation of the Peoples of Russia will be proclaimed in Prague, under the presidency of Vlasov, who has received the rank of a commander in chief. I, myself, can do no more for Vlasov than I could in the past. I wanted you to take charge of organizing Vlasov's divisions because of your experience. By any rational measure, it is too late. But who can see ahead even as far as the day after tomorrow?"

Immediately after this talk Herre returned to Berlin. First of all, he tried to find out where he stood. Putting together a small staff, which was all he would need, was a question of only twenty-four hours. He chose his men among officers who had served in previous years as liaison personnel with volunteer formations and had learned to live and work with Russians. For his operations officer he appointed Major Keiling, commander of Russian Artillery Battery 621, who had just received the Knight's Cross. He and his unit were still on the western front. Keiling received the order to meet Herre in Münsingen. There both men had a foretaste of the difficulties they would be encountering: shortage of equipment, shortage of clothing, unwillingness to give existing stocks for, of all things, Russian divisions. Even to put across the name "First Vlasov Division" was a struggle; the bureaucracy was reluctant to drop the term "600th Infantry Division (Russian)."

The old troop-training ground at Münsingen was too small for an entire division. The commander, General Weninger, could suggest nothing but putting up tents to supplement the barracks—this at the beginning of winter. There was also no fuel available for heating. The quartermasters thought it would be a pity to waste the limited stocks on Russians. Meanwhile, one telephoned order after another came from Potsdam and Berlin. The office of the commander of the Reserve Army had already started the first Russian formations, which were to be molded into the First Vlasov Division, on the march toward Münsingen. Herre learned that first of all he would be receiving a Kaminski Brigade and remnants of the 30th SS Sigling Division. Kaminski Brigade meant something to him, although he had no definite knowledge of the fate of Kaminski and his men after the fall of Lokoty. He had never heard of the SS Sigling Division; Major Keiling likewise knew nothing about it.

But that was not all. Herre received an order to report to Himmler personally on November 12. He was to go to Himmler's train, which was on a siding in the area between Zossen and Jüterbog. Hence, Herre could not even wait for the arrival of the Russian formations.

He left Keiling behind. In Potsdam he learned that Vlasov in the interval had proposed the commander and staff officers for his first division. The commander was to be Colonel Bunyachenko. Herre knew nothing as yet about Bunyachenko's fighting in the West. Bunyachenko's Ia was to be Lieutenant Colonel Nikolayev. Both men were already on their way to Münsingen.

Worn out from an almost sleepless night, Herre arrived at Himmler's command train next morning. Himmler's adjutant led him to a parlor car. A moment later he stood before Himmler. The Reichsführer struck him as extremely pale and nervous; his movements were quick and jerky.

Himmler said: "As you surely know, I have spoken with General . . ." He paused and made curiously fumbling movements with his hands. Then he went on: "General what'sisname, what'sis . . ."

It seemed incomprehensible that Himmler could not even remember the name of the man he was now backing. But Herre said, circumspectly: "You mean General Vlasov, sir?"

"That's right," Himmler said, relieved to have found the thread again. "General Vlasov. I liked the fellow. What the devil was the army doing with him for such a long time? Why wasn't he used in a sensible way? He could have raised whole armies."

"The Army General Staff," Herre replied, "tried for years to induce the political authority to set goals for the volunteers from the East. But the German political leadership refused to do so. And the SS—I must emphasize this fact, since you call me to account—had a great part in that refusal. I need only mention the *Untermensch* propaganda."

Himmler gave Herre an uncertain look. He was obviously at a loss for a reply. Then, with nervous abruptness, he said: "Yes, yes, I suppose some sins of omission were committed. But these mistakes must be amended now."

Herre hesitated. Finally, he blurted out what he was thinking: "The German armies no longer occupy much Russian soil at all. Reichsführer, for years I dealt with the volunteers. I know how disillusioned they feel. They will hardly believe anything any more. . . ."

"You sound extremely pessimistic," Himmler interrupted. "You sound almost as if you no longer believe in victory."

Herre realized he had gone too far. "Please consider," he said in his most politic tone, "that I have come from the Italian theater of war. For months we have not seen a German plane in the air."

"I see," Himmler said. "Then you are judging from the viewpoint of a minor sector of the front. But I can tell you that the war is about to take a decisive turn. The secret weapons are already in production. They will soon be employed, and will change the entire picture."

Herre was tempted to ask Himmler why, then, he was backing Vlasov at this time, if the turning point was all that close. But why provoke the man? There was something else that needed saying, and he said it: "One way or the other, we must be honest in our intentions toward Vlasov and his men."

"That goes without saying," Himmler answered with another jerky wave of his hand. He wanted to end this awkward conversation. "Go forward with the organization of the divisions as quickly as possible."

. . .

On November 11 Colonel Bunyachenko arrived in Camp Münsingen, accompanied by Nikolayev. Weninger and Keiling welcomed him and showed him his apartment in one of the officers' barracks. Keiling quickly realized that Bunyachenko was not a man to be trifled with. His keen eyes immediately spotted things that corroborated his distrust of the Germans' sincerity. Inspecting the quarters intended for the men, he saw at once that all sorts of necessities were lacking, and his frown deepened.

Soon afterward the arrival of the Kaminski Brigade was reported. And the scene at the Münsingen railroad station was not calculated to soothe Bunyachenko's feelings. Out of the trains poured a wild horde of armed and unarmed men dressed in all sorts of uniforms. Among them were women hung with jewelry. The officers, who seemed as disorganized as the majority of the soldiers, had three, four, and five wrist watches on their arms. Ever since Kaminski had left White Ruthenia with his men and their families, things had gone steadily downhill. Nothing had come of the transfer to Hungary. As a result of an uprising in Slovakia, the transport trains had been stuck in Silesia. There nobody felt responsible for Kaminski's men. Gauleiter Bracht of Upper Silesia had refused to have anything to do with "that pack of Russians." The consequence was marauding and clashes with Germans. Meanwhile, the Polish uprising in Warsaw had broken out. Hitler ordered that the Kaminski Brigade be sent to fight the Warsaw rebels under the command of SS Obergruppenführer (Lieutenant General) Bach-Zelewski. If the brigade had had any cohesion and discipline up to this point, it vanished in the savage Warsaw street battles. For Kaminski and his men the fighting for Warsaw meant the first direct contact with the world of Western comfort.

The men became intoxicated with looting. There was a ban against it, but Kaminski refused to discipline his men. He argued that his men and their families had lost everything while fighting loyally for the Germans for years. And now, on top of all, when they were only compensating themselves by taking from the filthy Poles, the Germans were trying to stop them. His attitude threatened to delay the capitulation of the Poles. Himmler, therefore, ordered him arrested.

Kaminski, however, was warned in time. Cheated of the opportunity to carry out his original mission, all sense of decency gone, corrupted to mere mercenary, he made a break for freedom. South of Tarnow in the foothills of the Carpathians he was caught by the security police and shot then and there. His car was smeared with blood from geese to simulate an attack by bandits.

Kaminski's leaderless men were still suffering the impact of these events when they arrived in Münsingen.

When Bunyachenko saw that wild horde, he flushed with fury. "So that's what you're giving me," he bellowed. "Bandits, robbers, thieves! You'll let me have what you can no longer use."

He stalked back to his small car and left it to the Germans to get the rowdy mob into the camp.

Keiling had a ghastly night. The soldiers made a rush for the barracks. Soon there were scenes of total confusion. Not until next morning did Bunyachenko come out of his fury. But then he began to show what he was capable of. With merciless toughness, he created order. He demanded the immediate removal of all the so-called "officers" who had come with the mob of Kaminski soldiers. Then he subjected the remaining 5000-odd men to his own brand of iron discipline.

The city of Prague, as yet quite untouched by the war, was just beginning to wake up when Vlasov's special train, coming from Berlin, arrived at the main railroad station at five o'clock in the morning on November 14, 1944. By seven o'clock the sleeping cars in which Vlasov and his entourage had traveled from Berlin were moved to another track. By this time everything was ready for the reception.

Shortly after seven o'clock, Vlasov passed through the station, his face showing no signs of whatever he might be feeling. To outsiders, who knew nothing of the wearing struggles and the endless disappointments, it might have seemed an unusual triumph for him that a German company was drawn up outside the railroad station to welcome a Russian general who had been a prisoner of war.

The lobby of the Hotel Alcron was jammed with onlookers and reporters. Vlasov, accompanied by Zhilenkov, Malyshkin, and the others, went up to his suite.

Shortly before nine o'clock, Köstring arrived to meet Vlasov for the first time. But he was the prisoner of his official status, especially at this time of clashes between Vlasov and the national committees. Köstring was in no position to express his fundamental sympathy with a Pan-Russian solution, and he also knew that there was no longer the slightest chance for such a solution. The two met and parted without having established any kind of relationship.

Herre was a witness of this encounter. After Köstring's departure he went up to Vlasov's room once more. Vlasov had propped his head in his right hand and was staring with his nearsighted eyes at his horn-rimmed glasses, which lay on the table in front of him. When he heard the sound of Herre's footsteps, he put on the glasses and looked up.

"Andrei Fedorovich—" that was how the Russians addressed Herre— "it's good that you're here today. We've tried for so long, and so long in vain. Do you think it is too late now?"

Herre avoided Vlasov's eyes. "Andrei Andreyevich," he said evasively, "if there is the slightest remaining chance, you must make use of it."

At eleven A.M. Frank received Vlasov and his entourage at breakfast. It was an outwardly brilliant reception, but one could detect that the Germans were nervous at fraternizing with "the Slavic element."

The majority of the Russian delegates, meanwhile, were assembling at the Prague Press Club. The representatives of the *Ostarbeiter,* who had been brought to Prague despite much obstruction by German authorities, looked around anxiously. They could not quite believe that they had been transported from the misery of their camps into all this splendor. They could not understand that the Gestapo should suddenly have become their benefactors and forced reluctant camp commanders to improve conditions. The delegates from Russian military units felt much the same way. Russian guards were obviously enjoying their assignment of checking the credentials of Germans.

Shortly before noon the automobiles rolled through Prague up to the citadel. The sunlight was refracted in the crystals of the ballroom chandeliers. Inside, everyone in charge was Russian.

By the time Herre drove into the courtyard, the majority of the participants had already assembled. There was a ghostly silence in the square. Herre saw one gray-haired civilian standing alone. He was Hilger, who had replaced Bräutigam as the Foreign Office's liaison to Vlasov. "Andrei Fedorovich," he said in Russian to Herre, "if we had experienced this day years ago, we would probably have no worries today."

A few minutes later Vlasov entered with his entourage.

It was as if there were a sharp intake of breath by everyone in the room.

Then Deputy Reich Protector Frank stepped to the speaker's platform to welcome Vlasov and the Russians. There was something oddly insubstantial about Frank's pencil-thin figure on the podium. He read his speech with great rapidity. He was followed by SS Obergruppenführer Werner Lorenz, who also read from a prepared text. A stir of uneasiness was spreading through the crowd: was this all they would get in the way of official welcome? For both Frank and Lorenz were second-raters. They saw that no important representative of the Berlin government had come. However, Lorenz at least spoke of Vlasov and his men as "allies."

After Lorenz had finished, the forty-nine members of the Committee for the Liberation of the Peoples of Russia took seats at a long table at the front end of the room. Vlasov was seated in the middle, to his right Zhilenkov and Trukhin, to his left Malyshkin and several civilian members of the committee.

The German text of the speeches had not been printed in time, so that all those who did not speak Russian could not follow a word.

Vlasov made a few introductory remarks in which he gave due respect to Germany but placed major emphasis on his own aims. When he said that this was no time to remember mistakes and personal insults, everyone knew just what he meant. His meaning was also clear when he spoke of Germany "today" as offering the only real chance for organizing an armed struggle. Or when he said that the manifesto, which expressed the determination of the peoples of Russia to continue the struggle, was being published to the entire world. That was a hidden "appeal to the West."

Trukhin followed, giving expression to the military hopes that he still felt strongly. At one point he said:

"For the sake of military secrecy we also cannot say when this or that contingent of volunteers will be summoned to the ranks of the Liberation Army of the Peoples of Russia. But those who have not been called up today will be tomorrow or the day after. Since the days of Peter the Great, the Russian army has learned from the military experience of Europe. In this respect we are in a favorable situation: we can learn from the experience of one of the world's best armies—the German army—and simultaneously draw on the fighting experience of the Red Army. Our military forces will be organized as a completely independent factor in the struggle against bolshevism!"

After Trukhin had ended, the executive board of the Committee for the Liberation of the Peoples of Russia was elected. Vlasov was elected chairman; among the members of the executive board were Major General Balabin, the Cossack deputy; Professor Bogatyrshuk, the Ukrainian deputy; N. N. Budsilovich; Brigadier General Malyshkin; Brigadier General Trukhin; and Professor Rudnev.

No one knew better than Vlasov that this election by people who had long ago forgotten or never learned the meaning of free elections was nothing but a farce, and that the committee was a temporary device that could not possibly last.

He rose slowly to read aloud the committee's manifesto:

"Fellow countrymen, brothers and sisters. In this hour of perilous trials we must decide the fate of our homeland, of our peoples, and our own personal fates as well. Humanity is living through an age of tremendous upheavals. The present war is a struggle to the death of antagonistic political systems."

He continued with political statements that once again made obeisance to Germany's political ideology. But the ambiguity of his words, and the real target of them, was quite plain when he said: "There is no greater crime than Stalin's in laying waste other countries and trampling upon peoples who are only trying to preserve the land they inherited from their forefathers and by their own work on it find their own happiness. And there is no greater crime than trampling another nation underfoot and imposing your own will upon it. . . ."

The few Germans who understood knew that these words on the surface referred to the advance of Stalin's armies beyond the frontiers to Russia into the West. But in reality they were a denunciation of Hitler's crimes upon the soil of Russia.

At this point, Vlasov went far afield—as was his wont—to explain once more that he was not imbued with reactionary ideas, but hoped to carry on the Russian Revolution and bring about the idealistic transformation of the Soviet Union into a socialist people's democracy. What he said indicated how far removed he was indeed from fascist doctrines and Nazi practices in government.

"In the February Revolution of 1917 the peoples of the Russian Empire sought justice, the common welfare, and national freedom. They rose up against the tsarist regime, which was neither willing nor able to abolish the remnants of serfdom and the economic and cultural backwardness of the country. But after tsarism was overthrown by the peoples of our country in February 1917, neither the political parties nor individual leaders had the courage to carry out bold and consistent reforms. By their ambiguous policy, their opportunism, and their hesitancy to take responsibility for the future, they lost credit with the people. The people spontaneously followed those who promised immediate peace, freedom, and bread, and who offered the most radical slogans. It is not the people's fault that the Bolshevik party seized power for themselves. For the Bolsheviks promised a rebuilding of the social order that would bring happiness to the people. For the sake of that rebuilding countless sacrifices were offered. But the Bolshevik party failed to keep its promises to the people. What is more, by forever consolidating its tyrannical system, it robbed the people of the rights they had won and plunged them into endless misery and oppression. . . . The Bolsheviks robbed the peoples of Russia of freedom of speech, freedom of opinion, freedom of individuality, freedom of movement, freedom in their choice of occupation; and they took from the individual his ability to seek a place within the community consonant with his abilities. In place of freedom they introduced terror, special privilege for the party, and arbitrariness.

"The Bolsheviks robbed the peasants of the land they had fought for, of the right to till the soil without interference, and to enjoy the fruits of their own labor. By imposing upon the peasants the fetters of the collective farm system, the Bolsheviks reduced them to slaves of the state, the most exploited and oppressed group of all.

"The Bolsheviks deprived the workers of the right to choose their own occupation and their own place to work, of the right to organize and fight for better working conditions and better pay for their work, as well as the right to share in the control of production. They reduced the workers to slaves of state capitalism.

"The Bolsheviks deprived the intellectuals of the right to create freely for the benefit of their own people. By using force, terror, and corruption, they tried to make the people instruments of their lying propaganda. . . .

"Two years ago Stalin was still able to fool the peoples with balderdash about the patriotic and libertarian meaning of the war. But now the Red Army has crossed the borders of the Soviet Union, has invaded Rumania, Bulgaria, Serbia, and Croatia, and is drowning those countries in torrents of blood.

"All this is covered up by lies about the democratic nature of Stalin's Constitution and the building of a socialist system. No nation in the world has known such a low standard of living with such tremendous material resources, such deprivation of rights and debasement of the individual, as bolshevism has imposed and will continue to impose.

"For more than a quarter of a century the peoples of our country have endured the whole burden of Bolshevik tyranny. . . . They have lost forever all faith in bolshevism. . . . Therefore, the efforts of all nations must be directed toward the annihilation of this monstrous apparatus, so that every man shall enjoy the right to a free life and to work and create according to his abilities, with the goal of building a social order that will protect the individual against despotism and will prohibit appropriation of the fruits of his work, even by the state itself.

"In full consciousness of their responsibility to their peoples, to history, and to posterity, the representatives of the peoples of our country have founded a Committee for the Liberation of the Peoples of Russia whose goal shall be the common struggle against bolshevism."

Vlasov had been repeatedly interrupted by applause. At first, however, the delegates of the *Ostarbeiter* had been very tentative in their applause, as if afraid to call attention to themselves.

Vlasov continued: "The Committee for Liberation of the Peoples of Russia has set the following aims . . ." And he proceeded to read the Fourteen Points of the program.

1. Equality of all the peoples of Russia and their right to national development, self-determination, and, should the case arise, political independence.

2. National labor reorganization, with all interests of the state subordinated to the effort to raise the standard of living and develop the nation.

3. Preservation of peace and establishment of amicable relations with all countries, together with the promotion of international cooperation.

4. Comprehensive government measures for strengthening the family and marriage. Equal rights for women.

5. Abolition of forced labor and guarantee of the right to work, assuring all workers a decent livelihood. Establishment of wage scales that will assure an appropriate standard of living for every kind of work.

6. Abolition of collective farms, the land to be turned over to the peasants as their private property without remittance to the state. Freedom to use agricultural land as the peasant himself decides. Every peasant shall be free to sell the products of his own labor. Abolition of forced deliveries and abrogation of debts owed to the Soviet state.

7. Inviolability of private property acquired by labor. Revival of commerce and crafts; guarantee of the right and the opportunity for individuals to participate in the economic life of the country.

8. Creation of opportunities for the intellectuals to work freely for the benefit of the people.

9. Guarantee of social justice and protection from all kinds of exploitation accorded to all workers, irrespective of their social origins or earlier activities.

10. Free education, medical care, vacations, and old-age pensions for all.

11. Eradication of the regime of terror and violence. Abolition of forced resettlement and mass deportation. Granting of freedom of religion and of conscience, of speech, of assembly, of the press. Guarantee of the inviolability of the individual, of property, of the home. Equality of all before the law. Independence of the judiciary. Public trials.

12. Freeing of all political prisoners and return to their homes from prisons and camps of all those who have been prosecuted for their struggle against bolshevism. No punishment or persecution of those who stopped fighting for Stalin and bolshevism, no matter whether they did so out of conviction or under coercion.

13. Restoration at government expense of the people's property destroyed by the war—cities, villages, factories, and workshops.

14. The government to care for disabled veterans and their families.

It was an idealistic, socialistic program. An icy realist like Stalin would have laughed scornfully at the possibility of its ever being put into practice. And certainly Hitler had allowed it to be presented only because he never imagined that socialist convictions could be honestly meant. As a matter of fact, democratic and social-minded politicians might find this manifesto well worth reading even decades later.

Once again, after he had read the Fourteen Points, Vlasov issued an appeal for unity: "Only the unity of all armed anti-Bolshevik military forces of our country's peoples will lead to victory." And he was speaking to the Americans and British when he said: "There is no doubt that the liberation of the peoples of Russia from Bolshevik oppression will be supported by all the freedom-loving peoples of the world." And finally, he once more raised the problem of the ties to Germany: "The Committee for the Liberation of the Peoples of Russia welcomes the help of Germany under conditions that do not infringe upon the honor or the independence of our country. This help represents *at present* the only realistic possibility of organizing armed struggle against the Stalinist clique. . . ." The phrase "at present" distinguished him from all the Quislings and the other actual mercenaries of Germany in the occupied countries of Europe—those who had put their bets on a Nazi Europe and were continuing to bet on it.

At four P.M. the doors opened. The other delegates entered the courtyard in solemn silence. Vlasov himself, his immediate entourage, and most of the German guests of honor, went to the banquet to which Frank had invited them. There was a macabre glitter about the long, ceremonial tables. Wine flowed freely; there were speeches and toasts.

Coffee, cognac, and vodka were served in an adjacent room with tall windows and red upholstery. Russian songs rang out. Vlasov listened as he downed glass after glass. At one point he put his arm around Herre's shoulders and said: "Andrei Fedorovich, if fate does decide to help us after all, you'll become military attaché in Moscow." And then he joined in the singing with his deep basso.

On November 19 Herre arrived in Münsingen.

The SS Thirtieth Sigling Division was just arriving, along with remnants of a wide variety of volunteer battalions who had been more or less battered in the fighting on the western front. They were squeezed into the inadequate quarters.

Herre heard complaints from General Weninger about the bands of Russians, who seemed to make mockery of all German notions of order. Complaints were also already coming in from the vicinity of Münsingen and from the gauleiter's office in Stuttgart. Kaminski Brigade men had poured out of the camp in the evenings to obtain liquor. The Russians had also been hunting up girls. Inevitably, they had come upon the Russian women who were working in a nearby factory. The superintendent of the women's camp had not allowed any contact between the Russians and their countrywomen. There had already been some clashes with Russian volunteers who had fought for years on various fronts, been awarded many medals, were for the first time able to move freely around in Germany, and were now discovering that Russian women were still denied their personal freedom.

Bunyachenko and Nikolayev received Herre in Bunyachenko's living room. As the German entered, a Russian woman left the room. Keiling whispered to Herre that she was Bunyachenko's "woman" and "maid."

Bunyachenko had just got up and was still unshaved. He put his tunic on over a yellowish undershirt. On the table stood a wooden plate with army canned sausage that had been dumped out of the cans and cut into thick slices. The inevitable onions were there, too. Alongside stood several bottles of vodka and empty water glasses.

Bunyachenko greeted Herre, filled the water glasses to the brim with vodka, and gestured at the sausage and onions.

"*Na zdorovye gospodin polkovnik*—to your health, Colonel," he said in a voice icy with mistrust. He watched as Herre ate a slice of sausage and drained the glass at one draught. Then he, too, ate and likewise drank his glass down in one draught. Only then did he sit down on his stiff wooden chair and begin the conversation with a torrent of complaints.

During the past few days the worst soldiers in the world had been sent to him, he griped. The camp administration regarded him as a kind of bandit captain. Germans were reluctant to salute him. Two of his officers had been deliberately jostled by German noncoms. He had not even received kettles for the mess. After their evenings off, his soldiers came back with reports on the humiliating treatment of their fellow countrymen in the labor camps of the vicinity.

Bunyachenko's tactics were intended to put the Germans in the wrong from the start. Herre had to take an appeasing line, promising investigations. He realized what a battle it was going to be for him to gain a degree of trust from this disillusioned man, even though he himself spoke Russian and thought he could point to a good many accomplishments for the Russian cause.

Herre reported to General Rudolf Veiel, deputy chief of the corps headquarters staff in Stuttgart. The general referred him to Gauleiter Wilhelm Murr of Württemberg.

Murr's notions of Russia and Russians were still those of 1941. After a good deal of fencing, he declared that written instructions from him to the labor camps would have little effect. It would be better if Herre gave a lecture to the district and local party leaders on the "delicate subject." Herre, therefore, addressed some fifty party leaders who already felt, although they would never say so, the cold breath of defeat on the napes of their necks. Hence, they were prepared to grant more freedom to the Russian women workers.

With this matter settled, technical difficulties of organizing divisions came to the fore. Air raids constantly hindered the work, but so also did lack of good will. It remained impossible to obtain proper uniforms. Before the First Vlasov Division left for a training march, trousers had to be "liberated" at night from German reserve units, so that Vlasov's men would have a proper field uniform in place of their cotton twills. There were days when Herre would have preferred to give Bunyachenko a wide berth. At night Herre dreamed of that shaven head and those narrow, reproachful eyes. Not a morning passed without Bunyachenko's presenting one accounting or another. And the worst of it was that he was right. He would say: "Andrei Fedorovich, it's clear you don't trust us. A soldier needs a rifle if he is to be able to fight. So we have rifles now. Soldiers also need steel helmets if they're to fight. We don't have those. We need machine guns. We don't have those. Andrei Fedorovich, how are my soldiers going to fight?"

Bunyachenko was rushing about from early morning until late at night. He was a genius at improvisation. The officers he chose were excellent, with few exceptions.

In the course of December Bunyachenko suffered from a dangerous case of phlebitis. But he paid little attention to it, continuing to work late into the night as if there were nothing wrong with him. Then he would vanish with that stocky, dark-haired woman who was both maid and wife, who trembled in his presence and nevertheless loved him. At nine o'clock in the morning he would once more be seated behind his desk, head propped in hands, in stockinged feet, his food within reach as he worked. On the desk lay heaps of papers with organizational charts and calculations.

On December 17 Herre had a shattering experience. He had tried to obtain wine and chocolates as Christmas presents for the Russian soldiers. For hours he vainly belabored the officials at the well-stocked army supply depot in Ulm. The clerks refused to hand out anything at all for Russians. Shortly afterward, American bombing squadrons appeared over Ulm and set the city afire. Herre telephoned Bunyachenko to send several units from Münsingen. The Russians rescued thousands of Germans from collapsed cellars and burning houses. The stocks of the army supply depot had been destroyed.

Coal for heating the Russian barracks could not be obtained. The administrative officers commented that Russians were used to cold, after all. Finally Köstring in person went to see the quartermaster general. After his interview it proved possible—but by then it was January of 1945—to bring a coal train to Münsingen.

In January new batches of officers and soldiers began coming directly from the prisoner-of-war camps. It seemed almost incomprehensible that at this stage of the game there should still have been volunteers for the

"Vlasov Army." These were men who, up to this point, had not fought on the German side. Nobody knew them, and both Herre and Bunyachenko rightly suspected that there were Soviet agents among them, who had allowed themselves to be captured in order to volunteer for "service with Vlasov."

But Bunyachenko had on his staff an intelligence officer named Olchovik who displayed knowledgeability, cunning, and ruthlessness in hunting down agents and provocateurs among the approximately 20,000 members of the First Division. He also screened the Russian laborers, both male and female, with whom the soldiers came in contact, and the women doctors, clerical helpers, and cooks who belonged to the division. Bunyachenko himself knew this was an eye-for-eye, tooth-for-tooth struggle, and he acted accordingly when it was a matter of punishing convicted, or even merely suspected, agents.

During the second week in January the organization of the First Vlasov Division was completed. The past several weeks had even seen deliveries of German artillery and captured Soviet tanks, and Herre received an additional assignment: to establish in Münsingen an officers' school for the Vlasov Army, and to get things ready for a second Vlasov Division to be organized at the troop-training grounds in Heuberg.

A Colonel Meandrov arrived in Münsingen from Dabendorf to serve as commander of the officers' school. Meandrov had been captured by the German 49th Mountain Corps in August 1941. At the time he had been chief of staff of a Soviet corps, and Herre had interviewed him. As he shook hands with Meandrov now, he recalled with painful clarity their conversation then. He had asked Meandrov whether Russian resistance would not soon be collapsing, and received the reply: "I have the highest respect for the German army. Nevertheless, the German army will never be able to defeat Russia unless it succeeds in mobilizing the Russian people against Stalin."

Now this man was here!

Meandrov proved to be a man of considerable intellect who had subscribed wholeheartedly to the ideals of the NTS. He was convinced that socialism as a principle had lost none of its original luster, but that it had been sadly misused by Stalin. He was able to tell Herre—who so far had not heard—what Vlasov and his entourage had been experiencing in Berlin since the heady days of Prague.

The SS had confirmed Vlasov's rank as an army commander in chief. The formation of the army's staff was more or less complete. Trukhin had done an excellent job. A Colonel Neryanin, who came from Dabendorf, had been appointed chief of the Operations Department. Herre knew him.

But Meandrov had rather more bad than good to report. Rosenberg was striking out in all directions like a desperate man, denouncing Vlasov as the future tsar of Russia. Taubert of the East Department of the Propaganda Ministry was demonstrating that he had learned nothing since the Vineta days of 1941. He protested that the Vlasov movement was not National Socialist, that it did not even recognize the importance of the Jewish question. These men had no power, but their criticism intensified Himmler's uncertainty.

Zhilenkov had traveled to Bratislava with a delegation to make a speech. He had given interviews, had stressed that Vlasov would fight only against Stalin and never against Englishmen, Americans, or Frenchmen, and that he was not in the employ of the Germans. Since then, a ban had been issued on any travels of this type and on granting interviews to foreign correspondents. On January 14 Herre sent Major Keiling to Heuberg to begin raising the Second Division there. On the morning of that same day the first detailed reports arrived from the eastern front on the beginning of the expected Russian winter offensive. It had begun on January 12 in the Baranov bridgehead on the Vistula River. Within a few days it was obvious to both the Russians and the Germans in Münsingen that a disaster was descending upon the German army group in the Vistula region. Marshal Zhukov's tank troops crossed the Oder River at Küstrin and Frankfurt. Sizable parts of Silesia were overrun, Breslau threatened.

The First Vlasov Division was gripped by a fearful, aching nervousness. For nights on end Bunyachenko conferred with Meandrov. Both men kept constantly in touch with Vlasov by courier. The Russian intelligence officers listened to Soviet broadcasts and reports whenever possible. And they likewise paid close attention to the operations of the British and Americans in the West.

Unlike Strik-Strikfeldt, Herre did not know that Vlasov's friends cherished hopes of being able to establish relations with the British or the Americans. He suspected, however, that the division leaders were considering such possibilities and even conferring with Vlasov on how to bring the division unharmed and with its full fighting effectiveness through a German debacle. But despite such suspicions, Herre did not interfere with Bunyachenko and his men.

In the first week of February, Zhukov's offensive on the Oder came to a standstill, at least for the time being, and the ferment among the Russians quieted somewhat. Herre went to Heuberg to see personally to the work of organizing the Second Division.

Some 18,000 Russian soldiers, the overwhelming majority of them men who had just come from the prison camps, were waiting for shelter. Everything Herre had been through in Münsingen was being repeated in Heuberg: the daily struggle with German administrative bureaus, the wearying hostility of the paymasters, the clashes in the surrounding area, and finally the deep mistrust of the Russians themselves and their daily more candid reproach: "Too late."

Vlasov had appointed as commander of the Second Russian Division Colonel Sveryev, who in February was promoted to general. On the surface, Sveryev was just the opposite of Bunyachenko. Of medium height, he was very lean and well groomed. He wore his hair slicked back without a part over this thin, wrinkled face. Although the deeply drooping corners of his mouth suggested the brutal strength of which he was capable, his whole manner was obliging. His slightly almond-shaped eyes were almost always smiling. But his resentments were even more deep-seated than Bunyachenko's, and he was equally intent on building up his division as quickly as possible. Like Bunyachenko, Sveryev asked daily: "What am I supposed to fight with? With clubs? With wooden rifles?" Both men were seared by the same worries.

On February 9 Bunyachenko's division undertook major exercises, and Herre returned to Münsingen to observe them. There he received an order from Köstring to organize, within a few days, several Russian antitank detachments which were to be equipped with bicycles and bazookas and sent to the Oder. Herre learned that at the end of January Himmler had been appointed commander in chief of the improvised Vistula Army Group, whose front extended from the Oder near Frankfurt and Küstrin through Pomerania to the vicinity of Danzig. The request for the antitank detachments came from Himmler personally.

Herre went to Bunyachenko, who was watching a company at target practice, with Nikolayev standing behind him. Herre had assumed that both officers would be glad for a chance to demonstrate the fighting spirit of their men. Instead, he encountered a mysterious reserve.

Herre would have understood the reasons for this attitude had he been aware of an incident that had taken place at this time in the Berlin SS hospital. D'Alquen had been lying alone in his sickroom one morning when the door suddenly opened and Vlasov, dressed in his brown uniform and long coat, entered, accompanied only by an interpreter. He placed a bouquet of flowers on the night table. Then he came up to the bed, embraced the sick man, kissed him, and reportedly said: "How are you? We've missed you very much, and we need you. . . . Things are not good. You're going to lose the war, and that will be a bad business for the SS in particular. But don't worry, I'll protect you. I've come to tell you that. The war is over for you, but for us it's only beginning. The Americans will give us the help we've been unable to get from the Germans— for all sorts of reasons." He added that d'Alquen had been a good friend of the Russian cause; he would not forget him and would give him a place on his personal staff as soon as the bitter end came. Then he embraced the sick man once more and left the room.

This episode indicated that Vlasov and at least the larger part of his entourage had finally buried their hopes of help from Germans and were staking everything on future collaboration with America and England. That was the motivation behind Bunyachenko's attitude. He had no desire to risk his one great stake, his division, in hopeless battles.

It took Herre several hours to convince first Nikolayev and then Bunyachenko that this was a priceless chance to show the German leadership how serious the Vlasov men were in their determination to fight against the Soviet power. "That is the only thing that will speed up the equipping of additional troops," Herre argued.

Finally Bunyachenko agreed, and assigned Lieutenant Korshenevski to take over organization of the detachments. Within a few days the units were ready to march.

The same evening that Herre reported to Köstring by telephone the departure of these detachments, he learned that Vlasov would arrive on February 16 in Münsingen with parts of his army staff. The commander in chief was coming to inspect his First Division.

February 16 was a cold winter day. The First Vlasov Division had assembled in the snow-covered open square. Deputations of Russian men and women workers from the vicinity had also gathered for the occasion.

Vlasov arrived accompanied by Trukhin, Neryanin, and Zhilenkov. In his long brown coat he looked even taller than usual. Bunyachenko stepped forward, saluted, and reported the readiness of the First Vlasov Division. Vlasov thanked him. At this moment his face bore an almost majestic expression. Suddenly his eyes filled with tears. With a noticeable effort he pulled himself together and with almost too rapid a stride paced off the fronts of the regiments and companies. After a while he slowed his step. He had regained his composure.

He was led to the reviewing stand, which was decorated with pine branches and flanked by two howitzers; here he was to watch the march-past of the First Division. On the stand he extended both hands to Herre.

"Andrei Fedorovich," he said, "couldn't we have had this a long time ago?"

Flurries of snow began falling, and one flake after another settled on his brown coat. "Andrei Fedorovich," Vlasov said, "you have been in on the training. What do you say to this division?"

"It will do its duty, Andrei Andreyevich," Herre replied, "if it is given a fair chance."

Herre's words were accompanied by the tramp of feet as the first soldiers in the approaching column marched up to the reviewing stand. The falling snow more and more blurred the division that had at last become a reality, as if to show that this belated reality was no more than a phantom. The eyes of every individual soldier were directed straight at Vlasov. The general stood immobile. To each of the passing companies he called out a few words in his booming voice: *"Vperyod, v boy, maladtsy* (Forward, my boys!); *Vperyod za osvoboshdeniye rodiny* (Forward for the liberation of the homeland)!"

As assault guns and T-34's rolled past, the falling snow had become so thick that those huge machines were visible only as ghostly shadows.

A few hours later all the Russian officers gathered with their German guests in the casino barrack. Sveryev had come over from Heuberg. The room was decorated in red, white, and blue. They had all been buoyed up by the parade. Nevertheless, Vlasov's address to the assembled officers took note of the gravity of the moment. He said that the division must prove itself in order to prepare the way for additional divisions of the Russian army of liberation. It must prove itself even though the situation on the eastern front certainly looked gloomy. Bunyachenko rose and toasted Vlasov. He said: "Andrei Andreyevich, you may rely on us. We will do it." It was as if the ceremony of reviewing his division had temporarily put his forebodings out of his mind, so that he was ready to make pledges he had avoided making only a few days ago.

The following day was cold and snowy, and brought a fresh onslaught of bad news from both the eastern and the western fronts. Accompanied by Herre, Vlasov drove over to Heuberg to visit the Second Division. Sveryev had preceded them.

As the columns of cars rolled slowly over the icy roads, Vlasov told Herre about what had been going on in Berlin during the past few months. Tensions with representatives of the various national groups were beginning to ease, he said. The Cossacks were seeking cooperation. Ostrovsky, the White Ruthenian leader, was still obstinate in his rejection of Vlasov, as was Chayum Khan and Khedia. But Vlasov found Ostrovsky's attitude all the more curious because much of the First Division was made up of White Ruthenians who had previously been members of the SS Sigling Division. He took this as proof that White Russian separatism was unnatural. But what had moved him most was that General Shandruk had come to him in January. The two generals had agreed that for the sake of the common cause they would forget all the disagreements of the past.

While Vlasov was talking, the foremost car in the small column skidded into the roadside ditch. The second car, in which Vlasov and Herre were seated, likewise skidded. Both men got out, and Herre loudly bawled out the drivers because it seemed to him that the whole Heuberg program was already threatened. Vlasov took his arm. Herre was taking things too hard, he said. And he spoke about Russian fatalism, his people's greatest strength in difficult times.

"Think of what I was just telling you, Andrei Fedorovich," he said. "What does Shandruk matter? What does Krasnov matter? Or Ostrovsky? What does it matter whether we quarrel or love each other? We've tried something impossible; we are all of us facing the same fate."

Herre disagreed. But Vlasov seemed to have been suddenly seized by a mood of resignation. "From our youth on we learned that bolshevism is invincible. That idea has been with us throughout our lives; only when we came over to your side could we begin to think differently. But maybe it really is true that bolshevism is unshakable and is creeping upon us like a serpent. . . ."

Again Herre tried to object. But he sensed that nothing he could say would change Vlasov's mood.

Vlasov stayed in Heuberg among his soldiers for a few days. It was as if he were living on a patch of Russian soil. On February 19 he returned to Münsingen with Herre. Once more Herre observed the charismatic effect Vlasov had upon people.

"If you can manage to advance twenty kilometers at any one point in the front, our victory is certain," Vlasov told his soldiers. On the face of it, he was thinking about the First Division's trial by fire, and how its performance would impress the Germans. But Herre felt, correctly, that

Vlasov was taking a longer view and that he had written off Germany and was somehow counting on America or England. Did Vlasov want some visible success for the First Division in order to show the Western powers that he was a force to be reckoned with?

For several nights Herre paid a late visit to Vlasov's barrack. In the darkened anteroom he usually found an adjutant or orderly who would say: *"Odnu minutoshku* (Wait a moment)." Shortly afterward, a half-dressed Russian girl would scurry through the anteroom. Once it was a young woman doctor, another time a stenographer. Then Herre would be shown into the bedroom. Usually he found Vlasov sprawled on the sofa or the bed. His face showed nothing of the keenness he liked to display to his soldiers. On a chair, bottles of vodka and large glasses would be standing. Vlasov would apologize; he was suffering from overwork, or from a cold. Then he would fill the glasses and begin a brooding conversation. Repeatedly he reviewed his life, as though he found it constantly necessary to justify the course he had chosen. Several times he said: "Andrei Fedorovich, Strik-Strikfeldt was right when he warned me against taking this last course. Himmler, too, has betrayed me. He, too, is not a strong man." Or else he would say: "Andrei Fedorovich, one must not demand too much of fate. When I think of it, I've had everything: fame, women, and a fine life for a long time."

These fits of fatalism troubled Herre. He kept asking Köstring almost daily for some opportunity to send the First Division into action. If only they could find the sort of situation where it might score a spectacular success while not running the danger of being annihilated by some overwhelmingly superior force. That was a tough nut to crack, and Köstring at last suggested that Herre talk to Himmler personally about it.

On February 21 Herre received word that Himmler would be expecting him on February 23 at the headquarters of Army Group Vistula in the municipal forest of Prenzlau.

When he reported there, Herre ran into two old friends from the Army General Staff, who filled him in on Himmler's disastrous record as commander in chief of the Army Group Vistula. His friends thought that Himmler's appointment represented a coup on Martin Bormann's part, the idea being to discredit Himmler in Hitler's eyes by giving the Reichsführer a job he could not possibly handle.

Himmler received Herre in the office of his barrack. He seemed even more fidgety than he had been at their November talk, but made an attempt to seem brisk.

"Well," he asked, "how is our friend Vlasov?"

This time, at least, the name rolled easily off his tongue.

"I've been having some long talks with him," Herre said. "He seems in a very gloomy state of mind. I suppose he keeps feeling, 'Too late.' In fact, you can't blame him for feeling that way."

"Why so?" Himmler asked distractedly. "After all, he now has his First Division. I understand that you're impatient for the chance to commit it to battle. The antitank detachments you sent me have been a great success. Many deserters have come over."

Herre noted the flickering light in Himmler's eyes, and a certain shiftiness in his whole tone. The mention of deserters was also disquieting. Why was he so interested in deserters? Had Strik-Strikfeldt and all the others been right after all when they insisted that behind Himmler's change of heart was nothing more than an opportunistic interest in exploiting Vlasov, and that if the tide of battle should once more change in Germany's favor, Vlasov would promptly be retired again?

"Still Vlasov has some grounds for pessimism," Herre said. "You will remember that when I saw you in November I spoke of two prerequisites for the success of his cause. Only one of those has been achieved."

"I don't follow."

"What I mean is this," Herre said. "We have given Vlasov and many of the Eastern volunteers a political goal by letting the Prague Manifesto be issued. But the second prerequisite is totally lacking. With the exception of Army Group Courland, German troops no longer occupy any Russian soil."

"Have you by any chance frightened Vlasov?" Himmler asked.

"No, I am trying to encourage him in every possible way. That is why I am here. We need to have the First Division go into action. And it ought to be somewhere on the eastern front where it could win a tangible success."

"What do you have in mind specifically?"

"The First Vlasov Division should be allowed to participate in a limited mission consistent with its strength. One possibility would be the elimination of a Soviet bridgehead. I've come directly to you, Reichsführer, in the hope that you can find some such mission for the division within the territory of your army group."

Himmler seemed to reflect for a while. At last he said: "I give you my word that the division will be assigned such a mission."

On February 24 Vlasov left Münsingen for Karlsbad. The members of the Liberation Committee were to meet there on February 27. Vlasov himself arrived in Karlsbad on that day and was given an effusive welcome by his followers.

Karlsbad had changed. The Richmond, Karlsbad's biggest hotel, was filled with various bureaus of the committee and the army. Malyshkin and Zhilenkov were working here. Many boarding houses, small hotels, and private homes were occupied by Russian officers and officials. Marienbad and Joachimsthal had also taken on a distinctly Russian aspect.

In Jäger, just to the west of Karlsbad, General Aschenbrenner, the former German air attaché in Moscow, along with his adjutant Buschmann and Russian Air Force Colonel Malytsev, had set up a mixed air division composed of former Russian air and anti-aircraft officers, noncoms, and enlisted men. The majority had previously served in German air units, many as ground personnel at airports and on flak batteries, but some had done actual flying, either delivering planes or in squadrons engaged in combatting partisans. In Jäger there now took shape a flak regiment, a parachute troop battalion, a communications regiment, an air force transport regiment, a reconnaissance echelon with readied planes, and a pilots' school. The division was officially subordinated to the German Luftwaffe, not to Vlasov. But Aschenbrenner had long known that the war was lost for Germany; he sympathized with Vlasov and on his own initiative was trying to find ways to "put Vlasov into touch with the Western powers."

The Liberation Committee met on February 27 in the Hotel Richmond. Vlasov managed to pull himself together for a major speech. Reports on the successes of his antitank detachments and on the numbers of deserters, insignificant as these matters were against the gigantic panorama of the eastern front, helped to boost his morale.

"Former officers and soldiers of the Red Army who had marched all the way to the Oder today entered the ranks of the Russian Liberation Army . . . doing so at a moment in which Stalin regards the question of victory as already decided. . . . The appearance at the front of the Liberation Army of the Peoples of Russia will be a glorious day for our countrymen."

The well-tried magic of his personality and his voice did not fail. Many members of the audience stood up to relate some encouraging experience at one of the fronts. A Cossack officer rose and described an incident which had occurred in Yugoslavia, where his corps was already in retreat. He reported that a Soviet bomber had dropped a note reading: "Brother Cossacks, we want to fight on your side. Prepare a landing runway for us." The runway was prepared. Up to the last moment the Cossacks feared some trick. But then one after another six planes had landed. That same night eight hundred and three members of a Soviet Guards Division had deserted to the Cossacks. And this had taken place at a stage in the war when Russian victory over the Germans was clearly in the cards.

A man stood up and identified himself as the first mayor of Kiev under the German occupation. In his excitement he spoke with a bluntness that had hardly ever been heard before among these former German captives: "I want to say to you Germans that the clock is striking twelve. Now there is no longer any talk about conquest—you won't be doing any more conquering—but about our saving our own people from Stalin's regime and your saving your people and averting the peril that now threatens you and the whole world. We received you as liberators. You trampled upon us. For three years we have waited for you to recognize where your true interest lies. . . . Isn't it time for you to come to your senses? Even now won't you unshackle our half-freed hands, so that we can really fight for our and your freedom? . . . The hour is late. Consider, before it is too late for you."

On March 2 Herre received the order to bring the Vlasov First Division to Army Group Vistula. But when he passed this order on to Bunyachenko, the Russian refused. His division's supply vehicles were not yet adequate, he said. This or that regiment was not ready. Finally, he made the point that General Vlasov was his commander. His division was part of General Vlasov's army and could be committed to action only within the framework of that army, which was not yet ready. Four days of tough arguing followed before Bunyachenko finally agreed to march. In fact, the decision finally came from Vlasov himself, who on March 5 personally confirmed the order to send the division into action within the area of Army Group Vistula.

On March 6 the first unit, the reconnaisance company, marched through the camp gate. This was the first time large numbers of Russian soldiers were leaving the isolation of Münsingen.

Herre drove ahead of the division. He visited mayors and district party leaders to prepare them for the division's passing through. As had been the case months earlier, in some places he met with understanding, in others with utter astonishment. But with few exceptions the march pro-

ceeded without difficulty or friction. The fact that Germans received the
soldiers in their homes, ate and talked with them as equals, made some
impression on the division's men. But there were other complications.
Major Helmut Schwenninger, who had been appointed head of the German liaison staff of the First Vlasov Division, arrived to take up his
duties, and Herre was able to return to Münsingen. Schwenninger then
discovered that the division's demand for rations was steadily increasing.

News of the march of the First Vlasov Division had spread like wildfire
through the camps of *Ostarbeiter* that lay along the route. By the hundreds the Russian workers and prisoners of war broke out of their camps
to join the division. And the division's regiments took them in. The
division had left Münsingen at a strength of 13,000 men. In the course of
its march its strength swelled to 18,000. Party leaders, camp commandants, and factory managers complained that their Russian workers were
melting away; the division was passing through the country like the Pied
Piper of Hamlin.

During this period Bunyachenko kept restlessly riding back and forth,
his leg in a plaster cast, his ponderous figure lying more than sitting in the
back of a jeep. He knew precisely what was going on in the division and
did his best to keep out of Schwenninger's way, letting Nikolayev do the
talking for him.

Schwenninger pointed out that he had done everything in his power to
correct the wrongheaded attitude of his fellow Germans. But now he must
insist that Bunyachenko do something to curb the influx of Russians.

Nikolayev shrugged. "What are we supposed to do?" he asked. "What
would you do if you were in our situation? Would you shoot them? Would
you drive them away?"

Schwenninger could think of no reply.

"Our soldiers obey orders," Nikolayev continued. "But would they
shoot their fellow countrymen? No, it's better for us to say nothing about
it. They don't just come to us. They have stories to tell. They tell about
everything they've experienced and suffered." He paused, then added with
a trace of bitterness and menace: "We cannot keep our soldiers from
listening to them."

The division marched by way of Donauwörth and Weissenburg. On
March 19 it assembled in several villages northwest of Nuremberg. All
the preparations for railroad transport were by this time complete. But
when Schwenninger came to Bunyachenko to discuss the transportation
of the division, he met with fresh reservations. According to the usual
arrangements, the units were to be divided up among a number of trains.

But Bunyachenko thought the division was being broken up deliberately, perhaps in order to place it once more under German administration. Schwenninger had a hard day persuading him otherwise. But finally all the trains were filled and departed. The first of them arrived at the Lieberose troop-training area on March 22.

Since Herre's visit to Himmler, the situation on the Oder had changed. On March 20 Himmler had resigned his post as commander of Army Group Vistula, alleging illness. In reality, he was ducking out of the assignment. On March 22 tough little General Gotthard Heinrici had assumed command on the Oder front. He had been fighting on the eastern front since 1941, and had never taken the slightest interest in political problems. The very name of Vlasov was unknown to him. When he heard that a Russian division was to be sent into battle in his area, he asked whether anybody seriously believed that as matters now stood a Russian division would fight. Himmler had arranged the transportation of the division, he concluded; let Himmler take the responsibility for it. Himmler was at the moment "taking the cure" in Hohenlychen. Consequently, on April 2 Schwenninger was received in Berlin by Obergruppenführer Berger. Berger sent him back to the Oder, this time to see the commander of the Ninth Army, General Theodor Busse.

On April 4 Schwenninger reported to Busse's chief of staff, General Hölz. He met with a degree of courteous understanding. Probably Berger had prepared the ground. At any rate, Hölz accepted Schwenninger's arguments and finally suggested a mission for the division which, if successfully carried out, could have the hoped-for political and propagandistic effect.

In addition to a large bridgehead at Küstrin, the Red Army had established a smaller bridgehead to the south of Frankfurt on the Oder. This bridgehead was called "Erlenhof." The previous week two German officer-candidate regiments had tried in vain to wipe out this bridgehead. On a front that was painfully girding itself against the new offensive which was clearly in the offing, Erlenhof represented the only chance for a limited attacking operation.

After Schwenninger's initial discussions, Bunyachenko himself went to see Busse and Hölz. Schwenninger fully realized that both Bunyachenko and Nikolayev suspected that the division was being assigned a hopeless mission in which it would be bled to death. This wall of suspicion was at least somewhat shaken by the attitudes of Busse and Hölz, who received

Bunyachenko as an ally. Bunyachenko went to the front and examined conditions carefully. Whenever the principal argument for sending the division into battle was raised—namely, that success would spur the Germans into organizing more Vlasov divisions—Bunyachenko would nod impassively, keeping his thoughts to himself. He showed the keenest interest, however, in the general situation. He asked about the strength of the Soviet forces across the Oder, about the strength of the German forces, and particularly whether anything was known about the date for the next Soviet offensive.

Busse assured Bunyachenko the best artillery support that the army could supply. A few Stukas would also be committed to the battle.

The attack was set for early in the morning on April 13, after a brief but heavy artillery barrage.

On April 11 Vlasov, accompanied by Trukhin, came to see Bunyachenko. He inquired about the situation and spent a long time alone with Bunyachenko. He addressed several of the battalions. Once more he told the men that everything would depend on the success of the attack, including the development of a liberation army and the victory of this army as an instrument in the struggle against Stalinism. But he chose his words carefully and there was a note of some hidden intention behind them.

Before Vlasov departed, he came upon Schwenninger alone. He had just been looking through a field telescope. The Soviet attacking forces were camped on the other side of the river. They seemed, if anything, too calm. No one had been able to tell him when the Soviet assault would erupt. It was expected in, perhaps, a week to ten days. But German air reconnaissance was almost paralyzed. The Russians were maintaining radio silence. So the offensive might come sooner. Vlasov tramped along the side of the road with Schwenninger for a while, and then said: "Join me in wishing that our fellows will have time for a successful attack. Once those boys across the river strike, it will be too late. We must carry out our action first. Otherwise, it will be better not to try. A lot hangs on Operation Erlenhof. But not so much that we ought to sacrifice our First Division for it. We must preserve it. We need it."

Schwenninger himself was so convinced of the need for a success that he did not understand Vlasov's much greater concern: the possibility that the division built up despite so many obstacles could be overwhelmed and go down to destruction in the initial waves of a Soviet offensive.

. . .

The attack began, as intended, in the early morning of April 13.

Bunyachenko with the divisional staff and Schwenninger with his liaison detachment stood at dawn on a height from which they could survey the bridgehead.

The artillery barrage roared and spat into the dawn. But the promised dive-bombers did not appear. They were grounded for lack of fuel. Nevertheless, at first the attack seemed to proceed according to plan. Everyone waited for the first penetration. Bunyachenko's eyes glittered as the flares rose, calling for the barrage to advance. Shortly afterward came the first reports of a penetration in the north and south as well. But now the engineers and infantrymen found themselves halted by tremendous barbed-wire entanglements. Several times they tried to get through. But they suffered considerable losses and made no progress. These were the same barbed-wire entanglements that had stopped the German officer candidates.

Schwenninger kept hoping for a breakthrough. He was so obsessed by the importance of this attack that he could not imagine it would fail. Uneasily he watched Bunyachenko, in whom a surprising change seemed to be taking place. Bunyachenko is switching sides, he suddenly thought. The division has failed; the great opportunity is lost.

The attack was broken off after four hours. The Russian regiments retreated to their starting positions, and Bunyachenko asked Schwenninger to obtain authorization from the army for the division to return to its quarters.

Schwenninger was horrified, but he carried out the request. Busse and Hölz refused, and ordered the First Division to remain in its starting position. Busse sent for Bunyachenko, so that he could deliver a report in person. But when Schwenninger returned, he found the Russian division with its wounded already on the march back to the quarters in Lieberose. Bunyachenko wore a cold and resolute air. He refused to report to Busse, stating that his superior officer was Vlasov and no one else. His only interest seemed to be in the question of whether Schwenninger had learned anything new about Zhukov's possible deadline for the offensive. When Schwenninger was unable to say, distrust flared in Bunyachenko's eyes. He asked Schwenninger to return to Busse's headquarters and obtain permission for the entire division to start out that same evening for the south, for the vicinity of Cottbus, say.

In all the previous weeks Schwenninger had honestly endeavored to understand the division's problems. Nevertheless, he could not help seeing the situation now with German eyes, and his concepts of the obedience owed to Busse or Hölz plunged him into profound conflicts. Evidently Bunyachenko had interpreted his inability to obtain information on the time of Zhukov's offensive, and Busse's refusal to allow retreat from the front lines, as signs of a malignant desire to keep the division where it was and "burn it up," as if in a crematorium. In his new surge of distrust Bunyachenko evidently envisaged the sudden outbreak of a Soviet offensive, in the turmoil of which the First Division would be helplessly destroyed. Consequently, he regarded putting distance between his division and the German front lines as more important than the spectacular conquest of a bridgehead or than obeying the orders of Germans from whom no further hope and no third division could reasonably be expected.

Schwenninger had no idea where Bunyachenko was bound and what he was still hoping to do. But when he saw Hölz he tried to offer a justification of the Russians' "mutinous" attitude. Hölz heard him out calmly. He had to admit that the Soviet offensive might begin at any moment and that nobody knew where the main thrust would be delivered. There were supposed concentrations at Küstrin and at Frankfurt on the Oder, but there was another further to the south. The British and American armies were marching almost unimpeded through Central, North, and South Germany. There was no saying whether they could be halted at the Elbe.

After some discussion back and forth, Hölz appeared almost relieved to be rid of the Russian "problem division" in his territory. He issued the order for it to march southward into the rear area of General Schörner's army group; its first destination would be just to the north of Cottbus. But he insisted that the division's artillery remain on his own front at the Oder.

When Schwenninger arrived in Lieberose, bringing the order for the march south, Bunyachenko said: "Very good. I did not doubt that the German authorities would be understanding. In view of this, I have already ordered the march."

Schwenninger replied: "But the order calls for the division's artillery to remain on the Oder front."

Bunyachenko reverted to his former slyness. "Look," he said, "what good is the division without artillery? It had better come with us."

. . .

268

At eight o'clock in the morning on April 14 Bunyachenko sent for Schwenninger. The Russian was sitting in the midst of his staff, his leg propped up on a chair. What further orders, he asked, did Schwenninger think would be issued once the division reached the area north of Cottbus?

Schwenninger did not understand the question. With sincere conviction he said: "From there the march will proceed to the south. Cottbus is only the first destination, as you know."

Bunyachenko poured himself a drink. Over the glass of vodka his eyes remained fixed on Schwenninger.

"Good," he said cunningly, "but what if my division were held there, after all? What if it were sent into a hopeless battle in the dangerous area it will then reach?"

Schwenninger realized that something unforeseen must have happened. "That would not be in keeping with the discussions I have had up to this point," he replied.

Bunyachenko reached under the desk and produced a document which he tossed into Schwenninger's lap. "And what may this be?"

It turned out to be an order from the 275th Infantry Division to the "600th Infantry Division (Russian)" which placed it under the Schörner Army Group, effective April 14. The commander of the 275th Infantry Division ordered the Russian division to create a backup position directly behind his division and prepare for defense against the expected Soviet major offensive.

As he stood there, the target of distrustful looks from all the Russians, Schwenninger feverishly tried to think out the situation. He had heard a great deal about Schörner, about his loyalty to Hitler and his brutality. And he could not help admiring the celerity with which Schörner's command apparatus had operated in order to commandeer the new division marching into the area for its own purposes. On the other hand, when Schwenninger thought of the respect the Russian division had always received from the Ninth Army, he could scarcely comprehend the thoughtless clumsiness with which the Russian division was now being subordinated to a German division.

He was not given time to think. Bunyachenko pounded his fist on the table. This was a breach of agreements, he declared. He was still Vlasov's subordinate; it was an insult to attempt to subordinate him to a German divisional commander. Then he subsided and became icy. He would stick to the order to march to the Cottbus area, he continued. He would carry out this order. As far as he was concerned, the order from the 275th

Infantry Division had no validity. His headquarters would be northwest of Peitz in the evening. Schwenninger could talk to him again there.

Schwenninger had no choice but to attempt to clarify the division's relations with the 275th Infantry Division. When he reached that division's headquarters at 11 A.M. he noticed at once that the atmosphere of Schörner's army group was extremely different from that in Busse's. Here any discussion of the military situation was out of line. By order, everyone had faith in German victory. It was defeatism to mention the possibility that the front might collapse—or to refer to the consequences for the Russian division of such a collapse. It proved impossible for Schwenninger to obtain any alteration of the existing order from the 275th Infantry Division, or from the Fifth Corps, to which it belonged. Only Field Marshal Schörner personally could make any such change. Schörner was expected to be at Fifth Corps Headquarters at 2 P.M.

This was Schwenninger's first meeting with the notorious field marshal. He had often heard that Schörner's slogan was "Strength through Fear—an interesting version of "Strength through Joy." And he quickly saw an example of the field marshal's behavior pattern when Schörner made a telephone call. He had a bad connection and began to shout, insisting on talking to the operator, and poured out a stream of the coarsest threats. Then he looked around the circle of his staff, who stood in embarrassed silence, and declared: "It's better already. You only have to make a stink."

He displayed the keenest interest in the Russian division, which seemed to him to have fallen from heaven just when he needed reinforcements for his front. When he heard that the division was 17,000 men strong, his eyes lit up.

"Well, what's up with those fellows?" he asked. "Do they want to fight or don't they?"

Schwenninger tried to explain. But Schörner interrupted him. "So your general doesn't want to. Well, suppose you let this Russky know I'll have him up against the wall if he doesn't obey my orders. It's for me to judge whether or not my front will hold. You tell the bastard that."

Schwenninger said it would not be so easy to pry Bunyachenko out of the midst of his 17,000 men. Schörner thundered, "So that's what you've accomplished, to make these boys a menace in my rear. But how would it be if I had a squadron of bombers smash him and his division?"

It was hopeless to try to explain a complex political problem to Schörner. Schwenninger did not even try. Instead, Schörner suddenly and unpredictably softened. Perhaps he did not have any such squadron of bombers at his disposal. At any rate, he said he had no more time now to waste on those Russians. The order for subordination to the 275th Infantry Division was rescinded. He had to go to the Führer's Headquarters. When he was back he would teach those Russkys how to obey orders.

That evening Schwenninger met Bunyachenko already on the march toward Peitz. When he gave his report, Bunyachenko's eyes glittered. "So," he said, "your field marshal talks of shooting me. I don't take that too seriously. Twice I've been threatened with a firing squad. Once in 1937 and then once more. He'll see."

Schwenninger "saw" by next morning. That was the morning of April 15. Bunyachenko with his staff sat in a farmhouse in Schonholz. He had removed the plaster cast from his leg. His mood seemed again to have changed; he welcomed Schwenninger with something approaching cordiality and thanked him for his previous cooperation. Schwenninger was puzzled.

"Do you think we're going to be able to go on cooperating?" Bunyachenko asked with that cunning look of his. Then he abruptly changed the subject. "Oh well, we'll see. Let's have a drink first." He raised the glass, but his eyes continued to bore into Schwenninger. After Schwenninger had finished his drink and set it down, Bunyachenko continued: "You were supposed to go back to the Fifth Corps today, to see about possible further orders. You know, before you leave you ought to see how I quartered my division last night. I picked this terrain for all eventualities."

Schwenninger understood. He made no comment, and Bunyachenko went on: "Any commitment of my division to battle requires the approval of General Vlasov. Report to General Schörner that my division is now completely assembled in this area; the artillery is here, too, along with the anti-aircraft units. We are feeling very well, thank you. The woods shield us from aviation. Our antitank units, assault batteries, and tanks are so arranged that we can defend ourselves against attacks of all kinds, for example, against the attacks of enemy tank forces that might achieve a breakthrough in this vicinity. . . ."

He waited—drinking—to observe the effect of these words on Schwenninger. For just a moment Schwenninger was tempted to say something about mutiny. But he controlled himself because he knew that it was pointless and that from Bunyachenko's point of view the dispute involved sheer self-preservation.

As Schwenninger went out, he noticed Nikolayev following him. The Russian took Schwenninger's arm and drew him into an adjoining room. "Do you really mean to transmit that message?" he asked. His angular face showed concern.

"I have no choice," Schwenninger replied.

"Don't take the message personally," Nikolayev urged. "Have it sent by radio. Otherwise you, Gelmut Fritzovich, will pay for what we are doing here."

Schwenninger waved away the warning. He himself was in no danger, he said, but he was worried about what decision Schörner would make in regard to the division.

Nikolayev countered. "What can he do? But I wouldn't want you to take the rap for us. If you insist on going personally, I'll have a radio team go with you, so we can hear if he comes down hard on you."

He insisted on having the radio team go along. At dawn on April 16 Schwenninger reached the battle headquarters of the Fifth Corps. But only a few hours before, the Soviet spring offensive on the Oder and Neisse had begun with a frightful artillery barrage. The front between Muskau and Guben was already crumbling. Schwenninger managed to persuade the chief of staff to telephone Josephstadt, Schörner's headquarters; but apparently everyone there had other things on his mind than the insubordination of the Russians. Without clearing it with Schörner, the army group authorized the Russian division to continue its march toward Senftenberg and Hoyerswerda.

As Schwenninger drove back, Soviet planes were in the air over the roads. Marshal Koniev's army was on the point of breaking through the German front between Muskau and Guben, then swinging north toward Berlin, and later south against the yielding left wing of Schörner's army group.

By April 17, after an extraordinary performance marching in constant readiness for battle, the First Vlasov Division reached the vicinity of Hoyerswerda. There a personal order from Schörner arrived. It read: "Division to march to the front for battle in the Kosel area, 6 kilometers northwest of Niesky." Bunyachenko behaved as if there were no such order. On April 18 he marched to the area west of Kamenz. On the morning of that day a new order from the army group reached Schwenninger. It read: "Division to reach area of Radeberg near Dresden for rail transport to action in Czechoslovakia."

During the night, however, Schwenninger had lost contact with Bunyachenko's staff. He searched for it for an entire day. In the course of his search he encountered bands of dispersing German troops. In Stölpchen, between Dresden and Hoyerswerda, Schwenninger finally came upon the division staff. He brought the order to Bunyachenko, who announced that he would carry it out, obviously because he in any case intended to continue marching in that direction. On April 19 the division actually reached the vicinity of Radeberg. But here Bunyachenko refused to let his division board the train. Fighting was already going on in the vicinity of Bautzen. Bunyachenko said cunningly, but with no less truthfulness, that entraining now was pointless; the division would be wiped out before half the men were aboard the trains. And that certainly would do Schörner no good. He preferred to continue marching on foot.

For three days after that, communications with Schörner's headquarters were broken. Bunyachenko continued south by forced marches, in exemplary order. By April 22 the entire division was assembled in the area around Bad Schandau. Here, on April 23, one of Schörner's personal liaison officers, a Major Neuner, arrived. Schörner obviously had had enough of this hide-and-seek game. He also no longer trusted Schwenninger. Major Neuner had the assignment of delivering orders to Bunyachenko to occupy a backup position in the Haida area, eight kilometers north of Böhmisch-Leipa. In addition, he ordered Bunyachenko to appear in Haida at 5 P.M. on April 24 to receive personal instructions from Schörner.

Bunyachenko displayed his most amiable side. He said that he would march to Haida. He also declared that it would be an honor for him to make the acquaintance of Schörner.

On the afternoon of April 24 Schwenninger drove ahead to Haida. That was the day Russian armies began to close their ring around Berlin and Schörner's front in Czechoslovakia was engaged in bitter defensive battles. Only a short distance separated the Americans and Russians in the neighborhood of Torgau on the Elbe. The entire countryside behind Schörner was in a state of upheaval. Refugees were wandering about. The first signs of Czech uprisings were appearing.

Schörner was waiting. But instead of Bunyachenko, who should appear but the commander of the First Division's reconnaissance company,

Kostyenko. With a wink at Schwenninger, he reported to Schörner that Bunyachenko had unfortunately been involved in an automobile accident and was in no condition to come.

Schörner controlled himself with an effort until Kostyenko had left. Then he raged: "Stinkers! Oh, that Luftwaffe! If only I had planes, I'd bomb those Russians till they knuckled under!"

On April 25 Schwenninger found Bunyachenko's staff again, this time in the vicinity of the Hoher Schneeberg northwest of Tetschen-Bodenbach. The entire division was assembled here. Bunyachenko wore heavy bandages around his head, his right arm, and his right leg. He gave Schwenninger a circumstantial account of the accident. But he was obviously suffering no pain at all, and Schwenninger had his suspicions.

The following afternoon Schörner announced by radio that he would arrive in person in a Storch reconnaissance plane at the Russian divisional headquarters at 10 A.M. on April 27.

Schwenninger fully realized the grotesque change in the situation. Here was the almighty field marshal condescending to visit a disobedient Russian general. Bunyachenko lined up an honor company and the regimental band. But Schörner had changed his mind after all. He sent his chief of staff, Brigadier General von Natzmer.

Natzmer sat for a long time negotiating with Bunyachenko. The Russian finally agreed to commit his division in the area of Brno, although it was patent, to anyone who knew him, that he had not the slightest intention of carrying out the agreement. Natzmer then tried to persuade him to entrain the division this time, so that it could be sent into battle in a few days. But this Bunyachenko refused. Then Natzmer tried to settle on a marching route which would keep the division close behind the front as it moved south. He argued on the basis of the stocks of ammunition and rations which were in the neighborhood of his proposed route, and without which the division could not manage. His unspoken reason was, undoubtedly, that the division would thus be kept as close as possible to the front. Bunyachenko smiled in his sly fashion. After Natzmer's Storch had taken off, he said to Nikolayev: "They want us to march behind our bread. . . . No, we don't need to." He was clearly implying that if necessary he and his men would seize what they needed.

Next day the division marched to Teplitz-Schönau. On April 29 it continued its march in a southerly direction. That evening Bunyachenko and his staff set up headquarters in Kosoyed.

In all the Czech towns and villages, the young men were gathering together in bands. Schwenninger for the first time noticed some sort of confabulation between Czechs and soldiers and officers of the division. The atmosphere was filled with suspense of a kind he had never observed before. And for the first time also there were clashes with German soldiers. A group of Germans who tried to restore the cut telephone lines in the division's area were stopped by Russian guards and arrested. Bunyachenko released them, declaring that of course they could carry out their assignment. But an hour later the Germans were found shot. They had been stopped once more by other Russian guards and had reached for their weapons.

On the evening of April 29 a radio message from Schörner arrived at the divisional headquarters. He had evidently learned that the division was not adhering to the route laid down by Natzmer. Schörner announced that at noon he would land in Klappai, eight kilometers south of Lobositz, and would visit Bunyachenko.

When Bunyachenko received this message he was sitting in a peasant's kitchen with his sleeves rolled up. Half an hour later he was in full uniform and welcomed Schörner in perfect military form. Schörner was trying the friendly approach. He was carrying a bottle of vodka and a box of cigars, which he extended to Bunyachenko. But the Russian displayed icy stiffness. Ignoring the gifts, he said: "I am pleased to have you call on me, Herr Generalfeldmarschall—all the more so since a few weeks ago you were considering a different sort of treatment."

Bunyachenko's eyes shone with the triumph of a man who had borne the slur "subhuman" for too many years.

Schörner was plainly baffled by the interpreter's words. "What do you mean?" he asked. "I don't recall."

Bunyachenko said: "May I remind the field marshal that he intended to have me shot."

Schörner threw a furious look at Schwenninger. "Who told you that?" he demanded.

"I did, Herr Generalfeldmarschall," Schwenninger said.

The field marshal glared at him. "That was extremely diplomatic," he growled. He turned back to Bunyachenko. "But that's ridiculous. Would I be coming to see you otherwise?"

Bunyachenko remained unmoved. He offered Schörner a seat. This was his big moment.

Schörner controlled his temper with difficulty. But he could not help realizing that the power and menace of his personality were leaking away rapidly. In fact, it was questionable whether he had any power at all. "I should like to hear from you directly what your real intentions are," he said. "Are you still willing to fight with your division or aren't you?"

Bunyachenko said: "Of course, I want to fight." But he refrained from saying for whom or where he meant to fight.

Relieved to have found an escape from his dilemma, Schörner took a hearty tone: "For me, that is the most important thing. In that case, I agree that you yourself settle your marching route to Brno. When will you be there?"

The answer he received was vague. But he did not press the point; he took his leave quickly and drove back to his plane, inwardly vowing vengeance on all and sundry. As soon as he had taken off, Bunyachenko held conferences with several of his officers. There was a mysterious amount of activity. That evening Schwenninger was informed that several Czechs in civilian dress had called on Bunyachenko and had talked with him for hours. What that might mean, Schwenninger had no idea. But he had an intimation that crucial events were in the offing.

A few days after the First Division had left Münsingen on March 6, the existing formations of the Second Division had been transferred from Heuberg to Münsingen. Trukhin remained behind in Heuberg with the army staff.

Heuberg had been unable to provide Sveryev's soldiers with small arms, machine guns, and bazookas. Only with great difficulty were requisitioned vehicles rounded up for the supply services. There were no longer any heavy arms to be had. It had been something of a miracle when ultimately a number of modern 12.2 cannon-howitzers of Russian origin, for which there was suitable German ammunition, arrived in Münsingen.

The artillery was unloaded while the German western front was receding more and more to the east and southeast. Soon afterward, an artillery officer from Army Group G, which was retreating through Württemberg, turned up in Münsingen to requisition arms for use on the western front. There was a grave crisis with Sveryev. He refused to give up the artillery pieces. Herre finally worked out a compromise; some of the howitzers were turned over to the officer; the rest were kept.

This crisis of confidence had long repercussions. It was not helped by reports on the unmistakable collapse of the German eastern front, and by the absence of any word on the fate of the First Vlasov Division. Days passed before it was learned that the division had been saved from the general disaster and was on the march to the south. Then all sources of information dried up. American troops were approaching Münsingen.

It seemed probable that Vlasov was still in the First Division's vicinity. Trukhin, Sveryev, Boyarski, Neryanin, and Meandrov showed growing uneasiness. Time and again, they had together given thought to the prospects and pitfalls of their situation. But now the moment was inexorably approaching when their fate would be decided.

On the morning of April 18, Herre met Meandrov. From him Herre heard for the first time a fully candid account of what the Russians were contemplating. Some were preparing to defend themselves against Soviet troops and, if necessary, against German attacks, but to surrender to the Americans and British. Meandrov indicated that he had other ideas. He believed that the alliance between the Soviet regime and the Western Allies would collapse in the foreseeable future. But he thought that it would hold together long enough for them to celebrate the victory together. He wanted to march all the Vlasov troops to the southeast and there link up with the Cossacks and with Shandruk's Ukrainians. Then he wanted to make contact with Michailovich and show the British and Americans down there an example of battle against bolshevism that might help to change the attitude of the Western powers and accelerate the process of their turning against bolshevism.

It was a sign of his desperate need for advice that Meandrov confided his thoughts to Herre.

Herre was very pale as he listened. The conflict of conscience that had been troubling him for a long time was reaching its pitch. What Meandrov said about the possibilities in Yugoslavia seemed to him as fantastic, coming from the other side, as the talk about an alpine redoubt where the Nazis could hide until the tide had turned.

"What about Andrei Andreyevich?" he asked, in what may have sounded like an attempt to dodge the question. "What does he think?"

Meandrov shrugged. "He is no longer the man he was," he said slowly. "Andrei Fedorovich, you Germans have destroyed his soul."

Herre remembered all too plainly Vlasov's words about the serpent and the inexorable fate coming upon them, that wintry day they had driven together to Heuberg. "Don't take it amiss," Herre said to Meandrov. "You will have to decide your course alone. But since you ask me—I see no hope in Serbia. The only way I see is to the West. The only way is to make the Americans and the British realize what you people mean for their future as well."

An hour later Herre received an order from the Armed Forces Operations Staff to direct the Second Vlasov Division, the officers' school, the replacement brigade, and the army staff to march immediately to the area around Linz where all were to be thrown into battle under the command of either Field Marshal Schörner or General Lothar Rendulic against the advancing Soviet armies. That meant moving the Vlasov forces further away from the Americans and putting them in danger of annihilation along with the collapse of the eastern front.

Herre needed advice. Meanwhile, General Köstring and his staff had arrived in Reichenhall. Köstring was the only one Herre could turn to, and so he telephoned Reichenhall. He spoke openly about the senseless order which could lead only to the capture of the Vlasov forces by the Red Army. Köstring seemed remarkably close-mouthed; he replied that he had done everything he could. Herre refused to take this for an answer. After a night drive, he turned up in Reichenhall and found Köstring and his staff established in an old hotel in the town.

"There's no sense discussing it," Köstring told him. "Drive back to Münsingen and see to it that the order is carried out as given. It will be the best thing for you, too." Köstring hesitated a moment. Then he turned away. "Of course, you're right. But that no longer matters. Your telephone calls yesterday afternoon were tapped here. If your absence becomes known, I won't be able to save you from arrest for defeatism or treason."

Toward dawn Herre drove back to Münsingen. In a few frank words he described the actual situation to Meandrov. But the Russian seemed prepared to obey the order. Back of this docility probably lay Meandrov's hopes for a union of forces in Yugoslavia.

At noon on April 19 the Second Vlasov Division set out on three march routes that ran parallel. They were to proceed on foot to the Landsberg-Fürstenfeldbruck area and there would be taken to Linz by rail.

The march proceeded without incident at first. In the evening on April

19 Herre learned from Meandrov that Vlasov, coming from Prague, had arrived at army staff headquarters. He brought word that the First Division was on the march south into Czechoslovakia. That was all Herre learned because he had to hurry on ahead to Defense District VII, through which the division would be marching, to make sure it would be supplied.

After another night drive, in the course of which he came upon straggling German supply columns everywhere, he found the staff of Defense District VII in Kempfenhausen on Lake Starnberg. A colonel glared at Herre. "Russians?" he said bluntly. "They won't get a gram of bread or a drop of gasoline from me."

Herre explained that in such an eventuality he could not promise there would be no acts of violence. He drove toward Memmingen-Landsberg to meet the Vlasov regiments and came upon them just at the critical moment. Parallel to the Vlasov contingents, remnants of German troops were moving along in a state of total dissolution. Within a few hours the aura that the German army had always had for these Russians was dissipated. But worse was to come. In another parallel movement, endless, wretched lines of concentration camp and penal camp prisoners were being marched eastward and southeastward. Their SS guards were driving them across the open fields.

Herre heard shots long before he reached the division. There were many Russians in the concentration camp columns. While they marched alongside the Vlasov units, often no more than a hundred and fifty to three hundred feet away, many of them ran across the fields to their countrymen. The wall of Russian soldiers closed around the fugitives. Trucks stopped, uniforms were pulled out, and the prisoners quickly dressed in them. The SS guards had then begun to shoot. The Russians answered their fire.

Herre found dead and wounded men. He asked his way to the Russian regimental commander who told him where Vlasov and the army staff could be found. Within a short time he came upon Vlasov who was with Trukhin and Boyarski in a small village southwest of Landsberg.

"What's the matter, Andrei Fedorovich?" Vlasov asked as he recognized Herre.

Herre described the situation. Vlasov shook his head absently. Then he got into the car with Herre and they drove back to the scene of the clash. When they arrived, firing was still continuing. It did not stop until Vlasov stepped out among his men. Herre ran across to the SS guards and tried to calm them.

After a half hour, the outbreak of a regular battle was averted. The march resumed.

Four days passed. Transportation proved impossible to procure. Parts of the rail line were destroyed. Whole trains had been smashed. Here and there the railroad men were already refusing to entrain troops. Meanwhile, the Vlasov division camped in the woods.

Sveryev objected to the entraining anyhow. He suspected that after the incidents at Landsberg the Germans wanted to break up his division. Once the men were loaded aboard railroad trains, they would be out of his control.

When Herre tried to appeal to Vlasov, he learned that Vlasov and Zhilenkov had gone to the Allgäu. Meandrov whispered to Herre that Vlasov had found out where Strik-Strikfeldt was staying and had gone there to see his "starets" one last time. General Aschenbrenner was said to be accompanying him.

But Trukhin and Neryanin demonstrated that they had their troops well in hand.

The entraining began on April 23 and continued until April 26. The trains were able to move only at night. When they started off at last, Trukhin, Sveryev, and parts of the army and divisional staffs drove ahead in automobiles to Linz. Herre, however, made a side trip to Reichenhall. He wanted to see Köstring once more before the end came.

It was clear to Köstring that Herre was tormented by the problem of his personal loyalty to the Russians. But Köstring himself was by now beyond caring about anything.

"Whatever you do," he told Herre, "you can no longer help them."

All along, Herre said, he had tried to keep the Russians loyal to a cause for which they must now suffer. He could not shed his responsibility for them. He had to remain with them.

With a shrug, Köstring shook hands with him. "When everything is over, I am going to Unterwössen. Maybe I'll make it to my farm. You can find me there."

Early in the morning on May 1, Herre and Trukhin met in Linz. As they were setting up a temporary headquarters in a half-bombed barracks, the news of Hitler's death reached them. While the Second Division and parts of the reserve brigade were marching to Budweis, and Sveryev with his division staff was setting up headquarters in Suchenthal, Trukhin and Herre drove together to the small hunting lodge called "Erla" where Rendulic's army group had its headquarters. On both sides of the road they saw hanged German soldiers with placards pinned to their chests reading: "I am a coward." Trukhin did not say a word.

General Rendulic invited Trukhin and Herre to dinner. From his behavior, no one would have known that total collapse was going on outside.

Rendulic had only scanty information about Vlasov. He talked with Trukhin about Russian literature and Russian music, and waited until after dinner to ask about the condition of the Russian formations. That gave Herre a "saving idea." Their problem was, he said, that they lacked arms. He had been told that Rendulic would see to that. And Rendulic actually assented and ordered reequipping of the troops at Budweis.

Relieved, Trukhin returned to Linz. Herre hurried to Budweis. There the seething ferment among the Czechs was plainly evident. Neryanin urged him to take a Russian bodyguard thirty-five men strong. Nevertheless, he found an almost unreal, exalted mood among the members of the Russian army staff and the officers' school and in the Second Division generally. News of the appointment of Dönitz as Hitler's successor had already come in. The word was that Dönitz was planning "armistice in the West, continuation of the struggle in the East." Rumors were flying to the effect that negotiations with the Western powers were already in progress and that it would be only a few days before German troops together with American and English troops turned against the Soviet armies. Had not Hitler's death removed the man whose obstinacy had for so long blocked Vlasov's hopes?

During the month of April Strik-Strikfeldt had taken refuge on a farm in the Allgäu. But with the restiveness of a man who had been so closely committed to the "Vlasov idea," he had watched from afar the development of the past month. In Prague the State Security Office [SD] had once again tried to transfer him from the army to the SS and make him Vlasov's constant companion. With Gehlen's aid he had ducked out of this. Given the odd assignment to write the history of the Vlasov movement for the Foreign Armies East Department, he had hidden out on an estate in Pomerania until Zhukov's offensive forced him to flee. On April 19 he had driven over to the farm of his friend Dwinger. It was a lovely day. In the afternoon a boy came running, calling out that many officers had come, all generals, and wanted to see Strik-Strikfeldt and Dwinger.

Among Malyshkin, Zhilenkov, Boyarski, and Aschenbrenner, Vlasov's tall form appeared.

All went into the house. There they spent half the night in discussions centering around the painful question of ways to save the Vlasov group from being caught in the whirlpool of the German collapse or from falling into the hands of Stalin.

Dwinger put forward some wild ideas. He proposed seizing a camp in the vicinity in which, among others, the French collaborator Pierre Laval had sought refuge from the Allies. Laval and men of his ilk should be held as hostages and offered to the Western powers in exchange for the personal security of the Russians. Vlasov shook his head, displeased. He called the project "dishonorable."

Then they discussed Meandrov's plan.

General Aschenbrenner warned against that one. German armies stronger than all the Vlasov and Cossack forces put together were still fighting in the southeast, he pointed out. They had control of supplies, and it was more than doubtful that the Russian divisions could succeed in uniting their own troops with the Cossacks. To reach that area, they would have to fight not only against Tito's partisans but also against the Red Army. If they failed to unite, the Cossacks would be destroyed, and that would be destruction of the "substance." It was this substance—the forces in being—that might interest the Western powers.

Aschenbrenner proposed that the Russians should straightway try to make contact with the Americans and British. They must do their utmost to correct the picture of Vlasov as a mercenary and ally of Hitler, a picture systematically spread by Soviet propaganda. He, too, was convinced that the alliance among Stalin, Churchill, and Roosevelt would break down after their common victory, and that in spite of all their asseverations of friendship the statesmen in the West were fully aware of the unnaturalness of this alliance. They had to be convinced that the Vlasov forces had developed the only attractive democratic and nonfascist program against Stalin and therefore their movement must not go under. Their aim should be to let the Western Allies take them prisoners of war. They should strive to win the right of asylum for all members of the movement, in order to have a base for the future.

At this moment none of them knew that on February 11, during the Yalta Conference among Stalin, Churchill, and Roosevelt, the latter two had agreed to deliver to the Soviet Union all persons who on September

1, 1939 had been citizens of the Soviet Union, or who had been members of the Red Army on June 22, 1941 and had been captured in German uniform, or had become voluntary collaborators with the Germans. Such persons were to be turned over even against their will, by force. The U.S. State Department had termed this agreement a violation of international law. But Churchill and Roosevelt had yielded to Stalin on this because they thought they would need additional aid from the Soviet Union in the war against Japan. They had reminded themselves of the many violations of law that Hitler had committed before and during the war—and, of course, they had not the slightest concept of the large numbers of those they were promising to surrender.

A number of volunteers captured in the invasion battles had already been turned over to the Soviet authorities. But Vlasov, Strik-Strikfeldt, and all the others missed the significance of this. They thought that the Western powers did not understand the situation. They never dreamed that a pact had already been made about returning all Russians. Consequently, they went along with Aschenbrenner's argument that the British and Americans could be "convinced."

The more Aschenbrenner talked, the more optimistic he became. It was all perfectly feasible. First, he would send Captain Oberländer, who spoke English and was deeply familiar with the whole Russian volunteer movement, through the thin German lines to some high-ranking British command post. Meanwhile, Strik-Strikfeldt would make his way to an American headquarters. Strik-Strikfeldt's English was as fluent as his Russian, and if there were anyone who could explain to the Americans what was at stake, it was he.

Vlasov had listened quietly to Aschenbrenner, occasionally throwing glances at Strik-Strikfeldt as if imploring his old associate to help him this one last time. But before he could reply, Boyarski spoke up. He thought that if there were to be negotiations with the Western powers, one of the Russians should be along in any case.

Vlasov also listened quietly to him. Again he looked at Strik-Strikfeldt, and when he read something like acquiescence in his expression, he said: "If Wilfried Karlovich is willing . . ."

Strik-Strikfeldt did not know how the Americans might receive him. He himself might be on some list of people to be turned over to the Soviets. But he saw no other possibility. He had already had too great a part in bringing Vlasov and his men to this point. "I'll try it," he said.

Vlasov gave him a grateful look. He said: "Then go. God will thank you. And Malyshkin will go with you."

He had not given the matter long reflection. He knew exactly why it had to be Malyshkin—the most likable, most engaging member of his entire entourage.

Next morning their ways parted. Vlasov and his staff set out for the east. Malyshkin and Strik-Strikfeldt drove northwest into uncertain conditions. They passed dispersed German columns and had no trouble at all making contact with an American unit. The young American officers to whom they showed their credentials knew nothing about Vlasov. Nevertheless, they blindfolded Malyshkin and Strik-Strikfeldt and took them to a divisional staff headquarters where they were received by a Lieutenant Colonel Snyder. After they had explained the reason for their presence, he telephoned higher authorities and meanwhile proposed calling in a Soviet liaison officer.

"No, Colonel," Strik-Strikfeldt said. "Not that."

For a moment, the colonel covered the mouthpiece of the telephone as if he wanted to say something. But then he spoke into it again: "No, they don't want that."

They stayed with the division staff one night. The following morning they were placed in a jeep, once more blindfolded, and taken to the headquarters of the American Seventh Army. Its commander, General Patch, received them in a large room. At his side stood a Russian interpreter named Artamonov, the son of a tsarist general.

Strik-Strikfeldt saw the nervous twitch in Malyshkin's sensitive face, and he wondered whether Malyshkin would have the strength to break through this wall of ignorance.

Malyshkin began by saying that thousands of armed Russian troops under the command of General Vlasov, who had hitherto fought against bolshevism, were caught in a hopeless predicament between the advancing Red Army and the advancing American front. They were willing to lay down their arms and submit to American imprisonment on condition that they would not be handed over to the Soviets.

Patch listened in bafflement to the words that Artamonov translated with obvious sympathy.

"What's this about Vlasov?" he asked.

Malyshkin repeated: "We are an independent armed force serving the Russian Liberation Committee under General Vlasov and engaged in struggle against Stalin and bolshevism in order to create a free Russia."

Patch recalled the volunteer troops his army had encountered in France. He asked: "Then why did you fight in the West against us in German uniforms and under German officers?"

"We never fought in the West."

"But we captured thousands of Russian prisoners in German uniforms who belonged to the Vlasov army."

Malyshkin replied: "These people were not part of General Vlasov's forces. To be sure, hundreds of thousands of Russian soldiers were seduced by Hitler's claim that he wanted to free their country from bolshevism and fought on his side against bolshevism. When they realized the deception and rebelled, they were shipped from the eastern to the western front and pitted against the Americans and British, whom they never wanted to fight."

Malyshkin could sense how hopeless his task was, attempting to explain these seeming contradictions to someone knowing nothing of the intricacies of the problem. He would have to go far afield if he hoped to make the American general understand the Russians' tragic dilemma. To his relief, he could see by Patch's expression that the general was listening with interest. And so he tried to tell the whole story.

According to the recollections Strik-Strikfeldt wrote years later, he came forth with an almost Machiavellian masterpiece in response to Patch's objection that Stalin and his Russians were America's allies. "We are your allies, General Patch. . . . We are all Russians and ex-Red Army men. But we had decided to choose the cause of freedom. What freedom means, you, General, as an American should know much better than I do." He recalled the Englishmen and Americans who had fought against the Bolshevik dictatorship after the First World War. "And your compatriots were allies of anti-Bolshevik Russians. And, therefore, our allies. But now we are not asking for military support but for the right of asylum. This right is laid down in the Charter of the United Nations.* And America is the citadel of freedom."

Patch replied: "Unfortunately, what you ask is outside my competence as army commander; but I promise to pass your request to General Eisenhower. I will willingly do my best. Thank you."

Twenty-four hours later they were taken to see General Patch again. He looked at them gravely, with a slight expression of regret.

* Strik-Strikfeldt, *op. cit.*, p. 234. The reference to the Charter of the United Nations seems a bit improbable. It is unlikely that Malyshkin would already have information on a charter that was only then being negotiated in San Francisco.

"Unfortunately," he said, "General Eisenhower cannot make the decision on your offer. The decision is a matter of politics and can only be taken in Washington."

Malyshkin raised his shoulders in a weary shrug.

Patch continued: "The Vlasov divisions can nevertheless surrender. Until the decision from Washington arrives they will be treated like German prisoners of war."

Malyshkin gave a sigh of relief. Strik-Strikfeldt, however, pricked up his ears. "Does this mean, General, that the Russians will be treated according to the provisions of the Geneva Convention?" he asked.

Patch threw an odd look at one of his staff officers, then a look at Strik-Strikfeldt. And he said: "No."

Strik-Strikfeldt was not surprised when he considered that Hitler had been the first to breach the provisions of the Geneva Convention in regard to the Soviet Union. But it shook him to realize that not only the Germans but also Vlasov and his men would have to bear the brunt of that in American imprisonment.

Patch held out his hand to Malyshkin. "As general of the American Army," he said, "I regret that this is all I can tell you. Speaking personally, I must express my very great regret at having to do so. I understand your point of view and I want to assure you of my personal respect. You will understand I am a soldier . . ."* Then he added: "As soon as the position at the front allows, you will be sent back to your staff."

Malyshkin and Strik-Strikfeldt were led from the room. But after twenty-four hours had passed they began to suspect that they were no longer negotiators but prisoners of war. Within another twenty-four hours they had no doubt of this. On May 8 an officer informed them that Germany had surrendered and that, therefore, they were prisoners from then on.

A few days later they were transferred to an American prison camp.

During the period from April 25 to 27 Vlasov, Zhilenkov, and the others who had been to visit Strik-Strikfeldt and Dwinger were constantly driving back and forth between Münsingen and Heuberg. On April 29 Vlasov went to Reichenhall. He had caught up with Herre and Sveryev, and met with Kroeger. A few hours later he was found by Sergei Fröhlich, his companion from Kiebitzweg, who had been hunting for him for three days. Fröhlich had come as an emissary from Aschenbrenner, who was at

* Strik-Strikfeldt, *op. cit.*, p. 236.

Spitzberg in the Böhmerwald. What he had to tell Vlasov could not be said in Kroeger's presence. Fröhlich waited impatiently until Vlasov went to a washroom. Only there could they have a confidential talk.

Fröhlich told Vlasov that Aschenbrenner had not managed to make contact with the British, but that he had been in touch with General Patton, commander of the American Third Army. He had made the offer to Patton that Vlasov and his troops would surrender without a fight in return for a promise not to turn them over to the Soviet Union. His negotiator had been released by the Americans on his word of honor and had brought the message that Patton was prepared to receive Vlasov personally and negotiate with him. Aschenbrenner, therefore, was inviting Vlasov to come to Spitzberg.

In the evening Vlasov once more drove over to Reit im Winkl to see Heidi, who in the meantime had become his wife. He wanted to bid good-by to her. When he left, he said with pretended confidence that everything would turn out all right; that Malyshkin was with the Americans now and he himself would only have to return to Czechoslovakia once more. She should expect him back. Then he left.

En route he was informed that Patton was no longer willing to receive him. No news at all had come from Malyshkin and Strik-Strikfeldt.

On April 30 Vlasov was on the road, searching for the First Division, which had set out after Schörner's meeting with Bunyachenko to march to the vicinity of Beraun, thirty kilometers from Prague.

Even before Vlasov reached the division, Kroeger transmitted alarming information to him. It seemed that Schörner had issued orders to a temporary assemblage of formations called Kampfgruppe "Erzgebirge," under General Hoth, to encircle Bunyachenko's division and disarm or destroy the Russian force. He was certain that Bunyachenko would fight, to the very end, if need be, and with all the hatred he felt for the "German tricksters." Vlasov himself was gripped with fear that his largest force would be annihilated by the Germans while there was still some hope in the offing.

He decided at all costs to reach Schörner and convince him of the senselessness of attacking the First Division. Kroeger ascertained that Schörner's headquarters was in Königsgrätz (Hradec Králove, a city in eastern Czechoslovakia). Without knowing that the district had already come under the control of Czech partisans, the two men set out. On May 1 they arrived at the headquarters and found only Brigadier General von

Natzmer, Schörner's chief of staff, still there. He told Vlasov that the order to disarm the Russians had already gone out. They waited until evening—until Schörner returned from one of his hectic visits to the front. Kroeger spoke with him first, heard him out while he thundered countless threats against Bunyachenko, but finally managed to persuade him at least to see Vlasov.

One of Vlasov's last achievements was talking Schörner into rescinding his disarmament order and releasing the First Division to Vlasov's command. The story goes that Vlasov impressed the unpredictable and hotheaded Schörner by pointing out that his, Vlasov's, movement and his divisions alone might cause the Western powers to see the necessity for struggle against the Soviet Union. But to do so, they must remain intact. That was what Bunyachenko had in mind, he argued, not insubordination.

Exhausted but relieved, Vlasov set out once more to find Bunyachenko. On the way to Kosojedy he finally passed the first of the division's marching columns. The soldiers, who had been covering an average of fifty and sixty kilometers a day on foot, recognized him, and he waved to them. At noon he reached Bunyachenko in Kosojedy.

Bunyachenko was at the moment talking with a delegation of Czech army officers. They had come to remind him that the uprising of the Czechs against the Germans was slated to begin on May 5, and that the Czechs were counting on the help of his division. The Czech people, they said, would never forget this aid, and would show their appreciation.

After the Czechs had left, Bunyachenko first insisted that Vlasov send Kroeger away. He would not be able to guarantee Kroeger's safety, he said; in his soldiers' eyes, the man's SS uniform was the symbol of German procrastination and treachery. And, in fact, shortly afterward a hand grenade exploded in the room where Kroeger was to have spent the night. So Kroeger went to Prague to find out about the situation there and did not return.

Meanwhile, in the farmhouse where Bunyachenko was billeted there began the most significant quarrel that Vlasov had ever had with the commander of his First Division. Bunyachenko stood in shirt sleeves, his clenched fists resting on the table and on the draft of an agreement he had negotiated with the Czech nationalist officers. The document promised him and all Russian soldiers who fought on their side against the Germans a free homeland in a resurrected Czechoslovakia.

"Andrei Andreyevich," Bunyachenko pleaded, "Germany has lost the war. We can no longer expect anything from the Germans. They've cheated and betrayed us too often for them to expect anything of us.

Andrei Andreyevich, you tried to negotiate with the Allies and arrange for us to become prisoners of the British or Americans. But have you had any success? They understand us less than the Germans did. We need a country in which we can remain soldiers together, for the sake of our aims, for the sake of the future. And the only chance we have of finding such a country is by cooperating with the Czechs. Suppose we help the anticommunist Czechs throw off German rule and establish an anticommunist national government? Afterward the Americans will back that government. They won't let the Bolsheviks move in here."

Vlasov listened with drooping head.

"Andrei Andreyevich," Bunyachenko went on, "the Czechs want to free themselves from the Germans. They are divided into a Communist and a Czech National Committee. The Communists are waiting for the Red Army to arrive. But the Nationalists hope that the Americans will come first. In any case, they want to have their country in hand and form a regime before the Red Army can get here. They themselves don't have enough arms to get rid of the Germans. We have the arms. I've been negotiating for days with emissaries of the nationalist Czechs. With our help, they'll be able to defeat the Germans in Prague and throughout the country. It's to be a struggle simultaneously against bolshevism and national socialism. And don't you see what it means, Andrei Andreyevich, that these Czech Nationalists will guarantee us a home in their country?"

Vlasov still said nothing.

"Put the other hopes out of your head," Bunyachenko urged, "the negotiations with the Americans and this plan of Meandrov's to march to Yugoslavia. There Tito is taking over. The Soviet armies are deep inside the country. Here the whole country lies open to us. Once we've liberated it, no Americans will dare to turn us over to the Bolsheviks."

An orderly came in with a message for Nikolayev. Nikolayev held the message out to Bunyachenko.

"Andrei Andreyevich," Bunyachenko said, raising his voice, "look at the news that has just come in. Hitler is dead. What is there to think about?"

Vlasov lifted his gray face. "I know he is dead," he replied. "What has that to do with us? The whole world regards us as traitors. And are we now to pile treason on treason?"

Bunyachenko seemed stunned. "Treason to the Germans?" he growled. "Is that what you mean?"

Vlasov nodded.

"Betrayal of those who have betrayed us a thousand times?" Bunyachenko asked. "You want to keep faith with these dogs who were too stupid to understand us, too arrogant to see us as human beings? These dogs who kicked and despised us, berated and betrayed us? You want to keep faith with the Germans to whom we owe our misery? Andrei Andreyevich, it isn't your business to think of the Germans, but of your soldiers, who need a place where they can live for the sake of the future. Are you listening to me, Andrei Andreyevich? Everyone in the division sees it my way."

But Vlasov slowly shook his head. "This is the wrong course to take," he said. "In the world's eyes it will brand us as traitors once and for all, to all our causes. Moreover, it cannot succeed. I considered it, too, weeks ago, and Sergei [he meant Sergei Fröhlich] put me in touch with Klecanda, the Czech general who once fought under Kolchak. But Klecanda says that most of the Czechs will hail the Red Army because their old president Beneš would be returning with it. Only too late will they realize they are delivering up their country to bolshevism. But the Americans will be deceived, just the way they have been deceived in Poland. However," he concluded, "I won't stand in the way of your hopes."

"Then we have a free hand!" Bunyachenko exclaimed.

At this time Major Schwenninger knew nothing about the things that were going on behind his back.

On May 4 he was again informed that the Czechs were secretly negotiating with Bunyachenko. The possibility of a Czech uprising did not yet occur to him. Nevertheless, he ordered part of his liaison detachment to lag behind the First Division, so that it would be out of reach of Bunyachenko's power. Since May 1 Vlasov had not been seen in the vicinity. Schwenninger had the impression that Vlasov, in his mood of fatalism, would hold aloof from whatever happened. He might stay within the division's area, but he would probably be out of touch with Bunyachenko.

Toward nine o'clock in the morning on May 5 Schwenninger heard a roll of drums outside on the village street, followed by the voice of the Czech town clerk reading a proclamation to the inhabitants. Schwenninger's intelligence officer understood some Czech. He thought it was a proclamation of the end of the war. Schwenninger and his Ic went to

Bunyachenko's house. They were received by Nikolayev who said: "Please wait here a moment. I'll be right back."

In his place, however, Bunyachenko's Ic, Lieutenant Olchovik, appeared. With an embarrassed expression he asked the Germans to hand over their side arms. Bunyachenko, he said, wished the Germans to understand that this measure was not intended aggressively; that it was unfortunately necessary in the interests of the Germans themselves.

An hour later Nikolayev reappeared. Schwenninger had just gone to the window and seen a small, stocky colonel of the Czech police force leave the house, accompanied by several civilians.

Nikolayev again apologized. He then informed the two Germans that since the early morning hours the Czechs in Prague and throughout the country had issued a call for an uprising against the German occupation. There was fighting in Prague. The Nationalist Czechs had just concluded a pact with the division for joint struggle against fascism and bolshevism. The division would begin marching in a few hours in order to intervene in the struggle for Prague.

"Gelmut Fritzovich," he continued, "please try to understand us. This is our sole chance. We have obtained a promise from the Czechs that the Germans who offer no resistance will be granted honorable imprisonment and transportation to Germany. As far as the German liaison detachment is concerned, you can choose whether you wish to be sent to Germany immediately; the Czechs have undertaken to carry out the transportation safely. Or you may stay with us if you wish. In that case, for the time being, you must regard yourselves as our prisoners."

Schwenninger knew Nikolayev well enough to feel no doubts of his sincerity. And he thought Nikolayev's sincerity more reliable than Czech promises. Consequently, he said that he and his men would remain with the division.

A few hours later the bulk of the division set out on the march toward Prague.

The Protectorate of Bohemia and Moravia and the German Sudetenland had remained, in the midst of chaos, virtually untouched by the raging forces all around, up until the beginning of May. Parts of the American First and Third Armies were approaching Czech soil from the west, and American fighter and dive-bomber squadrons had appeared over the area. Toward the east, the center and southern wing of Schörner's army group was still in being. On the northern border, the Fourth German Tank Army was desperately fighting against Marshal Koniev's superior forces.

As late as May 4 General Eisenhower had wired Moscow that his Third Army was now ready to advance beyond the Karlsbad-Pilsen-Budweis line as far as the Elbe and the Moldau in Czechoslovakia and "to clean up the entire area as far as the west bank of these rivers." But that same day Soviet Chief of Staff Antonov "in the greatest haste called upon" Eisenhower by way of the American military mission in Moscow "not to advance further than the Karlsbad-Pilsen-Budweis line." And Eisenhower complied, ordering his troops to stop at the line in question.

This meant—although the Germans, Russians, and Czechs knew nothing about it—removing the basis for any hopes that an independently nationalist Czechoslovakia could be established and could be supported and occupied by the Americans. Only the Communist underground movement, secretly led by Soviet parachute officers, knew that the Red Army would occupy Prague and Czechoslovakia. This group had kept a watchful eye on the nationalist Czechs' negotiations with Bunyachenko. It knew that such an uprising would speed the victory and with remarkable tactical sense was prepared to join temporarily with the Nationalists to unleash the uprising against the Germans. Nor had it any objection if Bunyachenko's division, impelled by false hopes, took part in the action.

On the morning of May 5, when Bunyachenko started his division marching toward Prague, the Czech Nationalists and Communists had risen throughout the country, but with particular force in Prague itself. They seized the Prague radio station by a coup. They took over German warehouses of clothing and ammunition. As far as anyone knew, the Germans were leaderless. Hitler was dead, and from Flensburg came news of negotiations on the terms of capitulation.

General Rudolf Toussaint, the German commandant of Prague, had no authority over the SS and the police. These forces were only halfhearted about fighting. Had they been aware of the bloody fate awaiting large numbers of them, they probably would have fought more resolutely. Only old-established SS and SD groups who had a clear conception of the fate in store for them fought ruthlessly.

The Germans did not pull themselves together for a counterattack until the morning of May 6. Then a number of SS troops moved into Prague from outside. But they were hardly strong enough to change the course of events decisively. Here and there, however, some Czechs found themselves in perilous situations as a consequence of this action. For the first time the Prague radio station broadcast to Bunyachenko and his division a public appeal for help.

On the morning of May 7 Bunyachenko reached the outskirts of Prague. The First Regiment seized Prague airport and captured forty-six German planes. The other regiments and the reconnaissance company entered the city in forced marches. For a short time the Russians fought fierce skirmishes with SS forces who muttered bitterly about the Vlasov traitors whom the SS had nurtured.

At five o'clock in the afternoon Vlasov's flag was raised beside the Czech national flag in the center of Prague. During the fighting Bunyachenko had lost three hundred men. His soldiers were exuberantly cheered by the Czech population. Even Schwenninger, who was lingering in the suburb of Jinonice where Bunyachenko had set up his headquarters, was embraced by Czech women. Certainly none of the Russian soldiers could have imagined that this storm of enthusiasm would vanish within twenty-four hours, to be replaced by hatred.

In the course of May 8 Bunyachenko received the news that Germany had capitulated, that American troops had ceased their advance in the vicinity of Pilsen and were waiting with lowered arms for the arrival of the Red Army, which had already approached close to Prague from the north.

Bunyachenko refused to believe that his plan had miscarried. But his soldiers in Prague observed that a reversal was impending. More and more red flags appeared in the city. The Nationalist Czechs concluded an armistice with the Germans. They wanted to end the fighting as quickly as possible in order to have control of Prague before the Red Army reached the city. For they were still hoping that by forming a government they could induce the Americans to continue their advance.

The armistice was not recognized everywhere. The Communists fought on while the German soldiers were withdrawing from the city to the west. Pictures of Vlasov disappeared from the streets and the first pictures of Stalin appeared.

When the news finally spread that a provisional government had been formed, Bunyachenko sent a delegation of officers to find out definitely what the situation was and what attitude the government would take toward his division. The officers discovered to their horror that eight out of twelve members of the new government were Communists. They were told that the government had not asked them to march into Prague. No help was needed from the mercenaries of the Germans. They could be made use of only if they were willing to surrender to the Red Army.

About the same time the commander of Bunyachenko's reconnaissance company, which was stationed in the center of Prague, sent a radio message reporting that the arrival of Soviet armored troops in Prague could be expected within the hour. A Soviet commissar, who had been dropped by parachute, had just come to him and cynically expressed Stalin's hope that he would shortly be able to take into his arms Bunyachenko's entire division.

Bunyachenko answered with a curse. Shortly afterward the Czech officers who had worked out the pact with him came to see him. They could tell him only that their cause was lost. Their hopes in the Americans had proved illusory. It was now certain that the Red Army would occupy Czechoslovakia and determine the nature of the coming regime. They were no longer in a position to keep the agreement they had drawn up with Bunyachenko.

It was unimaginable for tough, loud Bunyachenko to be weeping. But at this moment his eyes filled with tears. Then he signed the order for withdrawal from Prague.

It was a strange, ghostly parade.

On the roads leading southwest from Prague there marched alongside the units of the First Vlasov Division columns of German army soldiers and remnants of SS units that had escaped from Prague.

On the evening of May 9 the division again reached the quarters in the vicinity of Beraun that it had left on May 5. Here Schwenninger and his men had their side arms returned to them.

The hatred of many Czechs, who had cheered the Russians only a few days earlier, made the march a hell. In one place through which the division marched on the afternoon of May 9 the Czech mayor sent envoys to Bunyachenko to invite him to dinner. Bunyachenko and Nikolayev refused. But several officers of one regiment accepted the invitation. While dinner was being served, the house was surrounded. The officers were shot down or taken prisoner and handed over to Soviet troops. Only a single one escaped to report what had happened.

On the morning of May 10 the division continued its march in the direction of the American line of demarcation. The question was, would the Americans receive them or refuse to allow them to cross the line. Late in the afternoon the marching columns came to a halt.

Nikolayev drove up to the front of the column, accompanied by Schwenninger. At the head of the division they found the commander of the reconnaissance company talking with an American captain. The captain welcomed Nikolayev with remarkable cordiality, although with some embarrassment. Through his Czech interpreter he requested Nikolayev to confirm once more that the division was on the march to quarters west of the line of demarcation.

Nikolayev confirmed that that was the case.

"Beg pardon," the American then asked, "but don't you know that Marshal Stalin announced the end of the war yesterday?"

Nikolayev nodded.

The captain's astonishment increased. He would talk with his commanding general, he said.

After a lengthy telephone conversation he turned to Nikolayev again. The commanding general felt it was all right for the division to continue its march, he said. Would Nikolayev convey to the commander of the Russian division the commanding general's invitation to breakfast in the morning.

Schwenninger suddenly guessed what sort of misunderstanding was involved. And when the captain then introduced Schwenninger to another American with the words, "One of the officers of our great Russian ally," the mix-up became grotesquely clear. The captain had never heard of Vlasov. He thought the First Vlasov Division must be, in spite of its German uniforms, a division of the Red Army that had overshot its destination.

The mistake was cleared up that night. Still, its effect had been to let the division cross the demarcation line unhindered. Late that evening and night the members of the division assembled in an area six kilometers north of Schlüsselburg: a crowd of disillusioned, desperate, still hopeful, drowning men hovering between life and death, between freedom and doom.

The previous week, on May 4, Lieutenant Buschmann of Malytsev's Luftwaffe division had landed near Kosojedy in an old Storch. He had been sent by Trukhin to hear what Vlasov thought about raising a third division. But there was no longer any chance for that. Vlasov had something else he wanted to discuss with Buschmann. He was considering the plan of letting himself be taken captive by the Americans, then submitting voluntarily to extradition to the Soviet Union and certain death in Moscow. Perhaps, Vlasov thought, such an act might save the majority of his men from extradition.

Buschmann informed Malytsev of this conversation. And Malytsev sent word to Vlasov that under no circumstances must he sacrifice himself; that whatever happened a living Vlasov was more important for the continuance of their cause. He pleaded with Vlasov to find a refuge. One of his pilots, Captain Antelevski, a former "Hero of the Soviet Union" who like so many others had gone over to Vlasov's side, had a suitable plane at his disposal and stood ready to fly Vlasov to Spain.

Vlasov refused. "A leader who abandons his men at the crucial moment will not be good for anything later on," he said. "I had every chance of victory. The Germans, or fate if you will, did not permit it. Now I must go my way to the end."

On March 9 he followed the marching First Division toward the west. Here and there a unit recognized him. He did not try to find Bunyachenko, and Bunyachenko also did not ask to see him. On the evening of the same day that the First Division crossed the line of demarcation, Vlasov also arrived at this line. As his car approached the American road guards, he laid his hand on Antonov's arm. "Now we have another hundred paces to the end," he said. Then he returned to the matter he had discussed with Buschmann. "Now my life no longer means anything. But do you think it means enough for me to be able to offer it—for your sakes and for all those who believed in me?"

Meanwhile, they had reached the American guards. Once more there was a blessed misunderstanding. When Vlasov asked through an interpreter to be taken to the nearest American general, the Americans thought him a Red Army general and directed him and his escort to the American regimental commander in Pilsen. The commander made the same mistake. He had never heard of Vlasov. While awaiting instructions he assigned Vlasov and his men quarters in a villa.

On the morning of May 10 Vlasov was taken to the commanding general of the American corps in the area, whose headquarters was in Schlüsselburg. By the time he arrived there, the Red Army had reached the town. The line of demarcation ran right through it.

At 10 A.M. Vlasov stood facing the American general. At this time he knew nothing about what had happened to Malyshkin. He had no knowledge of the speech Malyshkin had made when he tried to explain to General Patch that they were not traitors hoping for mercy but men who had wanted to fight for the betterment of their native land and who hoped only for understanding and fairness. Consequently, Vlasov did not know that he was almost repeating the words Malyshkin had spoken. That magnificent bass voice of his once more sounded as vibrant as it had in his best days.

Perhaps his American interlocutor only half understood what he was saying. But he certainly caught something of the power of Vlasov's personality. Whether or not he thought Vlasov and his men traitors, he sensed that this was an unusual man who was deeply concerned for the soldiers who had followed him. When Vlasov said that as commander of his formations he would accept extradition if in return his soldiers were permitted to save themselves, the commanding general declared that the question of extradition did not lie within his authority. But if Vlasov surrendered unconditionally, he would try to send his troops into American imprisonment, since they obviously had not fought against Koniev's Soviet army group. He then had Vlasov returned to his quarters to consider his decision.

That afternoon an American officer turned up with the surprising news for Vlasov that Bunyachenko's division was near Schlüsselburg. He proposed driving Vlasov over to join it. Oddly, however, he added that Vlasov could go elsewhere if he wished; there was ample gasoline available. It remained open whether this was a tacit offer to help him escape. In any case, Vlasov did not avail himself of it; he asked to be taken to Schlüsselburg. A column of American cars dropped him and his men at a castle on the outskirts of Schlüsselburg that evening.

In a room on the ground floor an American captain named Donahue was waiting for him. "Well, general," he said, "I suppose it's all up with you, eh? It didn't do you any good to change masters and bet on the wrong horse."

"Captain," Vlasov replied, "all my life I have served only one master."

Donahue's face showed a trace of skepticism. "Who would that be?" he asked.

"The Russian people," Vlasov said.

In a different tone Donahue asked him to follow him. He led Vlasov and two of his men, including the interpreter, up to the next floor and showed Vlasov the two rooms that had been assigned to him. But he did not take his leave. As though there were something about Vlasov that fascinated him, he waited until Vlasov had settled down, then began asking questions. The interpreter translated. The conversation went on for hours. Donahue's naïve thirst for knowledge once again tempted Vlasov to make a profession of faith, to give a last accounting and justification of the course he had chosen and the goal he had sought.

When the captain bade good night, he said that the town was already partly occupied by Soviet partisans, who had been dropped in this area by parachute. But he would do everything he could to protect Vlasov, he said.

He kept his word. From the window Vlasov saw Red Army vehicles moving on the street that formed the line of demarcation. Cavalry detachments also rode by.

On the morning of May 11 the American captain informed Vlasov that the American troops were going to withdraw in a westerly direction, leaving Schlüsselburg to the Soviet army. He offered to sneak Vlasov and his closest associates into a group of Englishmen who had been liberated from German captivity and were being taken into the future British zone of occupation in northwest Germany. Vlasov said, "No thanks," and asked to be taken to Bunyachenko so that he could talk with him once more. Bunyachenko was still hoping that he would be able to withdraw to the west with his division, to American captivity. But Vlasov warned him that probably the only chance left would be for the men to try to make their way westward in small groups. Then he returned to the castle, where Red Army soldiers were already going in and out without recognizing him.

Donahue greeted him with the news that his army staff had inquired whether Vlasov was still staying in his quarters. Then he asked ambiguously: "Are you here?" This was another offer to help him escape. Once again Vlasov refused the offer with thanks. Yes, he said, he was there and was at the disposal of the Americans. The following night he wrote a memorandum for the American command. He stated that he and all the leading men of his following were prepared to face an international court; that they were not mercenaries of the Germans but members of an independent political and military organization, and that it would be a breach of international law to hand them over to the Soviet Union and certain death without a proper judicial procedure.

Once again Captain Donahue tried to help him. He radioed Vlasov's statement to his superiors. Shortly afterward he returned looking downcast and informed Vlasov that the American command had refused to take the First Division into American imprisonment and would not admit it to the future American zone of occupation in southern Germany. Vlasov himself and his staff were to be transferred to the American army headquarters in Pilsen at two o'clock.

At the appointed hour several cars drove up. Vlasov and Antonov got into the last of them. Two American tanks and a small squad accompanied the column. Donahue said good-by, expressing the hope that Vlasov would after all succeed in convincing his superiors. At this moment no one suspected that one of Vlasov's officers, Captain Kuchinsky, had turned traitor. He saw a chance of saving his own life and informed the staff of the Soviet corps then entering Schlüsselburg that a column of cars with Vlasov in one of them would be leaving the castle. Only two kilometers away from the castle a Soviet army car blocked the way. A Battalion Commissar Yakushev got out. The American column was vastly superior in arms and numbers to the Red Army unit. But they did nothing while Yakushev wrenched open the door of the car in which Vlasov was sitting and with raised submachine gun ordered him out.

The cat-and-mouse game of the last few days had robbed Vlasov of his remaining strength. He was unspeakably weary, ready to yield to fate.

Without a word, he got out of the car, while Antonov simply turned the car around and drove back toward the castle. The other cars also turned under the eyes of the indifferent Americans. Vlasov stood alone facing the commissar. The only person who stayed was an interpreter, a German Czech named Kessler who ran up to the Americans and tried to tell them they must intervene and stop this kidnapping of a prisoner. The Americans acted as if they had not heard. From a passing jeep someone called out: "Boys, don't get mixed up in Russian affairs."

Vlasov seemed no longer to notice anything. He opened his coat and said to Yakushev: "Fire!"

But Yakushev replied: "Not me. Comrade Stalin will judge you."

Meanwhile, 15,000 soldiers of the First Division had been waiting for three days for their fate to be decided.

On May 10 they had been disarmed. But for the time being American tanks protected them against Red partisans who were assembling in the woods all around them and shooting down every man who wandered into their ambushes.

On May 11 the first Red Army tanks appeared at the demarcation line. At night Soviet agents infiltrated the area occupied by the division. They called upon the soldiers to cross over to their "Soviet brothers." Some succumbed to the lure. They were shot. Thereafter, the remaining men in the division knew irrevocably what awaited them. All their thoughts circled around the question of whether or not they would be turned over to the Red Army. Somehow, news came through that Vlasov was negotiating with the Americans. Hopes alternated with fears.

Schwenninger was still with Bunyachenko and Nikolayev. He was unwilling to desert the Russians before a final decision was made. Bunyachenko was a defeated, captive animal still fighting to survive. He smoked and drank immoderately. He might well have thrown into Schwenninger's face all the incredible stupidity on the part of the Germans, all the Germans' sins and all their responsibility for what was now happening. But ready as he had been with reproaches and complaints in the past— now he held his peace. The Germans, too, had fallen. The people who could now destroy his men, and would do so if they were given the chance, were located elsewhere.

On May 12 the decision was made. Two American officers came to see Bunyachenko. They informed him that beginning at three o'clock in the afternoon the American line of demarcation would be shifted further westward. Soviet troops would advance into the resultant vacuum.

That was the verdict. Bunyachenko did not say a word, although scorn and hatred must have been burning on the tip of his tongue. He waited until the Americans had left. Then he summoned the officers of the division for the last time. He said little. But what he said covered everything, what their whole long course had been about, and his belief that this purpose had not been wrong and was not lost, even though they themselves might be lost. He released his soldiers from their oath, and concluded: "You will have to choose where you want to go, where you want to try to go. The Bolsheviks are coming from there. The Americans are going there. My way lies to the west as long as I have breath in my body."

He turned and went into his room. Nikolayev followed him. They found Schwenninger there; he had come to say good-by. Bunyachenko silently shook hands with Schwenninger. Nikolayev accompanied the German out the door. When they stepped out into the street, they heard isolated shots. Nikolayev listened.

"Gelmut Fritzovich," he said with his impassive face, "they're already dying."

Schwenninger held his hand for another moment. "You must not give up," he said. "Every man ought to try at least to escape. I don't believe it can all have been in vain."

More shots sounded. Nikolayev said: "You can make your way through to your home. But we cannot. You and the others who understood us and who know our situation no longer have any influence. The Americans don't want to help us. I hope to God they don't have to repent that some day."

While Schwenninger prepared to make his way through to Germany, isolated shots continued to be heard. He came upon a number of officers who were waiting to escape to the west in the confusion of the American withdrawal. Others, like Kostyenko, were digging out weapons they had hidden before the division was disarmed. They preferred to die fighting to letting themselves be helplessly carried off. Schwenninger saw the commander of the artillery regiment. He was leaning against the wall of a building waiting for the end.

"What can I do?" he said softly. "Even if they kill me, my country is back there. . . . I can't go on living in foreign places any longer."

Probably there were thousands who felt as he did. They lay in fields and in front of their quarters as though numbed into submission to a fate that was obviously inevitable. Only a few days ago in Prague they would have faced any kind of fighting. As Vlasov had once said, they were afflicted by more than the endless disappointments. The old fear had come over them once more, fear of the superior power of the political system from which they had escaped for a while.

A few hours later the tragedy ran its course. Schwenninger succeeded in escaping. Perhaps a thousand or two thousand others made their way westward in small groups. But the majority were taken prisoner, some shot on the spot, the rest transported to the east.

The hope that had temporarily encouraged the men of the army staff, the men of the Second Division, and the men of the other Russian units who had assembled at Budweis, Kaplitz, and Strakonitz, soon vanished. The American troops stopped in the vicinity of Krumau as though to wait for the Russians there. The Second Division had no communication with Vlasov or with the First Division.

In Strakonitz Herre urged Trukhin to hesitate no longer, but to offer the Americans surrender of all Vlasov troops. There no longer existed any German front against the Americans.

A small group of negotiators, whom Trukhin sent to the Americans with a white flag on May 4, reached their destination without any difficulty. They returned to Budweis on the morning of May 5. They brought back a proposal from the American corps commander with whom they had talked. He suggested that within the next thirty-six hours the Vlasov troops should cross a precisely defined line running north and south of Krumau and enter American imprisonment.

A feeling of relief passed through the army staff. Most of them thought that the American side had at last come to appreciate the hopeless situation of the Vlasov troops, caught as they were between East and West. Trukhin alone remained skeptical. "Are we trying to deceive ourselves?" he said to Herre. "Maybe this one general understands us. And maybe he also just wants to get rid of us because we are the only division still facing him that is capable of putting up a fight. What is he promising us? Imprisonment? Does he tell us what will happen afterward?"

He did not use the word "extradition." But he refused to act without Vlasov's approval, in spite of Herre's urging. As yet no one knew of the battle that had meanwhile broken out in Prague. The first news of it arrived that afternoon, at first in the form of confused radio messages. Gradually, the Second Division's area began to feel the first ripples of the uprising, which was slowly spreading to the south. Trukhin and Neryanin conferred on the question of whom to send northward into the rebelling Czech territory to search for Vlasov. Finally Trukhin's deputy, General Boyarski, declared his willingness to go. He promised to be back by the morning of May 6 at the latest and drove off to the north.

The night passed in restive anticipation. On the morning of May 6 came alarming radio reports of the battles in Prague. By noon Boyarski was not yet back. More than twenty-four of the thirty-six hours given by the Americans had already passed. Trukhin then decided to drive to the vicinity of Prague himself in order to obtain Vlasov's decision. He took with him General Shapovalov, the young adjutant Romashkin, and his driver.

They drove toward Prague by circling to the west. In almost all the Czech towns they passed through, the flags of revolution waved. In several towns Trukhin saw groups of men, women, and children who had obviously been arrested. He assumed they must be Germans. Several German soldiers were hanging from a tree. In one small place his car was stopped by a sizable group of heavily armed Czechs consisting of men with Nationalist badges and others with red armbands. But the Nationalists were in the majority and let the car pass.

There were several such stops until Trukhin reached Przibram, several kilometers southwest of Prague. Here the road was blocked by armed Communists. When the car stopped, a Soviet officer opened the door. He was one of those who had been dropped by parachute a few days earlier. He spat into the car and said: "Well, now isn't it nice that you've come of your own accord. The game is up, comrades."

Romashkin, who sat beside the driver in front of Trukhin, turned around. "Shall we drive on?" he queried resolutely. But there was no longer a chance to escape. Trukhin, Shapovalov, and Romashkin were marched into the command post. A Soviet captain was waiting for them. He reached into a desk drawer. "Do you recognize this, Comrade Trukhin?" he asked.

In his hand he had the map case that Boyarski had always carried with him. He shook its contents out on the table.

"You know who owned that, don't you, Comrade Trukhin," he said. "Another of you bastards. We hanged him yesterday."

They were taken to the prison. The following night Shapovalov was shot and Trukhin shipped to Moscow. Romashkin remained behind in his cell. Three days later soldiers of the First Division on its desperate retreat from Prague passed through Przibram and freed him.

In Budweis and Strakonitz the remaining members of the army staff waited for the chief to return. They succeeded in obtaining an extension of the American thirty-six hour deadline by another twelve hours. At midnight Trukhin had not yet returned. Neryanin, chief of the Operations Department, was now convinced that the only chance lay in the West, as Herre had been saying all along. On his insistence Generals Bogdanov and Blagoveshchensky volunteered to try to get in touch with Vlasov. By the morning of May 7 these two also had not returned.

Herre now turned to Meandrov. "Since we cannot make contact with Vlasov, it is now your task to issue the orders to march to Krumau. Mikhail Alekseyevich, you must issue this order. . . ." Herre knew what that meant to Meandrov—final abandonment of the plan to march to the southeast.

With the forty-eight hours almost at their end, Meandrov asked the Americans to set up procedures for receiving the Russian troops. His negotiators had not yet returned when Herre was informed that the armistice could come into force on all fronts at 0000 hours on May 9. There was still no contact with Schwenninger and the First Division. But toward evening Major Keiling arrived in Strakonitz. He reported that Sveryev was determined to sell his life as dearly as possible, but that he had no ammunition.

Herre instructed Keiling to see to it that the Second Division also marched over to the Americans.

The negotiators returned after dark. The Americans were expecting the Russians to arrive at the prearranged line the following morning. During the early hours of the night couriers brought orders signed by Meandrov to the units. In the early morning hours the army staff, the officers' school, and parts of the reserve brigade marched westward, but the Second Division did not move.

Herre, together with the army staff, reached Krumau. The surrender to the Americans proceeded smoothly. But as they were led into the vast gardens of Krumau castle, behind high, gloomy walls, the men had a premonition that their fate was by no means decided yet.

Late in the afternoon Meandrov and Neryanin sent word to Herre that they would like to see him.

"Andrei Fedorovich," Neryanin said, "now there is nothing much more than we can do but wait to see what fate has in store for us. We know that you have always tried to help us. The time has come for you to stop thinking of us and think of yourself. But perhaps there is one more thing you can do for us. Maybe you can find General Köstring. And maybe he can go to the Americans and tell them what we wanted and—that we are not traitors. He is an old and wise man who gains respect at once. Perhaps they'll listen to him."

Herre thought of the last conversation he had had with Köstring in Reichenhall. He knew that the old general could give no help at all. But Meandrov joined Neryanin's plea. General Assberg, of Vlasov's staff, and Colonel Posdnyakov, who had long been Vlasov's adjutant, along with Posdnyakov's wife, who was an interpreter, would accompany Herre.

That evening Herre decided to go to Köstring after all. To have another German with him, he took his orderly along. Before they left, Meandrov came up to the car door. "May God guide you, Andrei Fedorovich," he said. "Our last hopes are going with you."

A second car with Assberg and the Posdnyakovs drove behind Herre's. But they did not get far. After a few kilometers American guards stopped the cars. Madame Posdnyakov tried all her English and all her feminine charm; but the Americans directed the cars to drive into the yard of a small farm. Not until morning were they able to move again, and then only by accident—of a now familiar sort. Herre went up to the guard once more and explained in English, indicating Assberg, that he had to go to the corps headquarters with the Russian general. The American gave him a look akin to alarm.

"A Russian general? For heaven's sake, go ahead."

In this way Herre reached the commanding general's office. Here he explained the mistake. He tried in a few words to make clear what fate awaited the men of the Vlasov divisions. And he asked for passes for himself, or at least for Assberg and his companions, to go to see General Köstring. Not until he had reached this point did he become aware that a Soviet officer was sitting in the room. At this same moment the officer sprang at General Assberg. He spat at Assberg's uniform, exclaiming: "*My znakomiye* (We know each other)."

The American turned pale. Then he said to the Soviet officer: "Will you kindly leave this room. In my office the manners customary among gentlemen will be observed."

The Russian turned sharply and left the room. There was a moment of embarrassed silence. Then the American explained that he did not have the authority to issue passes. He asked the Russians to return to Krumau.

Herre would never forget the look with which Assberg and the Posdnyakovs bade good-by to him.

Eleven days later, after an adventurous march on foot, Herre climbed the winding road to Köstring's small estate near Marquartstein. It was a useless mission.

On the evening of May 8 the Second Division was still located in the area east of Kaplitz. Sveryev sat with a gloomy frown in the house which he occupied with his "wife" and drank steadily. He seemed to be actually wishing for imprisonment and execution in order to put an end to the nerve-wracking psychological stress of the past several years. Several times Major Keiling tried to persuade him to march. But he shook his head.

"Give me weapons. I don't need anything more from you people," he said.

At five o'clock in the morning Keiling went to Sveryev once more to urge him to leave; if he could not move the Russian, Keiling was planning to bid him good-by. Artillery fire could be heard. German supply lines were marching hastily toward the west.

For a moment Keiling glanced into the eyes of Sveryev's woman, and he was struck by the intensity of hatred glowing in them. Of course, she hated the Germans because they had ruined everything and had brought matters to this sad end. Sveryev once more said thickly: "Weapons." Then he told Keiling to leave with his men.

On the morning of May 9 Keiling reached Krumau. Here he waited for a while to see whether Sveryev might not after all come with his division. But only a regiment of the division came; it had marched to the west without orders.

On May 11 Keiling made his way still further to the west. He managed to find civilian clothes and smuggled his way into a band of civilian refugees. In this way he made it to Germany.

On that same May 11 Soviet troops were on the outskirts of Kaplitz. Possibly Sveryev might still have been able to order the march to the west on May 9 or 10. But a personal motive restrained him. His woman companion had taken poison and was dying. Now he did not want to leave her behind. He had loved her after his fashion. Nor did he stir after she was dead. On the night of May 11 Soviet units arrived at the farms where Sveryev's staff had its headquarters. Sveryev's adjutant opened fire, but was shot down. There was more firing. Sveryev's orderly shouted: "Medicos, the general is wounded!" Then it was all over.

Only two men out of Sveryev's entire staff, one of them Captain Tvardiyevich, escaped—they reported on the Second Division's last hours.

While Vlasov and his men were being captured, Pannwitz with his Cossack corps was embroiled in the chaos of the German retreat from Yugoslavia. Pressed by the overwhelmingly superior Red Army forces, by Bulgarians, and by Tito's partisans, the remnants of the German Southeast Army fought to keep the road northward open for the troops that were coming from Greece, and at the same time to retreat into Austria themselves.

Behind their front and among their columns rolled the dreary lines of refugee *Volksdeutsche* (Germans of foreign citizenship) who were fleeing their homes and heading north and northwest. There were ambushes on every mountain road. Nobody knew who was a friend and who a foe. In the midst of this retreat, with the soldiers inadequately supplied and almost without ammunition, the Cossacks also moved north and northwest.

Near Varaždin at the end of February they had won a river crossing from Red Army and Bulgarian troops and had mounted a cavalry attack in the old style that overran the enemy. At the beginning of May they secured the area north of Celje along the Drava River. Pannwitz no longer had any illusions about the imminence of the end. He had cherished hopes for a very long time. But ever since the close of March he had at last recognized the whole bitterness of inevitable doom. Early in April, in the midst of battles on various fronts, he had held a general Cossack congress in Virovitica. He had ranged himself with those who no longer wanted to hear of Cossack separatism and were willing to seek ties with Vlasov. At his suggestion Komonov, the leader of his Plastun Brigade who had recently been promoted to brigadier general, was appointed to bear a message to Vlasov offering Cossack subordination. Neither Pannwitz nor any of the other Cossacks knew anything about the "southeastern plan" that Meandrov was advocating at this same time. The Cossacks were more familiar with the turmoil in the Yugoslav region and therefore were trying to reach the north, hoping to unite with the Vlasov troops in Austria or Czechoslovakia.

During April Pannwitz dispatched four officers with international connections, including Prince Schwarzenberg, with orders to get in touch with the British. The instructions he gave them expressed his naïveté and ignorance of the world situation. They read in part: "The struggle against bolshevism is not yet over. The Cossack Corps must be preserved as it exists, even if it has to take refuge in Africa or Australia or some such place. Some day it will be needed."

In his simplistic fashion he hoped his plea would be heard. He placed the corps' single Storch reconnaissance plane at the disposal of one of his envoys to make sure the man would reach his destination. But he waited in vain for news from these envoys. Even then he did not altogether abandon hope.

On the evening of May 8 the corps, still fighting delaying actions, reached the areas around Slov, Gradac, and to the west of Varaždin. There the operations officer of the First Cossack Division received a telephone call—the lines were still intact—from a colonel of Tito's Eighth Partisan Army. Such telephone communications were nothing unusual in the partisan fighting. What was unusual was that the officer informed the German that Germany had capitulated and that from eleven o'clock on no marching movements were permitted on the German side. Half an hour later confirmation came from the German side. Pannwitz knew that his entire corps would be the helpless victims of the partisans and the nearby Soviet tank troops if he obeyed the conditions of the armistice. At eleven o'clock that night he had all his Cossack troops drawn up in marching order. His command was: Make your way through to the Austrian border and to Field Marshal Alexander's English army.

All night long the Cossacks marched, passing German, Croat, and Hungarian troops, headquarters, supply trains, and refugees. The partisans who tried to block the highway were driven off. The Second Cossack Division fought its way laboriously northwest from the vicinity of Varaž- din. Those Cossacks who lost touch with the main highway were cut down by the partisans.

Toward ten o'clock on the morning of May 9 two Cossack units made contact with advance units of the Eleventh British Armored Division. Pannwitz went to see the British commanders. While the Second Cossack Division was partly broken up in several battles, so that its regiments had to fight their way through the mountains north of the main line of retreat, the First Division closed ranks in the area around Griffen. It took a brief rest. Then the regiments rode on, past more scenes of flight and general dissolution.

On the morning of May 10 the First Cossack Division was marching along the road from Lavamünd to Völkermarkt when the vanguard suddenly saw a column of cars approaching it from the opposite direction. In the front car stood Pannwitz. Behind him were other cars in which rode British officers. The Cossacks thought they were saved. Sharp commands rang out. As though all the terrible marches of the past few days and nights, and all the fighting of the past week, had never been, the regiments turned from the highway, formed in lines, and dismounted. The officers galloped up. From regiment to regiment the command was passed on: "First Cossack Cavalry Division. Form up by regiments. March past in line."

It was a fantastic scene in the midst of the collapse. The bugle corps wheeled opposite Pannwitz and the British officers. Then the first squadrons came riding up: regimental commander and squadron chiefs in the van, the cavalry of the First Don Cossack Regiment, the Second Siberian Cossack Regiment, the Fourth Kuban Cossack Regiment, and the Mounted Artillery Battery. There was no trace of unreliability, no sign of a beaten army.

Pannwitz's broad face twitched. There alongside the road lay the weapons that German units had thrown away, and his Cossacks, who had become the mission and the meaning of his life, had marched past him in proud and orderly ranks.

That afternoon, east of Völkermarkt, the division laid down its arms. Then it marched into the Klagenfurt-St. Veit area. The remnants of the Second Division followed two days later. They had seen dozens of slain comrades caught in the weirs on the Drava. For them there was no doubt about the fate that awaited them in the east. Their lives were now in the hands of the British, who on the afternoon of May 12 assigned them camping grounds in one of the valleys further to the west.

The commander of the Eleventh British Armored Division and his men were distant but courteous. They left the leadership of the Cossack formations to Pannwitz and the division commanders, Colonels Wagner and von Schulz. And they spoke of "internment" rather than "imprisonment." Colonel Hills, the commander of the British artillery regiment, displayed a generosity beneath which one could have sensed pity for men hopelessly lost.

Several weeks passed in almost total isolation. Hopes mounted. When on May 26 Colonel Wagner went to Neumarkt to see Pannwitz, the Cossack general said nothing about the possibility of being handed over to the Russians. The fair treatment he and his men were receiving from the British had given him a false sense of security.

In fact, three days earlier in Vienna a special agreement had been signed between representatives of Field Marshal Alexander and the Soviet High Command in the Balkans. Alexander had undertaken to hand over all Cossacks to Soviet detachments, beginning May 28. In the agreement the Cossacks were defined as "special units of the German SS partisans" and "counterrevolutionary White gangs who were in the pay of the Germans." The belated renaming of Pannwitz's corps as the Fifteenth SS Cossack Cavalry Corps had made it easier for the Soviet negotiators to win consent from the British.

Twenty-four hours later, on May 27, Pannwitz was arrested and taken to Graz, where representatives of the Soviet Union were awaiting him. In Graz he found Generals Krasnov and Shkuro, the two old men who had been handed over the same day. Even by the terms of the Yalta Agreement, the extradition of these three would not have been required. At the same time a British general came to the headquarters of the First Cossack Division in Sirnitz. He told its commander, Colonel Wagner: "Tomorrow you are to march all your units to the camp at Weitensfeld, Germans and Cossacks separated. When can you fall in?"

His face was a mask. Wagner found it difficult to keep his composure. He stated a time, while his mind raced over what could be done to save the Cossacks. As soon as the British general had left, Wagner sent one of his officers to Weitensfeld to look over the terrain. The officer returned with the report that high barbed-wire fences were being set up, also guard towers with searchlights.

Surreptitiously, Wagner had the entire division informed that contrary to expectations the internment was about to be changed to imprisonment, and that this would probably be followed by surrender of the men to the Soviet authorities. He left it to every individual to act as he saw fit.

Two hours later the British general returned. He looked hard at the scene of frantic activity, as though surprised that preparations for departure were actually going forward. "Have you any questions?"

"The first step is prison camp, the second being handed over to the Soviet Union, the third the long ride to the Siberian mines. That's it, isn't it?"

The British general bowed his head. "You must understand, there are . . . political considerations."

He turned abruptly on his heel.

That evening British cordons formed around the camp, evidently to prevent the Cossacks or the German cadres from fleeing into the mountains. Nevertheless, during the night Wagner and sizable numbers of the Germans and Cossacks managed to escape. A British lieutenant helped them. The majority, who could not make up their minds to undertake the flight through the Alps, were transported to Weitensfeld on May 28. Members of the German liaison staff had been loaded on trucks in the morning and taken under guard to Judenburg. There the cars drove across a bridge that was occupied half by British and half by Red Army soldiers. They, too, were turned over to the Red Army. The following day, when they were crammed into tiny cells in the Graz jailhouse, Cossack officers were thrown in with them. These officers reported what had taken place in Weitensfeld and in the camps at Spittal, to which Pannwitz had sent relatives and invalids during the retreat.

The main camp at Spittal, with all its sick men and the women and children, had been placed under protection by the British. But on May 27 all those who had worn uniforms received orders to prepare for transfer to Graz where they would be turned over to the Red Army. The women and children threw themselves on the ground in front of the trucks on which the Cossacks were being loaded under blows from rifle-butts. They ran blindly into the muzzles of British submachine-guns. They let tanks drive over them, or threw themselves into the Drava. During the ride to Graz the Cossacks once more attempted to flee. Many of them were shot. Others managed to take poison at the last minute.

The survivors were taken under heavy guard to Vienna. From there they continued their march into the unknown. Pannwitz's name turned up years later when, in January 1947, the newspapers reported his death by hanging in Moscow.

310

. . .

During the last few days of April General von Heygendorff and his 162nd Turkic Division were fighting delaying actions in the vicinity of Padua. A few days earlier American tank forces had broken through the front of the German Tenth Army to the west of von Heygendorff's sector. They had smashed through as far as Verona.

Doggedly, the shrunken German forces continued their fighting retreat. Among them were Heygendorff's Turkistanis and Caucasians. Most of his men could guess what awaited them. They could draw conclusions from the experiences of one of their number—an Azerbaijani, who had returned to his division in March 1945. Earlier in the war this soldier had fallen into American captivity north of Rome. He had been extradited to the Soviet Union. There he had steadfastly insisted that he had belonged only to a labor-service unit, with the result that he had not been shot but sent to Siberia. In the winter of 1944–1945 he was placed in a penal battalion and sent into battle in Courland. There he had succeeded in deserting and finding his way back to his old division.

In April 1945 a Soviet propaganda officer at Lake Comachio, operating at the British front line, called on Heygendorff's men to desert, promising them the privilege of unrestricted return to their own country. Behind the German lines, the Azerbaijani went from sector to sector telling his fellow soldiers about his experiences. So they had some idea of what their fate would be. But just like Vlasov's soldiers and the Cossacks and all the rest, they went on hoping that some kind of last-minute miracle would save them.

On May 2 came word of the special armistice on the southern front. Heygendorff got in touch with the headquarters of Army Group South and pleaded that the fate of his volunteers be considered in any further negotiations with Field Marshal Alexander. The British field marshal should be urged not to turn them over to the Soviet Union.

Heygendorff did one thing more before he surrendered. He issued certificates to all the volunteers stating that they had not belonged to the fighting troops, but only to labor units. He also offered them the opportunity to obtain civilian clothes and try to disappear into the Italian population. Many followed his advice. Those who stayed waited fatalistically for what might come.

Heygendorff and his German liaison staff were separated from the volunteers. At Whitsuntide the Germans were being held, half starving, behind the barbed wire of Camp Modena, while the volunteers were living in the open fields, without barbed wire, a fairly short distance away. Many of them crept up to the barbed wire fence at night to hand a piece of bread or a glass of wine through to the Germans. But the morning came when the volunteers were no longer there. British soldiers had transferred them to a large camp near Taranto where Soviet reception commissions were waiting for them.

At the very sight of the waving Soviet flags, many of them committed suicide or made desperate attempts at escape. One of the mullahs and a number of soldiers poured gasoline over themselves and burned themselves in their tents. On the railroad journey to the ships, eighty men jumped out of the moving train. During unloading in Odessa several hundreds sought death by leaping into the Black Sea.

The mournful tale continued. The first sections of the Second Ukrainian Division fought in the northern part of Schörner's army group until the last days of the collapse. Up to the end they received no heavy guns. Colonel Diachenko had to make do with whatever weapons he could manage to capture. The disintegration of Schörner's army group carried Diachenko's formations into the maelstrom. Soviet search detachments caught the survivors who did not take the option of dying by their own hands.

The First Ukrainian Division was luckier. In March 1945 it had been thrown into a gap on the southeastern front, a gap resulting from the withdrawal of some Hungarian units. In this battle it demonstrated for the first time that it was a genuine field-hardened division, although it had to fight under the most difficult circumstances. At this time General Shandruk in person joined the division. As "Commander in Chief of the Military Forces of the Ukrainian National Committee," he assumed personal command of the division. Dr. Fritz Rudolf Arlt, the SS lieutenant colonel, now accompanied him. Shandruk clearly saw the imminence of the end. Nevertheless, he was still pinning his hopes on the British and Americans. His reason for this last-ditch action was no longer to impress the Germans but to show his hoped-for future allies that Ukrainians were able to fight under their own leaders.

On May 8 Shandruk's division fought its way over Tauern Pass into the Radstadt pocket. The reserve regiment reached the area around Klagenfurt after severe battles. While his men surrendered to the British and Americans, Shandruk tried to make contact with higher British and American authorities. Once more he demonstrated his tenacity, his cleverness, and his diplomatic agility. He persuaded the British and Americans that his forces were made up of Galicians, that is, Polish citizens whose homes had been occupied in 1939 by the invasion of the Soviet armies and the incorporation of eastern Poland into the Soviet Union.

He was not able to prevent the transfer of his men to the large camp in Rimini. But he succeeded in keeping their status that of internment rather than imprisonment. Extradition of the Ukrainians to the Soviet Union was refused.

But tens of thousands of others were caught in the gears of the reception camps and handed over to the Soviet authorities. No one even mentioned those countless thousands, Russian, Ukrainian, Georgian, Turkistani, Azerbaijani, Usbek, Tatar, Cossack, Armenian, and other volunteers or auxiliaries who fell into the hands of the Western Allies during the retreat from France or the fighting in western Germany and who were turned over to the Soviet Union. No one spoke of the battalions that were captured at the end of the war in Norway, in Denmark, in "Fortress Holland," and on the Aegean islands, and who were likewise handed over to the Soviet ally.

Inside Germany itself, Englishmen and Americans collected in camps all the Vlasov soldiers and all the volunteers who were either caught in German garrisons and hospitals or who had succeeded in making their way eastward into German. One of those camps, Plattling in Bavaria, in May 1945 held four thousand members of the Vlasov forces as well as men from a wide variety of volunteer formations. Some of them were taken from hospitals and sent to the camp.

The American camp command set up a file of prisoners. It divided the prisoners into a group of old emigrants and of those volunteers who were born outside the Soviet frontiers of 1939, and another group consisting of those whose birthplaces were inside the Soviet frontiers of 1939. In order not to stir up disturbances in the camp, American officers repeatedly gave assurances that there was no intention of handing anybody over to the Soviet Union. A great many of the prisoners desperately believed these assurances. Others refused to be deceived. Individuals succeeded in escaping. But the majority helplessly watched the approach of the inevitable.

The fateful hour struck months later. Overnight, American special detachments surrounded the Russian barracks with tanks. At five o'clock in the morning blinding searchlights and headlights were turned on.

Immediately afterward, trucks drove into the camp. The loaded trucks, accompanied by armored cars, were driven to the Plattling railroad station. Only those escaped who had belonged to the first group in the file—and those who had sewn razor blades into their coats. Standing outside the barracks in the glare of the searchlights, these cut their wrist arteries.

What happened in Plattling was repeated in all the other reception camps. The hunt for every man who had belonged to a volunteer formation in the Germany army was not restricted to Czechoslovakia, Germany, or Austria. It extended to Italy, France, Holland, Denmark, and Norway—wherever a volunteer formation had been stationed—and continued into 1947. In the view of later historians there is no other example in history of two such powers as Great Britain and the United States carrying out so unconditionally, and even beyond the terms of their treaty obligations, the vindictive wishes of a third power. At the end of the war, the High Command of the German Armed Forces still listed 700,000 Soviet citizens in German uniform. There are no records of how many of these were handed over to the Soviet authorities—we know only that the number who escaped was few and that no history will ever tell the full tale.

Among the generals, Malyshkin, Zhilenkov, Meandrov, Assberg, and Malytsev were held longest in American interrogation camps. They owed this reprieve to chance or to some glimmering on the part of American intelligence circles that there might be a political and even military confrontation with the wartime Soviet ally in the future. But the intelligence officers who were using their prisoners as sources of information on the still mysterious complexities of German policy in the Soviet Union, and on the operations and opportunities of the volunteer troops, did not have the power to keep the generals. In April 1946 Meandrov and Assberg were turned over to the Soviet authorities. In November of the preceding year Meandrov had still been able to write hopefully: "Again and again the question is asked me why I did not escape, whether I had had the chance to do so. I want to answer it. . . . We are not traitors . . . but members of a political movement aiming at a better future for our people. . . . Hundreds of thousands of persons without any leadership, prompted only by the falseness of their lives, rose up to fight against a tyranny that they recognized as not having its source in the people and as unjust. We are not criminals because there are hundreds of thousands who share our views and because we were seeking not our own advantage but the welfare of our people, of our country. . . . Men who fear justice escape from prison. But we bear no guilt and are ready to face the tribunals of truly democratic countries."

By January 1946 he knew that all his hopes were vain, and he wrote in his "Notes of a Man in Mortal Sorrow": "We are called German mercenaries. It may look so, on a superficial level, for we had to arm ourselves in the enemy's camp. But no one who knows the true spirit of Bolshevism can honestly maintain such a charge."

Late in the evening of Whitsunday, May 20, 1945, General Köstring and Colonel Herre were arrested by an American squad at the general's estate. The two men were permitted to spend one more night in Köstring's house. The following morning, at ten o'clock, they had to report to the prisoner-of-war camp of the 101st American Airborne Division. There Köstring was separated from Herre and taken to an interrogation center in Augsburg. A month passed before he was perfunctorily questioned by an American colonel who had apparently fought volunteer battalions during the invasion battles. The colonel had noticed that some had fought to the last ditch and wanted to know what coercive measures Köstring had employed to drive those men into fire for Germany.

The old general knew it was pointless to attempt to explain the complexities of what had really taken place. But after the conversation had drifted along on the surface for a while, he felt obliged to say something. In his quiet, old man's voice he remarked: "By incomprehension, insatiability, incompetence, and ignorance we Germans threw away the greatest asset anyone could have held in the struggle against bolshevism. In the minds of innumerable Russians we befouled their picture of European culture and civilization. You won't understand what I am telling you now: that in these two weeks you are destroying that asset for the second time, not only in a material sense. You are destroying it in the souls of all those who placed their hopes in your aid and understanding, after Germany had abandoned them to their fate."

Somewhat more than a year later, in August 1946, a brief item appeared in the Moscow newspaper *Pravda*. It read:

The Military Tribunal of the Supreme Court of the USSR has recently tried the case against A. A. Vlasov, V. F. Malyshkin, G. N. Zhilenkov, F. I. Trukhin, D. J. Zakutny, I. A. Blagoveschenski, W.

I. Meandrov, V. I. Malytsev, S. K. Bunychenko, G. A. Sveryev, V. D. Korbukov, and N. S. Shatov. They were accused of having committed high treason and, acting as agents of the German intelligence service, of having engaged in active espionage, diversionary and terroristic activities against the USSR that constitute crimes under Sections 58-1-"b," 58.8, 58.9, 58.10, and 15-II of the Penal Code of the USSR. All defendants confessed their guilt in the sense of the indictment. According to Point I of the order of the Supreme Soviet of the USSR of April 19, 1943, the Military Tribunal of the Supreme Court of the USSR condemned the defendants to death by the rope. The sentence has been carried out.

In January 1947 Generals Krasnov and von Pannwitz were found guilty of "having fought against the USSR and committed active espionage as well as terroristic acts on behalf of the German intelligence service with the aid of the units formed by them." The sentence—death by hanging—was likewise carried out.

Bibliography

I

Printed Sources: Books

Assmann, Kurt, *Deutsche Schicksalsjahre* (Wiesbaden, n.d.).
Ber, Hermann Weber, *Kosaken-Saga, Kampf und Untergang der Deutschen Kosaken-Division im 2. Weltkrieg* (Rastatt, 1966).
Bullock, Alan, *Hitler, A Study in Tyranny* (New York, 1953).
Carell, Paul, *Unternehmen Barbarossa* (Berlin, 1963).
Cookridge, E. H., *Gehlen, Spy of the Century* (New York, 1971).
Dallin, Alexander, *German Rule in Russia, 1941–1945.* (New York, 1957).
Dwinger, Edwin, *General Wlassow—Eine Tragödie unserer Zeit* (Frankfurt, 1951).
Fersen, Nicholas, *Im Zorn der Zeit* (Bern, 1961).
Fischer, George, *Soviet Opposition to Stalin* (Cambridge, Mass., 1952).
Gehlen, Reinhardt, *Der Dienst* (Mainz, 1971).
Görlitz, Walter, *Der Deutsche Generalstab* (Frankfurt, n.d.): *Der Zweite Weltkrieg, 1932–1945* (Stuttgart, 1951–1952).
Höhne, H., *Der Orden unter dem Totenkopf* (Gütersloh, 1967).
Huxley-Blythe, Peter, J., *The East Came West* (Caldwell, Idaho, 1964).
Kalinow, Kyrill D., *Sowietmarschälle haben das Wort* (Hamburg, 1950).
Kern, Erich, *Der grosse Rausch, Russlandfeldzug 1941–1945* (Zurich, 1948).
General Pannwitz und seine Kosaken (Göttingen, 1963).
Kerr, Walter, *The Russian Army* (New York, 1944).
Kleist, Peter, *Zwischen Hitler und Stalin 1939–1945* (Bonn, 1950).
Lang, Serge; Schenck, Ernst von, *Alfred Rosenberg, Porträt eines Menschheitsverbrechers* (St. Gallen, 1947).
Liddell Hart, Basil H., *The German Generals Talk* (New York, 1948).
Mackewicz, J., *Tragödie an der Drau* (Munich, 1957).

Michel, Karl, *Ost und West: Der Ruf Stauffenbergs* (Zurich, 1947).

Nycop, Carl-Adam, *Die grossen Kanonen* (Zurich/New York, n.d.).

von Oven, Wilfried, *Mit Goebbels bis zum Ende*. 2 Vols. (Buenos Aires, 1950).

Pawlas, Karl P. (Herausg.), *Fremde Heere unter Hitlers Fahne* (Nuremberg, n.d.).

Petrowskij, Anatolij, *Unvergessener Verrat! 1945: Roosevelt, Stalin, Churchill* (Munich, 1965).

Reile, O., *Geheime Ostfront* (Munich, 1963).

Schmidt, Axel, *Ukraine, Land der Zukunft* (Berlin, 1939).

Steenberg, Sven, *Vlasov* (New York, 1970).

Strik-Strikfeldt, Wilfried, *Against Stalin and Hitler* (New York, 1973).

Suduvis, N. E., *Ein Kleines Volk wird ausgelöscht* (Zurich, 1947).

U.S., Axis Criminology, Office of the Chief of Counsel for Prosecution: *Nazi Conspiracy and Aggression,* Vols. XXVI and XXXI (Washington, D.C., U.S. Government Printing Office, 1946).

Treguboff, Jurij, *Der letzte Ataman* (Velbert, 1967).

Von Tippelskirch, *Geschichte des Zweiten Weltkrieges* (Bonn, 1951).

Vlis, J. A. van der, *Tragedie op Texel* (Amsterdam, 1946).

Werth, Alexander, *Russia at War, 1940–1945* (New York, 1964).

Wheeler-Bennett, John, *The Nemesis of Power: The German Army in Politics, 1918–1945* (New York, 1954).

Zolling, Hermann, Hans Höhne, *Pullach Intern* (Hamburg, 1971).

II

Printed Sources: Articles

The German edition lists articles from German magazines and newspapers.
The following are the English-language citations or were published here.

Epstein, J. "Die Auslieferung der Wlassow-Truppen," *New Yorker Staats-Zeitung und Herold* (New York, March 12, 1955).

Fischer, George, "Vlasov and Hitler," *Journal of Modern History,* 23 (March, 1951); "General Vlasov's Official Biography," *Russian Review,* 8 (October, 1949).

Lyons, Eugene, "General Vlasov's Mystery Army," *The American Mercury* (February, 1948).

III

Original documents, copies, and translations of documents

The documents in the following lists exist only in German; their original titles are given in the German edition of this book. Translations of these titles are provided here to acquaint the reader with the sources for various portions of the narrative.

File entry of East Propaganda Department for Special Duty, dated March 17, 1943.

Speeches on the occasion of the anniversary of the Eastern Replacement Regiment, July 1943.

Draft paper by Specialist Officer Otto von Irmer: How Should I Treat Russian Prisoners of War.

Proclamation of a German commander to Russian peasants and workers, July 1941.

Evaluation of agents' reports from the occupied Eastern territories.

Evaluation of statements by Soviet agents and prisoners of war on the political situation in the occupied Russian areas.

Extracts from letters of Russian civilian workers employed in Germany, July 20, 1942.

Extract from a report of the Fourth Army Headquarters Staff Ic on Special Duty, October 15, 1942, concerning interrogations of the more educated Russian prisoners of war and deserters.

Extract from the report of the commandant of a rear echelon of experiences with the Russian population, November 8, 1942.

Extract from the report of two former Soviet officers (General Zhilenkov and Colonel Boyarski) on experiences with their Russian volunteer unit (experimental unit) on the German side, January 15, 1943.

Extracts from the memorandum of Major General Zhilenkov and Colonel Boyarski as prisoners of war, October 27, 1942.

Extract from reports of secret agents on the situation in the East, April 8, 1943.

Extract from the report of an army counterintelligence unit in the Orel district, February 20, 1943.

Extract from prisoner interrogations, March 1, 1943.

Extract from a conference with Stolpin, commander of the volunteer battalion attached to the Seventeenth Armored Division at Lyudonovo, north of Bryansk, October 3, 1942.

Extract from staff headquarters of Army Group Center on the increase in banditry (Ia/Ic/artillery officer No. 386/42), *geheime Kommandosache* ("top secret"), September 15, 1942.

Report to the commanding general of the security troops and commander in Army Group Center Ia/East on a conversation with General Vlasov in March 1943.

Report of the Keiling Artillery Group, with the Royal Hungarian Infantry Regiment 53, to the commandant of the Rear Army Area #532, December 25, 1942, concerning East Artillery Battery 621.

Report of Second Army Headquarters Staff, from Chief of Supply and Administration/Ic/A.O. No. 1353/43, secret, on the treatment of the civilian population, April 6, 1943.

Report of Major General Vlasov to Major General Hellmich, commander of the East troops.

Report of geologist-engineer Anatoli Kokovtsov-Andreyevski on the question: "What accounts for the battle morale of the Red Army?"

Report of Army Group B Headquarters Staff from Chief of Supply and Administration/VII on the employment of Russians and Ukrainians from the occupied territories for the conduct of the war, May 11, 1943.

Report of Army Group B Headquarters Staff from Chief of Supply and Administration VII (military government) Br.B. No. 83/43g to Army High Command/Army General Staff/ Quartermaster General on the treatment of the civilian population in the Ukraine, March 14, 1943.

Report of Cavalry Captain V. Khochenkov to the Second Army Headquarters Staff from the village of Rozhdestvenskoye, March 21, 1943.

Report of Russian Lieutenant Bragin of the First East Artillery Battery 621 of April 18, 1943 to the commander of Wagner Group on the East Propaganda Training Camp of Dabendorf from February 28 to March 27, 1943.

Report of a Ukrainian secret agent, March 22, 1943.

Report on the visit to East Artillery Battery 621, February 3, 1944, and on the relationship between German and Russian ranks.

Report on the interrogation of the terrorist group led by Jan Gurov which was arrested in Krasny Rog by Security Battalion 703.

Report on the interrogation of Soviet Brigadier General Krupyennikov, captured.December 21, 1942.

Report on impressions of travel with Major General Vlasov in Army Group Center.

Memorandum of Fourth Army Headquarters Staff Ic/A.B.O., May 1943, on "The German Soldier and his Political Tasks in the East."

Memorandum of Regional Chief Axyonoff in Ostrov.

Statement of prisoners, January 19, 1943: "Why the Russians Fight and What Propaganda Approach to Take Toward Them."

Commentary of Russians in Shanghai on General Vlasov's first proclamation.

Report of the Second Tank Army, December 17, 1942: "On the Effects of Mistreatment of Prisoners of War."

Communications from OKW WFSt/WPr (IV A), No. 264, May 1943, on the fighting troops.

OKH memorandum of October 21, 1942 on internal changes in the Soviet regime.

Russian commentary on the situation in the occupied areas of the Soviet Union, February 20, 1943.

Special orders for the German personnel of East Artillery Battery 621, January 20, 1943.

Description of morale based on reports from the occupied territories, January 23, 1943.

Translation of leaflet packages 480–482, RAB/IX 1942.

Translation of an address by the inhabitants of the city of Neftegorsk in the North Caucasus welcoming the German army, August 1942.

Proposal from three former political commissars on the formation of a Russian national government, November 1942.

Memorandum to the Minister for Occupied Eastern Territories and to Gauleiter Sauckel on the way mistreatment of Russian workers in Germany influences the attitudes of the population in the territory of the Second Tank Army, from Army Headquarters Staff.

Literal translation of an appeal to the peasants in the East, July 1943.

IV

Unpublished manuscripts and stenographic records of interviews conducted in 1951 and 1952. The names of the authors of manuscripts, and of interviewed witnesses, who wished to remain anonymous because of conditions at the time, especially in the Russian-occupied zone of Germany, are indicated only by asterisks (**).

Abriamov, The Assassination of Reichskommissar Kube.

Adler, The 162nd (Turkic) Infantry Division (commitment to battle within the framework of the Tenth Army).

D'Alquen, Gunter
1. The SS and Eastern Policy.
2. From Pan-Germanism to Pan-Europeanism.
3. The Subhuman.
4. Operations Scorpion and Winter's Tale.
5. The Path to Vlasov.

Arlt, Dr. Fritz Rudolf
1. Effect of the Vlasov Program on National Military Formations.
2. Bandera.
3. Berger's Part in the General Question of the Volunteer Formations with Particular Reference to the Vlasov Question.
4. Kaminski's Last Days.
5. The Truth about Kaminski's Death.
6. General von Pannwitz's Efforts to make his Formation part of the Waffen-SS.
7. The Roles of Kaltenbrunner, Schellenberg, and Ohlendorff in regard to Vlasov.

13. Some Observations on the Reliability of the Sources Underlying *The Vlasov Movement in the Light of Documents,* by B. Dvinov.

Breitner, Klaus

Report on the uprising on Texel in a letter dated April 18, 1950.

Cvikevic, George

1. Experiences in Dabendorf.
2. General A. A. Vlasov and his Army.

Dürksen, Eugen

1. The OKW and the Volunteers.
2. Some Remarks on the Development of the Vlasov Movement.
3. Addenda on the Subject of Vlasov.
4. Things Seen and Heard from 1941 to 1945.
5. Addenda.
6. Conferences on the Vlasov Problem at Army Group Center, June 1943.
7. NTS—Natsionalno-Trudovoy Soyus—"National League of Production."
8. OKW/WPr (Propaganda Bureau of the High Command of the Armed Forces) and Vlasov.
9. Individuals in OKW/WPr. "The Laboratory in Viktoriastrasse."
10. Propaganda Operation, Summer 1941.
11. Some Observations on the Reliability of the Sources Underlying *The Vlasov Movement in the Light of Documents,* by B. Dvinov.
12. "Vineta."

Eck, Armin

The Employment of Formations of Foreign Race in the area of the Wehrmacht Commander for the Netherlands, later Army Staff Headquarters 25.

Fröhlich, Sergei

1. As Vlasov's Escort from 1943 to the End.
2. Vlasov's Characteristics.
3. Expansion of Vlasov's Staff and Transfer of the Committee from Berlin to Karlsbad.
4. Zykov.
5. Why Vlasov Went over to the German Side.

Gabliani, Giwi

Report on the Caucasian Volunteers in the German Armed Forces.

von Glasenapp, Peter

Account of my Life.

von Grote, Dr. Nikolaus

1. The WPr Bureau of the OKW and the Vlasov Question.
2. Employment of Eastern Formations in the West.
3. Transfer of the Volunteer Formations to the West.

Hansen, Walther
1. Some General Information on the Eastern Volunteers.
2. Serving as Operations Officer (Ia) to the Commander of Eastern Force for Special Assignment 703, later: Headquarters of Volunteer Formation under Commander in Chief, West, in France: Part I.
3. Ditto, Part II.
4. Ditto, Part III.
5. Ditto, Part IV.
6. Ditto, Part V.
7. Ditto, Conclusion.
8. Serving as Ia and Deputy Chief of the Inspectorate, Series I.
9. Ditto, Series II.
10. Ditto, Series III.
11. The Convalescent Estate of Durinichi.
12. The Security Police in the area of Army Group Center.
13. The Eastern Replacement Regiment, Center; later Eastern Training Regiment.
14. Cossack Battalion 600 in Mogilev.
15. In the Territory of the Commanding General of the Security Troops and Commander of Army Group Center.

Herre, Heinz Danko
1. Organization of the Vlasov Division in the Winter of 1944–1945.
2. Remarks on Operation Zeppelin.
3. The First Himmler-Herre Conversation, November 12, 1944.
4. The Second Himmler-Herre Conversation.
5. German Experiences in using Prisoners of War against the Soviet Union.
6. Operation Silver Lining.
7. The Prague Congress.
8. The Staffing of Major General von Pannwitz's Fifteenth Cossack Cavalry Corps (Spring 1945).
9. The Employment of Volunteers in the East.
10. The Real Numbers of Soviet Prisoners of War.
11. The Vlasov Troops and the Burning of Ulm.
12. Addenda to My Report on the Organization of the Vlasov Divisions, Part I.
13. Ditto, Part II.
14. History of the Office of the General of the Volunteers and of the Troops under its Command.
15. General von Heygendorff.
16. In the OKH (Army High Command).
17. In the Ukraine, 1941.
18. Pannwitz.

19. Individuals Serving in the Office of the General of Eastern Troops or Volunteer Formations.
20. Russian Music during the War.
21. Position Paper on the Events in Prague, May 6 and 7, 1945 (Activities of the First Vlasov Division).
22. Diaries, 1940–1945.

von Herwarth, Hans
1. Germany and the Ukrainian Question, 1941–1945.
2. German Policy in the East [in English].

von Heygendorff, Ralph
1. The Fate of the 162nd (Turkic) Infantry Division.
2. Fighting Windmills.
3. The Origins of the Headquarters of the Commander of the Eastern Legions.
4. Commanding Foreign Nationalities.
5. Turkic and Caucasian Formations in the War.
6. Principal Missions of the 162nd (Turkic) Infantry Division.
7. How My Appointment as Commander of the Eastern Legions Came About.

Hoheisel, Klaus
Organization and Tasks of Former Group III of the Foreign Armies, East Department in the OKH.

Kaufmann, Günter
Propaganda Questions Involving Vlasov.

Keiling, Siegfried
1. The Organization of the 600th and 650th Infantry Divisions (Russian).
2. Addenda.
3. East Artillery Battery 621.
4. Speech for the Information of Party Functionaries.

Köstring, Ernst
1. The 162nd (Turkic) Division.
2. Experiences with Volunteers from Russian Territory in the Struggle against Bolshevism, 1941–1945.
3. Addenda.
4. Experiences as General of the Volunteers.
5. After my Capture, June 1945.
6. OKW and the Volunteers.

von Kraewel, Kurt
1. The Reception of the Representatives of the Army Groups from the Eastern Front in the Ministry for Eastern Affairs, December 18, 1942.
2. General von Schenckendorff.
3. In the Rear Echelon of Army Group Center.

Krause
1. Observations on a Chronicle.
2. Some Details Contributing to a Biography of Vlasov.
3. Propaganda Aimed at Smoothing the Transfer of the Volunteer Formations to the West.

Kunold, Hans Joachim
1. Conversations with and Impressions of Leading Members of the General Staff and of the Army on Native Auxiliaries in the East.
2. From Subhumans to Allied Soldiers.

Kurz, Dr. Heinrich
1. The Prague Congress.
2. Experiences on the Staff of Reichskommissar Kube.
3. Tragedies in Plattling.
4. "Vineta."

van der Milwe, Anatol
1. The Soviet Union and the West.
2. Experiences in the Ministry for Eastern Affairs.
3. Erich Koch.
4. Vlasov.

Preuss, Maximilian
Kaminski and his Brigade.

Rübesamen, Friedrich Wilhelm
1. The Partisan Situation on the Eastern Front.
2. Opinion of the Chief of Staff of the Commander, Rear Echelon of Army Group North, on the Volunteer Formations Serving There.

Schwenninger, Helmut
1. Report on the Events Involving the 600th Infantry Division (Russian) in the period from March 6 to May 14, 1945 (Parts I and II).
2. The Uprising in Prague.
3. Addenda.

Sperber
Vlasov—a General between Two Worlds.

Strik-Strikfeldt, Wilfried Karl
1. Remarks on Vlasov's Life and Career.
2. The Dabendorf Camp.
3. The Employment of Émigrés in Defense Sector (Wehrkreis) III.
4. Vlasov's Open Letter and its Consequences.
5. The Experimental Formation in Army Group Center.
6. The Efforts to Form a Russian Committee.
7. The Vlasov Concept.
8. General Hellmich and His Staff.
9. Heidi Vlasov.
10. Himmler—Vlasov.

326

Westhoff
Organization of the Prisoner-of-war System in the East.
Wohldran-Arokay, Prof. Dr. Kurt
General Ernst Köstring.
Zhilenkov, G. N.
"We are Prepared for Decisive Battles." From a manuscript dated March 8, 1944.
Zimmermann, Job
Experiences and Personalities in the Ministry of Eastern Affairs.

** As a Military Commander in the Ukraine.
** The Inception and the Tasks of Operation Zeppelin.
** Operation Zeppelin.
** On Operation Zeppelin.
** Experiences in Conjunction with Operation Zeppelin.
** The OKW and the Volunteers.
** Remarks on the Volunteer Formations in the Area of Army Group North.
** 1. Eastern Replacement Regiment Center, April to December 1943.
   2. Report on the Journey to Smolensk, Mogilev, and Bobruisk with Major General Vlasov.
   3. Journey with General Vlasov to area of Army Group Center, 1943.
** The Abwehr in the Russian Volunteer Formations of the German Armed Forces.
** Volunteer Formations of Eastern Races in the German Army from 1943 to 1945.
** Experiences with Eastern Volunteers.
** Details Regarding the Activities of the General of the Volunteer Formations (from about the spring of 1944 to abolition of the post).
** Frau Dr. Heidi Bielenberg (Vlasov) Today.
** Brigadier General von Wartenberg.
** Biographical Notes on Brigadier General Ivan Nikitich Kononov.
** Major Schrader, section commander of Abwehr in the Department of Military Affairs, OKH.
** My Meeting with General Bunyachenko, Commander of the First Vlasov Division.
** Colonel Tarasov.
** Rounding Up of Eastern Workers during Religious Services.
** Soviet Partisans.
** List of the Volunteer Formations from the East in the German Armed Forces.

** How Counterintelligence or Supervision of the Volunteer Formations was Organized.
** Table of Organization and Tasks of the General of the Volunteer Formations (status from summer of 1944 on).

Index

Bogatyrshuk, Professor, 246
Bogdanov, General, 303
Bohemia, 235, 291
bolshevism, 5, 19, 50, 83, 89, 118–19, 121, 155, 157, 215, 259, 277, 284, 289–91, 315; and collectivized farms, 36, 66, 87–88, 248, 249; German plans to eliminate, 6, 8, 9, 11, 13, 15, 24, 40, 68, 101–03, 115; and Jews, xiii, 4, 7, 37, 56, 97, 196, 236; Russian and Eastern opposition to, 13, 24, 68, 101–03, 109, 114–15, 120, 126, 149, 177, 232–33, 235, 236, 246–50; and SS, 185, 195, 213, 218; see also communism
Borisov, 119
Bormann, Martin, 144, 233, 260
Boyarski, Gen. Vladimir, 85–86, 87, 97, 98–100, 207, 231, 277, 279, 282–83, 302–03
Bracht, Fritz, 243
Bratislava, 255
Brauchitsch, Field Marshal Walther von, 32, 33, 50
Bräutigam, Dr. Otto, 15–17, 18–21, 42, 45–46, 65–68, 71, 76–78, 107, 130, 131–34, 225–27, 245
Breslau, 255
Briansk, 47
British Army, see England, British Army
Bubnov, Andrei, 59
Budsilovich, N. N., 246
Budweis, 281, 301, 303
Bukharin, Nikolai, 59
Bulgaria, 214, 248, 306
Bunyachenko, Gen. S. K., 221–23, 241, 243, 244, 251–53, 254, 255, 256–57, 263–76, 287–94, 296, 297, 298, 300, 316
Burchardt, Dr., 231
Burgdorf, Gen. Wilhelm, 145
Buschmann, Lt. G., 262, 295–96
Busse, Gen. Theodor, 265–66, 267–68, 270

Camp Modena, 311
Camp Plattling, 313–14
Caucasus, the, xiv, 88, 234; émigrés from, 6, 16, 40, 66, 232; German defeat in, 76–78; German plans for, 9, 12–13, 14, 16, 20, 40, 44, 52, 64–

68, 76; Germans welcomed in, xiv, 67–68, 76; and Red Army, 232; and SS, 44, 189, 193, 232, 233; volunteers from, 44, 67, 72, 159, 220, 224, 228, 232–33, 311; see also East, the
Chamalyan (Caucasian), 232
Chayum Khan, Veli, 44, 66, 193, 226, 259
Chiang Kai-shek, 79, 83
China, 83, 158; Communist, 83, 227
Chistyakovo, 30
Chokai, 44
Churchill, Winston, xvi, 85, 156–59, 282–83
Circassians, 72
Committee for the Liberation of the Peoples of Russia (KONR), 231–32, 245–50, 262; manifesto of, xv, 234–40, 246–50, 261
communism, 32, 33, 37, 44, 57, 59–60, 63, 69, 109, 159; see also bolshevism
Conflans, 181
Conrad, General, 26, 30
Cossacks, xix, 48, 67, 68–70, 71, 76, 77, 119–20, 142–43, 163, 168, 177–78, 193, 220, 228, 246, 259, 262–63, 277, 282, 306–10, 311, 313; see also East, the
Cranz (East Ministry), 23
Crete, 9
Crimea, 11, 47, 83, 88, 137
Croatia, 233, 248, 307
Czechoslovakia, xiii, 8, 170, 177, 235, 273, 275, 276, 279, 281, 287, 307; Communists of, 289, 292–94, 302; Nationalists of, 287, 288, 291, 292–93, 302; Russian Liberation Army in, 288–94, 301; Soviet Army in, 289–90, 292–94; uprising in, 273, 288–94, 302
Czestokowo camp, 44

Dabendorf camp, 116–19, 123, 124, 128, 156, 172, 175–76, 201, 207, 223, 229, 231–32, 234, 235, 236, 254
D'Alquen, Gunter, 194–207, 210–20, 230–31, 256–57
Dargel, Paul, 106
Deminsk, 47
Denikin, Gen, Anton J., 83
Denmark, 193, 194, 232, 313, 314
Diachenko, Colonel, 234, 312

265, 276–81, 286, 301–02, 303–05, 315
Herwarth, Lt. Hans von, 64
Heuberg camp, 240, 254, 255, 256, 258–59, 276, 286
Heydrich, Gen. Reinhard, 188
Heygendorff, Col. Ralph von, 72–74, 311
Hilger, Gustav, 225–27, 245
Hills, Colonel, 309
Himmler, Heinrich, xviii, 5, 12, 16, 17, 40, 52, 60, 125, 149, 150, 152, 153, 154, 160–62, 170–72, 183–84, 187, 189, 194–220 passim, 243, 256, 260, 265; and Vlasov, xv, 171–72, 193, 200–20 passim, 225, 226, 227–29, 230, 233, 234, 236–37, 241–42, 255, 260, 261; see also SS
Hitler, Adolf, xvi, xxii, 4, 5, 12, 14, 33, 66, 86–87, 92–94, 98, 104, 107, 145, 157, 161, 165, 199, 283, 286; ambivalence of officer corps toward, xv, 25, 33, 38, 39, 43, 51, 131; assassination attempt on, 206, 207–08, 211, 227; and associates, 3–6, 7–8, 22, 39–40, 260, 269; colonial ambitions of, xiii–xiv, xv, xviii–xix, xxi, 5, 7, 11, 16, 22, 106–07, 148, 149, 155; death of, 280–81, 289, 292; and German Army, 12, 140, 141; plans for East of, 9–15, 17, 18–21, 46, 64, 68, 108–09, 234; and Russian volunteers, 39–40, 49–51, 122, 144, 145, 161–70, 183, 229, 243, 285; and Soviet campaign, 15, 31–33, 39, 52, 63, 75–76, 78, 129, 160, 172, 204, 225, 247; Soviet policy of, 39–40, 49–50, 51, 54, 60, 102, 108–09, 110, 121–22, 126, 128–29, 137, 153; and Vlasov, 125, 127, 129–36, 138, 146–47, 150, 151–52, 154, 159, 160, 194, 200, 205, 206, 211, 216, 220, 226, 233, 235, 236–37, 250, 281, 282; see also German Army; Germany
Hitler Youth movement, 148, 150, 184
Hohenlychen, 265
Holland, 232, 313, 314
Hölz, General, 265, 267–68
Hoth, Gen. Hermann, 84, 287
Hrinyokh (Ukrainian), 234
Hungary, 109, 178, 243, 307

Ingushetes, 67
Italy, 109, 175, 193, 199–200, 232–33, 240, 242, 314

Jacobi, SS Maj. Walter, 239
Jäger, 262
Japan, xvi, 12, 83, 283
Jews, 12, 30, 33, 58, 59, 118, 187, 230, 255; and bolshevism, xiii, 4, 7, 37, 56, 97, 196, 236
Joachimsthal, 262
Jodl, Gen. Alfred, 131, 134, 138, 166, 169–70, 174–75, 176, 229
Judenburg, 310

Kabardians, 67
Kalmucks, 70–71, 78
Kaltenbrunner, Ernst, 230–31, 234–35
Kalugin, Major, 124
Kaminski, Gen. Mieczylav, 48–49, 178–79, 241, 243–44
Kantemir (Caucasian), 232
Kaplitz, 301, 305–06
Karachayevs, 67, 68, 72, 73
Kara-Kalpaks, 73
Karlovich, Wilfried, 158
Karlsbad, 261–62
Kaufmann, Günter, 148, 149–50
Kazaks, 73
Kazantsev, Alexander Stepanovich, 55, 60–61, 90–91, 92, 95, 100, 101, 143, 156–160, 172–74, 236
Keiling, Maj. Siegfried, 178, 241, 243, 244, 251, 255, 303, 305–06
Keitel, Field Marshal Wilhelm, 33, 42, 44, 51, 91, 92–93, 94, 111, 125, 126, 129, 131, 134–36, 138, 161, 167, 229, 233
Kesselring, Field Marshal Albert, 176
Kessler (interpreter), 299
Kharbin, 118
Kharkov, 129
Khedia, Mischa, 66, 193, 232, 234, 259
Kholm, 47
Kielce, 73
Kienzel, Lieutenant Colonel, 32, 33
Kiev, 22, 79, 84, 137, 263
Kinkelin, Wilhelm, 136
Kirgizes, 73
Klamroth, Maj. Bernhard, 144
Klecanda, Gen. Vladimir, 290
Kleinert, Maj. Johannes, 124

Poland (*cont.*)

from, 71–74, 135; partition of, 8, 10, 32, 40, 50, 73; prisoner-of-war camps in, 44, 71, 73–74

Poltava, 137

Poltermann, Captain, 70–71

Ponedyelin, General, 104–05

Posdnyakov, Colonel and Madame, 304

Posen, 170–71, 182

Potsdam, 234, 240, 241

Prague, 235, 236–37, 239, 244, 281, 288, 291, 292–94, 301, 302

Pravda, 84, 122, 315

prisoners of war: brutal camp conditions for, xiv, xxii, 26–30, 34, 38, 44, 48, 58, 70, 71, 86, 104, 105, 113, 151; interrogations of, 35, 37–38, 109, 199; and KONR, 231, 245; as laborers, 152; and Smolensk Committee, 104–05; used for propaganda, 56–60, 117–19; as volunteers, 52, 69–70, 71, 86, 96–100, 109, 205, 216, 224, 253–54, 256, 264, 285

propaganda: Antikomintern, 56; army, 195, 198–99, 265; Department of OKW, 54, 55, 111, 116, 117, 122; East Propaganda Department for Special Purposes, 116–19, 255; liberation from Stalin, xiv, 30, 38, 42, 56, 57, 60, 86–88, 92–93, 100–03, 111–38 *passim*, 148; Ministry of, 55, 117, 119; and prisoners of war, 56–60, 117–19; Russian, 175–76, 223, 231; Soviet, 91, 282; SS, 195, 196, 198–207, 211, 220, 225, 233, 237, 242; Vlasov used for, 86–88, 91–96, 126–36, 138, 171, 199–207, 211, 220, 225, 233, 237, 261; WPr IV, 55–62, 79, 90, 97, 100, 116

Przibram, 302–03

Pskov, 122

Rastenburg, 206

Rembertow, 72, 73, 74

Rendulic, Gen. Lothar, 278, 281

Ribbentrop, Joachim von, 4, 8, 17

Riecke, Hans Joachim, 16, 18, 45

Riedweg, Dr. Frank, 184

Riga, 122, 124, 157

Rily, Colonel, 100

Rimini, 313

Roenne, Col. Freiherr von, 35–39, 41, 50, 60, 61–62, 75, 79, 80, 85, 87, 90, 97, 117

Rohrbeck, Major, 144, 166–67, 169

Rokossovski, Konstantin, 61

Romashkin (adjutant), 302–03

Rommel, Field Marshal Erwin, 153

Roosevelt, Franklin D., xvi, 157–59, 282–83

Ropke, Major, 162–63

Ropp, Lt. Georg von der, 117

Rosenberg, Alfred, xviii, 3, 7–9; and Hitler, 3–6, 7–9, 107–08, 131, 133, 134, 137, 138; as Minister for Occupied Eastern Territories, 5–7, 15, 17–21, 45–46, 64, 65, 105–09, 129–35, 136–38, 150, 153, 189–90, 223, 255; *Myth of the Twentieth Century*, 4, 7; *Paths for German Foreign Policy*, 7; plans for East, 9–15, 16, 18–21, 22–23, 40, 130, 134, 190, 226, 228, 233, 234

Rostov, 76, 77, 104

Rovno, 26, 136–37

Rudnev, Professor, 246

Ruhpolding, 208–10

Rumania, 109, 214, 248

Rundstedt, Field Marshal Gerd von, 32, 33, 180

Russian and Eastern volunteers and auxiliaries (Hiwis), xiv–xxii, 34–42, *passim*, 47–54, 113, 117, 121, 130, 139–45, 161–70, 173–86, 189–90; disarming of, 161–66, 223, 224; Kaminski Brigade, 49, 178–79, 241, 243–44, 251; native legions, 44, 64, 67, 69–75, 108, 122, 130, 139, 142–43, 159, 177–78, 188, 193, 220–25, 228, 232–33, 246, 259, 306–14; prisoners of war, 52, 69–70, 71, 86, 96–100, 109, 205, 216, 224, 253–54, 256, 264, 285; Russian brigade, 96–100; in SS, 189–93 *passim*, 224, 227; and SS propaganda, 199–204, 206, 242; transferred to West, 166–70, 173–83, 206, 216, 217, 220–25, 232, 251, 285; and Vlasov and Russian Liberation Army, 49–50, 111–12, 116–19, 122, 124, 140–41, 167, 169–70, 172–76, 181, 183, 199, 200, 202–06 *passim*, 216–17, 222, 227–29, 242, 246, 251, 253–54, 262–63, 264; and Western powers, 221, 224, 229, 277, 282–315 *passim*

Russian Liberation Army, 49–51, 60, 61, 86–88, 92–96, 99, 100, 103–05, 109–138 *passim,* 153, 159–60, 161, 200, 207, 211, 215–19, 226, 231, 237, 240–44, 288; and British Army, xvi, 313; and Czech uprising, 288–94, 301; equipment for, 240, 241, 252–53, 254, 256, 276, 281; First Vlasov Division, 241, 252, 254, 255, 257–58, 259–61, 263–77 279, 287–301 *passim,* 303, 311, 313; and German Army, 241, 246, 251, 252, 253, 256, 275, 279, 287–88, 291; Kaminski Brigade, 241, 243–44, 251; and Red Army, 278, 282, 284, 295, 296–303, 305, 306, 313; and Russian workers in Germany, 216–17, 218–19, 251, 252, 254, 257, 264; Second Vlasov Division, 254, 255, 256, 258, 276, 278–81, 301–06, 311, 313; training sites for, 240–41, 265; and U.S. Army, xvi, 284–86, 294–95, 296–305, 313; and volunteers, 49–50, 111–12, 116–19, 122, 124, 140–41, 167, 169–70, 172–76, 181, 183, 199, 200, 202–06 *passim,* 216–17, 222, 227–29, 242, 246, 251, 253–54, 262–63, 264
Russian Social People's Party, 118
Rykov, Aleksei, 59

SA, 17, 195
Sakutny, General, 231
Salzburg, 203
Samsonov, Gen. Alexander, 89–90
Sauckel, Fritz, 3, 14, 46, 52–53, 145, 153
Schachen, 170–72, 200, 214
Schareck, Lieutenant, 164, 183–86
Schenckendorff, General von, 46–49, 52–54, 61, 106, 107–08, 111, 112–13, 129
Scherff, Col. Walther, 135
Schickendanz, Arne, 6, 14, 20–21, 65–66
Schirach, Baldur von, 148, 149–52
Schlotterer, Gustav, 16
Schlüsselburg, 296–99
Schmidt, Gen. Rudolf, 49, 178
Schmidt von Altenstadt, Lt. Col. H. G., 39, 41, 43–44, 117, 129, 131–32, 134
Schmundt, Gen. Rudolf, 135
Schonholz, 271

Schörner, Field Marshal Ferdinand, 268–76, 278, 287–88, 291–92, 312
Schubuth, Lieutenant Colonel, 112–13
Schulz, Colonel von, 309
Schwarze Korps, Das (magazine), 195
Schwarzenberg, Prince, 307
Schwenninger, Maj. Helmut, 264–76, 290–91, 293–95, 300–01, 303
Schwerdtner, Captain, 81
Schwerin von Graf, Gen. Gerhard, 70
Serbia, 143, 248, 278
Sevastopol, 47, 137
Shandruk, Gen. Pavlo, 190–92, 226, 234, 259, 277, 312
Shapovalov, General, 302–03
Shatov, N. S., 316
Sherebkov, Yury Sergeyevich, 153
Shkuro, General, 69, 309
Siberia, 9, 12, 13, 59, 311
Sigling, Hans, 193
Silesia, xvii, 78, 243, 255
Silgeilis, Colonel, 192
Simeis, 137
Simferopol, 137
Simmern, 200, 224
Slavs, xiv, 3, 7, 23, 40, 160, 171–72, 184, 196, 215, 216, 220, 230, 235, 245
Slovakia, 234, 243
Smolensk, 10, 17, 37, 50, 51, 96, 110, 112, 113
Smolensk Committee, 92–96, 100–05, 110–38 *passim,* 206, 219
Snyder, Lieutenant Colonel, 284
socialism, xiv, xv xxii, 59, 61, 86, 118–19, 160, 247–50, 254
Soviet Army, 25, 54, 63, 71, 84, 101, 118, 214, 221, 227, 232, 246, 247, 248; in Czechoslovakia, 289–90, 292–94; and German campaign, xi, xii, xiii, xiv, 5, 15, 17, 18, 21, 26, 31–33, 44, 47, 48, 50, 52, 63–64, 70, 75–76, 79, 80–82, 84–85, 100, 108, 121, 127, 128, 129, 160–61, 166–67, 196–99, 203–04, 206, 211, 213, 214, 215–16, 229, 231, 242, 254, 255–81 *passim,* 289; in German prison camps, xiv, xxii, 26–30, 34, 35, 37–38, 44, 48, 58, 70, 86, 104, 105, 113, 117, 151, 231; and native legions, 224, 306–07, 309–14; Ninety-ninth Division, 79, 84; opposition to Stalin in, xiii, xiv,

Soviet Army (*cont.*)

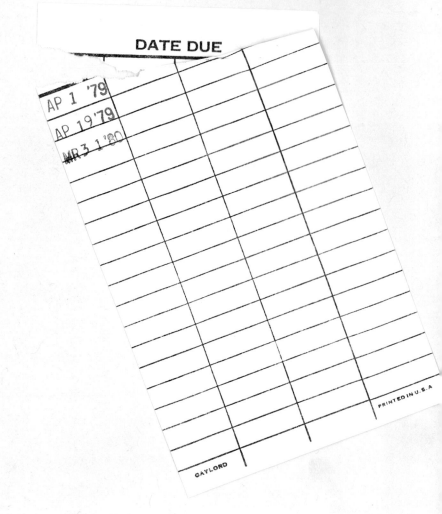

DATE DUE

AP 1 '79

AP 19 '79

MR 3 1 '80

GAYLORD

PRINTED IN U.S.A